THE HEATH INTRODUCTION TO
<u>POETRY</u>

THE HEATH INTRODUCTION TO
POETRY

SIXTH EDITION

Joseph DeRoche

Northeastern University

HOUGHTON MIFFLIN COMPANY   Boston   New York

Senior Sponsoring Editor: Dean Johnson
Associate Editor: Jennifer Roderick
Project Editor: Rebecca Bennett
Associate Production/Design Coordinator: Jodi O'Rourke
Senior Manufacturing Coordinator: Marie Barnes
Senior Marketing Manager: Nancy Lyman

Cover design: Minko T. Dimov, MinkoImages
Cover art: Richard Diebenkorn: *Ocean Park No. 24*. Yale University Art Gallery. Laila and Thurston Twigg-Smith, B. E. 1942.

Text credits continue on pages 571–577, which constitute an extension of the copyright page.

Library of Congress Catalog Card Number: 99-071997

ISBN: Student text 0-395-95824-5

3 4 5 6 7 8 9-DOC-03 02 01

LIST OF AUTHORS

CONTENTS

❦

---

*excerpt

3 A BRIEF HISTORY   93

5 A BRIEF HISTORY   267

6 A BRIEF HISTORY   357

PREFACE

The sixth edition of *The Heath Introduction to Poetry* continues to feature poets from the eighth century to the present, speaking in their own voices. Containing a wide range of poetry written in English from Great Britain, Ireland, Canada, and the United States, it provides students with a rich primary resource in a convenient, affordable anthology. The "Introduction to Poetry" and "Brief History" sections present a survey of technical terms and major developments in the history of poetry in the English language and discussions of the cultural and social contexts of the poems of various historical periods. As in previous editions, I gratefully acknowledge those who assisted me in locating and selecting some of the poems that appear in this historical anthology: Susan Alves, Kevin Gallagher, Anastasios Kozaitis, Mark Mantho, Jason Miranda, Robert Sapp, John Sullivan, and Diane Wald.

Forty selections are new to this edition. On the advice of respondents to our survey, we have included selected portions of epics translated by major English poets, and we have added more modern ballads to compare and contrast with earlier examples and as representatives of the popular poetry of the late nineteenth and early twentieth centuries. As in earlier editions, the representation of poems by women, Native Americans, and African Americans has been strengthened. Anthologized here for the first time are poems by Maxine Kumin, Isabella Gardner, Robert Pinsky, and Carl Phillips, as well as others. The poetry of major poets such as Yeats, Auden, and William Carlos Williams has been increased.

To make poems easier to find, we have placed them in general chronological sequence, as well as indexing them by titles and first lines and adding, new to this edition, a separate list of authors; however, a historical or an authorial approach to the poems is not the only possibility. Many of the poems can be grouped by theme, technique, or form for comparison and class discussion. Like the last edition, this one gives special emphasis to twentieth-century works, the sonnet, and longer lyric or narrative poems that are often anthologized piecemeal.

We thank the many instructors of poetry at colleges throughout North America for their helpful suggestions on previous editions. We appreciate the detailed survey responses from Sandra Bennett, Winona State University (MN); Karen Bevacqua, University of Iowa; Thomas E. Blom, University of British Columbia; Kevin Boyle, University of Iowa; Stavros Deligiorgis, University of

Iowa; Matts Djos, Mesa State College; Fidel Fajardo, University of Iowa; Jane M. Flick, University of British Columbia; Donald W. Foster, University of California, Santa Barbara; Edward Geist, Hofstra University; J. Kieran Kealy, University of British Columbia; Sheryll Luxton, Scott Community College (IA); Ben Moore, University of Iowa; Dan Morgan, Scott Community College (IA); Mark Newman, Scott Community College (IA); Paul R. Petrie, University of Connecticut; Elizabeth Renker, Ohio State University; Connie Re Rothwell, University of North Carolina—Charlotte; Carolyn Foster Segal, Lehigh University; Kenneth Scouten, Cayuga County Community College (NY); Sean Ward, Ryerson Polytechnic University (Ont.); Susan Wolstenholme, Cayuga County Community College (NY); Ed Zimmerman, Canisius College (NY); and Sherry Lutz Zivley, University of Houston—University Park. Additionally, we are especially grateful to the following reviewers for their help with this edition:

> Edward Foster, Stevens Institute of Technology (NJ)
> Renée Harlow, Southern Connecticut State University
> Kerry J. MacArthur, University of St. Thomas (TX)
> Jo Alyson Parker, St. Joseph's University (PA)
> Joyce Sutphen, Gustavus Adolphus College (MN)
> Richard S. Tomlinson, Richland Community College (IL)
> Sharon R. Yang, Eastern Connecticut State University

We trust that instructors will find this anthology comprehensive and teachable, that students will find the poetry included here an enlightening introduction to the scope and substance of poetry, and that all who use this edition will find the poems enjoyable. Throughout, the guiding aim of this anthology has been to present poetry as a crafted art, both as object and utterance, and to reveal poems that have flowed out of a great tradition, and have been molded by, added to, or reacted against that tradition and its changing historical and technical assumptions.

J. D.

INTRODUCTION: ON POETRY

We value poetry for what it shows us about our inner and outer lives. We find pleasure in its music, admire the power of its language and imagery, take pride and comfort in what it says. We think of the poet as something between a witch doctor and a magician. Poetry, we believe, is special, magical, spontaneous. Lightning strikes, the muse comes down, the poet gets possessed by a fit of high emotion or a tidal wave of feeling and sensibility and presto! a poem falls out of his or her head the way a star falls out of the summer sky. True, poets have a special talent. Some poets manipulate language with a juggler's ease. Others see a likeness between two things where the rest of us see only a difference. Some poets can take the substance of an ordinary day and cast it in such stunning images that it is changed forever. But, for all of this, the foundations of a poem are as practical, demanding, and precise as any hard labor. Inside a poem are spinning parts— words running against and with each other, the counterparts of the valves, pistons, hinges, and gears of more commonplace machinery, or the unseen electronic software of a personal computer.

Poems work like engines. The first thing to do with an automobile, for instance, is to turn the ignition key, engage the engine, and drive off. Most car drivers supposedly know how to shift the gears, understand how in some fashion or other the engine underneath the hood, if all is working well, will get them to where they want to go. On the other hand, most drivers don't know *how* the engine works. They know the engine has to be fed gasoline and lubricated with oil, but that's usually all. When anything goes wrong, the car goes to the garage where mechanics probe its mysterious innards and set things right again. The studying of the elements of poetry, in its way, seems much the same as examining a machine. If reading a poem is analogous to driving a car, then when we later discuss rhythm and meter, figures of speech, and the other apparatus of poetry, we'll be doing what mechanics do—looking into the workings to see what parts are doing what job. When we analyze a poem, lay bare its parts, we do so to make the poem mean more to us, not less. In the same way that attacking an engine with a sledgehammer not only breaks down the engine but also destroys it, looking at some parts of a poem without realizing how they fit with other parts makes the analysis of a poem destructive. We examine a poem to delight in it. When we read a poem that excites us, knowing the skill that makes the poem work can make the poem more alive and lasting.

"Ah," you say, "but I like what a poem *means,* how it makes me *feel,* not all this business about metaphors and feet and meters." Fair enough. But what you are saying really is that you like the message of the poem, the propaganda, the pictures and ideas you agree with. But there is a trick here. If you like what the poem means, then you can boil it down into one sentence of prose and be just as pleased. The point is you *won't* be just as pleased. The idea will be there, but something will be missing: the poem will have vanished. For instance, take this thought: "I think my girlfriend Julia looks beautiful when she wears silks." Let's agree that this is true. But look what happens when the poet Herrick writes the same thing in a poem:

> Whenas in silks my Julia goes,
> Then, then, methinks, how sweetly flows
> That liquefaction of her clothes.

Or take a universal truth: "I like to be kissed." Wyatt puts it this way:

> When her loose gown from her shoulders did fall,
> And she me caught in her arms long and small,
> And therewith all sweetly did me kiss
> And softly said, "Dear heart, how like you this?"

Obviously something has happened to the idea in both cases. Rhyme has been added, meter and regularity. Julia's beauty, for its part, suddenly shares in the fluid motions of every liquid and flowing thing. Wyatt's lady delivers a kiss with a charm, grace, and courtesy that is as much a part of the movement of the rhythms within the lines as it is a part of her disarmingly bright, easy whisper.

When we analyze poems like these, we note *how* the poem moves, as well as how we are moved *by* the poem. When the excitement of reading a poem we like for the first time is over, when the transport and intoxication of surprise fades, what remains behind in the lines of a well-made poem are the careful devices of poetry that can bring us again and again to pleasure and delight.

Still, if poems are like engines, they are also like jewels. Hold a stone cut by a fine jeweler up to the light. The facets of the stone were cut to bring out of the stone a fire and beauty that otherwise would have been locked in. The same holds true for the craftsmanship a poet puts into a poem. When we have finished analyzing a poem foot by foot, line by line, we must still face up to the fact that not everything in a poem can be tucked away in some tidy mental cubbyhole. Why a poet chooses one word over another, one rhyme scheme over another, one subject over another, adds the erratic spectacle of human choice. We discover a distinct, individual voice even in the most formal poems. In short, if a poem may move like an engine with the power of its parts pushing and pulling together, then like a precious stone cut into its most flattering shape, a poem may also shine inside with the personality, emotions, and desires of the man or woman who made it. So if some of you are worrying, as some of you usually are, that by looking at the parts of a poem we are destroying its mystery and taking away its spontaneity, then you should be made happy by the realization that poets in their grandeur or crankiness are beyond our grasp. After all is said and done, mystery remains.

From the far past of anonymous Anglo-Saxon poets to the present day, the single line of poetry, laid one upon another, has been the basic recognizable unit of a poem. We even say that a poem looks like a poem, meaning that we see lines standing individually apart and not, usually, running together as a prose paragraph would. On this frame, the various types and forms of poetry have been built. By examining lines of poetry, we can further break them down, a process we call **scanning** or **scansion,** into the common, small units that compose a poem: the consonant, the vowel, the syllable, the foot, the line. If for a time we can put aside all considerations such as what a poem means or what the poet is trying to say, we can find ourselves dealing with movement and sound on an extremely basic, almost abstract, level. Although it is difficult to be objective and scientific about ideas, we can more easily lay claim to being scientific about units of sound and movement. Looking at individual lines, we can divide poetry historically and stylistically according to four types of line scansion: **accentual, syllabic, accentual-syllabic,** and **free verse.**

The earliest Anglo-Saxon English poetry was measured by neither rhyme nor meter. From its beginning, the English language has been an **accented** language. When we speak English, the language demands that certain words or syllables be stressed over others, receive more emphasis, and thus stand out from the words around them. Anglo-Saxon poets used the normal accents of the language to determine the length of their lines of poetry. In English, then, accents are an inescapable part of the measurement of poetry, and the **ictus** [´] over a syllable means that syllable is to be accented, whereas the **breve** [˘] means that syllable is not stressed and takes a secondary place within the line. Whenever possible, a reader should read a line of poetry slowly and in a *normal* tone of voice, letting the accents fall naturally. No reader should force a word to be accented that normally would be unstressed, unless in peculiar cases (for example, Gerard Manley Hopkins) he is told to do so. Also, it's important to realize that some lines may be read in more than one way. A reader from Mississippi might read a line differently than a reader from Maine. Within reason and common sense, accenting a line leaves room for differences of opinion and pronunciation. In the following accentual passage from *Beowulf,* the beast Grendel creeps to the Dane's hall:

> When níght had fállen, the fiénd crépt near
> To the lófty háll, to leárn how the Dánes
> In Héorot faréd, when the feásting was dóne.

Notice how in the above passage, the first line has nine syllables; the second, ten; and the third line, ten or eleven. The syllable count of a line doesn't matter in accentual poetry; what matters is that each line have the same number of accents. In the first line, five words could possibly be accented, and only by progressing through the poem, line by line, would a reader new to the poem and to accentual verse be aware that a line of four accents should predominate. In fact, I have not accented the word *near,* but have given it a secondary **stress,** an accent with less importance than a full stress but more than an unstressed syllable. But no matter how we read the lines, it should still be impossible for anyone reading normally to stress such words as *had, the, to, in,* and so on.

Accentual verse, however, is not limited to Anglo-Saxon times. Coleridge's *Christabel,* for instance, is a Romantic experiment in accentuals. Gerard Manley Hopkins invented **sprung rhythm,** a nineteenth-century variation of accentual verse:

> Glóry bé to Gód for dáppled thíngs—
> For skíes of cóuple-cólor as a brínded ców . . .

Modern poets have returned to accentual verse in an attempt to escape the more rigid, formal patterns of scansion that developed after the coming of **syllabic verse** into the English language.

Unlike English, the French language makes little use of heavily accented words. Counting out accents to determine the length of lines in French poetry seldom occurred. Instead, the French devised a system of counting out the number of syllables to fix the length of their lines of poetry. When William the Conqueror invaded England in 1066, he brought with him not only the French Norman court but also French poets experienced in rhyme and syllabic rhythms. The next few centuries, culminating in Chaucer, witnessed the development of Old English into Middle English. Essentially what happened to the English language was a collision between Old English and French, which eventually developed into an amalgam of the two; the language of the peasants and the language of the court came slowly together to create Middle English, a midpoint between Old and Modern English. For a relatively short period the English court spoke French and listened to French poets reciting a poetry with a strict syllabic length of line. Although syllabic poetry swiftly evolved into accentual-syllabic poetry, English, and later American, poets occasionally wrote poems in which the line length was determined solely by counting out syllables, lines in which the number of accents could vary as long as the number of syllables remained the same. Modern poets have been especially fascinated with the syllabic line. Syllabic poetry, like accentual poetry, allows a poet to escape the rhythms and demands of more regulated, often sing-song, verse. Such freedom can result in a more rugged type of poem.

Dylan Thomas's *In My Craft or Sullen Art* is an example of a syllabic poem:

> In my craft or sullen art
> Exercised in the still night
> When only the moon rages
> And the lovers lie abed . . .

Although the accents may change from line to line, in both their number and their placement, each line has seven syllables. Syllabic poems often have an odd number of syllables to a line and can be richly complicated. *Fern Hill* by Thomas and *Poetry* by Marianne Moore are syllabic poems in which the line length differs within stanzas but the stanzas match each other line by line.

But the kind of poetry that most people would instantly recognize as poetry, poetry that often rhymes, has a definite beat (or meter), and can move with a clocklike regularity—this is what we call **accentual-syllabic** poetry. From the fourteenth century to the twentieth, accentual-syllabic poetry was predominant, becoming a convention and a tradition. Conventional poetry follows rules as strict as any laws, and the success of poets has sometimes been measured by the skill with which they can manipulate words within the tightest of circumstances.

Accentual-syllabic poetry evolved normally enough when the counting of accents and the counting of syllables in a line happened at the same time—the marriage of Anglo-Saxon and French traditions. Poetry written like this sounds, of course, crafted and artificial. For centuries the fact that poetry sounded artificial bothered hardly anyone. Poetry was allied to music, was understood to be a progression of beautiful sounds—sometimes simple, sometimes intricate—but nonetheless an artifact, a work of craftsmanship. Now and again poets have rebelled against the demands of what they felt to be such exclusive structure and have questioned the value of highly ordered, traditional verse. One outcry has it that conventional verse is artificial and therefore either insincere or hopelessly out of date. Conventional verse gains much of its power from the tension that exists when a syntactical language like English, a language in which word order plays a commanding role in the sense of a sentence, gets molded by the poet into a formal poem that moves effortlessly. The comparison is often made between formal and free-verse poems and horses. An untrained horse may be wild, free, and beautiful, but a trained horse, under a rider and a rein, gains in both purpose and power. Both have their virtues.

The counting out of accents and syllables together created the basic **foot** of English poetry. Because of the accentual base of the English language, when we divide syllables in a line into stressed and unstressed we soon discover that certain patterns keep recurring. As luck would have it, these patterns fit classical measures from Greek and Latin. Greek and Latin were quantitative languages: instead of counting stresses, these two classical languages counted duration—the length of time (quantity) it took to say something. Their syllables were differentiated by whether they were longer than one another or shorter, not by whether they were louder or softer, stressed or unstressed. Long and short syllables were supposed to be the near equivalent of what in English, a qualitative language, we call stressed or unstressed—the quality of a syllable. Therefore, counting in accentual-syllabic verse became measured in feet.

The four basic feet in English poetry are:

Iamb [˘ ´]   **Anapest** [˘ ˘ ´]
Trochee [´ ˘]   **Dactyl** [´ ˘ ˘]

Notice that a foot is composed of either two or three syllables, no more or less, and that the type of foot is determined by the placement of the accent. Every sentence of the English language, all prose and all poetry, even free verse, is composed of these feet. They determine **rhythm** by the nature of how they are placed side by side. More important, they determine **meter,** the nature of the metrical regularity in an accentual-syllabic poem. One or another of these feet will predominate in a line of metrical verse.

The following lines show examples of the four basic English feet:

Iamb	Ĭ táste ǀ ă líqu ǀ ŏr név ǀ ĕr bréwed
Trochee	Eárth, re ǀ céive ău ǀ hónŏred ǀ gúest
Anapest	The Assýr ǀ iăn căme dówn ǀ like thĕ wólf ǀ ŏn thĕ fóld
Dactyl	Oút ŏf thĕ ǀ crádlĕ ǀ éndlĕsslў ǀ róckiŇg

Note the divider [ǀǀ] that separates feet in a line.

The lines of a poem are seldom composed of only one kind of foot; this would sound as monotonous as a metronome. Substitutions are made, as in the dactyl above with its two trochees, in order to give a line a more interesting movement. Occasionally, rare feet, the **spondee** [΄ ΄] and the **pyrrhic** [˘ ˘], are interspersed with the four more common feet. An iambic line, therefore, can contain other feet—trochees, say, or anapests—just as a trochaic line could contain iambs. In lines like these, in which different feet are mixed together, whichever foot outnumbers the other determines the type of line. A line with four iambs and three trochees would become an iambic line.

Once we have discovered the predominant foot in a line by marking the accents and marking everything else as unstressed or secondary, we count the number of feet in order to find the total length of the line. For instance:

> Ĭ táste ǀ ă líqu ǀ ŏr név ǀ ĕr bréwed

has four iambic feet. We call this **iambic tetrameter.** The following chart shows the relationship between the number of feet and the length of the line:

Number of Feet	Line Length	
one	mono	meter
two	di	meter
three	tri	meter
four	tetra	meter
five	penta	meter
six	hexa	meter
seven	hepta	meter

Theoretically the number of feet could go on to infinity, but for practical purposes a **heptameter**—a line from fourteen to twenty-one syllables long—approaches the outer length limits of most poems. The most common foot in the English language happens to be the iamb, probably because the use of articles (*the, a, an*) almost always ensures that an unstressed accent will show up in the position before a stress. Children's verse, by contrast (*London Bridge is falling down, falling down, falling down*), often has trochaic feet dominating. Since children don't use as many articles in their speech as adults, their rhythms seem more primitive and emphatic. The most common line in English poetry is the **iambic pentameter,** probably because speaking anything longer than ten syllables in English usually requires an intake of breath, a pause, and often another line. In French, on the other hand, the most common line is one of twelve syllables, called in French, as in English, the **alexandrine.**

Precise as the measurement of an accentual-syllabic line can be, **elision** allows a poet to lengthen or shorten lines even within strict metrics. For instance, two vowels side by side can become a single syllable. Not only do we consider *a, e, i, o,* and *u* as vowels, but may also add *h, w,* and *v.* Look at these lines by Raleigh:

> The flowers do fade, and wanton fields
> To wayward winter reckoning yields;
> A honey tongue, a heart of gall,
> Is fancy's spring, but sorrow's fall.

The Nymph's Reply is written in iambic tetrameter, a poem which should have eight syllables to a line. The first two lines in the above stanza, however, count out to nine syllables apiece, whereas the second two lines count out to the anticipated eight syllables. We justify the extra syllable in the first line because in the word *flowers* the vowels *o, w,* and *e* fuse together, creating a **diphthong,** or two syllables which may be counted, and pronounced, as one syllable if the poet should so choose. In the second line, the word *reckoning* is commonly pronounced "reck'ning," thus compressing into two syllables what might have been, with more precise formal pronunciation, considered to be three syllables. In Milton's sonnet *On the Late Massacre* we see an example of an iambic pentameter line with eleven syllables instead of the normal ten:

>   . . . and they
> To Heaven. Their martyred blood and ashes sow
> O'er all th'Italian fields where still doth sway
> The triple tyrant;

Elision occurs with the words *To Heaven;* the two-syllable word *Heaven* is considered to be one syllable. In the next line, *Over* is written *O'er,* showing the elision in the spelling; likewise, in the same line, *the Italian fields* becomes *th'Italian fields.* Modern poems do not show the elision outright by contracting words as Milton did, following a seventeenth-century custom that is now considered old-fashioned. Elision is nevertheless present in modern accentual-syllabic poetry.

We can also use Milton to illustrate how another device, the **feminine ending,** allows a poet greater flexibility. A line is said to have a **masculine ending** when it ends on an accented syllable, a feminine ending when it ends on an unaccented syllable. The second of these lines from Book XII of *Paradise Lost,* because of its feminine ending, enjoys an extra syllable:

> Thus they in mutual accusation spent
> The fruitless hours, but neither self condemning

As an unaccented additional syllable at the end of the line, the *ing* may be discounted. Thus a line that counts out to eleven syllables may, at the poet's discretion, be considered a ten-syllable line, thanks to the feminine ending.

Accentual, syllabic, and accentual-syllabic poetry all find ways of counting, ways of measuring the length of a line, and ways of controlling the movement of accents. Such poetry is formal, strict, and demanding. The last type of poetry we consider here attempts to break away from strictness and formality; we call this **free verse.**

We could not have free verse without formal verse; it would make no sense. Free from what? we might well ask. Free from counting, free from measuring, free from meter. Free from accentual, syllabic, and accentual-syllabic verse. Free verse replaces the expected repetition of a particular foot with a looser movement we call rhythm. In this respect free verse shares something, as we have seen, with accentual and syllabic poetry. But to be truly free, free verse must also escape all predominant measurements—the placement of accents line to line must vary with no discernible pattern; the syllabic count, too, must follow no measurable regularity. Likewise the device of rhyme is employed, if at all, with freedom and irregularity. If, when we examine a poem, we can find no accentual or syllabic pattern, then we can safely say we have a free-verse poem. This poem by E. E. Cummings, *In Just-,* though it has other regularities, can serve as an example of a poem in which the accents and syllables in each line seem spontaneously and freely laid down:

> in Just-
> spring   when the world is mud-
> luscious the little
> lame balloonman
> whistles   far   and wee
>
> and eddieandbill come
> running from marbles and
> piracies and it's
> spring

In the French language, anything that simply doesn't conform to a regular syllabic count is free verse. English, because of its accentual base, complicates the issue. Indeed, by free verse, many contemporary poets simply mean poetry in which no conscious effort has been made to make the lines of a poem conform to a regular pattern, whether or not these patterns do in fact occur. Often what on the page looks like free verse—some of the poems of T. S. Eliot and Dylan

Thomas, for instance—under closer examination reveals itself to be syllabic or accentual verse. Other poems, like Ferlinghetti's The *pennycandy-store beyond the El,* move without discernible metric regularity but with plenty of rhythm.

Some poets have gone so far as to create poetry in which the shape matters and the words do not, poems divorced sometimes even from words. These **concrete poems,** sometimes just repeating one letter of the alphabet, rely on the eye to capture a significant or pleasing shape, leaving the ear in a vacuum.

Although we've explored the importance of rhythm and accents, syllables and lines, more obvious poetic elements can strike us when we first look at a poem. Thus far we have looked at lines mainly as single units, but it's obvious that the lines in a poem are strung together. Often these groupings of lines, symmetrical on the left-hand margin of the page and irregular on the right, arrange themselves in blocks of two lines, four lines, six lines, and so on. Generally we then have a space, followed by an equal block of lines. We call these groupings of lines **stanzas,** the rough equivalent of a prose paragraph. Two-line stanzas are **couplets;** four-line, **quatrains;** six-line, **sestets;** eight-line, **octets;** and so forth. The eye catches this visual regularity, but the ear is at work, too. Besides recognizing accents, the ear hears sounds, the music of words and syllables. Rhyme is the most obvious of these sounds.

Rhyme is the repetition of the same or similar sounds, often occurring at set intervals and most obviously appearing at the end of a line, where it is called **end rhyme.** For instance, the word *light* rhymes with *sight, fight, right,* etc. To make the rhyme, the consonant *l* changes to *s* or another consonant. The rhyming constant is the sound *ight,* on which constant echo the poet makes variations by changing the initial letter or letters. To some extent, the use of rhyme corresponds to the musical habit of returning to a familiar note or theme. In ancient folk poetry, before the widespread use of printing and the common ability to read, rhyme was an invaluable aid. Poetry could be more easily committed to memory when a consistent rhyme pattern jogged the mind. Thus, beyond pleasing the ear, rhyme may have had a very practical purpose. Today we can carry a portable radio or tape player with us wherever we go. At the touch of our fingertips we can command music, poetry, or drama. In times past, men and women relied upon their own memories and the songs and poems they carried with them.

The following poem by Thom Gunn, *Black Jackets,* gives us examples of various kinds of rhymes.

True or **perfect rhyme** occurs when the initial consonants change, but succeeding vowels and consonants remain the same:

> In the silence that prolongs the span
> Rawly of music when the record ends,
> The red-haired boy who drove a van
> In weekday overalls but, like his friends,

In this first stanza, *span* and *van* are perfect rhymes, as are *ends* and *friends.*

Ear rhyme occurs when words are spelled differently but sound the same. To continue Gunn's poem:

> Wore cycle boots and jacket here
> To suit the Sunday hangout he was in,
> Heard, as he stretched back from his beer,
> Leather creak softly round his neck and chin.

The ear rhymes are *here* and *beer, in* and *chin* being perfect rhymes.

Half-rhyme, near rhyme, or **slant rhyme,** occurs when there are changes within the vowel sounds of words meant to rhyme:

> Before him, on a coal-black sleeve
> Remote exertion had lined, scratched and burned
> Insignia that could not revive
> The heroic fall or climb where they were earned.

Sleeve and *revive* are half-rhymes; the initial vowel sound has changed from short to long, but the end *ve* sound has remained the same.

Assonance occurs when the vowels in a word agree, but the consonants do not—for instance, the words *seat* and *weak*. **Consonance** occurs when the consonants agree but the vowels do not, as in the words *lick* and *luck*. Assonance and consonance are both variations on half-rhyme. Within a line, the changing patterns of vowels add to the musical quality of a poem and are not necessarily occasions of rhyme. In this line of poetry, as the vowel *o* progresses in the line its sound quality changes and adds assonance:

> If all the world and love were young

Eye rhyme occurs when words are spelled the same and look alike but sound differently:

> These pretty pleasures might me move
> To live with thee and be thy love.

Move and *love* are eye rhymes. Such rhymes are also **historical rhymes** if, as in the above example by Raleigh, the pronunciation has changed over the years. The word *tea,* for instance, was once an ear rhyme with *day;* today the two words are, at best, a half-rhyme.

Internal rhyme occurs when rhyme appears not only at the end of a line, but within it:

> In the sun that is young once only,
>   Time let me play and be
> Golden in the mercy of his means

In this example by Dylan Thomas, *sun* and *young* are internal rhymes; the last syllable of *mercy* is an internal rhyme with the end rhyme *be.*

Masculine rhymes and **feminine rhymes** are the equivalents of masculine and feminine line endings. Rhymes that end on a stress (*van* and *span,* are masculine rhymes; rhymes ending on an unstressed syllable (*falling* and *calling*) are considered feminine.

Alliteration, the repetition of an initial sound, though not technically a form of rhyme, adds to the musical quality of any line or group of lines within a poem:

> About the lilting house and happy as the grass was green

The repetition of the *h* in *house* and *happy,* and the *gr* in *grass* and *green,* are both examples of alliteration. Accentual Anglo-Saxon poetry, already discussed, relied on alliteration and accents, not on rhyme, to create the music and balance of its lines.

Everything we have looked at so far may work simultaneously within any poem. An accentual-syllabic rhymed poem, for instance, may be filled with internal rhymes as well as with alliteration and assonance. One more element of sound, however, remains to be considered: *silence.* The punctuation marks in poems tell us when to fall silent and when to pause. A period or exclamation mark can be thought of as a whole rest in music—a full, heavy stop. A comma, on the other hand, gets perhaps a quarter rest—a half stop. The clear, rhythmic reading of a poem depends on close attention to its punctuation marks.

Some readers, for instance, stop at the end of every line of poetry. There's no reason to do this unless a comma, period, or other punctuation mark tells us to come to a complete stop. Such readings are unnatural and damage the sense and flow of a poem.

> Farewell, too little, and too lately known,
> Whom I began to think and call my own;
> For sure our souls were near allied, and thine
> Cast in the same poetic mold with mine.

These first four lines of John Dryden's *To the Memory of Mr. Oldham* show several uses of the pause in a tightly constructed accentual-syllabic poem. When a line of poetry has a pause at the end, as after *known, own,* and *mine,* we say the line is **end-stopped.** But when there are pauses called for within the line, as after *little* and *allied,* we call that pause a **caesura** (or cesura). When there is no pause at the end of a line, as after *thine,* and one line should flow into another, we call that a **run-on line** or an **enjambment.** These effects, common in modern verse, can be illustrated by this last stanza of a poem by Robert Lowell:

> The Aquarium is gone. Everywhere,
> giant finned cars nose forward like fish;
> a savage servility
> slides by on grease.

The caesura after *gone* precedes the lines end-stopped after *everywhere* and *fish,* whereas the last two lines are enjambed.

The examination of rhythm and sound within a poem can be the most difficult and demanding type of analysis. Such technical analysis requires close attention to the most minute parts of a poem and can remain independent of any meaning a poem may have—although punctuation goes hand in hand with a poem's meaning. When we isolate rhythms and meters, we use basically only one of our five senses: *hearing.* However, poems gain much of their power by engaging not only our sense of hearing but also our other four senses: *sight, touch, taste,* and *smell.* The objects, images, and sensations put into a line of poetry cause immediate reactions in a reader. **Imagism** builds on this reaction.

Imagist poetry, an early twentieth-century movement fostered by Ezra Pound, attempted to shed excess words and create poems of concise, clear, concrete detail. There should be "no ideas but in things," as William Carlos Williams put it. Imagist poets avoided the old accentual-syllabic rhythms and depended on the poem's image and the mind's eye of the reader to create their effect. **Didactic poetry,** poems with an obviously spelled-out moral or message like many of those by Pope or Tennyson, was to be avoided. Oriental forms of poetry such as the **haiku,** a syllabic poem of seventeen syllables and three lines, were admired models. Imagist poems became prized for their subtleties. Pound's *In a Station of the Metro* is a famous example of an imagist poem:

> The apparition of these faces in the crowd;
> Petals on a wet, black bough.

This couplet, along with its title, is the entire poem. The title informs a reader that the poem is about a metro, a European subway, but the poem makes its statement without directly telling the reader what conclusions to draw. The poem obviously means that the colorful faces of people in a dark subway are like flowers against dark branches. The poet selects his images and places them together, and the reader senses the relationships; the poem, like a small explosion, really occurs in the reader's brain.

The power of the haiku, its suggestiveness and directness of imagery, has been used by many modern poets to control and expand the limits of contemporary poetic forms. *Thirteen Ways of Looking at a Blackbird,* by Wallace Stevens, takes much of its form and structure from an understanding of, though not a slavish imitation of, the haiku. William Carlos Williams's *The Red Wheelbarrow* is a good example of the further development of the form in English, with its brief direct statement that "So much depends . . ."

Poems of all kinds contain **imagery,** the carefully described objects of the world. This horse by Auden performs unmistakably:

> . . . and the torturer's horse
> Scratches its innocent behind on a tree.

Or observe Roethke's woman:

> I knew a woman, lovely in her bones,
> When small birds sighed, she would sigh back at them . . .

The images are clear; the actions are clear. They mean what they say and, on one level, are no more or less than what we perceive them to be. These lines aren't difficult to understand; nothing is hidden or unrevealed. We know what a horse is, or a tree, a woman, bones, a bird.

Poems also often refer to special knowledge, allude to something we may need to have explained. Auden's *Musée des Beaux Arts,* quoted on the preceding page, contains specific **allusions.** The poem's title means "Museum of Fine Arts" in French. Within the poem, after Auden has described his itching horse, he immediately turns to a more specialized image: "In Brueghel's Icarus . . ." Who is Brueghel? Who is Icarus? Some of us will know this, others will not. Footnotes can help. But not everyone will know offhand that Brueghel is a sixteenth-century European painter, that "Icarus" is one of his paintings, and that, further, Icarus was a classical figure from mythology who flew too close to the sun on wax wings. Poems may allude to very obscure information or to more simple information. If I know nothing of carpentry, for instance, a poem by a carpenter could be as mysterious and difficult for me as a poem like Auden's about a part of art history.

Images make **tropes**—figures of speech that show relationships between different things. In poems relationships occur that we would not ordinarily expect. Sometimes one object is transformed into another. These metamorphoses take place largely through **metaphor** and **simile,** two figures of speech often considered the heart of poetry. A poet's fame can rest on his or her imaginative use of tropes.

Metaphor implies a relationship, a similarity, between two different objects. Once established, this relationship changes our perception of both objects. In the simplest metaphors, such as *my love is a rose,* both the idea *love* and the object *rose* become one and the same thing. Notice that love and rose are not *like* one another, they *are* one another; a magical change has taken place. The idea *love* has been made concrete—it is now not a vague internal feeling, an emotion, but a rose that theoretically could be picked, smelled, admired in a garden. We could make the identification even more exact, turn the rose red or white, describe the precise spicy quality of its smell. We call the subject of the comparison, in this case *love,* the **tenor;** we call the figure that completes the metaphor, the *rose,* the **vehicle.** In the following metaphor by John Donne, the poet's doctors become mapmakers of the heavens, and Donne's body becomes the map on which the ultimate destiny of his soul can be read:

> Whilst my physicians by their love are grown
> 　　Cosmographers, and I their map, who lie
> Flat on this bed . . .

When a metaphor becomes spun out, elaborated, complex, we call it an **extended metaphor.** When it extends itself beyond the original tenor and vehicle to other tenors and vehicles, we call it a **conceit.** In another example by Donne, the souls of two lovers become the same as the two legs of a draftsman's compass:

> If they be two, they are two so
>   As stiff twin compasses are two;
> Thy soul, the fixed foot, makes no show
>   To move, but doth, if th'other do.
>
> And though it in the center sit,
>   Yet when the other far doth roam,
> It leans and harkens after it,
>   And grows erect, as that comes home.

A **simile** is a more direct comparison. If I say "my love is like a red, red rose," I construct a simile. *A Red, Red Rose,* by Robert Burns, is the classic example. By using the words *like, as,* or an equivalent, I precisely point out the relationship between the tenor and the vehicle. The identification is not as total as it is in a metaphor because "love" and "rose" are *not* one another, but merely *like* one another. The resemblance, though real, becomes superficial; similar parts are compared, but not the whole. The essential point to remember is that the obvious difference between a simile and a metaphor lies in the use of the words *like* and *as.* When the relationship is pointed out directly we know we have a simile, as in these lines by Richard Wilbur:

> A cricket like a dwindled hearse
>   Crawls from the dry grass.

Or from Shakespeare:

> In me thou see'st the twilight of such day
> As after sunset fadeth in the west . . .

Along with metaphor and simile, other figures of speech may work within a poem.

Allegory occurs when one object or idea is represented in the shape of another. In medieval morality plays and in some poems, abstract virtues or vices appear as people. In this way a moral or lesson can more easily be made concrete and dramatic. Samson, for instance, could be an allegorical example of strength. In Emily Dickinson's poem *Because I Could Not Stop for Death,* death appears as the allegorical figure of a coachman, a chauffeur driving her through life into the eternity of death.

Ambiguity gives richness to a poem by allowing more than one interpretation to the meaning of a word or metaphor. Ambiguity does not mean that a word or image is unclear; instead, it means that a reader can recognize more than one possible reading at a time. **Puns,** for instance, offer ambiguity. These lines from Wyatt's *They Flee from Me* may be read simultaneously two ways:

> But since that I so kindely am served
> I fain would know what she hath deserved.

The word *kindely* means both "served by a group" and "courteously."

Connotation, like ambiguity, offers an additional richness to a word's meaning. In the line from Theodore Roethke's *I Knew a Woman,*

> She was the sickle; I, poor I, the rake

the word *rake* has a **denotative,** or exact, dictionary meaning—a gardening tool designed to gather up the clippings on a lawn that a sickle might have cut down. In the context of the whole poem, however, and not just the line, *rake* has an added, **connotative,** meaning—a debauched man. The two meanings bounce off one another, giving the poem a scope it would not ordinarily have.

Contrast, the opposite of comparison, shows the difference between two objects:

> My mistress' eyes are nothing like the sun;
> Coral is far more red than her lips' red;
> If snow be white, why then her breasts are dun;
> If hairs be wires, black wires grow on her head.

These lines by Shakespeare show what Shakespeare's mistress cannot be compared to and therefore, by elimination, what she can be compared to.

Hyperbole is purposeful exaggeration to create a specific effect. In Shakespeare's *Sonnet 97,* he writes:

> How like a winter hath my absence been
> From thee, the pleasure of the fleeting year!
> What freezings have I felt, what dark days seen!
> What old December's bareness everywhere!

We know that Shakespeare did not literally freeze with real cold when he was separated from his mistress. We know the days did not literally turn dark, or June turn into December, but we feel through the poet's deliberate exaggeration the depth of his unhappiness.

Irony achieves its effect by stating things in one tone of voice when in fact the opposite meaning is meant. Auden's *Unknown Citizen* ends ironically by making a statement that the reader knows to be false. The whole poem is an ironic exercise in condemning the state by using the state's own terms of praise:

> Was he free? Was he happy? The question is absurd;
> Had anything been wrong, we should certainly have heard.

Metonymy occurs when a word that merely relates to an object describes the object itself. When Sidney wrote in his sonnet *With How Sad Steps, O Moon,*

What, may it be that even in heav'nly place
That busy archer his sharp arrows tries?

"That busy archer" refers to Cupid, the god of love, shooting arrows into the hearts of unsuspecting men and women. Thus an archer, by relating to the god of love, describes love without specifically using that word.

Onomatopoeia refers to the repetition of a sound meant to resemble what it is describing. The famous last lines of Tennyson's *Come Down, O Maid*

The moan of doves in immemorial elms,
And murmuring of innumerable bees

are intended to echo the sounds of birds and bees amongst ancient trees.

Oxymoron combines two words whose meanings should nullify each other; instead, when brought together, they make sense. An example would be *sweet pain* to describe love.

Personification gives the attributes of human beings to ideas and objects. *Death, be not proud* by John Donne addresses death as if it were a person capable not only of hearing us but also of having the human emotion of pride. **Pathetic fallacy** is a form of personification in which inanimate objects are given human attributes. When we call falling rain "heaven's tears," we indulge in the pathetic fallacy.

Symbolism occurs when an image stands for something entirely different. The *ocean* may symbolize eternity; the phrase *river to the sea* could symbolize life flowing into death. Ordinarily, a symbol does not directly reveal what it stands for; the meaning must be deduced from a close reading of the poem and an understanding of conventional literary and cultural symbols. For instance, the Stars and Stripes is the flag of the United States—that is, the symbol of the United States. We know this because we are told so, not because the flag in any way resembles the country. Without communal agreement, the flag of any country would merely be a piece of colored cloth.

Synecdoche takes a part of an object to describe the whole. In the following stanza by Emily Dickinson, "morning" and "noon," parts of the day, refer to the whole day. In the same way, the "Rafter of Satin" refers to a coffin by describing not the whole coffin, but merely part of its inner lining:

Safe in their Alabaster Chambers—
Untouched by Morning—
And untouched by Noon—
Lie the meek members of the Resurrection—
Rafter of Satin—and Roof of Stone!

Synesthesia takes one of the five senses and creates an image or sensation perceived by another. For instance, *the golden cry of the trumpet* combines *golden,* a visual concept, with *cry,* an auditory concept.

Understatement, the opposite of hyperbole, achieves its effect by deliberately saying less than could be said either to diminish or to enhance a subject. Auden's ironic poem *The Unknown Citizen* contains numerous examples of understatement showing how statistics cannot evaluate the ultimate happiness of a citizen's life.

These figures of speech and many others, subdivisions and refinements of those we have already defined, work singly or in groups to create the total imaginative effect of a poem.

Along with figures of speech, however, *types* of poems challenged poets. As we've seen, the earliest English poetry, the Anglo-Saxon, relied on alliteration and accent as the keystones of its formal structure. Rhyme arrived later with French forms, becoming firmly established when Old English made the linguistic transformation to Middle English. The arrangement of poems into rhymed stanzas became the concern not only of court poets but also of folk balladeers. Chaucer would later establish the iambic pentameter line and the rhymed couplet. Traditionally, poets were expected to write within established forms. Even within these forms, though, poetry evolved and poets experimented. The long history of conventional verse is a history not of static forms but of generations of poets adding new perceptions and techniques to old certainties.

The **ballad,** genuine folk poetry, told simple, dramatic stories. Handed down by memory, these anonymous poems passed from person to person. Set to music and sung from generation to generation, ballads, unlike written poetry, underwent change. Once a poem is written down, its form is usually established forever. But **folk ballads,** composed before the ordinary man or woman could read or write, were altered and enriched by the imaginations of unnamed men and women. The tradition of the ballad runs through English and American verse. Ballads by Rudyard Kipling and Robert Service were among the most popular poems of the nineteenth and early twentieth centuries, and remained faithful to a poetry aimed at the expectations and beliefs of the ordinary unsophisticated common reader. The anonymous ballads of the fifteenth century have their counterparts in the ballads of twentieth-century America, songs of social protest and the narratives of ordinary men and women. When professional poets write in ballad stanzas, as in Auden's *As I Walked Out One Evening*, we call these poems **literary ballads.**

The ballad stanza rhymes *a b c b*—the letters *a* and *c* standing for unrhymed word sounds, the letter *b* for rhymes. Ballads, too, very often contain **refrains,** the musical repetition of words or phrases. Some believe the ballad was originally a two-line rhyming song, thus explaining why there are only two rhymes in a four-line stanza. The demands of printing presses and page size may have forced the original couplets to be broken in two at their natural caesuras and refrains. Because early ballads were nonliterary and came spontaneously from skilled, though unsophisticated, native poets, the rhymes are often half- and slant rhymes.

Epics—apparent fusions of myth and history—appear in the early stages of evolving cultures. *Beowulf* is the first English epic, a poem not of the common people but of cultural heroes involved in grand and significant adventures. Milton's *Paradise Lost* is a Christian epic, describing the expulsion of Adam and Eve from the Garden of Eden. The Augustan poets Alexander Pope and John Dryden, masters of the classical style, translated *The Iliad* and *The Aeneid* into English verse. Hart Crane's *The Bridge,* William Carlos Williams's *Patterson,* and Ezra Pound's *Cantos* are all attempts to create modern epics, in the first two cases for America, and in the latter case apparently for all of western civilization. T. S. Eliot's celebrated poem *The Waste Land* may be considered an epic of fragments, some of whose parts are often lines, images, and phrases gathered from world literature. Quotes are collected from works as diverse as Wagner's *Tristan and Isolde,* St. Augustine's *Confessions,* and the Buddha's *Fire Sermon.* Pound and Eliot make great intellectual demands on the reader. They represent poets who expect the reader to draw from a vast reservoir of education (or at least from footnotes climbing up the page, sometimes overwhelming the poem's text). Students often find it difficult to imagine these poems as they first appeared, with no or (in Eliot's case) minimal footnotes. Epics vary in structure; in *Beowulf* alliteration and accentual stress, not rhyme or stanza length, characterize the poem's structure.

Some poems receive their character from their **stanza patterns.** Two-line stanzas are called **couplets;** the iambic rhymed couplets of the Augustans Pope and Dryden, though not broken into separate stanzas, stand out as such forceful and integrated units that they are given the special name of **heroic couplets.** Three-line stanzas are **tercets** or, if they rhyme, **terza rima,** a term borrowed from the Italian. Four-line stanzas are called **quatrains.** A seven-line stanza, **rhyme royal,** *a b a b b c c,* introduced by Chaucer, determines the form of Wyatt's *They Flee from Me.* Many of the stanza forms, particularly the more complicated rhyming schemes, entered into English from Europe during the Renaissance. The most notable of these forms is the **sonnet.**

The sonnet is the best known, most recognized formal poem in the Western tradition. The poem was originally perfected in its **Italian sonnet** form by Petrarch in the 1300s as a "little song" about love. Since then, Petrarch's *sonettos* have evolved into sonnets that praise courtly and uncourtly love, that explore both sacred and profane love, and that examine subjects other than love.

Petrarch's sonnet was originally a poem of fourteen lines, rhyming *a b b a a b b a* in its first eight lines, the **octet** (or octave), and concluding with a six-line **sestet** rhyming *c d c d c d* or *c d e c d e.* The eight-line octave presents the theme of the poem, traditionally love and romance, and elaborates upon it. The six-line sestet then reflects upon the theme and comes to a conclusion about it, tying everything together. Sidney's sonnets are English examples of the **Petrarchan sonnet,** whereas Spenser's sonnets with linked rhymes are a variation. Italian, however, is a language especially rich in rhymes; English is not. The search for four or five rhymes to be repeated in each sonnet, particularly difficult in English, may account for the development of the Shakespearean sonnet.

The **English** or **Shakespearean sonnet** is composed of three quatrains rhyming *a b a b, c d c d, e f e f,* and a concluding couplet *g g.* In the Shakespearean sonnet, themes and recapitulations are developed in the same way as in the Petrarchan, but seven different rhymes are used instead of the more demanding four or five.

The **Miltonic sonnet** retains the Petrarchan rhyme scheme but introduces another innovation. Under Milton's refinement, the sonnet no longer breaks at the octet, but flows over, enjambs, from line to line and into the sestet. The sonnet appears to be more unified, structurally of one piece, beginning at one point and moving toward a seemingly inevitable controlled conclusion. Milton moves the theme of the sonnet away from love into larger intellectual and religious concerns, a development begun by Donne. Strict as its technical demands are, the sonnet shows, in its evolution and handling by different poets, the possibilities for change and variety within formal restraints. The sonnets of George Meredith from *Modern Love,* for instance, have sixteen lines rather than the traditional fourteen. Otherwise, in rhyme scheme and structure, the poems attempt to follow the traditional expectations of the sonnet. And succeed. In the twentieth century, Edna St. Vincent Millay, in her own sonnet sequences, explores romantic love as did Shakespeare. An examination of her poems, however, contrasts the male romantic perspective with a woman's viewpoint, adding elements of the modern temper: realism, skepticism, and fatalism.

The English poet Gerard Manley Hopkins attached his theories of accentual verse and sprung rhythm to the sonnet in *No Worse There Is None* and (*Carrion Comfort*). Moreover, the way sonnets often turn themselves at their end, either in explanation, summation, or surprise, reflects a characteristic of a vast proportion of poetry, formal or otherwise, ancient or new. This ability of the sonnet to encapsulate in fourteen lines the function of so many other types of poetry may account in part for its recurring vitality and fascination. Used as a training ground for young poets, the sonnet offers the challenge of technical restraints. At the same time the sonnet can take images and ideas and open them up like flowers in the sun. The long poem *The Fish* by Elizabeth Bishop brings us at its end, as a superbly handled sonnet would, to a surprising refreshment, which seems in retrospect inevitable. In another example by Bishop, her poem *Sonnet* breaks the sonnet's formal rules but keeps the form's theoretical premise and promise. The ability and desire of Elizabeth Bishop to use the "shadow" of the sonnet's structure can be something to remember in a time when the sonnet is no longer as popular and fashionable as it once was—and in a time when formal traditional poetry is often considered suspect, its rules (prosody) many times shrugged off as irrelevant and pointless.

Lastly, the original rigidity and predictability of the sonnet has been replaced with a chameleonlike adaptability, taking on a variety of forms as the lizard takes on a variety of colors: sonnets can contain more than fourteen lines; they are sometimes constructed in reverse; and they now are generally expandable and contractible into forms that pay allegiance to the theory of the original construct while building (or deconstructing) a new shape out of the recognizable skeleton of the original fourteenth-century artifact.

The **ode** was originally a classic Greek and Roman poem composed for serious occasions. In English, the ode remains a poem on elevated and exalted themes. In the **Pindaric ode,** named for the Greek poet Pindar, two structurally identical stanzas, the **strophe** and **antistrope** (Greek for "turn" and "counter-turn") are followed by a differently structured stanza, the **epode** (Greek for "stand"). The length of lines and the rhyming patterns are at the discretion of the poet. **Horatian odes,** named after the Latin poet Horace, are composed of matched regular stanzas, as in Keats' *Ode on a Grecian Urn.* The **irregular ode,** like Wordsworth's *Intimations of Immortality,* has stanzas of varying shapes, irregular rhyme schemes, and elaborate rhythms.

The **villanelle** not only rhymes but repeats lines in a predetermined manner, both as a refrain and as an integral part of the poem. Five stanzas of three lines each are followed by a quatrain. The first and third lines of the first stanza are repeated in a prescribed alternating order as the last lines of the remaining tercets, becoming the last two lines of the final quatrain. Dylan Thomas's poem *Do Not Go Gentle into That Good Night* is an example of a modern villanelle.

Emblematic poems, such as George Herbert's *Easter Wings,* take on the shape of the subject of the poem. An emblematic poem on swans, for instance, would have the shape of a swan.

Along with these forms, **blank verse** poems comprise a large body of poetry. Blank verse is simply poetry whose lines are composed of unrhymed iambic pentameter. Blank verse ranges all the way from Shakespeare's plays to a modern poem such as Wallace Stevens's *Sunday Morning.* And although the roots of these forms lie deep in the history of English and European poetry, sonnets, villanelles, and blank verse stanzas, like accentual and syllabic verse, are still alive and vital.

Of course, we also define poems according to their subject matter. We've already mentioned the heroic sweep of the epic. Everyone knows that love poems are legion; many people first come to poetry when they fall in or out of love. **Elegies,** on the other hand, deal solemnly with death. When someone falls in love or someone dies, poems written specifically to reflect on the event are called **occasional poems.** Occasional poems commemorate battles, anniversaries, coronations, the death of a goldfish; any occasion will do for an occasional poem.

Some poems are defined by the general manner in which they go about their task. **Narrative poems** (many of whose functions, like the epic, have been popularly replaced by film, novels, and short stories) tell a story, but, depending on how they tell it, narrative poems may be epics, ballads, or villanelles. A **satire** will hold up to ridicule or contempt anything the poet may despise, especially established institutions, attitudes, and people. **Parody,** a form of satire, closely imitates specific poems or poets in order to reveal their weaknesses and make light of them. Some poets, like Browning in *My Last Duchess,* wrote **dramatic monologues,** verse speeches delivered by a fictitious or historic person and designed to reveal character. Some of the greatest plays in the English language are, of course, poetry—poems to be delivered by actors and actresses from the stage. And alongside the poetic grandeur of a tragedy by Shakespeare exists the intensely personal **lyric,** usually a short, emotional poem meant to be sung or appreciated for its verbal music.

Harder to pin down, a poem's **tone** reveals the poet's attitude toward the subject and the reader. If a poet uses formal language, a strict meter, the restraints of a conventional stanza, tone will be affected in one way. If, on the other hand, a poet uses street speech, loose or jazzy rhythms, and finds images in back alleys and under the lids of trash cans while letting stanzas grow without rein or hindrance, then tone will be affected in another way. Tone tells us whether a poet is solemn or comic about the subject, whether the poet is being serious or clowning. How well or badly a poet handles imagery, technical effects, language—in short, everything the poet does in a poem—establishes tone.

The poetry of our times often moves readers not necessarily by technical brilliance or control, but by the theme, attitude, and diction of the poet. The easygoing diction in Edward Field's *Bride of Frankenstein* and his use of cinematic images, familiar to a whole generation of moviegoers, allows the poem to make its point. So, too, Allen Ginsberg's use of a suburban setting in *A Supermarket in California* both engages and disarms the modern reader. Nikki Giovanni's *Nikki-Rosa* makes use of tone, diction, and readers' attitudes, black or white, to make its point. We thus move into a new era of didactic, or teaching, poetry, in which the message of the environment reseen carries much of the power of the poem.

Finally, as the twentieth century draws to a close, new poetic theories and styles have created fresh attitudes and critical approaches to poetry. Poetry has climbed down from what some consider its "ivory tower" to enter the marketplace of social change and conflicting ideas and ideals. Critically, the influence of the Beat and Black Mountain poets, the rejection of the power of the traditional, and a rising suspicion of poetry that is not spontaneous, has radically changed contemporary views of poetry. African-American, feminist, and gay and lesbian poets have dramatically changed the sounds, attitudes, and themes of poetry. In some ways, like the Romantic poets of the eighteenth century, contemporary poets have come a long way toward redefining the subject matter of poetry, drawing it closer to "real" life, and dramatically shattering the notion that poetry (like the poetry of the nineteenth century) supports some canonical, conventional view of what the world and poetry should be about. Conflicting views of poetry, and styles of poetry, abound. Slammers concentrate on poetry as performance. Language poets explore the effects of disassociated syntax and imagery, often rejecting traditional logical and rhetorical movement in their poems. Increasingly, poetry that requires training, allusive subtlety, and special knowledge comes in conflict with poetry that prizes direct, uncensored utterance. In cyberspace, poetry has exploded into electronic publication in countless web sites and home pages, as well as experimenting with new hypertext innovations that change the shape and experience of poetry.

All that we have discussed, then—the scansion, metrics, and figures of speech—are only some of the structural supports and movements we may discover in a poem. What we have looked at allows us to discuss the structure within a poem, but nowhere, I hope you've noticed, have I attempted to tell what a poem *is*. A poem may be any and all of these things, but none of them in themselves will make a poem successful. Only the poet and his or her imagination can do that. Flying buttresses may hold up the walls of a cathedral, but they are only part of the cathedral. Rocks may make mountains, but they are not the mountain scenery. When two pairs of lips meet we have a kiss, but to claim that that *defines* a kiss courts the ridiculous. Above everything, we care for poems because they move us. Whether in the face of life poets are emotional or thoughtful, serious or coy, they extend our awareness of our lives. If poems use regular rhythms, so do we. Within ourselves, our pulses can quicken or grow calm. If the images we see in poems are fanciful, we too daydream and alter reality. As men and women differ, so do poets. When poets tend to write alike, we say they belong to schools and some critics, preferring one school to another, promote one kind of poetry over another. The truth remains that different kinds of poets live side by side, like crows and sparrows. Twenty years after Alexander Pope had finally stopped worrying with stately logic and statelier meters about the proper study of humanity, Christopher Smart was busy considering his cat Jeoffrey. Just as the formal poet and the romantic have always lived side by side, some of our days are made memorable by how they are structured and some by how they are free.

The novelist E. M. Forster once suggested we should think of writers not as men and women locked into different centuries, but as men and women sitting around a table carrying on a living conversation. In every century we will find exciting poets, even if, for a time, their language and imagery seem strange. Although the horse and buggy gave way to the automobile, the ecstasies and laments, heroics and follies of men and women remained remarkably the same. When the automobile, in turn, gives way to something else, its drivers will not go out-of-date with it; they will only have to find another way to travel. They may choose to ride a horse again or they may learn to fly. As some of us prefer horses to cars or planes, we will naturally prefer some poets and poems to others. Not everyone, after all, becomes our close friend. Nonetheless, the more we open our lives to experience, the richer our lives become. The more poets and poems we come to understand, the livelier the world becomes, no matter what century they, or we, have been fated to live in.

Joseph DeRoche

1

A BRIEF HISTORY

Obscured in the mists and fogs of Celtic Britain, the history of poetry in English began with the oral traditions of that island's first inhabitants and settlers: the Celts, the Angles, and the Saxons. Some forms of this poetry have been passed down to us through written manuscripts, but for most readers, these poems, like *Beowulf,* need to be translated from the original Anglo-Saxon into modern English.

The real written history of English began when William the Conqueror, crossing the English Channel from Normandy in France, defeated the Saxons at the battle of Hastings in the year 1066. William brought with him his French court, complete with a literary tradition, thus importing the poetic forms of France and the continent into Britain. Over the years, the gradual assimilation of French into the Anglo-Saxon language created Middle English, the language of Chaucer. Eventually, Middle English evolved into Modern English—a process that continued down through Shakespeare and Elizabethan England to today, obviously reflected by the differences in language between Great Britain and the United States today.

This period in British history was reflected in poetry. The life of the court, the traditions of courtly love, the dynastic Wars of the Roses were represented in courtly rhymed love poems and sonnets. Poems on the classical Roman and Greek themes of *carpe diem* ("seize the day") and *tempus fugit* ("time flies"), as well as pastoral poetry, were partly the result of the Renaissance. A cultural awakening in Europe to the art and literature of classical civilization, these Renaissance themes of mortality were given a poignant turn by the short life spans of most men and women. Political tumult also resulted in the execution of several poets, such as Tichborne and Raleigh, who found themselves out of favor and under the blade of the executioner's axe. The sonnet form was imported from Italy through France. The writing of poetry in established forms, meters, and subject matter became an expected part of an aristocratic gentleman's life. Even folk poetry, such as ballads, began to be written down, eventually to become part of the poetic tradition.

Anglo-Saxon poetry was composed on the twin bases of alliterative sound and accentual beat; the separate lines were balanced in halves by a strong mid-line pause, the caesura. Early English poetry was also noted for its kennings, or double-yoked metaphors—for example, whales'-road = the ocean. Perfect rhyme, a somewhat later development, added a new music to anonymous lyrics and ballads: the folk poetry passed on by word of mouth and changed anew with each passing generation until it was finally fixed in written form. As Anglo-Saxon evolved with the French language to create Middle English, a syllabic count, carried over from French prosody, combined with the Anglo-Saxon accentual count to create accentual-syllabic poetry, a poetry of specific feet and meters, regulated line lengths, and stanzas of established, conventionally recognized structure. Through practice and tradition, accentual-syllabic poetry became the accepted norm of English verse; verse forms like the villanelle and the sonnet, the rondeau and the ballad stanza, the various quatrains and sestets became established. Once introduced by Chaucer, the iambic pentameter line showed its versatility by becoming the basic line of poems as diverse in shape and size as love lyrics, the rhymed couplet, and the sonnet. Rhyme became an expected element of a poem, more common than not. Poets such as Wyatt delighted in elaborately conceived metaphors and similes. Pastoral poems—those by Raleigh and Marlowe, for instance, with rural scenery and characters—reflected older classical themes and traditional settings. Tichborne's *Elegy* is one example of a type of poem that reflects on mortality. The sonnet evolved from Sidney's obedience to the strict demands of the Petrarchan form to Shakespeare's use of the looser English sonnet. In the Petrarchan tradition, however, the sonnet concerns itself principally with love. Lyrics such as those from Shakespeare's plays represent the further development of poems meant to be sung and accompanied by music but which also stand by themselves.

Anonymous

(eighth century)

The Seafarer (modern version by Ezra Pound, 1912)

May I for my own self song's truth reckon,
Journey's jargon, how I in harsh days
Hardship endured oft.
Bitter breast-cares have I abided,
5 Known on my keel many a care's hold,
And dire sea-surge, and there I oft spent
Narrow nightwatch nigh the ship's head
While she tossed close to cliffs. Coldly afflicted,
My feet were by frost benumbed.
10 Chill its chains are; chafing signs
Hew my heart round and hunger begot.
Mere-weary mood. Lest man know not
That he on dry land loveliest liveth,
List how I, care-wretched, on ice-cold sea,
15 Weathered the winter, wretched outcast
Deprived of my kinsmen;
Hung with hard ice-flakes, where hail-scur flew,
There I heard naught save the harsh sea
And ice-cold wave, at whiles the swan cries,
20 Did for my games the gannet's clamor,
Sea-fowls' loudness was for me laughter,
The mews' singing all my mead-drink.
Storms, on the stone-cliffs beaten, fell on the stern
In icy feathers; full oft the eagle screamed
25 With spray on his pinion.
                    Not any protector
May make merry man faring needy.
This he little believes, who aye in winsome life
Abides 'mid burghers some heavy business,
30 Wealthy and wine-flushed, how I weary oft
Must bide above brine.
Neareth nightshade, snoweth from north,
Frost froze the land, hail fell on earth then,
Corn of the coldest. Nathless there knocketh now
35 The heart's thought that I on high streams
The salt-wavy tumult traverse alone.
Moaneth alway my mind's lust
That I fare forth, that I afar hence
Seek out a foreign fastness.

40 For this there's no mood-lofty man over earth's midst,
   Not though he be given his good, but will have in his youth greed;
   Nor his deed to the daring, nor his king to the faithful
   But shall have his sorrow for sea-fare
   Whatever his lord will.
45 He hath not heart for harping, nor in ring-having
   Nor winsomeness to wife, nor world's delight
   Nor any whit else save the wave's slash,
   Yet longing comes upon him to fare forth on the water.
   Bosque taketh blossom, cometh beauty of berries,
50 Fields to fairness, land fares brisker,
   All this admonisheth man eager of mood,
   The heart turns to travel so that he then thinks
   On flood-ways to be far departing.
   Cuckoo calleth with gloomy crying,
55 He singeth summerward, bodeth sorrow,
   The bitter heart's blood. Burgher knows not—
   He the prosperous man—what some perform
   Where wandering them widest draweth.
   So that but now my heart burst from my breastlock,
60 My mood 'mid the mere-flood,
   Over the whale's acre, would wander wide.
   On earth's shelter cometh oft to me,
   Eager and ready, the crying lone-flyer,
   Whets for the whale-path the heart irresistibly,
65 O'er tracks of ocean; seeing that anyhow
   My lord deems to me this dead life
   On loan and on land, I believe not
   That any earth-weal eternal standeth
   Save there be somewhat calamitous
70 That, ere a man's tide go, turn it to twain.
   Disease or oldness or sword-hate
   Beats out the breath from doom-gripped body.
   And for this, every earl whatever, for those speaking after—
   Laud of the living, boasteth some last word,
75 That he will work ere he pass onward,
   Frame on the fair earth 'gainst foes his malice,
   Daring ado, . . .
   So that all men shall honor him after
   And his laud beyond them remain 'mid the English,
80 Aye, for ever, a lasting life's-blast,
   Delight 'mid the doughty.
                              Days little durable,
   And all arrogance of earthen riches,

There come now no kings nor Caesars
85   Nor gold-giving lords like those gone.
Howe'er in mirth most magnified,
Whoe'er lived in life most lordliest,
Drear all this excellence, delights undurable!
Waneth the watch, but the world holdeth.
90   Tomb hideth trouble. The blade is layed low.
Earthly glory ageth and seareth.
No man at all going the earth's gait,
But age fares against him, his face paleth,
Grey-haired he groaneth, knows gone companions,
95   Lordly men, are to earth o'ergiven,
Nor may he then the flesh-cover, whose life ceaseth,
Nor eat the sweet nor feel the sorry,
Nor stir hand nor think in mid heart,
And though he strew the grave with gold,
100   His born brothers, their buried bodies
Be an unlikely treasure hoard.

Anonymous

(eighth century)

From **Beowulf** (translation by C. W. Kennedy)

"Oft in the hall I have heard my people,
Comrades and counsellors, telling a tale
Of evil spirits their eyes have sighted,
105   Two mighty marauders who haunt the moors.
One shape, as clearly as men could see,
Seemed woman's likeness, and one seemed man,
An outcast wretch of another world,
And huger far than a human form.
110   Grendel my countrymen called him, not knowing
What monster-brood spawned him, what sire begot.
Wild and lonely the land they live in,
Wind-swept ridges and wolf-retreats,
Dread tracts of fen where the falling torrent
115   Downward dips into gloom and shadow
Under the dusk of the darkening cliff.
Not far in miles lies the lonely mere
Where trees firm-rooted and hung with frost
Overshroud the wave with shadowing gloom.

120 And there a portent appears each night,
     A flame in the water; no man so wise
     Who knows the bound of its bottomless depth.
     The heather-stepper, the horned stag,
     The antlered hart hard driven by hounds,
125 Invading that forest in flight from afar
     Will turn at bay and die on the brink
     Ere ever he'll plunge in that haunted pool.
     'Tis an eerie spot! Its tossing spray
     Mounts dark to heaven when high winds stir
130 The driving storm, and the sky is murky,
     And with foul weather the heavens weep."

Anonymous—Middle English Lyrics

(thirteenth and fourteenth centuries)

Sumer Is Icumen In[1]

Sumer is icumen in,
    Lhude sing cuccu!
Groweth sed and bloweth med
    And springth the wude nu.
5   Sing cuccu!

Awe bleteth after lomb,
    Lhouth after calve cu,
Bulluc sterteth, bucke verteth;
    Murie sing cuccu!
10   Cuccu! cuccu!
Wel singes thu cuccu.
Ne swik thu naver nu!

Sing cuccu nu, Sing cuccu!
Sing cuccu, Sing cuccu nu!

---

[1]*Translation:*
Spring has come in,
    Loudly sing cuckoo!
Grows seed and blooms mead
    And springs the wood now.
        Sing cuckoo!

Ewe bleats after lamb,
    Lows after calf the cow,

Bullock starts, buck farts;
    Merrily sing cuckoo!
        Cuckoo! cuckoo!
Well sing thou cuckoo.
Cease thou never now!

Sing cuckoo now etc.

Alysoun[1]

Bytuene Mersh and Averil,
   When spray beginneth to springe,
The lutel foul hath hire wyl
   On hyre lud to synge.
     5   Ich libbe in lovelonginge
   For semlokest of alle thynge;
   He may me blisse bringe:
Icham in hire baundoun.
   An hendy hap ichabbe yhent—
10   Ichot from hevene it is me sent:
   From alle wymmen mi love is lent
And lyht on Alysoun.

On heu hire her is fayr ynoh,
   Hire browe broune, hire eye blake;
15 With lossum chere he on me loh;
   With middel small and wel ymake.
   Bote he me wolle to hire take
   Forte buen hire owen make,
   Longe to lyven ichulle forsake
20 And feye fallen adoun.
   An hendy hap etc.

---

[1]*Translation:*

Between March and April
   When twigs begin to spring,
The little bird has a will
   In her tongue to sing.
   I live in love-longing
   For the seemliest of all things;
   She may to me bliss bring:
I am in her power.
   A happy chance I have received—
   I know from heaven it is me sent:
   From all women my love is turned
And lights on Alison.

In hue her hair is fair enough,
   Her brow brown, her eye black;
With lovely face she on me laughed;
   With waist small and well-made.
   Unless she me will to her take
   To be her own mate,
   Long to live I shall forsake
And doomed fall down.
   A happy chance etc.

Nights when I turn and wake—
   So that my cheeks wax wan—
Lady, all for thy sake,
   Longing has come upon me,
   In the world there's not so wise a
     man
   That can all her goodness tell;
   Her neck is whiter than the swan,
And fairest maid in town.
   A happy chance etc.

I am from wooing all worn out,
   Weary as water on the beach;
Lest any take from me my mate
   Whom I have yearned for long.
   Better it is to suffer awhile sorely
   Than to mourn evermore.
   Fairest under gown,
Harken to my song.
   A happy chance etc.

Nihtes when y wende and wake—
 For-thi myn wonges waxeth won—
Levedi, al for thine sake,
25 Longinge is ylent me on.
 In world nis non so wyter mon
 That al hire bounte telle con;
 Hire swyre is whittore then the swon,
And feyrest may in toune.
30 An hendy hap etc.

Icham for wowyng al forwake,
 Wery so water in wore;
Lest eny reve me my make
 Ychabbe y-yyrned yore.
35 Betere is tholien whyle sore
 Then mournen evermore.
 Geynest under gore,
Herkne to my roun.
  An hendy hap etc.

All Night by the Rose

All night by the rose, rose—
 All night by the rose I lay;
Dared I not the rose steal,
 And yet I bore the flower away.

Western Wind

Western wind, when will thou blow,
 The small rain down can rain?
Christ, if my love were in my arms
 And I in my bed again.

The Lady Fortune

The lady Fortune is both freend and fo.
Of poure she maketh riche, of riche poure also;
She turneth wo al into wele, and wele al into wo.
Ne truste no man to this wele, the wheel it turneth so.

Geoffrey Chaucer

(c. 1343–1400)

From **The Legend of Good Women**

And as for me, though that I konne but lyte,[1]
30 On bokes for to rede I me delyte,
And to hem give I feyth and ful credence,
And in myn herte have hem in reverence
So hertely, that ther is game noon
That fro my bokes maketh me to goon,
35 But yt be seldom on the holy day,
Save, certeynly, whan that the monethe of May
Is comen, and that I here the foules[2] synge,
And that the floures gynnen for to sprynge,—
Fairewel my boke, and my devocioun!
40   Now have I thanne suche a condicioun,
That of alle the floures in the mede,
Thanne love I most thise floures white and rede,
Suche as men callen daysyes in her toune.
To hem have I so grete affeccioun,
45 As I seyde erst, whanne comen is the May,
That in my bed ther daweth me no day,
That I nam uppe and walkyng in the mede,
To seen this floure agein[3] the sonne sprede,
Whan it up rysith erly by the morwe;
50 That blisful sight softneth al my sorwe,
So glad am I, whan that I have presence
Of it, to doon it alle reverence,
As she that is of alle floures flour,
Fulfilled of al vertue and honour,
55 And evere ilike faire, and fresshe of hewe.
And I love it, and evere ylike newe,
And ever shal, til that myn herte dye;
Al swere I nat—of this I wol nat lye—
Ther lovede no wight hotter in his lyve.
60   And, whan that hit ys eve, I renne blyve,[4]

----

[1]know but little
[2]birds
[3]toward
[4]run quickly

As sone as evere the sonne gynneth weste,[5]
To seen this flour, how it wol go to reste,
For fere of nyght, so hateth she derkenesse!
Hire chere[6] is pleynly sprad in the brightnesse
65 Of the sonne, for ther yt wol unclose.
Allas, that I ne had Englyssh, ryme or prose,
Suffisant this flour to preyse aryght!

Anonymous—the Popular Ballads

(fourteenth and fifteenth centuries)

Get Up and Bar the Door

It fell about the Martinmas[1] time,
   And a gay time it was then,
When our good wife got puddings[2] to make,
   And she's boild them in the pan.

5 The wind sae cauld blew south and north,
   And blew into the floor;
Quoth our goodman to our goodwife,
   "Gae out and bar the door."

"My hand is in my hussyfskap,[3]
10   Goodman, as ye may see;
An it shoud nae be barrd this hundred year,
   It's no be barrd for me."

They made a paction tween them twa,
   They made it firm and sure,
15 That the first word whaeer shoud speak,
   Shoud rise and bar the door.

Then by there came two gentlemen,
   At twelve oclock at night,
And they could neither see house nor hall,
20   Nor coal nor candle-light.

"Now whether is this a rich man's house,
   Or whether is it a poor?"

---

[5]begins to go west
[6]countenance

---

[1]November 11
[2]sausages
[3]household chores

But neer a word wad ane o them speak,
    For barring of the door.

25 And first they ate the white puddings,
    And then they ate the black;
Tho muckle[4] thought the goodwife to hersel,
    Yet neer a word she spake.

Then said the one unto the other,
30   "Here, man, tak ye my knife;
Do ye tak aff the auld man's beard,
    And I'll kiss the goodwife."

"But there's nae water in the house,
    And what shall we do than?"
35 "What ails ye at the pudding-broo,
    That boils into the pan?"

O up then started our goodman,
    An angry man was he:
"Will ye kiss my wife before my een,
40   And scad me wi pudding-bree?"

Then up and started our goodwife,
    Gied three skips on the floor:
"Goodman, you've spoken the foremost word,
    Get up and bar the door."

Lord Randal

"O where ha you been, Lord Randal, my son?
And where ha you been, my handsome young man?"
"I ha been at the greenwood; mother, mak my bed soon,
For I'm wearied wi hunting, and fain wad lie down."

5 "An wha met ye there, Lord Randal, my son?
An wha met you there, my handsome young man?"
"O I met wi my true-love; mother, mak my bed soon,
For I'm wearied wi huntin, and fain wad lie down."

"And what did she give you, Lord Randal, my son?
10 And what did she give you, my handsome young man?"
"Eels fried in a pan; mother, mak my bed soon,
For I'm wearied wi huntin, and fain wad lie down."

"And wha gat your leavins, Lord Randal, my son?
And wha gat your leavins, my handsome young man?"

---

[4]much

15 "My hawks and my hounds; mother, mak my bed soon,
For I'm wearied wi hunting, and fain wad lie down."

"And what becam of them, Lord Randal, my son?
And what becam of them, my handsome young man?"
"They stretched their legs out and died; mother, mak my bed soon,
20 For I'm wearied wi huntin, and fain wad lie down."

"O I fear you are poisoned, Lord Randal, my son!
I fear you are poisoned, my handsome young man!"
"O yes, I am poisoned; mother, mak my bed soon,
For I'm sick at the heart, and I fain wad lie down."

25 "What d'ye leave to your mother, Lord Randal, my son?
What d'ye leave to your mother, my handsome young man?"
"Four and twenty milk kye[1]; mother, mak my bed soon,
For I'm sick at the heart, and I fain wad lie down."

"What d'ye leave to your sister, Lord Randal, my son?
30 What d'ye leave to your sister, my handsome young man?"
"My gold and my silver; mother, mak my bed soon,
For I'm sick at the heart, an I fain wad lie down."

"What d'ye leave to your brother, Lord Randal, my son?
What d'ye leave to your brother, my handsome young man?"
35 "My houses and my lands; mother, mak my bed soon,
For I'm sick at the heart, and I fain wad lie down."

"What d'ye leave to your true-love, Lord Randal, my son?
What d'ye leave to your true-love, my handsome young man?"
"I leave her hell and fire; mother, mak my bed soon,
40 For I'm sick at the heart, and I fain wad lie down."

The Three Ravens

There were three ravens sat on a tree,
    Downe a downe, hay down, hay downe,
There were three ravens sat on a tree,
    With a downe,
5 There were three ravens sat on a tree,
They were as blacke as they might be,
    With a downe derrie, derrie, derrie, downe, downe.

The one of them said to his mate,
"Where shall we our breakfast take?"[1]

---

[1]cows

---

[1]The line pattern and refrain of the first stanza recur throughout.

10 "Downe in yonder greene field,
    There lies a knight slain under his shield.

"His hounds they lie downe at his feete,
So well they can their master keepe.

"His hawkes they flie so eagerly,[2]
15 There's no fowle dare him come nie."

Downe there comes a fallow doe,
As great with yong as she might goe.

She lift up his bloody hed,
And kist his wounds that were so red.

20 She got him up upon her back,
And carried him to earthen lake.[3]

She buried him before the prime,
She was dead herselfe ere evensong time.

God send every gentleman
25 Such hawkes, such hounds, and such a leman.[4]

The Cherry-Tree Carol

Joseph was an old man,
    and an old man was he,
When he wedded Mary,
    in the land of Galilee.

5 Joseph and Mary walked
    through an orchard good,
Where was cherries and berries,
    so red as any blood.

Joseph and Mary walked
10   through an orchard green,
Where was berries and cherries,
    as thick as might be seen.

O then bespoke Mary,
    so meek and so mild:
15 "Pluck me one cherry, Joseph,
    for I am with child."

---

[2]fiercely
[3]grave
[4]lover

O then bespoke Joseph:
    with words most unkind:
"Let him pluck thee a cherry
20   that brought thee with child."

O then bespoke the babe,
    within his mother's womb:
"Bow down then the tallest tree,
    for my mother to have some."

25 Then bowed down the highest tree
    unto his mother's hand;
Then she cried, "See, Joseph,
    I have cherries at command."

O then bespoke Joseph:
30   "I have done Mary wrong;
But cheer up, my dearest,
    and be not cast down."

Then Mary plucked a cherry,
    as red as the blood,
35 Then Mary went home
    with her heavy load.

Then Mary took her babe,
    and sat him on her knee,
Saying, "My dear son, tell me
40   what this world will be."

"O I shall be as dead, mother,
    as the stones in the wall;
O the stones in the streets, mother,
    shall mourn for me all.

45 "Upon Easter-day, mother,
    my uprising shall be;
O the sun and the moon, mother,
    shall both rise with me."

The Unquiet Grave

"The wind doth blow today, my love,
    And a few small drops of rain;
I never had but one true-love,
    In cold grave she was lain.

5 "I'll do as much for my true-love
    As any young man may;

I'll sit and mourn all at her grave
    For a twelvemonth and a day."

The twelvemonth and a day being up,
10   The dead began to speak:
"Oh who sits weeping on my grave,
    And will not let me sleep?"

"'Tis I, my love, sits on your grave,
    And will not let you sleep;
15 For I crave one kiss of your clay-cold lips,
    And that is all I seek."

"You crave one kiss of my clay-cold lips;
    But my breath smells earthy strong;
If you have one kiss of my clay-cold lips,
20   Your time will not be long.

"'Tis down in yonder garden green,
    Love, where we used to walk,
The finest flower that e'er was seen
    Is withered to a stalk.

25 "The stalk is withered dry, my love,
    So will our hearts decay;
So make yourself content, my love,
    Till God calls you away."

Bonny Barbara Allan

It was in and about the Martinmas time,
    When the green leaves were a falling,
That Sir John Graeme, in the West Country,
    Fell in love with Barbara Allan.

5 He sent his man down through the town,
    To the place where she was dwelling:
"O haste and come to my master dear,
    Gin[1] ye be Barbara Allan."

O hooly,[2] hooly rose she up,
10   To the place where he was lying,
And when she drew the curtain by,
    "Young man, I think you're dying."

---

[1]if
[2]slowly

"O it's I'm sick, and very, very sick,
   And 'tis a' for Barbara Allan."
15 "O the better for me ye's never be,
   Tho your heart's blood were a spilling.

"O dinna ye mind,[3] young man," said she,
   "When ye was in the tavern a drinking,
That ye made the healths gae round and round,
20   And slighted Barbara Allan?"

He turnd his face unto the wall,
   And death was with him dealing:
"Adieu, adieu, my dear friends all,
   And be kind to Barbara Allan."

25 And slowly, slowly raise she up,
   And slowly, slowly left him,
And sighing said she could not stay,
   Since death of life had reft him.

She had not gane a mile but twa,
30   When she heard the dead-bell ringing;
And every jow[4] that the dead-bell geid,[5]
   It cry'd "Woe to Barbara Allan!"

"O mother, mother, make my bed!
   O make it soft and narrow!
35 Since my love died for me today,
   I'll die for him tomorrow."

Sir Thomas Wyatt

(1503–1542)

They Flee from Me

They flee from me that sometime did me seek
   With naked foot stalking in my chamber.
I have seen them gentle tame and meek
   That now are wild and do not remember
5   That sometime they put themself in danger
To take bread at my hand; and now they range
Busily seeking with a continual change.

---

[3]don't you remember
[4]stroke
[5]gave

Thanked be Fortune it hath been otherwise
   Twenty times better; but once in special,
10 In thin array after a pleasant guise,
   When her loose gown from her shoulders did fall,
   And she me caught in her arms long and small;[1]
And therewith all sweetly did me kiss,
And softly said, "Dear heart, how like you this?"

15 It was no dream: I lay broad waking.
   But all is turned thorough my gentleness
Into a strange fashion of forsaking;
   And I have leave to go of her goodness,
   And she also to use newfangleness.
20 But since that I so kindely[2] am served,
I fain would know what she hath deserved.

1557

Sir Walter Raleigh

(1552?–1618)

The Nymph's Reply to the Shepherd

If all the world and love were young,
And truth in every shepherd's tongue,
These pretty pleasures might me move
To live with thee and be thy love.

5 Time drives the flocks from field to fold
When rivers rage and rocks grow cold,
And Philomel becometh dumb;
The rest complains of cares to come.

The flowers do fade, and wanton fields
10 To wayward winter reckoning yields;
A honey tongue, a heart of gall,
Is fancy's spring, but sorrow's fall.

Thy gowns, thy shoes, thy beds of roses,
Thy cap, thy kirtle, and thy posies
15 Soon break, soon wither, soon forgotten—
In folly ripe, in reason rotten.

———
[1]slender
[2]in the manner of womankind; also "agreeably," in an ironic sense

Thy belt of straw and ivy buds,
Thy coral clasps and amber studs,
All these in me no means can move
20 To come to thee and be thy love.

But could youth last and love still breed,
Had joys no date nor age no need,
Then these delights my mind might move
To live with thee and be thy love.

1600

Edmund Spenser

(1552?–1599)

From **Amoretti**

Sonnet 15

Ye tradefull Merchants, that with weary toyle,
Do seeke most pretious things to make your gain,
And both the Indias of their treasure spoile,
What needeth you to seeke so farre in vaine?
5 For loe, my Love doth in her selfe containe
All this worlds riches that may farre be found:
If saphyres, loe her eies be saphyres plaine;
If rubies, loe hir lips be rubies sound;
If pearles, hir teeth be pearles both pure and round;
10 If yvorie, her forhead yvory weene;
If gold, her locks are finest gold on ground;
If silver, her faire hands are silver sheene:
   But that which fairest is but few behold:—
   Her mind, adornd with vertues manifold.

Sonnet 67

Lyke as a huntsman, after weary chace,
Seeing the game from him escapt away,
Sits downe to rest him in some shady place,
With panting hounds beguilèd of their pray,
5 So after long pursuit and vaine assay,
When I all weary had the chace forsooke,
The gentle deere returned the selfe-same way,
Thinking to quench her thirst at the next brooke.

There she beholding me with mylder looke
10 Sought not to fly, but fearlesse still did bide,
Till I in hand her yet halfe trembling tooke,
And with her owne goodwill her fyrmely tyde.
     Strange thing, me seemd, to see a beast so wyld
     So goodly wonne, with her owne will beguyld.

Sonnet 75

One day I wrote her name upon the strand,
But came the waves and washèd it away:
Agayne I wrote it with a second hand,
But came the tyde, and made my paynes his pray.
5 "Vayne man," sayd she, "that doest in vaine assay
A mortall thing so to immortalize;
For I my selve shall lyke to this decay,
And eek my name bee wypèd out lykewize."
"Not so," quod I, "let baser things devize[1]
10 To dy in dust, but you shall live by fame:
My verse your vertues rare shall eternize,
And in the hevens wryte your glorious name;
     Where, when as death shall all the world subdew,
     Our love shall live, and later life renew."

Sonnet 82

Joy of my life, full oft for loving you
I blesse my lot, that was so lucky placed.
But then the more your owne mishap I rew,
That are so much by so meane love embased.
5 For, had the equall hevens so much you graced
In this as in the rest, ye mote invent[1]
Som hevenly wit, whose verse could have enchased
Your glorious name in golden moniment.
But since ye deignd so goodly to relent
10 To me, your thrall, in whom is little worth,
That little that I am shall all be spent
In setting your immortall prayses forth:
     Whose lofty argument, uplifting me,
     Shall lift you up unto an high degree.

1595

---
[1]contrive

---
[1]might find

Sir Philip Sidney

(1554–1586)

Thou Blind Man's Mark

Thou blind man's mark,[1] thou fool's self-chosen snare,
Fond fancy's scum, and dregs of scattered thought,
Bands of all evils, cradle of causeless care,
Thou web of will whose end is never wrought;

5 Desire, Desire, I have too dearly bought
With prize of mangled mind thy worthless ware!
Too long, too long asleep thou hast me brought
Who should my mind to higher things prepare.

But yet in vain thou hast my ruin sought;
10 In vain thou madest me to vain things aspire;
In vain thou kindlest all thy smoky fire.

For Virtue hath this better lesson taught:
Within myself to seek my only hire,
Desiring nought but how to kill desire.

Leave Me, O Love

Leave me, O Love, which reachest but to dust,
And thou, my mind, aspire to higher things.
Grow rich in that which never taketh rust.
Whatever fades but fading pleasure brings.

5 Draw in thy beams and humble all thy might
To that sweet yoke where lasting freedoms be,
Which breaks the clouds and opens forth the light
That doth both shine and give us sight to see.

O take fast hold; let that light be thy guide
10 In this small course which birth draws out to death,
And think how evil becometh him to slide
Who seeketh heaven and comes of heavenly breath.
    Then farewell, world! The uttermost I see!
    Eternal Love, maintain thy life in me.

---

[1]target

Chidiock Tichborne

(1558?–1586)

Tichborne's Elegy

Written with His Own Hand in the Tower
Before His Execution

My prime of youth is but a frost of cares,
My feast of joy is but a dish of pain,
My crop of corn is but a field of tares,
And all my good is but vain hope of gain;
5   The day is past, and yet I saw no sun,
And now I live, and now my life is done.

My tale was heard and yet it was not told,
My fruit is fallen and yet my leaves are green,
My youth is spent and yet I am not old,
10   I saw the world and yet I was not seen;
My thread is cut and yet it is not spun,
And now I live, and now my life is done.

I sought my death and found it in my womb,
I looked for life and saw it was a shade,
15   I trod the earth and knew it was my tomb,
And now I die, and now I was but made;
My glass is full, and now my glass is run,
And now I live, and now my life is done.

1586

Robert Southwell

(1561?–1595)

The Burning Babe

As I in hoary winter's night stood shivering in the snow,
Surprised I was with sudden heat which made my heart to glow;
And lifting up a fearful eye to view what fire was near,
A pretty babe all burning bright did in the air appear;
5   Who, scorchèd with excessive heat, such floods of tears did shed
As though his floods should quench his flames which with his tears
        were fed.
"Alas," quoth he, "but newly born in fiery heats I fry,
Yet none approach to warm their hearts or feel my fire but I!

My faultless breast the furnace is, the fuel wounding thorns,
10 Love is the fire, and sighs the smoke, the ashes shame and scorns;
The fuel justice layeth on, and mercy blows the coals,
The metal in this furnace wrought are men's defilèd souls,
For which, as now on fire I am to work them to their good,
So will I melt into a bath to wash them in my blood."
15 With this he vanished out of sight and swiftly shrunk away,
And straight I callèd unto mind that it was Christmas day.

1595

Michael Drayton

(1563–1631)

From **Idea**

Sonnet 6

How many paltry, foolish, painted things
That now in coaches trouble every street
Shall be forgotten, whom no poet sings,
Ere they be well wrapped in their winding-sheet!
5 Where I to thee eternity shall give
When nothing else remaineth of these days,
And queens hereafter shall be glad to live
Upon the alms of thy superfluous praise.
Virgins and matrons, reading these my rimes,
10 Shall be so much delighted with thy story
That they shall grieve they lived not in these times
To have seen thee, their sex's only glory.
　　So shalt thou fly above the vulgar throng
　　Still to survive in my immortal song.

Sonnet 7

Since there's no help, come, let us kiss and part.
Nay, I have done, you get no more of me,
And I am glad, yea glad with all my heart
That thus so cleanly I myself can free;
5 Shake hands forever, cancel all our vows,
And when we meet at any time again
Be it not seen in either of our brows
That we one jot of former love retain.

Now at the last gasp of Love's latest breath,
10 When, his pulse failing, Passion speechless lies,
When Faith is kneeling by his bed of death
And innocence is closing up his eyes,
    Now if thou would'st, when all have given him over,
    From death to life thou might'st him yet recover.

1619

Christopher Marlowe

(1564–1593)

The Passionate Shepherd to His Love

Come live with me, and be my love,
And we will all the pleasures prove
That hills and valleys, dales and fields,
And all the craggy mountains yields.

5 And we will sit upon the rocks,
Seeing the shepherds feed their flocks,
By shallow rivers, to whose falls
Melodious birds sing madrigals.

And I will make thee beds of roses
10 And a thousand fragrant posies,
A cap of flowers, and a kirtle
Embroidered all with leaves of myrtle;

A gown made of the finest wool,
Which from our pretty lambs we pull,
15 Fair linèd slippers, for the cold,
With buckles of the purest gold;

A belt of straw and ivy-buds
With coral clasps and amber studs.
And if these pleasures may thee move,
20 Come live with me, and be my love.

The shepherds' swains shall dance and sing
For thy delight each May morning.
If these delights thy mind may move,
Then live with me, and be my love.

1599

William Shakespeare

(1564–1616)

From **The Sonnets**

Sonnet 18

Shall I compare thee to a summer's day?
Thou art more lovely and more temperate:
Rough winds do shake the darling buds of May,
And summer's lease hath all too short a date:
5   Sometime too hot the eye of heaven shines,
And often is his gold complexion dimmed;
And every fair from fair sometime declines,
By chance or nature's changing course untrimmed:
But thy eternal summer shall not fade
10   Nor lose possession of that fair thou ow'st,[1]
Nor shall Death brag thou wand'rest in his shade,
When in eternal lines to time thou grow'st.
    So long as men can breathe or eyes can see,
    So long lives this, and this gives life to thee.

Sonnet 20

A woman's face with Nature's own hand painted
Hast thou, the master-mistress of my passion;
A woman's gentle heart, but not acquainted
With shifting change, as is false women's fashion;
5   An eye more bright than theirs, less false in rolling,
Gilding the object whereupon it gazeth;
A man in hue, all hues in his controlling,
Which steals men's eyes and women's souls amazeth.
And for a woman wert thou first created,
10   Till Nature, as she wrought thee, fell a-doting,
And by addition me of thee defeated,
By adding one thing to my purpose nothing.
    But since she pricked thee out for women's pleasure
    Mine be thy love and thy love's use their treasure.

Sonnet 29

When, in disgrace with Fortune and men's eyes,
I all alone beweep my outcast state,
And trouble deaf heaven with my bootless cries,
And look upon myself and curse my fate,

---

[1]ownest

5 Wishing me like to one more rich in hope,
  Featured like him, like him with friends possessed,
  Desiring this man's art, and that man's scope,
  With what I most enjoy contented least;
  Yet in these thoughts myself almost despising,
10 Haply I think on thee, and then my state,
  Like to the lark at break of day arising
  From sullen earth, sings hymns at heaven's gate;
    For thy sweet love remembered such wealth brings
    That when I scorn to change my state with kings.

Sonnet 30

When to the sessions[1] of sweet silent thought
I summon up remembrance of things past,
I sigh the lack of many a thing I sought,
And with old woes new wail my dear time's waste.
5 Then can I drown an eye, unused to flow,
  For precious friends hid in death's dateless night,
  And weep afresh love's long since canceled woe,
  And moan th' expense of many a vanished sight.
  Then can I grieve at grievances foregone,
10 And heavily from woe to woe tell o'er
  The sad account of fore-bemoanèd moan,
  Which I new pay as if not paid before.
    But if the while I think on thee, dear friend,
    All losses are restored and sorrows end.

Sonnet 73

That time of year thou mayst in me behold
When yellow leaves, or none, or few, do hang
Upon those boughs which shake against the cold,
Bare ruined choirs where late the sweet birds sang.
5 In me thou see'st the twilight of such day
  As after sunset fadeth in the west,
  Which by and by black night doth take away,
  Death's second self that seals up all in rest.
  In me thou see'st the glowing of such fire
10 That on the ashes of his youth doth lie,
  As the deathbed whereon it must expire,
  Consumed with that which it was nourished by.
    This thou perceiv'st, which makes thy love more strong
    To love that well which thou must leave ere long.

---

[1]English court of law

Sonnet 97

How like a winter hath my absence been
From thee, the pleasure of the fleeting year!
What freezings have I felt, what dark days seen!
What old December's bareness everywhere!
5 And yet this time removed[1] was summer's time,
The teeming autumn, big with rich increase,
Bearing the wanton burden of the prime,
Like widowed wombs after their lords' decease.
Yet this abundant issue seemed to me
10 But hope of orphans and unfathered fruit,
For summer and his pleasures wait on thee,
And, thou away, the very birds are mute;
   Or, if they sing, 'tis with so dull a cheer
   That leaves look pale, dreading the winter's near.

Sonnet 104

To me, fair friend, you never can be old,
For as you were when first your eye I eyed,
Such seems your beauty still. Three winters cold
Have from the forests shook three summers' pride,
5 Three beauteous springs to yellow autumn turned
In process of the seasons have I seen,
Three April perfumes in three hot Junes burned,
Since first I saw you fresh which yet are green.
Ah yet doth beauty like a dial hand
10 Steal from his figure, and no pace perceived!
So your sweet hue, which methinks still doth stand,
Hath motion, and mine eye may be deceived;
   For fear of which, hear this thou age unbred:
   Ere you were born was beauty's summer dead.

Sonnet 116

Let me not to the marriage of true minds
Admit impediments. Love is not love
Which alters when it alteration finds,
Or bends with the remover to remove.
5 O no! it is an ever-fixèd mark
That looks on tempests and is never shaken;
It is the star to every wand'ring bark,
Whose worth's unknown, although his height be taken.
Love's not Time's fool, though rosy lips and cheeks

---

[1] time we were apart

10 Within his bending sickle's compass come.
    Love alters not with his brief hours and weeks,
    But bears it out even to the edge of doom.
       If this be error, and upon me proved,
       I never writ, nor no man ever loved.

Sonnet 129

    Th' expense of spirit in a waste of shame
    Is lust in action; and, till action, lust
    Is perjured, murd'rous, bloody, full of blame,
    Savage, extreme, rude, cruel, not to trust;
5 Enjoyed no sooner but despisèd straight;
    Past reason hunted, and no sooner had,
    Past reason hated, as a swallowed bait
    On purpose laid to make the taker mad;
    Mad in pursuit, and in possession so;
10 Had, having, and in quest to have, extreme;
    A bliss in proof—and proved, a very woe;
    Before, a joy proposed; behind, a dream.
       All this the world well knows; yet none knows well
       To shun the heaven that leads men to this hell.

Sonnet 130

    My mistress' eyes are nothing like the sun;
    Coral is far more red than her lips' red;
    If snow be white, why then her breasts are dun;[1]
    If hairs be wires, black wires grow on her head.
5 I have seen roses damasked, red and white,
    But no such roses see I in her cheeks;
    And in some perfumes is there more delight
    Than in the breath that from my mistress reeks.
    I love to hear her speak, yet well I know
10 That music hath a far more pleasing sound.
    I grant I never saw a goddess go;
    My mistress, when she walks, treads on the ground.
       And yet, by heaven, I think my love as rare
       As any she belied with false compare.

Sonnet 144

    Two loves I have, of comfort and despair,
    Which like two spirits do suggest me still:
    The better angel is a man right fair,

---

[1]brownish dark gray

The worser spirit a woman colored ill.
5   To win me soon to hell, my female evil
Tempteth my better angel from my side,
And would corrupt my saint to be a devil,
Wooing his purity with her foul pride.
And whether that my angel be turned fiend
10   Suspect I may, yet not directly tell;
But being both from me, both to each friend,
I guess one angel in another's hell.
　　Yet this shall I ne'er know, but live in doubt
　　Till my bad angel fire my good one out.

Sonnet 151

Love is too young to know what conscience is,—
Yet who knows not conscience is born of love?
Then, gentle cheater, urge not my amiss,
Lest guilty of my faults thy sweet self prove.
5   For, thou betraying me, I do betray
My nobler part to my gross body's treason;
My soul doth tell my body that he may
Triumph in love: flesh stays no farther reason,
But rising at thy name doth point out thee
10   As his triumphant prize. Proud of this pride,
He is contented thy poor drudge to be,
To stand in thy affairs, fall by thy side.
　　No want of conscience hold it that I call
　　Her "love" for whose dear love I rise and fall.

1609

Anonymous—Elizabethan Lyrics

(sixteenth and seventeenth centuries)

Back and Side Go Bare

Back and side go bare, go bare,
　　Both foot and hand go cold;
But, belly, God send thee good ale enough,
　　Whether it be new or old.

5   I cannot eat but little meat,
　　My stomach is not good;
But sure I think that I can drink
　　With him that wears a hood.

Though I go bare, take ye no care,
10   I am nothing a-cold;
I stuff my skin so full within
    Of jolly good ale and old.
        Back and side go bare, go bare, &c.

I love no roast but a nutbrown toast,
15   And a crab laid in the fire;
A little bread shall do me stead,
    Much bread I not desire.
No frost nor snow, no wind, I trow,
    Can hurt me if I would,
20 I am so wrapt, and throughly lapt
    Of jolly good ale and old.
        Back and side go bare, go bare, &c.

And Tib my wife, that as her life
    Loveth well good ale to seek,
25 Full oft drinks she, till ye may see
    The tears run down her cheek.
Then doth she troll to me the bowl,
    Even as a maltworm should;
And saith, "Sweetheart, I took my part
30   Of this jolly good ale and old."
        Back and side go bare, go bare, &c.

Now let them drink, till they nod and wink,
    Even as good fellows should do;
They shall not miss to have the bliss
35   Good ale doth bring men to.
And all poor souls that have scourèd bowls,
    Or have them lustily trolled,
God save the lives of them and their wives,
    Whether they be young or old.
40   Back and side go bare, go bare,
            Both foot and hand go cold;
            But, belly, God send thee good ale enough,
                Whether it be new or old.

April Is in My Mistress' Face

April is in my mistress' face,
And Jùly in her eyes hath place,
Within her bosom is September,
But in her heart a cold December.

My Love in Her Attire

My love in her attire doth show her wit,
    It doth so well become her.
For every season she hath dressings fit,
    For winter, spring, and summer.
5 No beauty she doth miss
    When all her robes are on;
But Beauty's self she is
    When all her robes are gone.

1602

There Is a Lady Sweet and Kind

There is a lady sweet and kind,
Was never face so pleased my mind;
I did but see her passing by,
And yet I love her till I die.

5 Her gesture, motion and her smiles,
Her wit, her voice, my heart beguiles,
Beguiles my heart, I know not why,
And yet I love her till I die.

Her free behavior, winning looks,
10 Will make a lawyer burn his books.
I touched her not, alas, not I,
And yet I love her till I die.

Had I her fast betwixt mine arms,
Judge you that think such sports were harms,
15 Were't any harm? No, no, fie, fie!
For I will love her till I die.

Should I remain confinèd there,
So long as Phoebus in his sphere,
I to request, she to deny,
20 Yet would I love her till I die.

Cupid is wingèd and doth range;
Her country so my love doth change,
But change she earth, or change she sky,
Yet will I love her till I die.

1607

The Silver Swan

The silver swan, who living had no note,
When death approached, unlocked her silent throat;
Leaning her breast against the reedy shore,
Thus sung her first and last, and sung no more:
5 "Farewell, all joys; Oh death, come close mine eyes;
More geese than swans now live, more fools than wise."

1612

Thomas Nashe

(1567–1601)

Adieu, Farewell Earth's Bliss

Adieu, farewell earth's bliss!
This world uncertain is;
Fond are life's lustful joys:
Death proves them all but toys.
5 None from his darts can fly;
I am sick, I must die.
    Lord, have mercy on us!

Rich men, trust not in wealth;
Gold cannot buy you health;
10 Physic himself must fade.
All things to end are made;
The plague full swift goes by;
I am sick, I must die.
    Lord, have mercy on us!

15 Beauty is but a flower,
Which wrinkles will devour;
Brightness falls from the air;
Queens have died young and fair;
Dust hath closed Helen's eye.
20 I am sick, I must die.
    Lord, have mercy on us!

Strength stoops unto the grave;
Worms feed on Hector brave;
Swords may not fight with fate;
25 Earth still holds ope her gate;

"Come, come!" the bells do cry.
I am sick, I must die.
   Lord, have mercy on us!

Wit with his wantonness
30 Tasteth death's bitterness;
Hell's executioner
Hath no ears for to hear
What vain art can reply.
I am sick, I must die.
35   Lord, have mercy on us!

Haste, therefore, each degree,
To welcome destiny!
Heaven is our heritage,
Earth but a player's stage;
40 Mount we unto the sky.
I am sick, I must die.
   Lord, have mercy on us!

1600

Thomas Campion

(1567–1620)

My Sweetest Lesbia

My sweetest Lesbia, let us live and love;
And though the sager sort our deeds reprove,
Let us not weigh them: heaven's great lamps do dive
Into their west, and straight again revive;
5 But soon as once set is our little light,
Then must we sleep one ever-during night.

If all would lead their lives in love like me,
Then bloody swords and armor should not be;
No drum nor trumpet peaceful sleeps should move,
10 Unless alarm came from the camp of love.
But fools do live, and waste their little light,
And seek with pain their ever-during night.

When timely death my life and fortune ends,
Let not my hearse be vexed with mourning friends;
15 But let all lovers, rich in triumph, come

And with sweet pastimes grace my happy tomb;
And, Lesbia, close up thou my little light,
And crown with love my ever-during night.

1601

There Is a Garden in Her Face

There is a garden in her face,
    Where roses and white lilies grow;
A heavenly paradise is that place,
    Wherein all pleasant fruits do flow.
5 There cherries grow, which none may buy
Till "Cherry ripe!" themselves do cry.

Those cherries fairly do enclose
    Of orient pearl a double row,
Which when her lovely laughter shows,
10   They look like rose-buds filled with snow.
Yet them nor peer nor prince can buy,
Till "Cherry ripe!" themselves do cry.

Her eyes like angels watch them still;
    Her brows like bended bows do stand,
15 Threat'ning with piercing frowns to kill
    All that attempt with eye or hand
Those sacred cherries to come nigh,
Till "Cherry ripe!" themselves do cry.

1617

2

A BRIEF HISTORY

England, like Europe, was convulsed by the religious controversies of the Reformation. The religious passions that swept the Western world resulted in a flood of poetry on religious themes. The worldly concerns of Renaissance poetry were replaced increasingly with themes of redemption and salvation. John Donne had hoped to have a career at court, but was convinced by the king, under pressure, to become an Anglican priest. Donne's priestly career changed his earlier secular love poems into the equally fiery poetry of his Holy Sonnets. At the same time, the discoveries of seventeenth-century science provided him with many of the metaphors and conceits that make his poems engines of density and intellect, characteristic of the Metaphysical school of poetry.

The religious controversies that beheaded King Charles I brought Oliver Cromwell to power in the period known as the Commonwealth and gave way in turn to weariness with Puritan rules and regulations. The Restoration brought back a monarchy considerably weakened by Parliament. Interest in classical themes returned. A period known as the Enlightenment, part of the Age of Reason, brought to birth the Augustan Period. Overseen by the poetry of Dryden and Pope, whose poems were marked by elegance and refinement, a poetry of reason, intellect, and tradition reflected the established views of the upper class. At the same time these poets, along with Jonathan Swift, wrote satirical poetry that ridiculed the superficial manners and morals of their society.

Across the Atlantic in the Colonies, American literature began by modeling its poetry and prose on the literature of England, the mother country. The work of women poets like Anne Bradstreet began to appear. The printing press, along with the slow but steady rise of literacy, increased the audience for poetry, novels, short stories, and political tracts and essays. The ideas of the Enlightenment spread, carrying the political ferment of equality and democracy.

The works of John Donne display numerous famous examples of tropes, figures of speech, which lend his poetry the elaborate quality of the conceit. Along with extended metaphors, devices such as personification, alliteration, and apostrophe combine with complicated meters, irregular line lengths, and eccentric stanza structure. Another Metaphysical poet, Herbert, not only created conceits for his effects but sometimes used visual shapes as well. His *Easter Wings* is an example of an emblematic poem. Earth-bound metaphors allowed the Metaphysical poets to arrive at supernatural, religious, and emotional visions ordinarily beyond the five senses. The sonnets of John Donne concern themselves not only with love, their traditional mode, but also with religion and mortality. Milton's sonnets break away from the usual octet and sestet divisions to create a poem that seems to be a more unified whole. Poems continued to be written on classical models from the Greek and Latin. Some poets wrote on classical themes. Robert Herrick's *To the Virgins, to Make Much of Time* and Andrew Marvell's *To His Coy Mistress* are examples of poems built up not only on elaborate conceits but also on the ancient idea of *carpe diem* ("seize the day"). John Milton composed his epic *Paradise Lost* in blank verse and used technical devices such as elision to lengthen and shorten individual lines of otherwise standardized length. Alexander Pope showed another way to avoid monotony in a long poem when he varied the rhythm of his heroic couplets by moving the caesura to various positions within individual lines. The poems of John Dryden and Pope are often didactic—poems written not only to entertain but also to teach and instruct the reader. Such poems appeal directly to the intellect as well as to the five senses; the life of the mind is considered equal to the emotional and sensational life.

John Donne

(1572–1631)

Song

Go and catch a falling star,
   Get with child a mandrake[1] root,
Tell me where all past years are
   Or who cleft the devil's foot,
5 Teach me to hear mermaids singing
Or to keep off envy's stinging,
      And find
      What wind
Serves to advance an honest mind.

10 If thou be'st born to strange sights,
   Things invisible to see,
Ride ten thousand days and nights
   Till age snow white hairs on thee.
Thou, when thou return'st, wilt tell me
15 All strange wonders that befell thee,
      And swear
      No where
Lives a woman true, and fair.

If thou find'st one, let me know;
20   Such a pilgrimage were sweet.
Yet do not; I would not go,
   Though at next door we might meet.
Though she were true, when you met her,
And last, till you write your letter,
25   Yet she
     Will be
False ere I come, to two, or three.

                                        1633

The Sun Rising

   Busy old fool, unruly sun,
     Why dost thou thus
Through windows and through curtains call on us?
Must to thy motions lovers' seasons run?

---

[1]The large forked root of the mandrake was often credited with human attributes, because of its fancied resemblance to the human body.

5   Saucy, pedantic wretch, go chide
        Late schoolboys and sour 'prentices,
    Go tell court huntsmen that the king will ride,
    Call country ants to harvest offices.
Love, all alike, no season knows nor clime,
10 Nor hours, days, months, which are the rags of time.

      Thy beams, so reverend and strong
        Why shouldst thou think?
I could eclipse and cloud them with a wink,
But that I would not lose her sight so long.
15   If her eyes have not blinded thine,
        Look, and tomorrow late tell me
    Whether both th' Indias of spice and mine
    Be where thou left'st them, or lie here with me;
Ask for those kings whom thou saw'st yesterday,
20 And thou shalt hear: All here in one bed lay.

      She's all states, and all princes I;
        Nothing else is.
Princes do but play us; compared to this,
All honor's mimic, all wealth alchemy.
25   Thou, sun, art half as happy as we,
        In that the world's contracted thus;
    Thine age asks ease, and since thy duties be
    To warm the world, that's done in warming us.
Shine here to us, and thou art everywhere;
30 This bed thy center is, these walls thy sphere.

                                        1633

A Valediction: Of Weeping

      Let me pour forth
My tears before thy face whilst I stay here,
For thy face coins them, and thy stamp they bear,
And by this mintage they are something worth,
5   For thus they be
      Pregnant of thee;
Fruits of much grief they are, emblems of more—
When a tear falls, that Thou falls which it bore,
So thou and I are nothing then, when on a divers shore.

10   On a round ball
A workman that hath copies by can lay
An Europe, Afrique, and an Asia,
And quickly make that which was nothing, all;

So doth each tear
15   Which thee doth wear,
A globe, yea world, by that impression grow,
Till thy tears mixed with mine do overflow
This world; by waters sent from thee, my heaven dissolvèd so.

O more than moon,
20 Draw not up seas to drown me in thy sphere;
Weep me not dead in thine arms, but forbear
To teach the sea what it may do too soon;
       Let not the wind
       Example find,
25 To do me more harm than it purposeth;
Since thou and I sigh one another's breath,
Whoe'er sighs most is cruelist, and hastes the other's death.

1633

A Valediction: Forbidding Mourning

As virtuous men pass mildly away,
And whisper to their souls to go,
Whilst some of their sad friends do say,
"The breath goes now," and some say, "No,"

5 So let us melt and make no noise,
No tear-floods, nor sigh-tempests move;
'Twere profanation of our joys
To tell the laity our love.

Moving of th' earth brings harm and fears;
10 Men reckon what it did and meant.
But trepidation of the spheres,
Though greater far, is innocent.

Dull sùblunary lovers' love
(Whose soul is sense) cannot admit
15 Absence, because it doth remove
Those things which elemented it.

But we by a love so much refined
That ourselves know not what it is,
Inter-assurèd of the mind,
20 Care less eyes, lips, and hands to miss.

Our two souls, therefore, which are one,
Though I must go, endure not yet
A breach, but an expansion,
Like gold to airy thinness beat.

25 If they be two, they are two so
   As stiff twin compasses are two;
   Thy soul, the fixed foot, makes no show
   To move, but doth if th' other do.

   And though it in the center sit,
30 Yet when the other far doth roam,
   It leans and hearkens after it,
   And grows erect as that comes home.

   Such wilt thou be to me, who must,
   Like th' other foot, obliquely run;
35 Thy firmness makes my circle just,
   And makes me end where I begun.

1633

The Funeral

   Whoever comes to shroud me, do not harm
       Nor question much
   That subtle wreath of hair which crowns mine arm:
   The mystery, the sign, you must not touch,
5   For 'tis my outward soul,
   Viceroy to that which, then to heaven being gone,
       Will leave this to control
   And keep these limbs, her provinces, from dissolutiön.

   For if the sinewy thread my brain lets fall
10   Through every part
   Can tie those parts, and make me one of all,
   These hairs which upward grew, and strength and art
       Have from a better brain,
   Can better do't—except she meant that I
15   By this should know my pain,
   As prisoners then are manacled when they're condemned to die.

   Whate'er she meant by it, bury it with me;
       For since I am
   Love's martyr, it might breed idolatry
20 If into others' hands these relics came.
       As 'twas humility
   To afford to it all that a soul can do,
       So, 'tis some bravery,
   That since you would have none of me, I bury some of you.

1633

From **Holy Sonnets**

Sonnet 7

At the round earth's imagined corners, blow
Your trumpets, angels, and arise, arise
From death, you numberless infinities
Of souls, and to your scattered bodies go;
5 All whom the flood did, and fire shall o'erthrow;
All whom war, dearth, age, agues, tyrannies,
Despair, law, chance, hath slain, and you whose eyes
Shall behold God, and never taste death's woe.
But let them sleep, Lord, and me mourn a space,
10 For if above all these my sins abound,
'Tis late to ask abundance of thy grace
When we are there; here on this lowly ground
Teach me how to repent; for that's as good
As if thou hadst sealed my pardon with thy blood.

Sonnet 10

Death, be not proud, though some have callèd thee
Mighty and dreadful, for thou art not so;
For those whom thou think'st thou dost overthrow
Die not, poor Death, nor yet canst thou kill me.
5 From rest and sleep, which but thy pictures be,
Much pleasure; then from thee much more must flow;
And soonest our best men with thee do go,
Rest of their bones and souls' delivery.
Thou'rt slave to fate, chance, kings, and desperate men,
10 And dost with poison, war, and sickness dwell;
And poppy or charms can make us sleep as well
And better than thy stroke. Why swell'st thou then?
One short sleep past, we wake eternally,
And Death shall be no more: Death, thou shalt die.

Sonnet 14

Batter my heart, three-personed God; for you
As yet but knock, breathe, shine, and seek to mend;
That I may rise, and stand, o'erthrow me, and bend
Your force, to break, blow, burn, and make me new.
5 I, like an usurped town, to another due,
Labor to admit you, but Oh, to no end,
Reason your viceroy in me, me should defend,
But is captived, and proves weak or untrue.
Yet dearly I love you, and would be loved fain,

10 But am betrothed unto your enemy:
Divorce me, untie, or break that knot again,
Take me to you, imprison me, for I
Except you enthral me, never shall be free,
Nor ever chaste, except you ravish me.

1610–1611

Hymn to God My God, in My Sickness

Since I am coming to that holy room,
   Where, with thy choir of Saints for evermore,
I shall be made thy music; as I come
   I tune the instrument here at the door,
5   And what I must do then, think now before.

Whilst my physicians by their love are grown
   Cosmographers, and I their map, who lie
Flat on this bed, that by them may be shown
   That this is my Southwest discovery
10   *Per fretum febris,*[1] by these straits to die,

I joy, that in these straits, I see my west;[2]
   For, though their currents yield return to none,
What shall my west hurt me? As west and east
   In all flat maps (and I am one) are one,
15   So death doth touch the Resurrection.

Is the Pacific Sea my home? Or are
   The eastern riches? Is Jerusalem?
Anyan,[3] and Magellan, and Gibraltàr,
   All straits, and none but straits, are ways to them,
20   Whether where Japhet dwelt, or Cham, or Shem.[4]

We think that Paradise and Calvary,
   Christ's Cross, and Adam's tree, stood in one place;
Look Lord, and find both Adams met in me;
   As the first Adam's sweat surrounds my face,
25   May the last Adam's blood my soul embrace.

So, in his purple wrapped receive me, Lord,
   By these his thorns give me his other crown;
And as to others' souls I preached thy word,

---

[1]through the straits of fever
[2]my death
[3]modern Annam, then thought of as a strait between Asia and America
[4]sons of Noah, said to have settled Europe, Asia, and Africa after the flood

Be this my text, my sermon to mine own,
30   Therefore that he may raise, the Lord throws down.

1635

Robert Herrick

(1591–1674)

Delight in Disorder

A sweet disorder in the dress
Kindles in clothes a wantonness:
A lawn[1] about the shoulders thrown
Into a fine distraction,
5 An erring lace which here and there
Enthralls the crimson stomacher,[2]
A cuff neglectful and thereby
Ribbands to flow confusedly,
A winning wave (deserving note)
10 In the tempestuous petticoat,
A careless shoestring in whose tie
I see a wild civility,
Do more bewitch me than when art
Is too precise in every part.

1648

Upon Julia's Clothes

Whenas in silks my Julia goes,
Then, then, methinks, how sweetly flows
That liquefaction of her clothes.

Next, when I cast mine eyes and see
5 That brave vibration each way free,
O how that glittering taketh me!

1648

To the Virgins, to Make Much of Time

Gather ye rosebuds while ye may:
   Old Time is still a-flying;
And this same flower that smiles today,
   Tomorrow will be dying.

---

[1] a scarf of fine linen
[2] bodice

5 The glorious lamp of heaven, the sun,
    The higher he's a-getting,
The sooner will his race be run,
    And nearer he's to setting.

That age is best which is the first,
10   When youth and blood are warmer;
But being spent, the worse, and worst
    Times, still succeed the former.

Then be not coy, but use your time;
    And while ye may, go marry:
15 For, having lost but once your prime,
    You may for ever tarry.

1648

George Herbert

(1593–1633)

The Pulley

    When God at first made man,
Having a glass of blessings standing by,
    "Let us," said he, "pour on him all we can:
Let the world's riches, which dispersèd lie,
5   Contract into a span."

    So Strength first made a way;
Then Beauty flowed; then Wisdom, Honor, Pleasure.
    When almost all was out, God made a stay,
Perceiving that alone of all his treasure
10   Rest in the bottom lay.

    "For if I should," said he,
"Bestow this jewel also on my creature,
    He would adore my gifts instead of me,
And rest in Nature, not the God of Nature;
15   So both should losers be.

    "Yet let him keep the rest,
But keep them with repining restlessness:
    Let him be rich and weary, that at least,
If goodness lead him not, yet weariness
20   May toss him to my breast."

1633

The Collar[1]

I struck the board[2] and cried, "No more!
     I will abroad!
What, shall I ever sigh and pine?
My lines and life are free: free as the road,
5   Loose as the wind, as large as store.
      Shall I be still in suit?[3]
Have I no harvest but a thorn
To let me blood, and not restore
What I have lost with cordial[4] fruit?
10   Sure there was wine
Before my sighs did dry it; there was corn
    Before my tears did drown it.
Is the year only lost to me?
Have I no bays[5] to crown it,
15 No flowers, no garlands gay? all blasted?
      All wasted?
Not so, my heart; but there is fruit,
     And thou hast hands.
Recover all thy sigh-blown age
20 On double pleasures. Leave thy cold dispute
Of what is fit and not. Forsake thy cage,
     Thy rope of sands,
Which petty thoughts have made and made to thee
    Good cable, to enforce and draw,
25   And be thy law,
While thou didst wink and wouldst not see.
      Away! take heed!
      I will abroad!
Call in thy death's-head there! Tie up thy fears!
30   He that forbears
    To suit and serve his need,
     Deserves his load."
But as I raved, and grew more fierce and wild
     At every word,
35   Methought I heard one calling, "Child!"
     And I replied, "My Lord."

1633

---

[1] the iron band encircling the neck of a prisoner or slave; also perhaps a pun on "choler" as "rebellious anger"
[2] dining table
[3] always petitioning
[4] restorative
[5] laurels

Easter Wings

Lord, who createdst man in wealth and store,
  Though foolishly he lost the same,
    Decaying more and more,
      Till he became
5   Most poor:
      With thee
    O let me rise
  As larks, harmoniously,
  And sing this day thy victories:
10 Then shall the fall further the flight in me.

My tender age in sorrow did begin:
  And still with sicknesses and shame
    Thou didst so punish sin,
      That I became
15   Most thin.
      With thee
    Let me combine,
  And feel this day thy victory:
  For, if I imp[1] my wing on thine,
20 Affliction shall advance the flight in me.

1633

Virtue

Sweet day, so cool, so calm, so bright,
The bridal of the earth and sky,
The dew shall weep thy fall tonight,
    For thou must die.

5 Sweet rose, whose hue, angry and brave,
Bids the rash gazer wipe his eye,
Thy root is ever in its grave,
    And thou must die.

Sweet spring, full of sweet days and roses,
10 A box where sweets compacted lie,
My music shows ye have your closes,[1]
    And all must die.

Only a sweet and virtuous soul,
Like seasoned timber, never gives;

---

[1] in falconry, to graft feathers on a damaged wing

---

[1] musical cadences

15 But though the whole world turn to coal,
    Then chiefly lives.

1633

Love (III)

Love bade me welcome; yet my soul drew back,
    Guilty of dust and sin.
But quick-eyed Love, observing me grow slack
    From my first entrance in,
5 Drew nearer to me, sweetly questioning
    If I lacked anything.

"A guest," I answered, "worthy to be here."
    Love said, "You shall be he."
"I, the unkind, ungrateful? Ah my dear,
10   I cannot look on Thee."
Love took my hand, and smiling, did reply,
    "Who made the eyes but I?"

"Truth, Lord, but I have marred them; let my shame
    Go where it doth deserve."
15 "And know you not," says Love, "who bore the blame?"
    "My dear, then I will serve."
"You must sit down," says Love, "and taste my meat."
    So I did sit and eat.

1633

John Milton

(1608–1674)

How Soon Hath Time

How soon hath Time, the subtle thief of youth,
Stolen on his wing my three-and-twentieth year!
My hasting days fly on with full career,
But my late spring no bud or blossom shew'th.
5 Perhaps my semblance might deceive the truth
That I to manhood am arrived so near;
And inward ripeness doth much less appear,
That some more timely-happy spirits endu'th.[1]

---

[1]endoweth

Yet be it less or more, or soon or slow,
10 It shall be still in strictest measure even
To that same lot, however mean or high,
Toward which Time leads me, and the will of Heaven;
All is, if I have grace to use it so,
As ever in my great Taskmaster's eye.

1645

On His Blindness

When I consider how my light is spent,
Ere half my days, in this dark world and wide,
And that one talent which is death to hide
Lodged with me useless, though my soul more bent
5 To serve therewith my Maker, and present
My true account, lest he returning chide,
"Doth God exact day labor, light denied?"
I fondly ask; but Patience, to prevent
That murmur, soon replies: "God doth not need
10 Either man's work or his own gifts; who best
Bear his mild yoke, they serve him best. His state
Is kingly: thousands at his bidding speed
And post o'er land and ocean without rest.
They also serve who only stand and wait."

1673

At a Solemn Music

Blest pair of Sirens, pledges of Heaven's joy,
Sphere-born harmonious sisters, Voice and Verse,
Wed your divine sounds, and mixed power employ
Dead things with inbreathed sense able to pierce,
5 And to our high-raised fantasy present
That undisturbed song of pure consent,[1]
Aye sung before the sapphire-colored throne
To him that sits thereon
With saintly shout and solemn jubilee,
10 Where the bright seraphim in burning row
Their loud uplifted angel-trumpets blow,
And the cherubic host in thousand choirs
Touch their immortal harps of golden wires,
With those just spirits that wear victorious palms,
15 Hymns devout and holy psalms

––––––––––
[1]harmony

Singing everlastingly;
That we on earth with undiscording voice
May rightly answer that melodious noise;
As once we did, till disproportioned sin
20 Jarred against nature's chime, and with harsh din
Broke the fair music that all creatures made
To their great Lord, whose love their motion swayed
In perfect diapason,[2] whilst they stood
In first obedience, and their state of good.
25 O may we soon again renew that song,
And keep in tune with Heaven, till God ere long
To his celestial consort us unite.
To live with him, and sing in endless morn of light.

On the Late Massacre in Piedmont

Avenge, O Lord, thy slaughtered saints, whose bones
Lie scattered on the Alpine mountains cold;
Even them who kept thy truth so pure of old
When all our fathers worshipped stocks and stones,
5 Forget not: in thy book record their groans
Who were thy sheep and in their ancient fold
Slain by the bloody Piedmontese, that rolled
Mother with infant down the rocks. Their moans
The vales redoubled to the hills, and they
10 To heaven. Their martyred blood and ashes sow
O'er all the Italian fields where still doth sway
The triple tyrant;[1] that from these may grow
A hundredfold, who, having learnt thy way,
Early may fly the Babylonian woe.[2]

1673

From **Paradise Lost,** Book 12

He[1] ended; and thus Adam last replied:
"How soon hath thy prediction, seer blest,
Measured this transient world, the race of time,
Till time stand fixed! Beyond is all abyss,
555 Eternity, whose end no eye can reach.
Greatly instructed I shall hence depart,

---

[2]concord

---

[1]the pope, whose tiara has three crowns
[2]The Roman Catholic Church was identified by the Puritans with the Babylon of Revelation 17–18.

---

[1]the angel Michael

Greatly in peace of thought, and have my fill
Of knowledge, what this vessel can contain,
Beyond which was my folly to aspire.
560 Henceforth I learn that to obey is best,
And love with fear the only God, to walk
As in his presence, ever to observe
His providence, and on him sole depend,
Merciful over all his works, with good
565 Still overcoming evil, and by small
Accomplishing great things, by things deemed weak
Subverting worldly strong, and worldly wise
By simply meek; that suffering for truth's sake
Is fortitude to highest victory,
570 And to the faithful death the gate of life,
Taught this by his example whom I now
Acknowledge my Redeemer ever blest."
    To whom thus also the angel last replied:
"This having learned, thou hast attained the sum
575 Of wisdom; hope no higher, though all the stars
Thou knew'st by name, and all the ethereal powers,
All secrets of the deep, all Nature's works,
Or works of God in heaven, air, earth, or sea,
And all the riches of this world enjoy'dst,
580 And all the rule, one empire. Only add
Deeds to thy knowledge answerable; add faith;
Add virtue, patience, temperance; add love,
By name to come called charity, the soul
Of all the rest: then wilt thou not be loath
585 To leave this Paradise, but shalt possess
A paradise within thee, happier far.
Let us descend now, therefore, from this top
Of speculation; for the hour precise
Exacts our parting hence; and, see, the guards,
590 By me encamped on yonder hill, expect
Their motion, at whose front a flaming sword
In signal of remove waves fiercely round.
We may no longer stay. Go, waken Eve;
Her also I with gentle dreams have calmed,
595 Portending good, and all her spirits composed
To meek submission: thou at season fit
Let her with thee partake what thou hast heard,
Chiefly what may concern her faith to know,
The great deliverance by her seed to come
600 (For by the woman's seed) on all mankind,

That ye may live, which will be many days,
Both in one faith unanimous; though sad
With cause for evils past, yet much more cheered
With meditation on the happy end."
605   He ended, and they both descend the hill;
Descended, Adam to the bower where Eve
Lay sleeping ran before, but found her waked;
And thus with words not sad she him received:
   "Whence thou return'st and whither went'st I know;
610 For God is also in sleep, and dreams advise,
Which he hath sent propitious, some great good
Presaging, since, with sorrow and heart's distress
Wearied, I fell asleep: but now lead on;
In me is no delay; with thee to go,
615 Is to stay here; without thee here to stay,
Is to go hence unwilling; thou to me
Art all things under heaven, all places thou,
Who for my willful crime art banished hence.
This further consolation yet secure
620 I carry hence: though all by me is lost,
Such favor I unworthy am vouchsafed,
By me the promised seed shall all restore."
   So spake our mother Eve, and Adam heard
Well pleased, but answered not; for now too nigh
625 The Archangel stood, and from the other hill
To their fixed station, all in bright array,
The Cherubim descended, on the ground
Gliding metèorous, as evening mist
Risen from a river o'er the marish glides
630 And gathers ground fast at the laborer's heel
Homeward returning. High in front advanced,
The brandished sword of God before them blazed
Fierce as a comet, which with torrid heat,
And vapor as the Libyan air adust,
635 Began to parch that temperate clime; whereat
In either hand the hastening Angel caught
Our lingering parents, and to the eastern gate
Led them direct, and down the cliff as fast
To the subjected plain; then disappeared.
640 They, looking back, all the eastern side beheld
Of Paradise, so late their happy seat,
Waved over by that flaming brand, the gate
With dreadful faces thronged and fiery arms.
Some natural tears they dropped, but wiped them soon;

645 The world was all before them, where to choose
       Their place of rest, and Providence their guide:
       They hand in hand, with wandering steps and slow,
       Through Eden took their solitary way.

                    THE END

                                                        1667

Anne Bradstreet

(1612?–1672)

To My Dear and Loving Husband

If ever two were one, then surely we.
If ever man were lov'd by wife, then thee;
If ever wife was happy in a man,
Compare with me ye women if you can.
5 I prize thy love more than whole Mines of gold,
Or all the riches that the East doth hold.
My love is such that Rivers cannot quench,
Nor ought but love from thee, give recompence.
Thy love is such I can no way repay,
10 The heavens reward thee manifold I pray.
Then while we live, in love lets so persever,
That when we live no more, we may live ever.

                                                        1678

A Letter to Her Husband, Absent upon
Publick Employment

My head, my heart, mine Eyes, my life, nay more,
My joy, my Magazine of earthly store,
If two be one, as surely thou and I,
How stayest thou there, whilst I at *Ipswich* lye?
5 So many steps, head from the heart to sever
If but a neck, soon should we be together:
I like the earth this season, mourn in black,
My Sun is gone so far in's Zodiack,
Whom whilst I 'joy'd, nor storms, nor frosts I felt,
10 His warmth such frigid colds did cause to melt.
My chilled limbs now nummed lye forlorn;
Return, return sweet *Sol* from *Capricorn;*

In this dead time, alas, what can I more
Then view those fruits which through thy heat I bore?
15 Which sweet contentment yield me for a space,
True living Pictures of their Fathers face.
O strange effect! now thou art *Southward* gone,
I weary grow, the tedious day so long;
But when thou *Northward* to me shalt return,
20 I wish my Sun may never set, but burn
Within the Cancer of my glowing breast,
The welcome house of him my dearest guest.
Where ever, ever stay, and go not thence,
Till natures sad decree shall call thee hence;
25 Flesh of thy flesh, bone of thy bone,
I here, thou there, yet both but one.

1678

Andrew Marvell

(1621–1678)

To His Coy Mistress

Had we but world enough, and time,
This coyness, lady, were no crime.
We would sit down, and think which way
To walk, and pass our long love's day.
5 Thou by the Indian Ganges' side
Shouldst rubies find; I by the tide
Of Humber would complain. I would
Love you ten years before the Flood,
And you should, if you please, refuse
10 Till the conversion of the Jews.
My vegetable love should grow
Vaster than empires, and more slow;
An hundred years should go to praise
Thine eyes and on thy forehead gaze,
15 Two hundred to adore each breast,
But thirty thousand to the rest:
An age at least to every part,
And the last age should show your heart.
For, lady, you deserve this state,
20 Nor would I love at lower rate.

But at my back I always hear
Time's wingèd chariot hurrying near;
And yonder all before us lie
Deserts of vast eternity.
25 Thy beauty shall no more be found,
Nor in thy marble vault shall sound
My echoing song; then worms shall try
That long preserved virginity,
And your quaint honor turn to dust,
30 And into ashes all my lust.
The grave's a fine and private place,
But none, I think, do there embrace.
       Now, therefore, while the youthful hue
Sits on thy skin like morning dew,
35 And while thy willing soul transpires
At every pore with instant fires,
Now let us sport us while we may,
And now, like am'rous birds of prey,
Rather at once our time devour
40 Than languish in his slow-chapped power.
Let us roll all our strength and all
Our sweetness up into one ball,
And tear our pleasures with rough strife
Through the iron gates of life.
45 Thus, though we cannot make our sun
Stand still, yet we will make him run.

                                                    1681

The Garden

       How vainly men themselves amaze
To win the palm, the oak, or bays,
And their incessant labors see
Crowned from some single herb, or tree,
5 Whose short and narrow-vergèd shade
Does prudently their toils upbraid;
While all flowers and all trees do close
To weave the garlands of repose!

       Fair Quiet, have I found thee here,
10 And Innocence, thy sister dear?
Mistaken long, I sought you then
In busy companies of men.
Your sacred plants, if here below,

Only among the plants will grow;
15 Society is all but rude
To this delicious solitude.

No white nor red was ever seen
So amorous as this lovely green.
Fond lovers, cruel as their flame,
20 Cut in these trees their mistress' name:
Little, alas, they know or heed
How far these beauties hers exceed!
Fair trees, wheresoe'er your barks I wound,
No name shall but your own be found.

25 When we have run our passion's heat,
Love hither makes his best retreat.
The gods, that mortal beauty chase,
Still in a tree did end their race:
Apollo hunted Daphne so,
30 Only that she might laurel grow;
And Pan did after Syrinx speed,
Not as a nymph, but for a reed.

What wondrous life is this I lead!
Ripe apples drop about my head;
35 The luscious clusters of the vine
Upon my mouth do crush their wine;
The nectarine and curious peach
Into my hands themselves do reach;
Stumbling on melons, as I pass,
40 Insnared with flowers, I fall on grass.

Meanwhile the mind, from pleasure less,
Withdraws into its happiness;
The mind, that ocean where each kind
Does straight its own resemblance find;
45 Yet it creates, transcending these,
Far other worlds and other seas,
Annihilating all that's made
To a green thought in a green shade.

Here at the fountain's sliding foot,
50 Or at some fruit tree's mossy root,
Casting the body's vest aside,
My soul into the boughs does glide:
There, like a bird, it sits and sings,
Then whets and combs its silver wings,

55 And, till prepared for longer flight,
   Waves in its plumes the various light.

   Such was that happy garden-state,
   While man there walked without a mate:
   After a place so pure and sweet,
60 What other help could yet be meet!
   But 'twas beyond a mortal's share
   To wander solitary there:
   Two paradises 'twere in one
   To live in paradise alone.

65   How well the skillful gardener drew
   Of flowers and herbs this dial new,
   Where, from above, the milder sun
   Does through a fragrant zodiac run;
   And as it works, th' industrious bee
70 Computes its time as well as we!
   How could such sweet and wholesome hours
   Be reckoned but with herbs and flowers?

                                        1681

John Dryden

(1631–1700)

From the **Aeneid**[1]

The Death of Dido

Then to Sichæus'[2] nurse she briefly said
(For, when she left her country, hers was dead):
"Go, Barce, call my sister. Let her care
910 The solemn rites of sacrifice prepare;
The sheep, and all th' atoning off'rings, bring,
Sprinkling her body from the crystal spring
With living drops; then let her come, and thou
With scared fillets bind they hoary brow.
915 Thus will I pay my vows to Stygian Jove,[3]
And end the cares of my disastrous love;

---

[1]In this section of the *Aeneid*, Dido commits suicide over the lost love of Aeneis.
[2]murdered husband of Dido
[3]king of the Olympian gods

Then cast the Trojan image on the fire,
And, as that burns, my passion shall expire."
   The nurse moves onward, with officious care,
920 And all the speed her aged limbs can bear.
But furious Dido, with dark thoughts involv'd,
Shook at the mighty mischief she resolv'd.
With livid spots distinguish'd was her face;
Red were her rolling eyes, and discompos'd her pace;
925 Ghastly she gaz'd, with pain she drew her breath,
And nature shiver'd at approaching death.
   Then swiftly to the fatal place she pass'd,
And mounts the fun'ral pile with furious haste;
Unsheathes the sword the Trojan left behind
930 (Not for so dire an enterprise design'd).
But when she view'd the garments loosely spread,
Which once he wore, and saw the conscious bed,
She paus'd, and with a sigh the robes embrac'd;
Then on the couch her trembling body cast,
935 Repress'd the ready tears, and spoke her last:
"Dear pledges of my love, while Heav'n so pleas'd,
Receive a soul, of mortal anguish eas'd:
My fatal course is finish'd; and I go,
A glorious name, among the ghosts below.
940 A lofty city by my hands is rais'd,
Pygmalion punish'd, and my lord appeas'd.
What could my fortune have afforded more,
Had the false Trojan never touch'd my shore!"
Then kiss'd the couch; and, "Must I die," she said,
945 "And unreveng'd? 'T is doubly to be dead!
Yet ev'n this death with pleasure I receive
On any terms, 't is better than to live.
These flames, from far, may the false Trojan view;
These boding omens his base flight pursue!"
950   She said, and struck; deep enter'd in her side
The piercing steel, with reeking purple dyed:
Clogg'd in the wound the cruel weapon stands;
The spouting blood came streaming on her hands.
Her sad attendants saw the deadly stroke,
955 And with loud cries the sounding palace shook.
Distracted, from the fatal sight they fled,
And thro' the town the dismal rumor spread.
First from the frighted court the yell began;
Redoubled, thence from house to house it ran:
960 The groans of men, with shrieks, laments, and cries

Of mixing women, mount the vaulted skies.
Not less the clamor, than if — ancient Tyre,
Or the new Carthage, set by foes on fire —
The rolling ruin, with their lov'd abodes,
965 Involv'd the blazing temples of their gods.
    Her sister hears; and, furious with despair,
She beats her breast, and rends her yellow hair,
And, calling on Eliza's[4] name aloud,
Runs breathless to the place, and breaks the crowd.
970 "Was all that pomp of woe for this prepar'd:
These fires, this fun'ral pile, these altars rear'd?
Was all this train of plots contriv'd," said she,
"All only to deceive unhappy me?
Which is the worst? Didst thou in death pretend
975 To scorn thy sister, or delude thy friend?
Thy summon'd sister, and thy friend, had come;
One sword had serv'd us both, one common tomb:
Was I to raise the pile, the pow'rs invoke,
Not to be present at the fatal stroke?
980 At once thou hast destroy'd thyself and me,
Thy town, they senate, and thy colony!
Bring water; bathe the wound; while I in death
Lay close my lips to hers, and catch the flying breath."
This said, she mounts the pile with eager haste,
985 And in her arms the gasping queen embrac'd;
Her temples chaf'd; and her own garment tore,
To stanch the streaming blood, and cleanse the gore.
Thrice Dido tried to raise her drooping head,
And, fainting thrice, fell grov'ling on the bed;
990 Thrice op'd her heavy eyes, and sought the light,
But, having found it, sicken'd at the sight,
And clos'd her lids at last in endless night.
    Then Juno,[5] grieving that she should sustain
A death so ling'ring, and so full of pain,
995 Sent Iris[6] down, to free her from the strife
Of lab'ring nature, and dissolve her life.
For since she died, not doom'd by Heav'n's decree,
Or her own crime, but human casualty,
And rage of love, that plung'd her in despair,
1000 The Sisters had not cut the topmost hair,

---

[4]another name for Dido
[5]wife of Jove
[6]messenger of Juno

Which Proserpine and they can only know;
Nor made her sacred to the shades below.
Downward the various goddess took her flight,
And drew a thousand colors from the light;
1005 Then stood above the dying lover's head,
And said: "I thus devote thee to the dead.
This off'ring to th' infernal gods I bear."
Thus while she spoke, she cut the fatal hair:
The struggling soul was loos'd, and life dissolv'd in air.

Edward Taylor

(1642–1729)

Meditation Six

CANTICLES II: 1: *I am . . . the lily of the valleys.*

Am I thy gold? Or Purse, Lord, for thy Wealth;
    Whether in mine or mint refinde for thee?
Ime counted so, but count me o're thyselfe,
    Lest gold washt face, and brass in Heart I bee.
5   I Feare my Touchstone touches when I try
    Mee, and my Counted Gold too overly.

Am I new minted by thy Stamp indeed?
    Mine Eyes are dim; I cannot clearly see.
Be thou my Spectacles that I may read
10   Thin Image and Inscription stampt on mee.
    If thy bright Image do upon me stand,
    I am a Golden Angell[1] in thy hand.

Lord, make my Soule thy Plate: thine Image bright
    Within the Circle of the same enfoile.
15 And on its brims in golden Letters write
    Thy Superscription in an Holy style.
    Then I shall be thy Money, thou my Hord:
    Let me thy Angell bee, bee thou my Lord.

                                        1683

-----
[1]gold coin

Upon a Spider Catching a Fly

Thou sorrow, venom Elfe:
    Is this thy play,
To spin a web out of thyselfe
    To Catch a Fly?
5   For why?

I saw a pettish wasp
    Fall foule therein:
Whom yet thy whorle pins¹ did no[t hasp]
    Lest he should fling
10   His sting.

But as afraid, remote
    Didst stand hereat,
And with thy little fingers stroke
    And gently tap
15   His back.

Thus gently him didst treate
    Lest he should pet,
And in a froppish, aspish heate
    Should greatly fret
20   Thy net.

Whereas the silly Fly,
    Caught by its leg,
Thou by the throate took'st hastily,
    And 'hinde the head
25   Bite Dead.

This goes to pot, that not
    Nature doth call.
Strive not above what strength hath got,
    Lest in the brawle
30   Thou fall.

This Frey seems thus to us:
    Hells Spider gets
His intrails spun to whip Cords thus,
    And wove to nets,
35   And sets.

To tangle Adams race
    In's stratagems

---

¹web spinning

To their Destructions, Spoil'd, made base
   By venom things,
40   Damn'd Sins.

But mighty, Gracious Lord,
   Communicate
Thy Grace to breake the Cord; afford
   Us Glorys Gate
45   And State.

We'l Nightingaile sing like,
   When pearcht on high
In Glories Cage, thy glory, bright:
   [Yea,] thankfully,
50   For joy.

ca. 1673

Jonathan Swift

(1667–1745)

A Description of the Morning

Now hardly here and there an hackney-coach
Appearing, showed the ruddy morn's approach.
Now Betty from her master's bed had flown,
And softly stole to discompose her own.
5 The slipshod 'prentice from his master's door,
Had pared the dirt, and sprinkled round the floor.
Now Moll had whirled her mop with dext'rous airs,
Prepared to scrub the entry and the stairs.
The youth with broomy stumps began to trace
10 The kennel edge, where wheels had worn the place.
The small-coal man was heard with cadence deep,
'Till drowned in shriller notes of chimney sweep,
Duns at his lordship's gate began to meet,
And brickdust Moll had screamed through half a street.
15 The turnkey now his flock returning sees,
Duly let out a-nights to steal for fees.
The watchful bailiffs take their silent stands;
And schoolboys lag with satchels in their hands.

1709

A Description of a City Shower

Careful observers may foretell the hour
(By sure prognostics) when to dread a show'r.
While rain depends, the pensive cat gives o'er
Her frolics, and pursues her tail no more.
5 Returning home at night, you'll find the sink
Strike your offended sense with double stink.
If you be wise, then go not far to dine;
You'll spend in coach-hire more than save in wine.
A coming show'r your shooting corns presage,
10 Old aches throb, your hollow tooth will rage:
Saunt'ring in coffee-house is Dulman seen;
He damns the climate, and complains of spleen.
    Meanwhile the South, rising with dabbled wings,
A sable cloud athwart the welkin flings,
15 That swill'd more liquor than it could contain,
And, like a drunkard, gives it up again.
Brisk Susan whips her linen from the rope,
While the first drizzling show'r is born aslope:
Such is that sprinkling, which some careless quean
20 Flirts on you from her mop, but not so clean:
You fly, invoke the gods; then turning, stop
To rail; she singing, still whirls on her mop.
Not yet the dust had shunn'd th' unequal strife,
But, aided by the wind, fought still for life,
25 And wafted with its foe by vi'lent gust,
'Twas doubtful which was rain, and which was dust.
Ah! where must needy poet seek for aid,
When dust and rain at once his coat invade?
Sole coat, where dust cemented by the rain
30 Erects the nap, and leaves a cloudy stain.
Now in contiguous drops the flood comes down,
Threat'ning with deluge this *devoted* town.
To shops in crowds the daggled females fly,
Pretend to cheapen goods, but nothing buy.
35 The Templar spruce, while ev'ry spout's abroach,
Stays till 'tis fair, yet seems to call a coach.
The tuck'd-up sempstress walks with hasty strides,
While streams run down her oil'd umbrella's sides.
Here various kinds, by various fortunes led,
40 Commence acquaintance underneath a shed.
Triumphant Tories, and desponding Whigs,
Forget their feuds, and join to save their wigs.
Box'd in a chair the beau impatient sits,

While spouts run clatt'ring o'er the roof by fits,
45 And ever and anon with frightful din
The leather sounds; he trembles from within.
So when Troy chairmen bore the wooden steed,
Pregnant with Greeks impatient to be freed
(Those bully Greeks, who, as the moderns do,
50 Instead of paying chairmen, ran them through),
Laocoön struck the outside with his spear,
And each imprison'd hero quak'd for fear.
    Now from all parts the swelling kennels flow,
And bear their trophies with them as they go:
55 Filth of all hues and odor seem to tell
What street they sail'd from, by their sight and smell.
They, as each torrent drives with rapid force,
From Smithfield to St. Pulchre's shape their course,
And in huge confluence join'd at Snowhill ridge,
60 Fall from the conduit prone to Holborn bridge.
Sweeping from butcher's stalls, dung, guts, and blood,
Drown'd puppies, stinking sprats, all drench'd in mud,
Dead cats, and turnip-tops, come tumbling down the flood.

1709

Alexander Pope

(1688–1744)

Ode on Solitude

Happy the man whose wish and care
    A few paternal acres bound,
Content to breathe his native air,
                In his own ground.

5 Whose herds with milk, whose fields with bread,
    Whose flocks supply him with attire,
Whose trees in summer yield him shade,
                In winter fire.

Blest, who can unconcernedly find
10   Hours, days, and years slide soft away,
In health of body, peace of mind,
                Quiet by day,

Sound sleep by night; study and ease;
    Together mixed; sweet recreation;

15 And innocence, which most does please
                    With meditation.

    Thus let me live, unseen, unknown;
        Thus unlamented let me die;
    Steal from the world, and not a stone
20   Tell where I lie.

                                                      1736

From **An Essay on Man**

        VI. What would this Man? Now upward will he soar,
    And, little less than angel, would be more;
175 Now, looking downwards, just as grieved appears
    To want the strength of bulls, the fur of bears.
    Made for his use all creatures if he call,
    Say what their use, had he the powers of all?
    Nature to these without profusion kind,
180 The proper organs, proper pow'rs assigned;
    Each seeming want compènsated of course,
    Here with degrees of swiftness, there of force;
    All in exact proportion to the state;
    Nothing to add, and nothing to abate.
185 Each beast, each insect, happy in its own:
    Is heav'n unkind to man, and man alone?
    Shall he alone, whom rational we call,
    Be pleased with nothing if not blessed with all?
        The bliss of man (could pride that blessing find)
190 Is not to act or think beyond mankind;
    No pow'rs of body or of soul to share,
    But what his nature and his state can bear.
    Why has not man a microscopic eye?
    For this plain reason, man is not a fly.
195 Say what the use, were finer optics giv'n,
    T' inspect a mite, not comprehend the heav'n?
    Or touch, if tremblingly alive all o'er,
    To smart and agonize at ev'ry pore?
    Or, quick effluvia darting through the brain,
200 Die of a rose in aromatic pain?
    If nature thundered in his op'ning ears,
    And stunned him with the music of the spheres,
    How would he wish that heav'n had left him still
    The whisp'ring zephyr and the purling rill!
205 Who finds not Providence all good and wise,
    Alike in what it gives and what denies?

VII. Far as creation's ample range extends,
The scale of sensual, mental pow'rs ascends:
Mark how it mounts to man's imperial race
210　From the green myriads in the peopled grass;
What modes of sight betwixt each wide extreme,
The mole's dim curtain and the lynx's beam:
Of smell, the headlong lioness between,
And hound sagacious on the tainted green:
215　Of hearing, from the life that fills the flood
To that which warbles through the vernal wood:
The spider's touch, how exquisitely fine!
Feels at each thread, and lives alone the line:
In the nice[1] bee what sense, so subtly true,
220　From pois'nous herbs extracts the healing dew?
How instinct varies in the grov'ling swine,
Compared, half-reas'ning elephant, with thine!
'Twixt that and reason what a nice[2] barrièr!
For ever sep'rate, yet for ever near!
225　Remembrance and reflection how allied;
What thin partitions sense from thought divide:
And middle natures how they long to join,
Yet never pass th' insuperable line!
Without this just gradation could they be
230　Subjected, these to those, or all to thee?

1733–1734

From the **Iliad,** Book 18

The Grief of Achilles, and His Mother's Reply

Thus like the rage of fire the combat burns,
And now it rises, now it sinks by turns.
Meanwhile, where Hellespont's broad waters flow
Stood Nestor's son, the messenger of woe:
5　There sate Achilles, shaded by his sails,
On hoisted yards extended to the gales;
Pensive he sate; for all that fate designed,
Rose in sad prospect to his boding mind.
Thus to his soul he said: "Ah! what constrains
10　The Greeks, late victors, now to quit the plains?
Is this the day, which heaven so long ago
Ordained, to sink me with the weight of woe?

---

[1]discriminating
[2]fine

(So Thetis warned) when by a Trojan hand,
The bravest of the Myrmidonian band
15 Should lose the light? Fulfilled is that decree;
Fallen is the warrior, and Patroclus he!
In vain I charged him soon to quit the plain,
And warned to shun Hectorean force in vain!"
    Thus while he thinks, Antilochus appears,
20 And tells the melancholy tale with tears.
"Sad tidings, son of Peleus! thou must hear;
And wretched I, th' unwilling messenger!
Dead is Patroclus! For his corpse they fight;
His naked corpse: his arms are Hector's right."
25   A sudden horror shot through all the chief,
And wrapped his senses in the cloud of grief;
Cast on the ground, with furious hands he spread
The scorching ashes o'er his graceful head;
His purple garments, and his golden hairs,
30 Those he deforms with dust, and these he tears:
On the hard soil his groaning breast he threw,
And rolled and grovelled, as to earth he grew.
The virgin captives, with disordered charms,
(Won by his own, or by Patroclus' arms)
35 Rushed from the tents with cries; and gathering round
Beat their white breasts, and fainted on the ground:
While Nestor's son sustains a manlier part,
And mourns the warrior with a warrior's heart;
Hangs on his arms, amidst his frantic woe,
40 And oft prevents the meditated blow.
    Far in the deep abysses of the main,
With hoary Nereus, and the watery train,
The mother goddess from her crystal throne
Heard his loud cries, and answered groan for groan.
45 The circling Nereids[1] with their mistress weep,
And all the sea-green sisters of the deep.
Thalia, Glauce, (every watery name)
Nesaea mild, and silver Spio came.
Cymothoe and Cymodoce were nigh,
50 And the blue languish of soft Alia's eye.
Their locks Actaea and Limnoria rear,
Then Proto, Doris, Panope appear;
Thoa, Pherusa, Doto, Melita;
Agave gentle, and Amphithoe gay:

_____
[1]water nymphs

55 Next Callianira, Callianassa show
   Their sister looks; Dexamene the slow,
   And swift Dynamene, now cut the tides:
   Iaera now the verdant wave divides;
   Nemertes with Apseudes lifts the head:
60 Bright Galatea quits her pearly bed:
   These Orythia, Clymene, attend,
   Maera, Amphinome, the train extend,
   And black Janira, and Janassa fair,
   And Amatheia with her amber hair.
65 All these, and all that deep in ocean held
   Their sacred seats, the glimmering grotto filled;
   Each beat her ivory breast with silent woe,
   Till Thetis' sorrows thus began to flow.
      "Hear me, and judge, ye sisters of the main!
70 How just a cause has Thetis to complain?
   How wretched, were I mortal, were my fate!
   How more than wretched in th' immortal state!
   Sprung from my bed a godlike hero came,
   The bravest far that ever bore the name;
75 Like some fair olive, by my careful hand
   He grew, he flourished, and adorned the land:
   To Troy I sent him; but the fates ordain
   He never, never must return again.
   So short a space the light of heaven to view,
80 So short alas! and filled with anguish too.
   Hear how his sorrows echo through the shore!
   I cannot ease them, but I must deplore;
   I go at least to bear a tender part,
   And mourn my loved one with a mother's heart."
85   She said, and left the caverns of the main.
   All bathed in tears, the melancholy train
   Attend her way. Wide-opening part the tides,
   While the long pomp the silver wave divides.

1720

From **The Rape of the Lock**

   But when to mischief mortals bend their will,[1]
   How soon they find fit instruments of ill?
   Just then, Clarissa drew with tempting grace
   A two-edged weapon from her shining case:

----

[1] In this mock heroic epic, a lord cuts off a lock of a woman's hair and begins a social scandal.

So ladies in romance assist their knight,
130 Present the spear, and arm him for the fight.
He takes the gift with reverence, and extends
The little engine on his finger's ends;
This just behind Belinda's neck he spread,
As o'er the fragrant steams she bends her head.
135 Swift to the lock a thousand sprites repair,
A thousand wings, by turns, blow back the hair;
And thrice they twitched the diamond in her ear;
Thrice she looked back, and thrice the foe drew near.
Just in that instant, anxious Ariel sought
140 The close recesses of the virgin's thought;
As on the nosegay in her breast reclined,
He watched th' ideas rising in her mind,
Sudden he viewed, in spite of all her art,
An earthly lover lurking at her heart.
145 Amazed, confused, he found his power expired,
Resigned to fate, and with a sign retired.
     The peer now spreads the glittering forfex wide,
T' enclose the lock; now joins it, to divide.
Ev'n then, before the fatal engine closed,
150 A wretched sylph too fondly interposed;
Fate urged the shears, and cut the sylph in twain,
(But airy substance soon units again)[2]
The meeting points the sacred hair dissever
From the fair head, for ever, and for ever!
155   Then flashed the living lightning from her eyes,
And screams of horror rend th' affrighted skies.
Not louder shrieks to pitying heaven are cast,
When husbands, or when lapdogs breathe their last,
Or when rich china vessels, fallen from high,
160 In glittering dust, and painted fragments lie!
     "Let wreaths of triumph now my temples twine,"
The victor cried, "the glorious prize is mine!
While fish in streams, or birds delight in air,
Or in a coach and six the British fair,
165 As long as *Atalantis* shall be read,
Or the small pillow grace a lady's bed,
While visits shall be paid on solemn days,
When numerous wax-lights in bright order blaze,
While nymphs take treats, or assignations give,

---

[2]See Milton, lib. vi. of Satan cut asunder by the angel Michael.

170 So long my honour, name, and praise shall live!
What time would spare, from steel receives its date,
And monuments, like men, submit to fate!
Steel could the labour of the Gods destroy,
And strike to dust th' imperial towers of Troy;
175 Steel could the works of mortal pride confound,
And hew triumphal arches to the ground.
What wonder then, fair nymph! thy hairs should feel
The conquering force of unresisted steel?"

1712

3

A BRIEF HISTORY

The Romantic movement and revolution swept over America and Europe in the eighteenth century. The Romantic movement swerved away from the intellectual and formal poetry of the Augustan Age. The Romantics explored the natural world as a source of spiritual strength. The lives of ordinary men and women, and their language, became an abiding principle. Poems were modeled not from classical Renaissance patterns but from simpler folk sources such as the ballad. As a bridge to the Romantic movement, William Blake combined the spiritual and the commonplace in his *Songs of Innocence* and *Songs of Experience.* The publication of *The Lyrical Ballads* in 1789 by Wordsworth and Coleridge marked both the official beginning of the Romantic movement and its manifesto.

The American and French Revolutions spread the ideals of democracy and republicanism across Europe, and spread fear into the hearts of the English aristocracy. Lord Byron and Shelley scandalized and thrilled England with the irregularities of their personal lives and fled to Europe to escape the confines of English society. Keats died at the age of twenty-five in Rome from tuberculosis—the white plague of the eighteenth and nineteenth centuries. Shelley drowned at thirty. Byron succumbed to fever at thirty-five, fighting for the freedom of Greece from the Turkish Empire. All three became instant legends of the Romantic era.

The Industrial Revolution brought wealth to the middle class and misery to workers trapped in the mills and factories. The rise of overcrowded industrial cities like London, with its slums, poverty, and suffocating pollution, intensified the nostalgia for the simpler life of the countryside and the simpler virtues of ordinary men and women. At the same time, the seeds were planted for the Victorian era, with its respect for social stability, hard work, and the claims of Empire.

Some Romantic poets experimented within established forms. Other poets worked in more irregular and personal veins. In Christopher Smart's *Rejoice in the Lamb* the lines are composed roughly as sentences arranged in parallels. Gray's *Elegy,* on the other hand, combines a sober reflective tone with a pastoral English churchyard setting to create a conventionally rhymed and structured poem. Thus the sonnet, ode, and elegy continue to be written side by side with more experimental and evolutionary poetry. Wordsworth's irregular ode *Intimations of Immortality* and Keats's Horatian *Ode on a Grecian Urn* may be contrasted with the personal symbolism of William Blake's *The Sick Rose* or *The*

Tyger. Blake is also an example of a poet who turns his attention to subjects not previously considered to be poetic: *The Little Black Boy* and *The Chimney Sweeper*. Although Coleridge creates a drug-induced landscape in the exotic pleasure dome of *Kubla Khan,* a lyric poet like Robert Burns will write about a subject as simple as a mouse. The older poetic dictions, dictions in which the language of poetry was ordinarily different from that of prose or the market-place, begin to give up their exclusive hold. Instead of using formal language, some poets—like their anonymous forebears the balladeers—find a language closer to home. Burns's poems echo the sounds of ordinary speech. Even while poets are writing about their contemporary scene, however, they also hark back to other times. In a nineteenth-century poem, Wordsworth's sonnet *Composed upon Westminster Bridge* alludes to the classic myths and the ancient pagan gods Proteus and Triton. Keats, of course, turns to an antique artifact to buttress his ode to beauty and truth—a case again of anchoring an idea, beauty, to the reality of an image, the Grecian urn.

Thomas Gray

(1716–1771)

Elegy Written in a Country Churchyard

The curfew tolls the knell of parting day;
The lowing herd wind slowly o'er the lea;
The plowman homeward plods in his weary way,
And leaves the world to darkness and to me.

5 Now fades the glimmering landscape on the sight,
And all the air a solemn stillness holds,
Save where the beetle wheels his droning flight,
And drowsy tinklings lull the distant folds;

Save that from yonder ivy-mantled tow'r,
10 The moping owl does to the moon complain
Of such as, wand'ring near her secret bow'r,
Molest her ancient solitary reign.

Beneath those rugged elms, that yew tree's shade,
Where heaves the turf in many a mold'ring heap,
15 Each in his narrow cell for ever laid,
The rude forefathers of the hamlet sleep.

The breezy call of incense-breathing Morn,
The swallow twitt'ring from the straw-built shed,
The cock's shrill clarion, or the echoing horn,
20 No more shall rouse them from their lowly bed.

For them no more the blazing hearth shall burn,
Or busy housewife ply her evening care;
No children run to lisp their sire's return,
Or climb his knees the envied kiss to share.

25 Oft did the harvest to their sickle yield;
Their furrow oft the stubborn glebe has broke;
How jocund did they drive their team afield!
How bowed the woods beneath their sturdy stroke!

Let not Ambition mock their useful toil,
30 Their homely joys, and destiny obscure;
Nor Grandeur hear with a disdainful smile,
The short and simple annals of the poor.

The boast of heraldry, the pomp of pow'r,
And all that beauty, all that wealth, e'er gave

35   Awaits alike th' inevitable hour.
     The paths of glory lead but to the grave.

     Nor you, ye proud, impute to these the fault
     If Mem'ry o'er their tomb no trophies raise,
     Where, through the long-drawn aisle and fretted vault,
40   The pealing anthem swells the note of praise.

     Can storied urn[1] or animated[2] bust
     Back to its mansion call the fleeting breath?
     Can Honor's voice provoke[3] the silent dust,
     Or Flattery soothe the dull cold ear of Death?

45   Perhaps in this neglected spot is laid
     Some heart once pregnant with celestial fire;
     Hands that the rod of empire might have swayed,
     Or waked to ecstasy the living lyre.

     But Knowledge to their eyes her ample page,
50   Rich with the spoils of time, did ne'er unroll;
     Chill Penury repressed their noble rage,[4]
     And froze the genial[5] current of the soul.

     Full many a gem of purest ray serene
     The dark unfathomed caves of ocean bear;
55   Full many a flower is born to blush unseen,
     And waste its sweetness on the desert air.

     Some village Hampden,[6] that with dauntless breast
     The little tyrant of his fields withstood;
     Some mute inglorious Milton here may rest,
60   Some Cromwell guiltless of his country's blood.

     Th' applause of list'ning senates to command,
     The threats of pain and ruin to despise,
     To scatter plenty o'er a smiling land,
     And read their hist'ry in a nation's eyes,

65   Their lot forbade: nor circumscribed alone
     Their growing virtues, but their crimes confined;

------

[1]funeral urn
[2]lifelike
[3]call forth
[4]inspiration
[5]creative
[6]John Hampden, leader of the opposition to the tyranny of Charles I

Forbade to wade through slaughter to a throne
And shut the gates of mercy on mankind,

The struggling pangs of conscious truth to hide,
70   To quench the blushes of ingenuous shame,
Or heap the shrine of Luxury and Pride
With incense kindled at the Muse's flame.

Far from the madding crowd's ignoble strife,
Their sober wishes never learned to stray;
75   Along the cool sequestered vale of life
They kept the noiseless tenor of their way.

Yet ev'n these bones from insult to protect,
Some frail memorial still erected nigh,
With uncouth rimes and shapeless sculpture decked,
80   Implores the passing tribute of a sigh.

Their name, their years, spelt by th' unlettered Muse,
The place of fame and elegy supply;
And many a holy text around she strews,
That teach the rustic moralist to die.

85   For who, to dumb Forgetfulness a prey,
This pleasing anxious being e'er resigned,
Left the warm precincts of the cheerful day,
Nor cast one longing ling'ring look behind?

On some fond breast the parting soul relies,
90   Some pious drops the closing eye requires;
Ev'n from the tomb the voice of Nature cries,
Ev'n in our ashes live their wanted fires.

For thee who, mindful of th' unhonored dead,
Dost in these lines their artless tale relate,
95   If chance, by lonely contemplation led,
Some kindred spirit shall inquire thy fate,

Haply some hoary-headed swain may say,
"Oft have we seen him at the peep of dawn
Brushing with hasty steps the dews away
100   To meet the sun upon the upland lawn.

"There at the foot of yonder nodding beech
That wreathes its old fantastic roots so high,
His listless length at noontide would he stretch,
And pore upon the brook that babbles by.

105 "Hard by yon wood, now smiling as in scorn,
     Mutt'ring his wayward fancies he would rove,
     Now drooping, woeful wan, like one forlorn,
     Or crazed with care, or crossed in hopeless love.

     "One morn I missed him on the customed hill,
110 Along the heath and near his fav'rite tree;
     Another came; nor yet beside the rill,
     Nor up the lawn, nor at the wood was hie;

     "The next, with dirges due in sad array
     Slow through the church-way path we saw him borne.
115 Approach and read (for thou canst read) the lay,
     Graved on the stone beneath yon aged thorn."

                 The Epitaph

     Here rests his head upon the lap of Earth
     A youth to fortune and to fame unknown.
     Fair Science frowned not on his humble birth,
120 And Melancholy marked him for her own.

     Large was his bounty, and his soul sincere,
     Heav'n did a recompense as largely send:
     He gave to Misery all he had, a tear;
     He gained from heav'n ('twas all he wished) a friend.

125 No farther seek his merits to disclose,
     Or draw his frailties from their dread abode
     (There they alike in trembling hope repose),
     The bosom of his Father and his God.

                                             1751

Christopher Smart

(1722–1771)

From **Rejoice in the Lamb**

For I will consider my Cat Jeoffry.
For he is the servant of the Living God, duly and daily serving him.
For at the first glance of the glory of God in the East he worships in his way.
For is this done by wreathing his body seven times round with elegant
        quickness.
  5 For then he leaps up to catch the musk, which is the blessing of God upon his
        prayer.

For he rolls upon prank to work it in.
For having done duty and received blessing he begins to consider himself.
For this he performs in ten degrees.
For first he looks upon his forepaws to see if they are clean.
10   For secondly he kicks up behind to clear away there.
For thirdly he works it upon stretch with the forepaws extended.
For fourthly he sharpens his paws by wood.
For fifthly he washes himself.
For sixthly he rolls upon wash.
15   For seventhly he fleas himself, that he may not be interrupted upon the beat.[1]
For eighthly he rubs himself against a post.
For ninthly he looks up for his instructions.
For tenthly he goes in quest of food.
For having considered God and himself he will consider his neighbor.
20   For if he meets another cat he will kiss her in kindness.
For when he takes his prey he plays with it to give it chance.
For one mouse in seven escapes by his dallying.
For when his day's work is done his business more properly begins.
For he keeps the Lord's watch in the night against the adversary.
25   For he counteracts the powers of darkness by his electrical skin and glaring
         eyes.
For he counteracts the Devil, who is death, by brisking about the life.
For in his morning orisons he loves the sun and the sun loves him.
For he is of the tribe of Tiger.
For the Cherub Cat is a term of the Angel Tiger.
30   For he has the subtlety and hissing of a serpent, which in goodness he
         suppresses.
For he will not do destruction, if he is well-fed, neither will he spit without
         provocation.
For he purrs in thankfulness, when God tell him he's a good Cat.
For he is an instrument for the children to learn benevolence upon.
For every house is incomplete without him and a blessing is lacking in the
         spirit.
35   For the Lord commanded Moses concerning the cats at the departure of the
         Children of Israel from Egypt.
For every family had one cat at least in the bag.
For the English Cats are the best in Europe.
For he is the cleanest in the use of his forepaws of any quadruped.
For the dexterity of his defense is an instance of the love of God to him
         exceedingly.

---

[1]on his daily rounds

40 For he is the quickest to his mark of any creature.
    For he is tenacious of his point.
    For he is a mixture of gravity and waggery.
    For he knows that God is his Saviour.
    For there is nothing sweeter than his peace when at rest.
45 For there is nothing brisker than his life when in motion.
    For he is of the Lord's poor and so indeed is he called by benevolence
        perpetually—Poor Jeoffry! poor Jeoffry! the rat has bit thy throat.
    For I bless the name of the Lord Jesus that Jeoffry is better.
    For the divine spirit comes about his body to sustain it in complete cat.
    For his tongue is exceeding pure so that it has in purity what it wants in
        music.
50 For he is docile and can learn certain things.
    For he can set up with gravity, which is patience upon approbation.
    For he can fetch and carry, which is patience in employment.
    For he can jump over a stick, which is patience upon proof positive.
    For he can spraggle upon waggle at the word of command.
55 For he can jump from an eminence into his master's bosom.
    For he can catch the cork and toss it again.
    For he is hated by the hypocrite and miser.
    For the former is afraid of detection.
    For the latter refuses the charge.
60 For he camels his back to bear the first notion of business.
    For he is good to think on, if a man would express himself neatly.
    For he made a great figure in Egypt for his signal services.
    For he killed the ichneumon-rat[2] very pernicious by land.
    For his ears are so acute that they sting again.
65 For from this proceeds the passing quickness of his attention.
    For by stroking him I have found out electricity.
    For I perceived God's light about him both wax and fire.
    For the electrical fire is the spiritual substance, which God sends from
        heaven to sustain the bodies both of man and beast.
    For God has blessed him in the variety of his movements.
70 For, though he cannot fly, he is an excellent clamberer.
    For his motions upon the face of the earth are more than any other
        quadruped.
    For he can tread to all the measures upon the music.
    For he can swim for life.
    For he can creep.

                                                            ca. 1760

---

[2]Mongoose; it was, however, generally regarded as beneficial.

William Blake

(1757–1827)

From **Songs of Innocence**

Introduction

Piping down the valleys wild
Piping songs of pleasant glee
On a cloud I saw a child,
And he laughing said to me,

5 "Pipe a song about a Lamb";
So I piped with merry chear;
"Piper pipe that song again"—
So I piped, he wept to hear.

"Drop thy pipe thy happy pipe
10 Sing thy songs of happy chear";
So I sung the same again
While he wept with joy to hear.

"Piper sit thee down and write
In a book that all may read"—
15 So he vanish'd from my sight.
And I pluck'd a hollow reed,

And I made a rural pen,
And I stain'd the water clear,
And I wrote my happy songs
20 Every child may joy to hear.

The Lamb

Little Lamb, who made thee?
    Dost thou know who made thee?
Gave thee life & bid thee feed,
By the stream & o'er the mead;
5 Gave thee clothing of delight,
Softest clothing wooly bright;
Gave thee such a tender voice,
Making all the vales rejoice!
    Little Lamb who made thee?
10   Dost thou know who made thee?

Little Lamb I'll tell thee,
Little Lamb I'll tell thee!

He is callèd by thy name,
For he calls himself a Lamb:
15 He is meek & he is mild,
He became a little child:
I a child & thou a lamb,
We are callèd by his name.
    Little Lamb God bless thee.
20   Little Lamb God bless thee.

The Chimney-Sweeper

When my mother died I was very young,
And my father sold me while yet my tongue
Could scarcely cry "'weep! 'weep! 'weep! 'weep!"
So your chimneys I sweep & in soot I sleep.

5 There's little Tom Dacre, who cried when his head
That curl'd like a lambs back, was shav'd, so I said,
"Hush, Tom! never mind it, for when your head's bare,
You know that the soot cannot spoil your white hair."

And so he was quiet, & that very night,
10 As Tom was a-sleeping he had such a sight!
That thousands of sweepers, Dick, Joe, Ned & Jack,
Were all of them lock'd up in coffins of black;

And by came an Angel who had a bright key,
And he open'd the coffins & set them all free;
15 Then down a green plain, leaping, laughing they run,
And wash in a river and shine in the Sun;

Then naked & white, all their bags left behind,
They rise upon clouds, and sport in the wind.
And the Angel told Tom, if he'd be a good boy,
20 He'd have God for his father & never want joy.

And so Tom awoke; and we rose in the dark
And got with our bags & our brushes to work.
Tho' the morning was cold, Tom was happy & warm;
So if all do their duty, they need not fear harm.

The Little Black Boy

My mother bore me in the southern wild,
And I am black, but O! my soul is white;
White as an angel is the English child:
But I am black as if bereav'd of light.

5 My mother taught me underneath a tree,
And sitting down before the heat of day,
She took me on her lap and kissèd me,
And pointing to the east, began to say:

"Look on the rising sun: there God does live,
10 And gives his light, and gives his heat away;
And flowers and trees and beasts and men receive
Comfort in morning, a joy in the noon day.

"And we are put on earth a little space,
That we may learn to bear the beams of love,
15 And these black bodies and this sun-burnt face
Is but a cloud, and like a shady grove.

"For when our souls have learn'd the heat to bear,
The cloud will vanish; we shall hear his voice,
Saying, 'Come out from the grove, my love & care,
20 And round my golden tent like lambs rejoice.'"

Thus did my mother say, and kissèd me;
And thus I say to little English boy:
When I from black and he from white cloud free,
And round the tent of God like lambs we joy,

25 I'll shade him from the heat till he can bear
To lean in joy upon our father's knee;
And then I'll stand and stroke his silver hair,
And be like him, and he will then love me.

1789

From **Songs of Experience**

The Sick Rose

O Rose, thou art sick.
The invisible worm
That flies in the night
In the howling storm

5 Has found out thy bed
Of crimson joy,
And his dark secret love
Does thy life destroy.

The Tyger

Tyger! Tyger! burning bright
In the forests of the night,

What immortal hand or eye
Could frame thy fearful symmetry?

5   In what distant deeps or skies
Burnt the fire of thine eyes?
On what wings dare he aspire?
What the hand, dare seize the fire?

And what shoulder, & what art,
10   Could twist the sinews of thy heart?
And when thy heart began to beat,
What dread hand? & what dread feet?

What the hammer? what the chain?
In what furnace was thy brain?
15   What the anvil? what dread grasp
Dare its deadly terrors clasp?

When the stars threw down their spears,
And water'd heaven with their tears,
Did he smile his work to see?
20   Did he who made the Lamb make thee?

Tyger! Tyger! burning bright
In the forests of the night,
What immortal hand or eye
Dare frame thy fearful symmetry?

London

I wander thro' each charter'd street,
Near where the charter'd Thames does flow,
And mark in every face I meet
Marks of weakness, marks of woe.

5   In every cry of every Man,
In every Infant's cry of fear,
In every voice, in every ban,
The mind-forg'd manacles I hear.

How the Chimney-sweeper's cry
10   Every blackning Church appalls;
And the hapless Soldier's sigh
Runs in blood down Palace walls.

But most thro' midnight streets I hear
How the youthful Harlot's curse

15 Blasts the new-born Infant's tear,
   And blights with plagues the Marriage hearse.

1794

To the Muses

Whether on Ida's shady brow,
Or in the chambers of the East,
The chambers of the sun, that now
From antient melody have ceased;

5 Whether in Heaven ye wander fair,
Or the green corners of the earth,
Or the blue regions of the air,
Where the melodious winds have birth;

Whether on chrystal rocks ye rove,
10 Beneath the bosom of the sea
Wandering in many a coral grove,
Fair Nine, forsaking Poetry!

How have you left the antient love
That bards of old enjoyed in you!
15 The languid strings do scarcely move!
The sound is forced, the notes are few!

1783

From **Milton**

And did those feet in ancient time
Walk upon England's mountains green?
And was the holy Lamb of God
On England's pleasant pastures seen?

5 And did the Countenance Divine
Shine forth upon our clouded hills?
And was Jerusalem builded here,
Among these dark Satanic Mills?

Bring me my Bow of burning gold:
10 Bring me my Arrows of desire:
Bring me my Spear: O clouds unfold!
Bring me my Chariot of fire!

I will not cease from Mental Fight,
Nor shall my Sword sleep in my hand,
15 Till we have built Jerusalem
In England's green & pleasant Land.

1804–1810

Robert Burns

(1759–1796)

To a Mouse

*On Turning Her Up in Her Nest with
the Plough, November 1785*

Wee, sleekit[1] cow'rin', tim'rous beastie,
O, what a panic's in thy breastie!
Thou need na start awa sae hasty,
        Wi' bickering brattle![2]
5 I wad be laith to rin[3] an' chase thee,
        Wi' murdering pattle![4]

I'm truly sorry man's dominion
Has broken Nature's social union,
An' justifies that ill opinion
10   Which makes thee startle
At me, thy poor earth-born companion,
        An' fellow-mortal!

I doubt na, whyles,[5] but thou may thieve;
What then? poor beastie, thou maun live!
15 A daimen icker in a thrave[6]
        'S a sma' request;
I'll get a blessin wi' the lave,[7]
        And never miss 't!

Thy wee-bit housie, too, in ruin!
20 It's silly wa's the win's are strewin'!
An' naething, now, to big[8] a new ane,
        O' foggage[9] green!
An' bleak December's win's ensuin',
        Baith snell[10] an' keen!

25 Thou saw the fields laid bare an' waste,
An' weary winter comin' fast,

---

[1]sleek
[2]hasty scamper
[3]loath to run
[4]plowstaff
[5]sometimes
[6]an occasional ear in 24 sheaves
[7]remainder
[8]build
[9]moss
[10]harsh

An' cozie here, beneath the blast,
   Thou thought to dwell,
Till crash! the cruel coulter past
30   Out thro' thy cell.

That wee bit heap o' leaves an' stibble
Has cost thee monie a weary nibble!
Now thou's turned out, for a' thy trouble,
   But house or hald,[11]
35 To thole[12] the winter's sleety dribble,
   An' cranreuch[13] cauld!

But, Mousie, thou art no thy lane,[14]
In proving foresight may be vain:
The best-laid schemes o' mice an' men
40   Gang aft agley,[15]
An' lea'e us nought but grief an' pain,
   For promis'd joy!

Still thou art blest, campared wi' me!
The present only toucheth thee:
45 But och! I backward cast my e'e,
   On prospects drear!
An' forward, tho' I canna see,
   I guess an' fear!

           1785

John Anderson, My Jo

John Anderson my jo,[1] John,
 When we were first acquent,
Your locks were like the raven,
 Your bonie brow was brent,[2]
5 But now your brow is beld, John,
 Your locks are like the snow;
But blessings on your frosty pow,[3]
 John Anderson, my jo.

John Anderson my jo, John,
10 We clamb the hill thegither;

---

[11]without house or hold
[12]endure
[13]hoarfrost
[14]not alone
[15]go oft awry

---

[1]joy
[2]straight
[3]poll

And mony a canty⁴ day, John,
    We've had wi' ane anither:
Now we maun totter down, John,
    And hand in hand we'll go,
15 And sleep thegither at the foot,
    John Anderson, my jo.

                                          1790

A Red, Red Rose

O my luve's like a red, red rose,
    That's newly sprung in June;
O my luve's like the melodie
    That's sweetly played in tune.

5 As fair art thou, my bonnie lass,
    So deep in luve am I;
And I will luve thee still, my dear,
    Till a' the seas gang dry.

Till a' the seas gang dry, my dear,
10   And the rocks melt wi' the sun:
O I will love thee still, my dear,
    While the sands o' life shall run.

And fare thee weel, my only luve,
    And fare thee weel awhile!
15 And I will come again, my luve,
    Though it were ten thousand mile.

                                          1796

William Wordsworth

(1770–1850)

Lines

*Composed a few miles above Tintern Abbey,
on revisiting the banks of the Wye
during a Tour. July 13, 1798*

Five years have passed; five summers, with the length
Of five long winters! and again I hear
These waters, rolling from their mountain-springs

---

⁴merry

With a soft inland murmur.—Once again
5 Do I behold these steep and lofty cliffs,
That on a wild secluded scene impress
Thoughts of more deep seclusion; and connect
The landscape with the quiet of the sky.
The day is come when I again repose
10 Here, under this dark sycamore, and view
These plots of cottage-ground, these orchard-tufts,
Which at this season, with their unripe fruits,
Are clad in one green hue, and lose themselves
'Mid groves and copses. Once again I see
15 These hedge-rows, hardly hedge-rows, little lines
Of sportive wood run wild: these pastoral farms,
Green to the very door; and wreaths of smoke
Sent up, in silence, from among the trees!
With some uncertain notice, as might seem
20 Of vagrant dwellers in the houseless woods,
Or of some Hermit's cave, where by his fire
The Hermit sits alone.
                              These beauteous forms,
Through a long absence, have not been to me
25 As is a landscape to a blind man's eye:
But oft, in lonely rooms, and 'mid the din
Of towns and cities, I have owed to them,
In hours of weariness, sensations sweet,
Felt in the blood, and felt along the heart;
30 And passing even into my purer mind,
With tranquil restoration:—feelings too
Of unremembered pleasure: such, perhaps,
As have no slight or trivial influence
On that best portion of a good man's life,
35 His little, nameless, unremembered, acts
Of kindness and of love. Nor less, I trust,
To them I may have owed another gift,
Of aspect more sublime; that blessèd mood,
In which the burthen of the mystery,
40 In which the heavy and the weary weight
Of all this unintelligible world,
Is lightened:—that serene and blessèd mood,
In which the affections gently lead us on,—
Until, the breath of this corporeal frame
45 And even the motion of our human blood
Almost suspended, we are laid asleep
In body, and become a living soul:

While with an eye made quiet by the power
Of harmony, and the deep power of joy,
50 We see into the life of things.
                              If this
Be but a vain belief, yet, oh! how oft—
In darkness and amid the many shapes
Of joyless daylight; when the fretful stir
55 Unprofitable, and the fever of the world,
Have hung upon the beatings of my heart—
How oft, in spirit, have I turned to thee,
O sylvan Wye! thou wanderer thro' the woods,
How often has my spirit turned to thee!
60   And now, with gleams of half-extinguished thought,
With many recognitions dim and faint,
And somewhat of a sad perplexity,
The picture of the mind revives again:
While here I stand, not only with the sense
65 Of present pleasure, but with pleasing thoughts
That in this moment there is life and food
For future years. And so I dare to hope,
Though changed, no doubt, from what I was when first
I came among these hills; when like a roe
70 I bounded o'er the mountains, by the sides
Of the deep rivers, and the lonely streams,
Wherever nature led: more like a man
Flying from something that he dreads than one
Who sought the thing he loved. For nature then
75 (The coarser pleasures of my boyish days,
And their glad animal movements all gone by)
To me was all in all.—I cannot paint
What then I was. The sounding cataract
Haunted me like a passion: the tall rock,
80 The mountain, and the deep and gloomy wood,
Their colors and their forms, were then to me
An appetite; a feeling and a love,
That had no need of a remoter charm,
By thought supplied, nor any interest
85 Unborrowed from the eye.—That time is past,
And all its aching joys are now no more,
And all its dizzy raptures. Not for this
Faint I, nor mourn nor murmur; other gifts
Have followed; for such loss, I would believe,
90 Abundant recompense. For I have learned

To look on nature, not as in the hour
Of thoughtless youth; but hearing oftentimes
The still, sad music of humanity,
Nor harsh nor grating, though of ample power
95 To chasten and subdue. And I have felt
A presence that disturbs me with the joy
Of elevated thoughts; a sense sublime
Of something far more deeply interfused
Whose dwelling is the light of setting suns,
100 And the round ocean and the living air,
And the blue sky, and in the mind of man:
A motion and a spirit, that impels
All thinking things, all objects of all thought,
And rolls through all things. Therefore am I still
105 A lover of the meadows and the woods,
And mountains; and of all that we behold
From this green earth; of all the mighty world
Of eye, and ear,—both what they half create,
And what perceive; well pleased to recognize
110 In nature and the language of the sense
The anchor of my purest thoughts, the nurse,
The guide, the guardian of my heart, and soul
Of all my moral being.
                        Nor perchance,
115 If I were not thus taught, should I the more
Suffer my genial spirits to decay:
For thou[1] art with me here upon the banks
Of this fair river; thou my dearest Friend,
My dear, dear Friend; and in thy voice I catch
120 The language of my former heart, and read
My former pleasures in the shooting lights
Of thy wild eyes. Oh! yet a little while
May I behold in thee what I was once,
My dear, dear Sister! and this prayer I make,
125 Knowing that Nature never did betray
The heart that loved her; 'tis her privilege,
Through all the years of this our life, to lead
From joy to joy: for she can so inform
The mind that is within us, so impress
130 With quietness and beauty, and so feed

---

[1]Wordsworth's sister Dorothy

With lofty thoughts, that neither evil tongues,
Rash judgments, nor the sneers of selfish men,
Nor greetings where no kindness is, nor all
The dreary intercourse of daily life,
135 Shall e'er prevail against us, or disturb
Our cheerful faith, that all which we behold
Is full of blessings. Therefore let the moon
Shine on thee in thy solitary walk;
And let the misty mountain-winds be free
140 To blow against thee: and, in after years,
When these wild ecstasies shall be matured
Into a sober pleasure; when thy mind
Shall be a mansion for all lovely forms,
Thy memory be as a dwelling-place
145 For all sweet sounds and harmonies; oh! then,
If solitude, or fear, or pain, or grief,
Should be thy portion, with what healing thoughts
Of tender joy wilt thou remember me,
And these my exhortations! Nor, perchance—
150 If I should be where I no more can hear
Thy voice, nor catch from thy wild eyes these gleams
Of past existence—wilt thou then forget
That on the banks of this delightful stream
We stood together; and that I, so long
155 A worshipper of Nature, hither came
Unwearied in that service: rather say
With warmer love—oh! with far deeper zeal
Of holier love. Nor wilt thou then forget
That after many wanderings, many years
160 Of absence, these steep woods and lofty cliffs,
And this green pastoral landscape, were to me
More dear, both for themselves and for thy sake!

                                              1798

She Dwelt Among the Untrodden Ways

She dwelt among the untrodden ways
    Beside the springs of Dove.
A Maid whom there were none to praise
    And very few to love;

5 A violet by a mossy stone
    Half hidden from the eye!

—Fair as a star, when only one
  Is shining in the sky.

She lived unknown, and few could know
10   When Lucy ceased to be;
But she is in her grave, and, oh,
    The difference to me!

                                    1800

A Slumber Did My Spirit Seal

A slumber did my spirit seal;
  I had no human fears:
She seemed a thing that could not feel
  The touch of earthly years.

5 No motion has she now, no force;
  She neither hears nor sees;
Rolled round in earth's diurnal course,
  With rocks, and stones, and trees.

                                    1800

It Is a Beauteous Evening

It is a beauteous evening, calm and free,
The holy time is quiet as a Nun
Breathless with adoration; the broad sun
Is sinking down in its tranquility;
5 The gentleness of heaven broods o'er the Sea:
Listen! the mighty Being is awake,
And doth with his eternal motion make
A sound like thunder—everlastingly.
Dear Child! dear Girl! that walkest with me here,
10 If thou appear untouched by solemn thought,
Thy nature is not therefore less divine:
Thou livest in Abraham's bosom all the year;
And worshipp'st at the Temple's inner shrine,
God being with thee when we know it not.

                                    1802

London, 1802

Milton! thou shouldst be living at this hour:
England hath need of thee: she is a fen
Of stagnant waters: altar, sword, and pen,

Fireside, the heroic wealth of hall and bower,
5   Have forfeited their ancient English dower
Of inward happiness. We are selfish men;
Oh! raise us up, return to us again;
And give us manners, virtue, freedom, power.
Thy soul was like a Star, and dwelt apart;
10 Thou hadst a voice whose sound was like the sea:
Pure as the naked heavens, majestic, free,
So didst thou travel on life's common way,
In cheerful godliness; and yet thy heart
The lowliest duties on herself did lay.

1807

Composed upon Westminster Bridge, September 3, 1802

Earth has not anything to show more fair:
Dull would he be of soul who could pass by
A sight so touching in its majesty;
This City now doth, like a garment, wear
5   The beauty of the morning; silent, bare,
Ships, towers, domes, theaters, and temples lie
Open unto the fields, and to the sky;
All bright and glittering in the smokeless air.
Never did sun more beautifully steep
10 In his first splendor, valley, rock, or hill;
Ne'er saw I, never felt, a calm so deep!
The river glideth at his own sweet will:
Dear God! the very houses seem asleep;
And all that mighty heart is lying still!

1807

Ode

Intimations of Immortality from Recollections of Early Childhood

The Child is father of the Man;
And I could wish my days to be
Bound each to each by natural piety.

1

There was a time when meadow, grove, and stream,
The earth, and every common sight,
        To me did seem

Apparelled in celestial light,
5 The glory and the freshness of a dream.
It is not now as it hath been of yore;—
        Turn wheresoe'er I may,
            By night or day,
The things which I have seen I now can see no more.

                        2

10   The Rainbow comes and goes,
        And lovely is the Rose,
        The Moon doth with delight
    Look round her when the heavens are bare;
        Waters on a starry night
15   Are beautiful and fair;
    The sunshine is a glorious birth;
    But yet I know, where'er I go,
That there hath past away a glory from the earth.

                        3

    Now, while the birds thus sing a joyous song,
20   And while the young lambs bound
            As to the tabor's sound,
    To me alone there came a thought of grief:
    A timely utterance gave that thought relief,
            And I again am strong:
25 The cataracts blow their trumpets from the steep;
    No more shall grief of mine the season wrong;
    I hear the Echoes through the mountains throng,
    The Winds come to me from the fields of sleep,
            And all the earth is gay;
30   Land and sea
        Give themselves up to jollity,
            And with the heart of May
        Doth every Beast keep holiday;—
            Thou Child of Joy,
35 Shout round me, let me hear thy shouts, thou happy Shepherd-boy!

                        4

    Ye blessèd Creatures, I have heard the call
        Ye to each other make; I see
    The heavens laugh with you in your jubilee;
        My heart is at your festival,
40   My head hath its coronal,

The fulness of your bliss, I feel—I feel it all.
      Oh evil day! if I were sullen
      While Earth herself is adorning,
         This sweet May-morning,
45   And the Children are culling
         On every side,
      In a thousand valleys far and wide,
      Fresh flowers; while the sun shines warm,
And the Babe leaps up on his Mother's arm;—
50   I hear, I hear, with joy I hear!
      —But there's a Tree, of many, one,
A single Field which I have looked upon,
Both of them speak of something that is gone:
      The Pansy at my feet
55   Doth the same tale repeat:
Whither is fled the visionary gleam?
Where is it now, the glory and the dream?

5

Our birth is but a sleep and a forgetting:
The Soul that rises with us, our life's Star,
60   Hath had elsewhere its setting,
         And cometh from afar:
      Not in entire forgetfulness,
      And not in utter nakedness,
But trailing clouds of glory do we come
65   From God, who is our home:
Heaven lies about us in our infancy!
Shades of the prison-house begin to close
      Upon the growing Boy,
        But He
70 Beholds the light, and whence it flows,
      He sees it in his joy;
The Youth, who daily farther from the east
      Must travel, still is Nature's Priest,
      And by the vision splendid
75   Is on his way attended;
At length the Man perceives it die away,
And fade into the light of common day.

6

Earth fills her lap with pleasures of her own;
Yearnings she hath in her own natural kind,

80 And, even with something of a Mother's mind,
     And no unworthy aim,
     The homely Nurse doth all she can
To make her Foster-child, her Inmate Man,
     Forget the glories he hath known,
85 And that imperial palace whence he came.

                        7

Behold the Child among his new-born blisses,
A six years' Darling of a pigmy size!
See, where 'mid work of his own hand he lies,
Fretted by sallies of his mother's kisses,
90 With light upon him from his father's eyes!
See, at his feet, some little plan or chart,
Some fragment from his dream of human life,
Shaped by himself with newly-learnèd art;
     A wedding or a festival,
95   A mourning or a funeral;
          And this hath now his heart,
          And unto this he frames his song:
              Then will he fit his tongue
To dialogues of business, love, or strife;
100   But it will not be long
             Ere this be thrown aside,
             And with new joy and pride
The little Actor cons another part;
Filling from time to time his "humorous stage"
105 With all the Persons, down to palsied Age,
That Life brings with her in her equipage;
          As if his whole vocation
          Were endless imitation.

                        8

Thou, whose exterior semblance doth belie
110   Thy Soul's immensity;
Thou best Philosopher, who yet dost keep
Thy heritage, thou Eye among the blind,
That, deaf and silent, read'st the eternal deep,
Haunted for ever by the eternal mind,—
115   Mighty Prophet! Seer blest!
          On whom those truths do rest,
Which we are toiling all our lives to find,
In darkness lost, the darkness of the grave;

Thou, over whom thy Immortality
120 Broods like the Day, a Master o'er a Slave,
A Presence which is not to be put by;
Thou little Child, yet glorious in the might
Of heaven-born freedom on thy being's height,
Why with such earnest pains dost thou provoke
125 The years to bring the inevitable yoke,
Thus blindly with thy blessedness at strife?
Full soon thy Soul shall have her earthly freight,
And custom lie upon thee with a weight,
Heavy as frost, and deep almost as life!

9

130   O joy! that in our embers
Is something that doth live,
That nature yet remembers
What was so fugitive!
The thought of our past years in me doth breed
135 Perpetual benediction: not indeed
· For that which is most worthy to be blest;
Delight and liberty, the simple creed
Of Childhood, whether busy or at rest,
With new-fledged hope still fluttering in his breast:—
140   Not for these I raise
The song of thanks and praise;
But for those obstinate questionings
Of sense and outward things,
Falling from us, vanishings;
145   Blank misgivings of a Creature
Moving about in worlds not realized,
High instincts before which our mortal Nature
Did tremble like a guilty Thing surprised:
But for those first affections,
150   Those shadowy recollections,
Which, be they what they may,
Are yet the fountain-light of all our day,
Are yet a master-light of all our seeing;
Uphold us, cherish, and have power to make
155 Our noisy years seem moments in the being
Of the eternal Silence: truths that wake,
To perish never:
Which neither listlessness, nor mad endeavor,
Nor Man nor Boy,

160   Nor all that is at enmity with joy,
      Can utterly abolish or destroy!
          Hence in a season of calm weather
              Though inland far we be,
      Our Souls have sight of that immortal sea
165   Which brought us hither,
          Can in a moment travel thither,
      And see the Children sport upon the shore,
      And hear the mighty waters rolling evermore.

                              10

      Then sing, ye Birds, sing, sing a joyous song!
170   And let the young Lambs bound
              As to the tabor's sound!
      We in thought will join your throng,
              Ye that pipe and ye that play,
              Ye that through your hearts to-day
175   Feel the gladness of the May!
      What though the radiance which was once so bright
      Be now for ever taken from my sight,
          Though nothing can bring back the hour
      Of splendor in the grass, of glory in the flower;
180   We will grieve not, rather find
              Strength in what remains behind;
              In the primal sympathy
              Which having been must ever be;
              In the soothing thoughts that spring
185   Out of human suffering;
              In the faith that looks through death,
      In years that bring the philosophic mind.

                              11

      And O, ye Fountains, Meadows, Hills, and Groves,
      Forebode not any severing of our loves!
190   Yet in my heart of hearts I feel your might;
      I only have relinquished one delight
      To live beneath your more habitual sway.
      I love the Brooks which down their channels fret,
      Even more than when I tripped lightly as they;
195   The innocent brightness of a new-born Day
                  Is lovely yet;
      The Clouds that gather round the setting sun
      Do take a sober coloring from an eye

That hath kept watch o'er man's mortality;
200 Another race hath been, and other palms are won.
Thanks to the human heart by which we live,
Thanks to its tenderness, its joys, and fears,
To me the meanest flower that blows can give
Thoughts that do often lie too deep for tears.

1807

She Was a Phantom of Delight

She was a Phantom of delight
When first she gleamed upon my sight;
A lovely Apparition, sent
To be a moment's ornament;
5 Her eyes as stars of Twilight fair;
Like Twilight's, too, her dusky hair;
But all things else about her drawn
From May-time and the cheerful Dawn;
A dancing Shape, an Image gay,
10 To haunt, to startle, and way-lay.

I saw her upon nearer view,
A Spirit, yet a Woman too!
Her household motions light and free,
And steps of virgin-liberty;
15 A countenance in which did meet
Sweet records, promises as sweet;
A Creature not too bright or good
For human nature's daily food;
For transient sorrows, simple wiles,
20 Praise, blame, love, kisses, tears, and smiles.

And now I see with eyes serene
The very pulse of the machine;
A Being breathing thoughtful breath,
A Traveller between life and death;
25 The reason firm, the temperate will,
Endurance, foresight, strength, and skill;
A perfect Woman, nobly planned,
To warn, to comfort, and command;
And yet a Spirit still, and bright
30 With something of angelic light.

1807

The World Is Too Much with Us

The world is too much with us; late and soon,
Getting and spending, we lay waste our powers:
Little we see in Nature that is ours;
We have given our hearts away, a sordid boon!
5 This Sea that bares her bosom to the moon;
The winds that will be howling at all hours,
And are up-gathered now like sleeping flowers;
For this, for everything, we are out of tune;
It moves us not.—Great God! I'd rather be
10 A Pagan suckled in a creed outworn;
So might I, standing on this pleasant lea,
Have glimpses that would make me less forlorn;
Have sight of Proteus rising from the sea;
Or hear old Triton blow his wreathèd horn.

1807

I Wandered Lonely as a Cloud

I wandered lonely as a cloud
That floats on high o'er vales and hills,
When all at once I saw a crowd,
A host, of golden daffodils;
5 Beside the lake, beneath the trees,
Fluttering and dancing in the breeze.

Continuous as the stars that shine
And twinkle on the Milky Way,
They stretched in never-ending line
10 Along the margin of a bay:
Ten thousand saw I at a glance,
Tossing their heads in sprightly dance.

The waves beside them danced; but they
Outdid the sparkling waves in glee;
15 A poet could not but be gay,
In such a jocund company;
I gazed—and gazed—but little thought
What wealth the show to me had brought:

For oft, when on my couch I lie
20 In vacant or in pensive mood,
They flash upon that inward eye
Which is the bliss of solitude;

And then my heart with pleasure fills,
And dances with the daffodils.

1807

Scorn Not the Sonnet

Scorn not the sonnet; critic, you have frowned,
Mindless of its just honors; with this key
Shakespeare unlocked his heart; the melody
Of this small lute gave ease to Petrarch's wound;
5   A thousand times this pipe did Tasso sound;
With its Camöens soothed an exile's grief;
The sonnet glittered a gay myrtle leaf
Amid the cypress with which Dante crowned
His visionary brow; a glow-worn lamp,
10 It cheered mild Spenser, called from Faeryland
To struggle through dark ways; and, when a damp
Fell round the path of Milton, in his hand
The thing became a trumpet; whence he blew
Soul-animating strains—alas, too few!

1827

Samuel Taylor Coleridge

(1772–1834)

Kubla Khan

In Xanadu did Kubla Khan
A stately pleasure-dome decree:
Where Alph, the sacred river, ran
Through caverns measureless to man
5   Down to a sunless sea.
So twice five miles of fertile ground
With walls and towers were girdled round:
And there were gardens bright with sinuous rills,
Where blossomed many an incense-bearing tree;
10 And here were forests ancient as the hills,
Enfolding sunny spots of greenery.

But oh! that deep romantic chasm which slanted
Down the green hill athwart a cedarn cover!
A savage place! as holy and enchanted

15 As e'er beneath a waning moon was haunted
By woman wailing for her demon-lover!
And from this chasm, with ceaseless turmoil seething,
As if this earth in fast thick pants were breathing,
A mighty fountain momently was forced:
20 Amid whose swift half-intermitted burst
Huge fragments vaulted like rebounding hail,
Or chaffy grain beneath the thresher's flail:
And 'mid these dancing rocks at once and ever
It flung up momently the sacred river.
25 Five miles meandering with a mazy motion
Through wood and dale the sacred river ran,
Then reached the caverns measureless to man,
And sank in tumult to a lifeless ocean:
And 'mid this tumult Kubla heard from far
30 Ancestral voices prophesying war!

    The shadow of the dome of pleasure
    Floated midway on the waves;
    Where was heard the mingled measure
    From the fountain and the caves.

35 It was a miracle of rare device,
A sunny pleasure-dome with caves of ice!

    A damsel with a dulcimer
    In a vision once I saw:
    It was an Abyssinian maid,
40   And on her dulcimer she played,
    Singing of Mount Abora.
    Could I revive within me
    Her symphony and song,
    To such a deep delight 'twould win me,

45 That with music loud and long,
I would build that dome in air,
That sunny dome! those caves of ice!
And all who heard should see them there,
And all should cry, Beware! Beware!
50 His flashing eyes, his floating hair!
Weave a circle round him thrice,
And close your eyes with holy dread,
For he on honey-dew hath fed,
And drunk the milk of Paradise.

1797

The Rime of the Ancient Mariner

Facile credo, plures esse Naturas invisibiles quam visibiles in rerum universitate. Sed horum omnium familiam quis nobis enarrabit? et gradus et cognationes et discrimina et singulorum munera? Quid agunt? quae loca habitant? Harum rerum notitiam semper ambivit ingenium humanum, nunquam attigit. Juvat, interea, non diffiteor, quandoque in animo, tanquam in tabulà, majoris et melioris mundi imaginem contemplari: ne mens assuefacta hodiernae vitae minutiis se contrahat nimis, et tota subsidat in pusillas cogitationes. Sed veritati interea inviglandum est, modusque servandus, ut certa ab incertis, diem a nocte, distinguamus.

T. BURNET, *ARCHAEOL. PHIL.* P. 68[1]

Argument

How a Ship, having first sailed to the Equator, was driven by Storms to the cold Country towards the South Pole; how the Ancient Mariner cruelly and in contempt of the laws of hospitality killed a Seabird and how he was followed by many and strange Judgements: and in what manner he came back to his own Country. [*Lyrical Ballads*. ed. of 1800.]

Part I

It is an ancient Mariner,
And he stoppeth one of three.
"By thy long grey beard and glittering eye,
Now wherefore stopp'st thou me?

An ancient Mariner meeteth three Gallants bidden to a wedding-feast, and detaineth one.

5   The Bridegroom's doors are opened wide,
And I am next of kin;
The guests are met, the feast is set:
May'st hear the merry din."

He holds him with his skinny hand,
10   "There was a ship," quoth he.
"Hold off! unhand me, grey-beard loon!"
Eftsoons his hand dropt he.

He holds him with his glittering eye—
The Wedding-Guest stood still,

The Wedding-Guest is spellbound by the eye of the old seafaring man, and constrained to hear his tale.

---

[1] I readily believe that there are more invisible than visible things in the universe. But who will tell us of their families, ranks, similarities and differences? What do they do? Where do they live? Human knowledge has always circled around the understanding of these things but has never achieved it. It is pleasant, however, to contemplate at times, as in a picture, the image of a greater and better world lest the mind, too accustomed to the details of everyday life, become contracted and dwell completely on trivial things. But meanwhile we must be watchful of truth and keep within certain limits so that we may distinguish truth from opinion, day from night. (Coleridge)

15 And listens like a three years' child:
   The Mariner hath his will.

The Wedding-Guest sat on a stone:
He cannot choose but hear;
And thus spake on that ancient man,
20 The bright-eyed Mariner.

"The ship was cheered, the harbour cleared,
Merrily did we drop
Below the kirk, below the hill,
Below the lighthouse top.

25 The Sun came up upon the left,
   Out of the sea came he!
   And he shone bright, and on the right
   Went down into the sea.

Higher and higher every day,
30 Till over the mast at noon—"
   The Wedding-Guest here beat his breast,
   For he heard the loud bassoon.

The bride hath paced into the hall,
Red as a rose is she;
35 Nodding their heads before her goes
   The merry minstrelsy.

The Wedding-Guest he beat his breast,
Yet he cannot choose but hear;
And thus spake on the ancient man,
40 The bright-eyed Mariner.

"And now the STORM-BLAST came, and he
Was tyrannous and strong:
He struck with his o'ertaking wings,
And chased us south along.

45 With sloping masts and dipping prow,
   As who pursued with yell and blow
   Still treads the shadow of his foe,
   And forward bends his head,
   The ship drove fast, loud roared the blast,
50 And southward aye we fled.

And now there came both mist and snow,
And it grew wondrous cold:
And ice, mast-high, came floating by,
As green as emerald.

The Mariner tells how the ship sailed southward with a good wind and fair weather, till it reached the line.

The Wedding-Guest heareth the bridal music; but the Mariner continueth his tale.

The ship driven by a storm toward the south pole.

55 And through the drifts the snowy clifts
    Did send a dismal sheen:
    Nor shapes of men nor beasts we ken—
    The ice was all between.

    The ice was here, the ice was there,
60 The ice was all around:
    It cracked and growled, and roared and howled,
    Like noises in a swound!²

    At length did cross an Albatross,
    Thorough the fog it came;
65 As if it had been a Christian soul,
    We hailed it in God's name.

    I ate the food it ne'er had eat,
    And round and round it flew.
    The ice did split with a thunder-fit;
70 The helmsman steered us through!

    And a good south wind sprung up behind;
    The Albatross did follow,
    And every day, for food or play,
    Came to the mariners' hollo!

75 In mist or cloud, on mast or shroud,³
    It perched for vespers nine;
    Whiles all the night, through fog-smoke white,
    Glimmered the white Moon-shine."

    "God save thee, ancient Mariner!
80 From the fiends, that plague thee thus!—
    Why look'st thou so?"—With my cross-bow
    I shot the ALBATROSS.

The land of ice, and of fearful sounds where no living thing was to be seen.

Till a great sea-bird, called the Albatross, came through the snow-fog, and was received with great joy and hospitality.

And lo! the Albatross proveth a bird of good omen, and followeth the ship as it returned northward through fog and floating ice.

The ancient Mariner inhospitably killeth the pious bird of good omen.

Part II

    The Sun now rose upon the right:
    Out of the sea came he,
85 Still hid in mist, and on the left
    Went down into the sea.

    And the good south wind still blew behind,
    But no sweet bird did follow,
    Nor any day for food or play
90 Came to the mariners' hollo!

------

²swoon
³the rope that supports the masthead

And I had done a hellish thing,
And it would work 'em woe:
For all averred, I had killed the bird
That made the breeze to blow.
95 Ah wretch! said they, the bird to slay,
That made the breeze to blow!

His shipmates cry out against the ancient Mariner, for killing the bird of good luck.

Nor dim nor red, like God's own head,
The glorious Sun uprist:
Then all averred, I had killed the bird
100 That brought the fog and mist.
'Twas right, said they, such birds to slay,
That bring the fog and mist.

But when the fog cleared off, they justify the same, and thus make themselves accomplices in the crime.

The fair breeze blew, the white foam flew,
The furrow followed free;
105 We were the first that ever burst
Into that silent sea.

The fair breeze continues; the ship enters the Pacific Ocean, and sails northward, even till it reaches the Line.

Down dropt the breeze, the sails dropt down,
'Twas sad as sad could be;
And we did speak only to break
110 The silence of the sea!

The ship hath been suddenly becalmed.

All in a hot and copper sky,
The bloody Sun, at noon,
Right up above the mast did stand,
No bigger than the Moon.

115 Day after day, day after day,
We stuck, nor breath nor motion;
As idle as a painted ship
Upon a painted ocean.

Water, water, every where,
120 And all the boards did shrink;
Water, water, every where,
Nor any drop to drink.

And the Albatross begins to be avenged.

The very deep did rot: O Christ!
That ever this should be!
125 Yea, slimy things did crawl with legs
Upon the slimy sea.

About, about, in reel and rout
The death-fires danced at night;
The water, like a witch's oils,
130 Burnt green, and blue and white.

A Spirit had followed them; one of the invisible inhabitants of this planet, neither departed souls nor angels;

And some in dreams assurèd were
Of the Spirit that plagued us so;
Nine fathom deep he had followed us
From the land of mist and snow.

135 And every tongue, through utter drought,
Was withered at the root;
We could not speak, no more than if
We had been choked with soot.

Ah! well a-day! what evil looks
140 Had I from old and young!
Instead of the cross, the Albatross
About my neck was hung.

Part III

There passed a weary time. Each throat
Was parched, and glazed each eye.
145 A weary time! a weary time!
How glazed each weary eye,
When looking westward, I beheld
A something in the sky.

At first it seemed a little speck,
150 And then it seemed a mist;
It moved and moved, and took at last
A certain shape, I wist.

A speck, a mist, a shape, I wist!
And still it neared and neared:
155 As if it dodged a water-sprite,
It plunged and tacked and veered.

With throats unslaked, with black lips baked,
We could nor laugh nor wail;
Through utter drought all dumb we stood!
160 I bit my arm, I sucked the blood,
And cried, A sail! a sail!

With throats unslaked, with black lips baked,
Agape they heard me call:
Gramercy! they for joy did grin,
165 And all at once their breath drew in,
As they were drinking all.

See! see! (I cried) she tacks no more!
Hither to work us weal;

concerning whom the learned Jew, Josephus, and the Platonic Constantinopolitan, Michael Psellus, may be consulted. They are very numerous, and there is no climate or element without one or more.

The shipmates, in their sore distress, would fain throw the whole guilt on the ancient Mariner: in sign whereof they hang the dead sea-bird round his neck.

The ancient Mariner beholdeth a sign in the element afar off.

As its nearer approach, it seemeth him to be a ship; and at a dear ransom he freeth his speech from the bonds of thirst.

A flash of joy;

And horror follows. For can it be a ship that comes onward without wind or tide?

Without a breeze, without a tide,
170 She steadies with upright keel!

The western wave was all a-flame.
The day was well nigh done!
Almost upon the western wave
Rested the broad bright Sun;
175 When that strange shape drove suddenly
Betwixt us and the Sun.

And straight the Sun was flecked with bars,
(Heaven's Mother send us grace!)
As if through a dungeon-grate he peered
180 With broad and burning face.

> It seemeth him but the skeleton of a ship.

Alas! (thought I, and my heart beat loud)
How fast she nears and nears!
Are those *her* sails that glance in the Sun,
Like restless gossameres?

> And its ribs are seen as bars on the face of the setting Sun.

185 Are those *her* ribs through which the Sun
Did peer, as through a grate?
And is that Woman all her crew?
Is that a DEATH? and are there two?
Is DEATH that woman's mate?

> The Spectre-Woman and her Deathmate, and no other on board the skeleton ship.

190 *Her* lips were red, *her* looks were free,
Her locks were yellow as gold:
Her skin was as white as leprosy,
The Night-mare LIFE-IN-DEATH was she,
Who thicks man's blood with cold.

> Like vessel, like crew!

195 The naked hulk alongside came,
And the twain were casting dice;
"The game is done! I've won! I've won!"
Quoth she, and whistles thrice.

> Death and Life-in-Death have diced for the ship's crew, and she (the latter) winneth the ancient Mariner.

The Sun's rim dips; the stars rush out:
200 At one stride comes the dark;
With far-heard whisper, o'er the sea,
Off shot the spectre-bark.

> No twilight within the courts of the Sun.

We listened and looked sideways up!
Fear at my heart, as at a cup,
205 My life-blood seemed to sip!
The stars were dim, and thick the night,
The steersman's face by his lamp gleamed white;
From the sails the dew did drip—

> At the rising of the Moon,

Till clomb above the eastern bar
210 The hornèd Moon, with one bright star
Within the nether tip.

One after one, by the star-dogged Moon,   One after another,
Too quick for groan or sigh,
Each turned his face with a ghastly pang,
215 And cursed me with his eye.

Four times fifty living men,   His shipmates drop down
(And I heard nor sigh nor groan)   dead.
With heavy thump, a lifeless lump,
They dropped down one by one.

220 The souls did from their bodies fly,—   But Life-in-Death begins her
They fled to bliss or woe!   work on the ancient Mariner.
And every soul, it passed me by,
Like the whizz of my cross-bow!

Part IV

"I fear thee, ancient Mariner!   The Wedding-Guest feareth
225 I fear thy skinny hand!   that a Spirit is talking to him;
And thou art long, and lank, and brown,
As is the ribbed sea-sand.[4]

I fear thee and thy glittering eye,
And thy skinny hand, so brown."—
230 Fear not, fear not, thou Wedding-Guest!
This body dropt not down.

Alone, alone, all, all alone,   But the ancient Mariner
Alone on a wide wide sea!   assureth him of his bodily
And never a saint took pity on   life, and proceedeth to relate
235 My soul in agony.   his horrible penance.

The many men, so beautiful!   He despiseth the creatures of
And they all dead did lie: the calm,
And a thousand thousand slimy things
Lived on; and so did I.

240 I looked upon the rotting sea,   And envieth that *they* should
And drew my eyes away;   live, and so many lie dead.
I looked upon the rotting deck,
And there the dead men lay.

---

[4]For the last two lines of this stanza I am indebted to Mr. Wordsworth. It was on a delightful walk
from Nether Stowey to Dulverton, with him and his sister, in the Autumn of 1797, that this poem
was planned, and in part composed. (Coleridge)

I looked to heaven, and tried to pray;
245 But or ever a prayer had gusht,
A wicked whisper came, and made
My heart as dry as dust.

I closed my lids, and kept them close,
And the balls like pulses beat;
250 For the sky and the sea, and the sea and the sky
Lay like a load on my weary eye,
And the dead were at my feet.

The cold sweat melted from their limbs,
Nor rot nor reek did they:
255 The look with which they looked on me
Had never passed away.

But the curse liveth for him
in the eye of the dead men.

An orphan's curse would drag to hell
A spirit from on high;
But oh! more horrible than that
260 Is the curse in a dead man's eye!
Seven days, seven nights, I saw that curse,
And yet I could not die.

The moving Moon went up the sky,
And no where did abide:
265 Softly she was going up,
And a star or two beside—

In his loneliness and
fixedness he yearneth
towards the journeying
Moon, and the stars that
still sojourn, yet still move
onward; and every where the
blue sky belongs to them, and
is their appointed rest, and
their native country and their
own natural homes, which
they enter unannounced, as
lords that are certainly
expected and yet there is a
silent joy at their arrival.

Her beams bemocked the sultry main,
Like April hoar-frost spread;
But where the ship's huge shadow lay,
270 The charmèd water burnt alway
A still and awful red.

Beyond the shadow of the ship,
I watched the water-snakes:
They moved in tracks of shining white,
275 And when they reared, the elfish light
Fell off in hoary flakes.

By the light of the Moon he
beholdeth God's creatures of
the great calm.

Within the shadow of the ship
I watched their rich attire:
Blue, glossy green, and velvet black,
280 They coiled and swam; and every track
Was a flash of golden fire.

O happy living things! no tongue
Their beauty might declare:

Their beauty and their
happiness.

A spring of love gushed from my heart,
285　And I blessed them unaware: He blesseth them in his heart.
Sure my kind saint took pity on me,
And I blessed them unaware.

The self-same moment I could pray;   The spell begins to break.
And from my neck so free
290　The Albatross fell off, and sank
Like lead into the sea.

Part V

Oh sleep! it is a gentle thing,
Beloved from pole to pole!
To Mary Queen the praise be given!
295　She sent the gentle sleep from Heaven,
That slid into my soul.

The silly buckets on the deck,   By grace of the holy Mother,
That had so long remained,   the ancient Mariner is
I dreamt that they were filled with dew;   refreshed with rain.
300　And when I awoke, it rained.

My lips were wet, my throat was cold,
My garments all were dank;
Sure I had drunken in my dreams,
And still my body drank.

305　I moved, and could not feel my limbs:
I was so light—almost
I thought that I had died in sleep,
And was a blessèd ghost.

And soon I heard a roaring wind: He heareth sounds and
310　It did not come anear;   seeth, strange sights and
But with its sound it shook the sails,   commotions in the sky and
That were so thin and sere.   the element.

The upper air burst into life!
And a hundred fire-flags sheen,
315　To and fro they were hurried about!
And to and fro, and in and out,
The wan stars danced between.

And the coming wind did roar more loud,
And the sails did sigh like sedge;
320　And the rain poured down from one black cloud;
The Moon was at its edge.

The thick black cloud was cleft, and still
The Moon was at its side:
Like waters shot from some high crag,
325   The lightning fell with never a jag,
A river steep and wide.

The loud wind never reached the ship,
Yet now the ship moved on!
Beneath the lightning and the Moon
330   The dead men gave a groan.

The bodies of the ship's crew are inspired and the ship moves on;

They groaned, they stirred, they all uprose,
Nor spake, nor moved their eyes;
It had been strange, even in a dream,
To have seen those dead men rise.

335   The helmsman steered, the ship moved on;
Yet never a breeze up-blew;
The mariners all 'gan work the ropes,
Where they were wont to do;
They raised their limbs like lifeless tools—
340   We were a ghastly crew.

The body of my brother's son
Stood by me, knee to knee:
The body and I pulled at one rope,
but he said nought to me.

345   "I fear thee, ancient Mariner!"
Be calm, thou Wedding-Guest!
'Twas not those souls that fled in pain,
Which to their corses came again,
But a troop of spirits blest:

But not by the souls of the men, nor by daemons of earth or middle air, but by a blessed troop of angelic spirits, sent down by the invocation of the guardian saint.

350   For when it dawned—they dropped their arms,
And clustered round the mast;
Sweet sounds rose slowly through their mouths,
And from their bodies passed.

Around, around, flew each sweet sound,
355   Then darted to the Sun;
Slowly the sounds came back again,
Now mixed, now one by one.

Sometimes a-dropping from the sky
I heard the sky-lark sing;
360   Sometimes all little birds that are,
How they seemed to fill the sea and air
With their sweet jargoning!

And now 'twas like all instruments,
Now like a lonely flute;
365 And now it is an angel's song,
That makes the heavens be mute.

It ceased; yet still the sails made on
A pleasant noise till noon,
A noise like of a hidden brook
370 In the leafy month of June,
that to the sleeping woods all night
Singeth a quiet tune.

Till noon we quietly sailed on,
Yet never a breeze did breathe:
375 Slowly and smoothly went the ship,
Moved onward from beneath.

Under the keel nine fathom deep,
From the land of mist and snow,
The spirit slid: and it was he
380 That made the ship to go.
The sails at noon left off their tune,
And the ship stood still also.

The lonesome Spirit from the south-pole carries on the ship as far as the Line, in obedience to the angelic troop, but still requireth vengeance.

The Sun, right up above the mast,
Had fixed her to the ocean:
385 But in a minute she 'gan stir,
With a short uneasy motion—
Backwards and forwards half her length
With a short uneasy motion.

Then like a pawing horse let go,
390 She made a sudden bound:
It flung the blood into my head,
And I fell down in a swound.

How long in that same fit I lay,
I have not to declare;
395 But ere my living life returned,
I heard and in my soul discerned
Two voices in the air.

The Polar Spirit's fellow-daemons, the invisible inhabitants of the element, take part in his wrong; and two of them relate, one to the other, that penance long and heavy for the ancient Mariner hath been accorded to the Polar Spirit, who returneth southward.

"Is it he?" quoth one, "Is this the man?
By him who died on cross,
400 With his cruel bow he laid full low
The harmless Albatross.

The spirit who bideth by himself
In the land of mist and snow,

He loved the bird that loved the man
405 Who shot him with his bow."

The other was a softer voice,
As soft as honey-dew:
Quoth he, "The man hath penance done,
And penance more will do."

Part VI

FIRST VOICE

410 "But tell me, tell me! speak again,
Thy soft response renewing—
What makes that ship drive on so fast?
What is the ocean doing?"

SECOND VOICE

"Still as a slave before his lord,
415 The ocean hath no blast;
His great bright eye most silently
Up to the Moon is cast—

If he may know which way to go;
For she guides him smooth or grim.
420 See, brother, see! how graciously
She looketh down on him."

FIRST VOICE

"But why drives on that ship so fast,
Without or wave or wind?"

The Mariner hath been cast into a trance; for the angelic power causeth the vessel to drive northward faster than human life could endure.

SECOND VOICE

"The air is cut away before,
425 And closes from behind.

Fly brother, fly! more high, more high!
Or we shall be belated:
For slow and slow that ship will go,
When the Mariner's trance is abated."

430 I woke, and we were sailing on
As in a gentle weather:
'Twas night, calm night, the moon was high;
The dead men stood together.

The supernatural motion is retarded; the Mariner awakes, and his penance begins anew.

All stood together on the deck,
435 For a charnel-dungeon fitter:
All fixed on me their stony eyes,
That in the Moon did glitter.

The pang, the curse, with which they died,
Had never passed away:
440 I could not draw my eyes from theirs,
Nor turn them up to pray.

And now this spell was snapt: once more   The curse is finally expiated.
I viewed the ocean green,
And looked far forth, yet little saw
445 Of what had else been seen—

Like one, that on a lonesome road
Doth walk in fear and dread,
And living once turned round walks on,
And turns no more his head;
450 Because he knows, a frightful fiend
Doth close behind him tread.

But soon there breathed a wind on me,
Nor sound nor motion made:
Its path was not upon the sea,
455 In ripple or in shade.

It raised my hair, it fanned my cheek
Like a meadow-gale of spring—
It mingled strangely with my fears,
Yet it felt like a welcoming.

460 Swiftly, swiftly flew the ship,
Yet she sailed softly too:
Sweetly, sweetly blew the breeze—
On me alone it blew.

Oh! dream of joy! is this indeed   And the ancient Mariner
465 The light-house top I see?   beholdeth his native country.
Is this the hill? is this the kirk?
Is this mine own countree?

We drifted o'er the harbour-bar,
And I with sobs did pray—
470 O let me be awake, my God!
Or let me sleep alway.

The harbour-bay was clear as glass,
So smoothly it was strewn!

And on the bay the moonlight lay,
475   And the shadow of the Moon.

The rock shone bright, the kirk no less,
That stands above the rock:
The moonlight steeped in silentness
The steady weathercock.

480   And the bay was white with silent light,
Till rising from the same,
Full many shapes, that shadows were,
In crimson colours came.

A little distance from the prow
485   Those crimson shadows were:
I turned my eyes upon the deck—
Oh, Christ! what saw I there!

Each corse lay flat, lifeless and flat,
And, by the holy rood!
490   A man all light, a seraph-man,
On every corse there stood.

This seraph-band, each waved his hand:
It was a heavenly sight!
They stood at signals to the land,
495   Each one a lovely light;

This seraph-band, each waved his hand,
No voice did they impart—
No voice; but oh! the silence sank
Like music on my heart.

500   But soon I heard the dash of oars,
I heard the Pilot's cheer;
My head was turned perforce away
And I saw a boat appear.

The Pilot and the Pilot's boy,
505   I heard them coming fast:
Dear Lord in Heaven! it was a joy
The dead men could not blast.

I saw a third—I heard his voice:
It is the Hermit good!
510   He singeth loud his godly hymns
That he makes in the wood.
He'll shrieve my soul, he'll wash away
The Albatross's blood.

The angelic spirits leave the
dead bodies,

And appear in their own
forms of light.

Part VII

This Hermit good lives in that wood   The Hermit of the Wood,
515 Which slopes down to the sea.
How loudly his sweet voice he rears!
He loves to talk with marineres
That come from a far countree.

He kneels at morn, and noon, and eve—
520 He hath a cushion plump:
It is the moss that wholly hides
The rotted old oak-stump.

The skiff-boat neared: I heard them talk,
"Why, this is strange, I trow!
525 Where are those lights so many and fair,
That signal made but now?"

"Strange, by my faith!" the Hermit said—   Approacheth the ship with
"And they answered not our cheer!   wonder.
The planks looked warped! and see those sails,
530 How thin they are and sere!
I never saw aught like to them,
Unless perchance it were

Brown skeletons of leaves that lag
My forest-brook along;
535 When the ivy-tod[5] is heavy with snow,
And the owlet whoops to the wolf below,
That eats the she-wolf's young."

"Dear Lord! it hath a fiendish look—
(The Pilot made reply)
540 I am a-feared"—"Push on, push on!"
Said the Hermit cheerily.

The boat came closer to the ship,
But I nor spake nor stirred;
The boat came close beneath the ship,
545 And straight a sound was heard.

Under the water it rumbled on,   The ship suddenly sinketh.
Still louder and more dread:
It reached the ship, it split the bay;
The ship went down like lead.

———————
[5]ivy-bush

550 Stunned by that loud and dreadful sound,
Which sky and ocean smote,
Like one that hath been seven days drowned
My body lay afloat;
But swift as dreams myself I found
555 Within the Pilot's boat.

The ancient Mariner is saved in the Pilot's boat.

Upon the whirl, where sank the ship,
The boat spun round and round;
And all was still, save that the hill
Was telling of the sound.

560 I moved my lips—the Pilot shrieked
And fell down in a fit;
The holy Hermit raised his eyes,
And prayed where he did sit.

I took the oars: the Pilot's boy,
565 Who now doth crazy go,
Laughed loud and long, and all the while
His eyes went to and fro.
"Ha! ha!" quoth he, "full plain I see,
The Devil knows how to row."

570 And now, all in my own countree,
I stood on the firm land!
The Hermit stepped forth from the boat,
And scarcely he could stand.

"O shrieve me, shrieve me, holy man!"
575 The Hermit crossed his brow.
"Say quick," quoth he, "I bid thee say—
What manner of man art thou?"

The ancient Mariner earnestly entreateth the Hermit to shrieve him; and the penance of life falls on him.

Forthwith this frame of mine was wrenched
With a woeful agony,
580 Which forced me to begin my tale;
And then it left me free.

Since then, at an uncertain hour,
That agony returns:
And till my ghastly tale is told,
585 This heart within me burns.

And ever and anon through out his future life an agony constraineth him to travel from land to land;

I pass, like night, from land to land;
I have strange power of speech;
That moment that his face I see,

I know the man that must hear me:
590   To him my tale I teach.

What loud uproar bursts from that door!
The wedding-guests are there:
But in the garden-bower the bride
And bride-maids singing are:
595   And hark the little vesper bell,
Which biddeth me to prayer!

O Wedding-Guest! this soul hath been
Alone on a wide wide sea:
So lonely 'twas that God himself
600   Scarce seemèd there to be.

O sweeter than the marriage-feast,
'Tis sweeter far to me,
To walk together to the kirk
With a goodly company!—

605   To walk together to the kirk,
And all together pray,
While each to his great Father bends,
Old men, and babes, and loving friends
And youths and maidens gay!

610   Farewell, farewell! but this I tell   And to teach, by his own
To thee, thou Wedding-Guest!   example, love and reverence
He prayeth well, who loveth well   to all things that God made
Both man and bird and beast.   and loveth.

He prayeth best, who loveth best
615   All things both great and small;
For the dear God who loveth us,
He made and loveth all.

The Mariner, whose eye is bright,
Whose beard with age is hoar,
620   Is gone: and now the Wedding-Guest
Turned from the bridegroom's door.

He went like one that hath been stunned,
And is of sense forlorn:
A sadder and a wiser man,
625   He rose the morrow morn.

1797

Dejection: An Ode

Written April 4, 1802

Late, late yestreen I saw the new Moon,
With the old Moon in her arms;
And I fear, I fear, my Master dear!
We shall have a deadly storm.

BALLAD OF SIR PATRICK SPENCE

I

Well! If the Bard was weather-wise, who made
    The grand old ballad of Sir Patrick Spence,
    This night, so tranquil now, will not go hence
Unroused by winds, that ply a busier trade
5 Than those which mould yon cloud in lazy flakes,
Or the dull sobbing draft, that moans and rakes
Upon the strings of this Æolian lute,
       Which better far were mute.
    For lo! the New-moon winter-bright!
10   And overspread with phantom light,
     (With swimming phantom light o'erspread
     But rimmed and circled by a silver thread)
I see the old Moon in her lap, foretelling
    The coming-on of rain and squally blast.
15 And oh! that even now the gust were swelling,
    And the slant night-shower driving loud and fast!
Those sounds which oft have raised me, whilst they awed,
       And sent my soul abroad,
Might now perhaps their wonted impulse give,
20 Might startle this dull pain, and make it move and live!

II

A grief without a pang, void, dark, and drear,
    A stifled, drowsy, unimpassioned grief,
    Which finds no natural outlet, no relief,
       In word, or sigh, or tear—
25 O lady! in this wan and heartless mood,
To other thoughts by yonder throstle woo'd,
    All this long eve, so balmy and serene,
Have I been gazing on the western sky,
    And its peculiar tint of yellow green:
30 And still I gaze—and with how blank an eye!
And those thin clouds above, in flakes and bars,
That give away their motion to the stars;

Those stars, that glide behind them or between,
Now sparkling, now bedimmed, but always seen:
35 Yon crescent Moon, as fixed as if it grew
In its own cloudless, starless lake of blue;
I see them all so excellently fair,
I see, not feel, how beautiful they are!

III

My genial spirits fail;
40   And what can these avail
To lift the smothering weight from off my breast?
It were a vain endeavour,
Though I should gaze for ever
On that green light that lingers in the west:
45 I may not hope from outward forms to win
The passion and the life, whose fountains are within.

IV

O Lady! we receive but what we give,
And in our life alone does Nature live:
Ours is her wedding garment, ours her shroud!
50   And would we aught behold, of higher worth,
Than that inanimate cold world allowed
To the poor loveless ever-anxious crowd,
Ah! from the soul itself must issue forth
A light, a glory, a fair luminous cloud
55   Enveloping the Earth—
And from the soul itself must there be sent
A sweet and potent voice, of its own birth,
Of all sweet sounds the life and element!

V

O pure of heart! thou need'st not ask of me
60 What this strong music in the soul may be!
What, and wherein it doth exist,
This light, this glory, this fair luminous mist,
This beautiful and beauty-making power.
Joy, virtuous Lady! Joy that ne'er was given,
65 Save to the pure, and in their purest hour,
Life, and Life's effluence, cloud at once and shower,
Joy, Lady! is the spirit and the power,
Which wedding Nature to us gives in dower
A new Earth and new Heaven,
70 Undreamt of by the sensual and the proud—

Joy is the sweet voice, Joy the luminous cloud—
    We in ourselves rejoice!
And thence flows all that charms or ear or sight,
    All melodies the echoes of that voice,
75 All colours a suffusion from that light.

VI

There was a time when, though my path was rough,
    This joy within me dallied with distress,
And all misfortunes were but as the stuff
    Whence Fancy made me dreams of happiness:
80 For hope grew round me, like the twining vine,
And fruits, and foliage, not my own, seemed mine.
But now afflictions bow me down to earth:
Nor care I that they rob me of my mirth;
    But oh! each visitation
85 Suspends what nature gave me at my birth,
    My shaping spirit of Imagination.
For not to think of what I needs must feel,
    But to be still and patient, all I can;
And haply by abstruse research to steal
90   From my own nature all the natural man—
    This was my sole resource, my only plan:
Till that which suits a part infects the whole,
And now is almost grown the habit of my soul.

VII

Hence, viper thoughts, that coil around my mind,
95   Reality's dark dream!
I turn from you, and listen to the wind,
    Which long has raved unnoticed. What a scream
Of agony by torture lengthened out
That lute sent forth! Thou Wind, that rav'st without,
100   Bare crag, or mountain-tairn, or blasted tree,
Or pine-grove whither woodman never clomb,
Or lonely house, long held the witches' home,
    Methinks were fitter instruments for thee,
Mad Lutanist! who is this month of showers,
105 Of dark-brown gardens, and of peeping flowers,
Mak'st Devils' yule, with worse than wintry song,
The blossoms, buds, and timorous leaves among.
    Thou Actor, perfect in all tragic sounds!
Thou mighty Poet, e'en to frenzy bold!
110   What tell'st thou now about?

'Tis of the rushing of an host in rout,
  With groans, of trampled men, with smarting wounds—
At once they groan with pain, and shudder with the cold!
But hush! there is a pause of deepest silence!
115   And all that noise, as of a rushing crowd,
  With groans, and tremulous shudderings—all is over—
    It tells another tale, with sounds less deep and loud!
      A tale of less affright,
      And tempered with delight,
120   As Otway's self had framed the tender lay,—
        'Tis of a little child
        Upon a lonesome wild,
Not far from home, but she hath lost her way:
And now moans low in bitter grief and fear,
125   And now screams loud, and hopes to make her mother hear.[1]

VIII

'Tis midnight, but small thoughts have I of sleep:
Full seldom may my friend such vigils keep!
Visit her, gentle Sleep! with wings of healing,
  And may this storm be but a mountain-birth,
130   May all the stars hang bright above her dwelling,
    Silent as though they watched the sleeping Earth!
      With light heart may she rise,
      Gay fancy, cheerful eyes,
      Joy lift her spirit, joy attune her voice;
135   To her may all things live, from pole to pole,
Their life the eddying of her living soul!
    O simple spirit, guided from above,
Dear Lady! friend devoutest of my choice,
Thus mayest thou ever, evermore rejoice.

1802

George Gordon, Lord Byron

(1788–1824)

So We'll Go No More A-Roving

So we'll go no more a-roving
  So late into the night,
Though the heart be still as loving,
  And the moon be still as bright.

---

[1]Lines 121–125 tell the story of Wordsworth's *Lucy Gray*.

5 For the sword outwears its sheath,
 And the soul wears out the breast,
And the heart must pause to breathe,
 And Love itself have rest.

Though the night was made for loving,
10 And the day returns too soon,
Yet we'll go no more a-roving
 By the light of the moon.

1817

She Walks in Beauty

She walks in beauty, like the night
 Of cloudless climes and starry skies;
And all that's best of dark and bright
 Meet in her aspect and her eyes:
5 Thus mellowed to that tender light
 Which heaven to gaudy day denies.

One shade the more, one ray the less,
 Had half impaired the nameless grace
Which waves in every raven tress,
10 Or softly lightens o'er her face;
Where thoughts serenely sweet express
 How pure, how dear their dwelling place.

And on that cheek, and o'er that brow,
 So soft, so calm, yet eloquent,
15 The smiles that win, the tints that glow,
 But tell of days in goodness spent,
A mind at peace with all below,
 A heart whose love is innocent!

1814

The Destruction of Sennacherib[1]

The Assyrian came down like the wolf on the fold,
And his cohorts were gleaming in purple and gold;
And the sheen of their spears was like stars on the sea,
When the blue wave rolls nightly on deep Galilee.

5 Like the leaves of the forest when summer is green,
That host with their banners at sunset were seen:
Like the leaves of the forest when autumn hath blown,
That host on the morrow lay wither'd and strown.

---

[1]For an account of the episode see II Kings 18–19 in the Bible.

For the Angel of Death spread his wings on the blast,
10 And breathed in the face of the foe as he pass'd
And the eyes of the sleepers wax'd deadly and chill,
And their hearts but once heaved, and forever grew still!

And there lay the steed with his nostril all wide,
But through it there roll'd not the breath of his pride;
15 And the foam of his gasping lay white on the turf,
And cold as the spray of the rock-beating surf.

And there lay the rider distorted and pale,
With the dew on his brow, and the rust on his mail:
And the tents were all silent, the banners alone,
20 The lances unlifted, the trumpet unblown.

And the widows of Ashur are loud in their wail,
And the idols are broke in the temple of Baal;
And the might of the Gentile, unsmote by the sword,
Hath melted like snow in the glance of the Lord!

1815

Lydia Sigourney

(1791–1865)

The Mother of Washington

On the laying of the Corner-stone of her Monument at Fredericksburg, Virginia

Long hast thou slept unnoted. Nature stole
In her soft ministry around thy bed,
Spreading her vernal tissue, violet-gemmed,
And pearled with dews.
5   She bade bright Summer bring
Gifts of frankincense, with sweet song of birds,
And Autumn cast his reaper's coronet
Down at thy feet, and stormy Winter speak
Sternly of man's neglect.
10   But now we come
To do thee homage—mother of our chief!
Fit homage—such as honoreth him who pays.
    Methinks we see thee—as in olden time—
Simple in garb—majestic and serene,
15 Unmoved by pomp or circumstance—in truth
Inflexible, and with a Spartan zeal
Repressing vice and making folly grave.
Thou didst not deem it woman's part to waste

Life in inglorious sloth—to sport awhile
20 Amid the flowers, or on the summer wave,
Then fleet, like the ephemeron, away,
Building no temple in her children's hearts,
Save to the vanity and pride of life
Which she had worshipped.
25   For the might that clothed
The "Pater Patriæ," for the glorious deeds
That make Mount Vernon's tomb a Mecca shrine
To all the earth, what thanks to thee are due,
Who, 'mid his elements of being, wrought,
30 We know not—Heaven can tell.
                              Rise, sculptured pile!
And show a race unborn who rests below;
And say to mothers what a holy charge
Is theirs—with what a kingly power their love
35 Might rule the fountains of the new-born mind.
Warn them to wake at early dawn—and sow
Good seed before the world hath sown her tares;
Nor in their toil decline—that angel bands
May put the sickle in, and reap for God,
40 And gather to his garner.
                              Ye, who stand,
With thrilling breast, to view her trophied praise,
Who nobly reared Virginia's godlike chief—
Ye, whose last thought upon your nightly couch,
45 Whose first at waking, is your cradled son,
What though no high ambition prompts to rear
A second Washington; or leave your name
Wrought out in marble with a nation's tears
Of deathless gratitude;—yet may you raise
50 A monument above the stars—a soul
Led by your teachings, and your prayers to God.

Death of an Infant

Death found strange beauty on that polished brow,
And dashed it out. There was a tint of rose
On cheek and lip. He touched the veins with ice,
And the rose faded. Forth from those blue eyes
5 There spake a wishful tenderness, a doubt
Whether to grieve or sleep, which innocence
Alone may wear. With ruthless haste he bound
The silken fringes of those curtaining lids
For ever. There had been a murmuring sound

10 With which the babe would claim its mother's ear,
Charming her even to tears. The spoiler set
The seal of silence. But there beamed a smile,
So fixed, so holy, from that cherub brow,
Death gazed, and left it there. He dared not steal
15 The signet ring of Heaven.

Female Education

Addressed to a South American Poet

Thou, of the living lyre,
   Thou, of the lavish clime,
Whose mountains mix their lightning-fire
   With the storm-cloud sublime,
5 We, of thy sister-land,
   The empire of the free,
Joy as those patriot-breasts expand
   With genial Liberty.

Thy flowers their fragrant breast
10   Unfold to catch its ray,
And Nature's velvet-tissued vest
   With brighter tint is gay,
More blest thy rivers roll
   Full tribute to the Sea,
15 And even Woman's cloister'd soul
   Walks forth among the free.

Aid with thy tuneful strain
   Her bold, adventurous way,
Bid the long-prisoned mind attain
20   A sphere of dazzling day,
Bid her unpinion'd foot
   The cliffs of knowledge climb,
And search for Wisdom's sacred root
   That mocks the blight of time.

Percy Bysshe Shelley

(1792–1822)

Ozymandias

I met a traveler from an antique land
Who said: Two vast and trunkless legs of stone
Stand in the desert . . . Near them, on the sand,

Half sunk, a shattered visage lies, whose frown,
5 And wrinkled lip, and sneer of cold command,
Tell that its sculptor well those passions read
Which yet survive, stamped on these lifeless things,
The hand that mocked them, and the heart that fed:
And on the pedestal these words appear:
10 "My name is Ozymandias, king of kings:
Look on my works, ye Mighty, and despair!"
Nothing beside remains. Round the decay
Of that colossal wreck, boundless and bare
The lone and level sands stretch far away.

1818

Ode to the West Wind

1

O wild West Wind, thou breath of Autumn's being,
Thou, from whose unseen presence the leaves dead
Are driven, like ghosts from an enchanter fleeing,

Yellow, and black, and pale, and hectic red,
5 Pestilence-stricken multitudes: O thou,
Who chariotest to their dark wintry bed

The wingèd seeds, where they lie cold and low,
Each like a corpse within its grave, until
Thine azure sister of the Spring shall blow

10 Her clarion o'er the dreaming earth, and fill
(Driving sweet buds like flocks to feed in air)
With living hues and odors plain and hill:

Wild Spirit, which art moving everywhere;
Destroyer and preserver; hear, oh, hear!

2

15 Thou on whose stream, mid the steep sky's commotion,
Loose clouds like earth's decaying leaves are shed,
Shook from the tangled boughs of Heaven and Ocean,

Angels of rain and lightning: there are spread
On the blue surface of thine aery surge,
20 Like the bright hair uplifted from the head

Of some fierce Maenad, even from the dim verge
Of the horizon to the zenith's height,
The locks of the approaching storm. Thou dirge

Of the dying year, to which this closing night
25 Will be the dome of a vast sepulcher,
Vaulted with all thy congregated might

Of vapors, from whose solid atmosphere
Black rain, and fire, and hail will burst: oh, hear!

3

Thou who didst waken from his summer dreams
30 The blue Mediterranean, where he lay,
Lulled by the coil of his crystàlline streams,

Beside a pumice isle in Baiae's bay,
And saw in sleep old palaces and towers
Quivering within the wave's intenser day,

35 All overgrown with azure moss and flowers
So sweet, the sense faints picturing them! Thou
For whose path the Atlantic's level powers

Cleave themselves into chasms, while far below
The sea-blooms and the oozy woods which wear
40 The sapless foliage of the ocean, know

Thy voice, and suddenly grow gray with fear,
And tremble and despoil themselves: oh, hear!

4

If I were a dead leaf thou mightest bear;
If I were a swift cloud to fly with thee;
45 A wave to pant beneath thy power, and share

The impulse of thy strength, only less free
Than thou, O uncontrollable! If even
I were as in my boyhood, and could be

The comrade of thy wanderings over Heaven,
50 As then, when to outstrip thy skiey speed
Scarce seem a vision; I would ne'er have striven

As thus with thee in prayer in my sore need.
Oh, lift me as a wave, a leaf, a cloud!
I fall upon the thorns of life! I bleed!

55 A heavy weight of hours has chained and bowed
One too like thee: tameless, and swift, and proud.

5

Make me thy lyre, even as the forest is:
What if my leaves are falling like its own!
The tumult of thy mighty harmonies

60 Will take from both a deep, autumnal tone,
Sweet though in sadness. Be thou, Spirit fierce,
My spirit! be thou me, impetuous one!

Drive my dead thoughts over the universe
Like withered leaves to quicken a new birth!
65 And, by the incantation of this verse,

Scatter, as from an unextinguished hearth
Ashes and sparks, my words among mankind!
Be through my lips to unawakened earth

The trumpet of a prophecy! O Wind,
70 If Winter comes, can Spring be far behind?

1820

To—

Music, when soft voices die,
Vibrates in the memory—
Odors, when sweet violets sicken,
Live within the sense they quicken.

5 Rose leaves, when the rose is dead,
Are heaped for the belovèd's bed;
And so thy thoughts, when thou art gone,
Love itself shall slumber on.

1824

John Keats

(1795–1821)

On First Looking into Chapman's Homer[1]

Much have I travelled in the realms of gold,
   And many goodly states and kingdoms seen;
   Round many western islands have I been

---
[1] a translation by George Chapman, a contemporary of Shakespeare

Which bards in fealty to Apollo hold.
5   Oft of one wide expanse had I been told
     That deep-browed Homer ruled as his demesne;
     Yet did I never breathe its pure serene
   Till I heard Chapman speak out loud and bold:
   Then felt I like some watcher of the skies
10   When a new planet swims into his ken;
   Or like stout Cortez[2] when with eagle eyes
     He stared at the Pacific—and all his men
   Looked at each other with a wild surmise—
     Silent, upon a peak in Darien.

               1816

When I Have Fears

When I have fears that I may cease to be
   Before my pen has gleaned my teeming brain,
Before high-piled books, in charactery,[1]
   Hold like rich garners the full ripened grain;
5 When I behold, upon the night's starred face,
   Huge cloudy symbols of a high romance,
And think that I may never live to trace
   Their shadows, with the magic hand of chance;
And when I feel, fair creature of an hour,
10   That I shall never look upon thee more,
Never have relish in the faery power
   Of unreflecting love;—then on the shore
Of the wide world I stand alone, and think
Till love and fame to nothingness do sink.

               1818

Ode on a Grecian Urn

1

Thou still unravished bride of quietness,
   Thou foster-child of silence and slow time,
Sylvan historian, who canst thus express
   A flowery tale more sweetly than our rhyme:
5 What leaf-fringed legend haunts about thy shape
   Of deities or mortals, or of both,

---

[2]It was actually Balboa who discovered the Pacific in 1513.

---

[1]characters, writing

In Tempe or the dales of Arcady?[1]
   What men or gods are these? What maidens loath?
What mad pursuit? What struggle to escape?
10   What pipes and timbrels? What wild ecstasy?

2

Heard melodies are sweet, but those unheard
   Are sweeter; therefore, ye soft pipes, play on;
Not to the sensual ear, but, more endeared,
   Pipe to the spirit ditties of no tone:
15 Fair youth, beneath the trees, thou canst not leave
   Thy song, nor ever can those trees be bare;
     Bold Lover, never, never canst thou kiss,
Though winning near the goal—yet, do not grieve;
     She cannot fade, though thou hast not thy bliss,
20   Forever wilt thou love, and she be fair!

3

Ah, happy, happy boughs! that cannot shed
   Your leaves, nor ever bid the Spring adieu;
And, happy melodist, unwearièd,
   Forever piping songs forever new;
25 More happy love! more happy, happy love!
   Forever warm and still to be enjoyed,
     Forever panting, and forever young;
All breathing human passion far above,
   That leaves a heart high-sorrowful and cloyed,
30   A burning forehead, and a parching tongue.

4

Who are these coming to the sacrifice?
   To what green altar, O mysterious priest,
Lead'st thou that heifer lowing at the skies,
   And all her silken flanks with garlands dressed?
35 What little town by river or sea shore,
   Or mountain-built with peaceful citadel,
     Is emptied of this folk, this pious morn?
And, little town, thy streets for evermore
   Will silent be; and not a soul to tell
40   Why thou art desolate, can e'er return.

---

[1]The vale of Tempe and Arcady (Arcadia) in Greece are symbolic of pastoral beauty.

5

O Attic[2] shape! Fair attitude! with brede[3]
   Of marble men and maidens overwrought,
With forest branches and the trodden weed;
   Thou, silent form, dost tease us out of thought
45 As doth eternity: Cold Pastoral!
   When old age shall this generation waste,
      Thou shalt remain, in midst of other woe
   Than ours, a friend to man, to whom thou say'st,
"Beauty is truth, truth beauty,—that is all
50   Ye know on earth, and all ye need to know."

                                      1819

La Belle Dame sans Merci

O, what can ail thee, knight-at-arms,
   Alone and palely loitering?
The sedge has wither'd from the lake,
   And no birds sing.

5 O, what can ail thee, knight-at-arms,
   So haggard and so woe-begone?
The squirrel's granary is full,
   And the harvest's done.

I see a lilly on thy brow,
10   With anguish moist and fever dew,
And on thy cheeks a fading rose
   Fast withereth too.

I met a lady in the meads,
   Full beautiful—a faery's child,
15 Her hair was long, her foot was light,
   And her eyes were wild.

I made a garland for her head,
   And bracelets too, and fragrant zone;
She look'd at me as she did love,
20   And made sweet moan.

I set her on my pacing steed,
   And nothing else saw all day long,

---

[2]Grecian, especially Athenian
[3]embroidery

For sidelong would she bend and sing
    A faery's song.

25 She found me roots of relish sweet,
    And honey wild, and manna dew,
And sure in language strange she said
    "I love thee true."

She took me to her elfin grot,
30   And there she wept and sigh'd full sore,
And there I shut her wild wild eyes
    With kisses four.

And there she lullèd me asleep,
    And there I dream'd—Ah! woe betide!
35 The latest dream I ever dream'd
    On the cold hill side.

I saw pale kings and princes too,
    Pale warriors, death-pale were they all;
They cried, "La Belle Dame sans Merci
40   Hath thee in thrall!"

I saw their starved lips in the gloam,
    With horrid warning gapèd wide,
And I awoke, and found me here,
    On the cold hill's side.

45 And this is why I sojourn here,
    Alone and palely loitering,
Though the sedge is wither'd from the lake,
    And no birds sing.

                                                   1819

To Autumn

I

Season of mists and mellow fruitfulness,
    Close bosom-friend of the maturing sun;
Conspiring with him how to load and bless
    With fruit the vines that round the thatch-eves run;
5 To bend with apples the moss'd cottage-trees,
    And fill all fruit with ripeness to the core;
        To swell the gourd, and plump the hazel shells
    With a sweet kernel; to set budding more,

And still more, later flowers for the bees,
10 Until they think warm days will never cease,
    For Summer has o'er-brimm'd their clammy cells.

II

Who hath not seen thee oft amid thy store?
    Sometimes whoever seeks abroad may find
Thee sitting careless on a granary floor,
15   Thy hair soft-lifted by the winnowing wind;
Or on a half-reap'd furrow sound asleep,
    Drows'd with the fume of poppies, while thy hook
        Spares the next swath and all its twinèd flowers:
And sometimes like a gleaner thou dost keep
20   Steady thy laden head across a brook;
    Or by a cyder-press, with patient look,
        Thou watchest the last oozings hours by hours.

III

Where are the songs of Spring? Ay, where are they?
    Think not of them, thou hast thy music too,—
25 While barrèd clouds bloom the soft-dying day,
    And touch the stubble-plains with rosy hue;
Then in a wailful choir the small gnats mourn
    Among the river sallows, borne aloft
        Or sinking as the light wind lives or dies;
30 And full-grown lambs loud bleat from hilly bourn;
    Hedge-crickets sing; and now with treble soft
    The red-breast whistles from a garden-croft;
        And gathering swallows twitter in the skies.

1819

4

A BRIEF HISTORY

While Victorian England in the nineteenth century enlarged an empire and congratulated itself on its prudence, military power, and industry, the United States began to come of age. The most popular poets in America were those like Longfellow, Emerson, and Bryant who supported the middle class, idealized the American past, and promoted the twin virtues of unending progress and republican certitude. Nonetheless, the Abolitionist movement and the ominous cloud of slavery would find no solution but the eruption of the Civil War.

With twentieth-century hindsight, however, the two greatest poets of the nineteenth century were Whitman and Dickinson. Dickinson labored as a recluse in her family home in Amherst, Massachusetts, barely noticed in her lifetime but recognized posthumously as one of the greatest American poets.

Whitman's *Leaves of Grass,* with its optimism about American democracy and its celebration of the American people and landscape, became in time the great American poem. Whitman's realism and inclusiveness, his poems of the Civil War, and his celebration of the self unfold with a free-verse style that turned its back on the restraints and demands of traditional poetry.

In England, the Victorian era discovered itself represented most optimistically in Browning and Tennyson. Still, a poet like Matthew Arnold in *Dover Beach* began anxiously to sense a decline in traditional virtues and to feel the gathering winds of some great social and cultural change. Optimism for the future, and a respect for tradition and established order, began to be tempered with an uncertainty about the future. Thomas Hardy's and A. E. Housman's pessimistic fatalism colored their poems, which were otherwise studied examples of traditional verse. As in the United States with Whitman and Dickinson, English poets experimented. Hopkins stretched the reach of language, rhythm, and syntax. Robert Browning began to reach psychologically into poetic studies of motive and ambition.

In both countries, women poets began to make reputations and build audiences for themselves. Although at first glance their poetry appears to reflect conventional lives, a closer examination reveals a new perspective. They not only questioned the roles they were assigned by the social order, but also began to speak for themselves, asking their own questions and finding their own answers.

The poems of England and America during the years of the Victorian era and the Industrial Revolution show simultaneous examples of experimentation and tradition. For a time American poetry imitated the traditional verse of England. Although the subject matter and imagery changed on the new-world side of the Atlantic ocean, Emerson's *Concord Hymn* and Longfellow's *The Jewish Cemetery at Newport* sound as English as they do American. In this poetry, experience is formalized, elevated. In England Tennyson recalled the Greece of Homer in his *Ulysses* and *The Lotos-Eaters.* Robert Browning recreated historical characters in the blank verse of his dramatic monologues. Walt Whitman charged into this tradition like a locomotive, a new American voice. Whitman's unrhymed free verse, arranged in parallel structure and energized with American speech patterns and slang, builds up a catalog of images drawn from the technology and democracy of America. Whereas Whitman supported his poetry on the two props of American speech and experience, Emily Dickinson found another poetic voice in New England hymn meters and the New England countryside. She personified death as a coachman, dying as the buzzing of a fly. Her deliberate use of half-rhymes, misunderstood in her day and considered an imperfection, adds to the distinctiveness of her verse and makes her seem especially modern to our ears. In England, Matthew Arnold experimented with rhymed free verse in *Dover Beach.* The rhythms of Matthew Arnold, however, flow with the regularity of scanned metrics, missing the deliberate common roughness often found in Whitman. Hopkins experimented with more complex rhythms, and he looked backward to accentual verse, writing in what he referred to as "sprung rhythm." At the same time that these experiments were going on, A. E. Housman wrote like a classicist, in conventional stanzas. Housman's poems, their diction a mixture of the formal and colloquial, capture the English countryside while alluding to Ancient Greece and classical mythology.

Ralph Waldo Emerson

(1803–1882)

Concord Hymn

Sung at the Completion of the Battle
Monument, July 4, 1837

By the rude bridge that arched the flood,
    Their flag to April's breeze unfurled,
Here once the embattled farmers stood
    And fired the shot heard round the world.

5 The foe long since in silence slept;
    Alike the conqueror silent sleeps;
And Time the ruined bridge has swept
    Down the dark stream which seaward creeps.

On this green bank, by this soft stream,
10   We set to-day a votive stone;
That memory may their deed redeem,
    When, like our sires, our sons are gone.

Spirit, that made those heroes dare
    To die, and leave their children free,
15 Bid Time and Nature gently spare
    That shaft we raise to them and thee.

1837

Days

Daughters of Time, the hypocritic Days,
Muffled and dumb like barefoot dervishes,
And marching single in an endless file,
Bring diadems and fagots in their hands.
5 To each they offer gifts after his will,
Bread, kingdoms, stars, and sky that holds them all.
I, in my pleached garden, watched the pomp,
Forgot my morning wishes, hastily
Took a few herbs and apples, and the Day
10 Turned and departed silent. I, too late,
Under her solemn fillet saw the scorn.

1857

Elizabeth Barrett Browning

(1806–1861)

On a Portrait of Wordsworth by B. R. Haydon[1]

Wordsworth upon Helvellyn![2] Let the cloud
Ebb audibly along the mountain-wind
Then break against the rock, and show behind
The lowland valleys floating up to crowd
5   The sense with beauty. He with forehead bowed
And humble-lidded eyes, as one inclined
Before the sovran thought of his own mind,
And very meek with inspirations proud,
Takes here his rightful place as poet-priest
10 By the high altar, singing prayer and prayer
To the higher Heavens. A nobler vision free
Our Haydon's hand has flung out from the mist:
No portrait this, with Academic air!
This is the poet and his poetry.

Grief

I tell you, hopeless grief is passionless;
That only men incredulous of despair,
Half-taught in anguish, through the midnight air
Beat upward to God's throne in loud access
5   Of shrieking and reproach. Full desertness,
In souls as countries, lieth silent-bare
Under the blanching, vertical eye-glare
Of the absolute Heavens. Deep-hearted man, express
Grief for thy Dead in silence like to death—
10 Most like a monumental statue set
In everlasting watch and moveless woe
Till itself crumble to the dust beneath.
Touch it; the marble eyelids are not wet:
If it could weep, it could arise and go.

Sonnets from the Portuguese

Sonnet 14

If thou must love me, let it be for nought
Except for love's sake only. Do not say,
"I love her for her smile—her look—her way

---

[1]English painter, friend of Wordsworth
[2]a peak in the English Lake Country

Of speaking gently,—for a trick of thought
5 That falls in well with mine, and certes brought
A sense of pleasant ease on such a day"—
For these things in themselves, Belovèd, may
Be changed, or change for thee,—and love, so wrought,
May be unwrought so. Neither love me for
10 Thine own dear pity's wiping my cheeks dry,—
A creature might forget to weep, who bore
Thy comfort long, and lose thy love thereby!
But love me for love's sake, that evermore
Thou may'st love on, through love's eternity.

Sonnet 43

How do I love thee? Let me count the ways.
I love thee to the depth and breadth and height
My soul can reach, when feeling out of sight
For the ends of Being and ideal Grace.
5 I love thee to the level of everyday's
Most quiet need, by sun and candle-light.
I love thee freely, as men strive for Right;
I love thee purely, as they turn from Praise.
I love thee with the passion put to use
10 In my old griefs, and with my childhood's faith.
I love thee with a love I seemed to lose
With my lost saints,—I love thee with the breath,
Smiles, tears, of all my life!—and, if God choose,
I shall but love thee better after death.

1850

Henry Wadsworth Longfellow

(1807–1882)

The Jewish Cemetery at Newport

How strange it seems! These Hebrews in their graves,
    Close by the street of this fair seaport town,
Silent beside the never-silent waves,
    At rest in all this moving up and down!

5 The trees are white with dust, that o'er their sleep
    Wave their broad curtains in the southwind's breath,
While underneath these leafy tents they keep
    The long, mysterious Exodus of Death.

And these sepulchral stones, so old and brown,
10   That pave with level flags their burial-place,
Seem like the tablets of the Law, thrown down
    And broken by Moses at the mountain's base.

The very names recorded here are strange,
    Of foreign accent, and of different climes;
15 Alvares and Rivera interchange
    With Abraham and Jacob of old times.

"Blessed be God! for he created Death!"
    The mourners said, "and Death is rest and peace";
Then added, in the certainty of faith,
20   "And giveth Life and nevermore shall cease."

Closed are the portals of their Synagogue,
    No Psalms of David now the silence break,
No Rabbi reads the ancient Decalogue
    In the grand dialect the Prophets spake.

25 Gone are the living, but the dead remain,
    And not neglected; for a hand unseen,
Scattering its bounty, like a summer rain,
    Still keeps their graves and their remembrance green.

How came they here? What burst of Christian hate,
30   What persecution, merciless and blind,
Drove o'er the sea—that desert desolate—
    These Ishmaels and Hagars of mankind?

They lived in narrow streets and lanes obscure,
    Ghetto and Judenstrass,[1] in mirk and mire;
35 Taught in the school of patience to endure
    The life of anguish and the death of fire.

All their lives long, with the unleavened bread
    And bitter herbs of exile and its fears,
The wasting famine of the heart they fed,
40   And slaked its thirst with marah[2] of their tears.

Anathema maranatha![3] was the cry
    That rang from town to town, from street to street;
At every gate the accursed Mordecai[4]
    Was mocked and jeered, and spurned by Christian feet.

---

[1]German for "Street of Jews"
[2]"bitter" in Hebrew
[3]a curse
[4]See the biblical Old Testament book of Esther.

45 Pride and humiliation hand in hand
 Walked with them through the world wher'er they went;
Trampled and beaten were they as the sand,
 And yet unshaken as the continent.

For in the background figures vague and vast
50 Of patriarchs and of prophets rose sublime,
And all the great traditions of the Past
 They saw reflected in the coming time.

And thus forever with reverted look
 The mystic volume of the world they read,
55 Spelling it backward, like a Hebrew book,
 Till life became a Legend of the Dead.

But ah! what once has been shall be no more!
 The growing earth in travail and in pain
Brings forth its races, but does not restore,
60 And the dead nations never rise again.

            1854

Chaucer

An old man in a lodge within a park;
 The chamber walls depicted all around
 With portraitures of huntsman, hawk, and hound,
 And the hurt deer. He listeneth to the lark,
5 Whose song comes with the sunshine through the dark
 Of painted glass in leaden lattice bound;
 He listeneth and he laugheth at the sound,
 Then writeth in a book like any clerk.
He is the poet of the dawn, who wrote
10 The Canterbury Tales, and his old age
 Made beautiful with song; and as I read
I hear the crowing cock, I hear the note
 Of lark and linnet, and from every page
 Rise odors of ploughed field or flowery mead.

            1873

The Cross of Snow

In the long, sleepless watches of the night
 A gentle face—the face of one long dead—[1]
 Looks at me from the wall, where round its head
 The night-lamp casts a halo of pale light.
5 Here in this room she died; and soul more white

---

[1]Frances Appleton, Longfellow's second wife, died of burns in 1861.

Never through martyrdom of fire was led
To its repose; nor can in books be read
The legend of a life more benedight.[2]
There is a mountain in the distant West
10   That, sun-defying, in its deep ravines
Displays a cross of snow upon its side.
Such is the cross I wear upon my breast
These eighteen years, through all the changing scenes
And seasons, changeless since the day she died.

1886

Edgar Allan Poe

(1809–1849)

To Helen

Helen, thy beauty is to me
Like those Nicèan barks of yore,
That gently, o'er a perfumed sea,
The weary, way-worn wanderer bore
5   To his own native shore.

On desperate seas long wont to roam,
Thy hyacinth hair, thy classic face,
Thy Naiad airs have brought me home
To the glory that was Greece,
10 And the grandeur that was Rome.

Lo! in yon brilliant window-niche
How statue-like I see thee stand,
The agate lamp within thy hand!
Ah, Psyche, from the regions which
15   Are Holy Land!

1831

The Raven

Once upon a midnight dreary, while I pondered, weak and weary,
Over many a quaint and curious volume of forgotten lore—
While I nodded, nearly napping, suddenly there came a tapping,
As of some one gently rapping, rapping at my chamber door.
5   "'Tis some visiter," I muttered, "tapping at my chamber door—
                    Only this and nothing more."

---

[2]blessed

Ah, distinctly I remember it was in the bleak December;
And each separate dying ember wrought its ghost upon the floor.
Eagerly I wished the morrow;—vainly I had sought to borrow
10   From my books surcease of sorrow—sorrow for the lost Lenore—
For the rare and radiant maiden whom the angels name Lenore—
            Nameless *here* for evermore.

And the silken, sad, uncertain rustling of each purple curtain
Thrilled me—filled me with fantastic terrors never felt before;
15   So that now, to still the beating of my heart, I stood repeating
" 'Tis some visiter entreating entrance at my chamber door—
Some late visiter entreating entrance at my chamber door;—
            That it is and nothing more."

Presently my soul grew stronger; hesitating then no longer,
20   "Sir," said I, "or Madam, truly your forgiveness I implore;
But the fact is I was napping, and so gently you came rapping,
And so faintly you came tapping, tapping at my chamber door,
That I scarce was sure I heard you"—here I opened wide the door:—
            Darkness there and nothing more.

25   Deep into that darkness peering, long I stood there wondering, fearing,
Doubting, dreaming dreams no mortal ever dared to dream before;
But the silence was unbroken, and the stillness gave no token,
And the only word there spoken was the whispered word, "Lenore?"
            Merely this and nothing more.

30   Back into the chamber turning, all my soul within me burning,
Soon again I heard a tapping somewhat louder than before.
"Surely," said I, "surely that is something at my window lattice;
Let me see, then, what thereat is, and this mystery explore—
Let my heart be still a moment and this mystery explore;—
35   'Tis the wind and nothing more!"

Open here I flung the shutter, when, with many a flirt and flutter
In there stepped a stately Raven of the saintly days of yore;
Not the least obeisance made he; not a minute stopped or stayed he;
But, when mien of lord or lady, perched above my chamber door—
40   Perched upon a bust of Pallas[1] just above my chamber door—
            Perched, and sat, and nothing more.

Then this ebony bird beguiling my sad fancy into smiling,
By the grave and stern decorum of the countenance it wore,
"Though thy crest be short and shaven, thou," I said, "art sure no craven,
45   Ghastly grim and ancient Raven wandering from the Nightly shore—

---

[1]Pallas Athena was the Greek goddess of wisdom and the arts.

Tell me what thy lordly name is on the Night's Plutonian[2] shore!
                    Quoth the Raven "Nevermore."

Much I marvelled this ungainly fowl to hear discourse so plainly,
Though its answer little meaning—little relevancy bore;
50 For we cannot help agreeing that no living human being
Ever yet blessed with seeing bird above this chamber door—
Bird or beast upon the sculptured bust above his chamber door,
                    With such name as "Nevermore."

But the Raven, sitting lonely on the placid bust, spoke only
55 That one word, as if his soul in that one word he did outpour.
Nothing farther then he uttered—not a feather then he fluttered—
Till I scarcely more than muttered "Other friends have flown before—
On the morrow *he* will leave me, as my Hopes have flown before."
                    Then the bird said "Nevermore."

60 Startled at the stillness broken by reply so aptly spoken,
"Doubtless," said I, "what it utters is its only stock and store
Caught from some unhappy master whom unmerciful Disaster
Followed fast and followed faster till his songs one burden bore—
Till the dirges of his Hope that melancholy burden bore
65   Of 'Never-nevermore.'"

But the Raven still beguiling all my fancy into smiling,
Straight I wheeled a cushioned seat in front of bird, and bust and door;
Then, upon the velvet sinking, I betook myself to linking
Fancy unto fancy, thinking what this ominous bird of yore—
70 What this grim, ungainly, ghastly, gaunt, and ominous bird of yore
                    Meant in croaking "Nevermore."

This I sat engaged in guessing, but no syllable expressing
To the fowl whose fiery eyes now burned into my bosom's core;
This and more I sat divining, with my head at ease reclining
75 On the cushion's velvet lining that the lamp light gloated o'er,
But whose velvet-violet lining with the lamp-light gloating o'er,
                    She shall press, ah, nevermore!

Then, methought, the air grew denser, perfumed from an unseen censer
Swung by Seraphim[3] whose foot-falls tinkled on the tufted floor.
80 "Wretch," I cried, "thy God hath lent thee—by these angels he hath sent thee
Respite—respite and nepenthe[4] from thy memories of Lenore;
Quaff, of quaff this kind nepenthe and forget this lost Lenore!"
                    Quoth the Raven "Nevermore."

---

[2]Infernal; the Greek god Pluto ruled the underworld.
[3]angels of the highest of the nine orders
[4]a drug that induces forgetfulness and oblivion when drunk

"Prophet!" said I, "thing of evil!—prophet still, if bird or devil!—
85 Whether Tempter sent, or whether tempest tossed thee here ashore,
Desolate yet all undaunted, on this desert land enchanted—
On this home by Horror haunted—tell me truly, I implore—
Is there—*is* there balm in Gilead?[5]—tell me—tell me, I implore!"
                    Quoth the Raven "Nevermore."

90 "Prophet!" said I, "thing of evil!—prophet still, if bird or devil!
By that Heaven that bends above us—by that God we both adore!—
Tell this soul with sorrow laden if, within the distant Aidenn,[6]
It shall clasp a sainted maiden whom the angels name Lenore—
Clasp a rare and radiant maiden whom the angels name Lonore."
95   Quoth the Raven "Nevermore."

"Be that word our sign of parting, bird or fiend!" I shrieked, upstarting—
"Get thee back into the tempest and the Night's Plutonian shore!
Leave no black plume as a token of that lie thy soul hath spoken!
Leave my loneliness unbroken!—quit the bust above my door!
100 Take thy beak from out my heart, and take thy form from off my door!"
                    Quoth the Raven "Nevermore."

And the Raven, never flitting, still is sitting, *still* is sitting
On the pallid bust of Pallas just above my chamber door;
And his eyes have all the seeming of a demon's that is dreaming,
105 And the lamp-light o'er him streaming throws his shadow on the floor;
And my soul from out that shadow that lies floating on the floor
                    Shall be lifted—nevermore!

                                            1845

Annabel Lee

It was many and many a year ago,
            In a kingdom by the sea,
That a maiden there lived whom you may know
            By the name of Annabel Lee;—
5 And this maiden she lived with no other thought
            Than to love and be loved by me.

She was a child and *I* was a child,
            In this kingdom by the sea,
But we loved with a love that was more than love—
10   I and my Annabel Lee—
With a love that the wingèd seraphs of Heaven
            Coveted her and me.

---

[5]resin from evergreen trees in Palestine, used to heal wounds and ease pain
[6]Eden

And this was the reason that, long ago,
        In this kingdom by the sea,
15 A wind blew out of a cloud by night
        Chilling my Annabel Lee;
So that her highborn kinsmen came
        And bore her away from me,
To shut her up in a sepulchre
20   In this kingdom by the sea.

The angels, not half so happy in Heaven,
        Went envying her and me—
Yes!—that was the reason (as all men know,
        In this kingdom by the sea)
25 That the wind came out of the cloud chilling
        And killing my Annabel Lee.

But our love it was stronger by far than the love
    Of those who were older than we—
    Of many far wiser than we—
30 And neither the angels in Heaven above,
    Nor the demons down under the sea,
Can ever dissever my soul from the soul
    Of the beautiful Annabel Lee:—

For the moon never beams without bringing me dreams
35   Of the beautiful Annabel Lee;
And the stars never rise but I see the bright eyes
    Of the beautiful Annabel Lee;
And so, all the night-tide, I lie down by the side
Of my darling, my darling, my life and my bride,
40   In her sepulchre there by the sea—
    In her tomb by the side of the sea.

                                        1849

Alfred, Lord Tennyson

(1809–1892)

Song

                1

A spirit haunts the year's last hours
Dwelling amid these yellowing bowers.
        To himself he talks;
For at eventide, listening earnestly,

5 At his work you may hear him sob and sigh
      In the walks;
   Earthward he boweth the heavy stalks
Of the moldering flowers.
      Heavily hangs the broad sunflower
10   Over its grave i' the earth so chilly;
      Heavily hangs the hollyhock,
        Heavily hangs the tiger-lily.

2

The air is damp, and hushed, and close,
As a sick man's room when he taketh repose
15   An hour before death;
My very heart faints and my whole soul grieves
At the moist rich smell of the rotting leaves,
      And the breath
Of the fading edges of box[1] beneath,
20 And the year's last rose.
      Heavily hangs the broad sunflower
        Over its grave i' the earth so chilly;
      Heavily hangs the hollyhock,
        Heavily hangs the tiger-lily.

1830

Ulysses

It little profits that an idle king,
By this still hearth, among these barren crags,
Matched with an aged wife, I mete and dole
Unequal laws unto a savage race,
5 That hoard, and sleep, and feed, and know not me.
I cannot rest from travel; I will drink
Life to the lees. All times I have enjoyed
Greatly, have suffered greatly, both with those
That loved me, and alone; on shore, and when
10 Through scudding drifts the rainy Hyades[1]
Vexed the dim sea: I am become a name;
For always roaming with a hungry heart
Much have I seen and known—cities of men
And manners, climates, councils, governments,
15 Myself not least, but honored of them all;
And drunk delight of battle with my peers,

---

[1]boxwood

---

[1]a group of stars in the constellation Taurus, whose rise with the sun heralded the spring rains

Far on the ringing plains of windy Troy.
I am a part of all that I have met;
Yet all experience is an arch wherethrough
20 Gleams that untraveled world whose margin fades
For ever and for ever when I move.
How dull it is to pause, to make an end,
To rust unburnished, not to shine in use!
As though to breathe were life! Life piled on life
25 Were all too little, and of one to me
Little remains; but every hour is saved
From that eternal silence, something more,
A bringer of new things; and vile it were
For some three suns to store and hoard myself,
30 And this gray spirit yearning in desire
To follow knowledge like a sinking star,
Beyond the utmost bound of human thought.

     This is my son, mine own Telemachus,
To whom I leave the scepter and the isle—
35 Well-loved of me, discerning to fulfil
This labor, by slow prudence to make mild
A rugged people, and through soft degrees
Subdue them to the useful and the good.
Most blameless is he, centered in the sphere
40 Of common duties, decent not to fail
In offices of tenderness, and pay
Meet adoration to my household gods,
When I am gone. He works his work, I mine.

     There lies the port; the vessel puffs her sail;
45 There gloom the dark, broad seas. My mariners,
Souls that have toiled, and wrought, and thought with me—
That ever with a frolic welcome took
The thunder and the sunshine, and opposed
Free hearts, free foreheads—you and I are old;
50 Old age hath yet his honor and his toil.
Death closes all; but something ere the end,
Some work of noble note, may yet be done,
Not unbecoming men that strove with Gods.
The lights begin to twinkle from the rocks:
55 The long day wanes: the slow moon climbs: the deep
Moans round with many voices. Come, my friends,
'Tis not too late to seek a newer world.
Push off, and sitting well in order smite
The sounding furrows; for my purpose holds
60 To sail beyond the sunset, and the baths

Of all the western stars, until I die.
It may be that the gulfs will wash us down;
It may be we shall touch the Happy Isles,
And see the great Achilles, whom we knew.
65 Though much is taken, much abides; and though
We are not now that strength which in old days
Moved earth and heaven, that which we are, we are;
One equal temper of heroic hearts,
Made weak by time and fate, but strong in will
70 To strive, to seek, to find, and not to yield.

1833

From **The Lotos-Eaters**

Choric Song

1

There is sweet music here that softer falls
Than petals from blown roses on the grass,
Or night-dews on still waters between walls
Of shadowy granite, in a gleaming pass;
5 Music that gentlier on the spirit lies,
Than tired eyelids upon tired eyes;
Music that brings sweet sleep down from the blissful skies.
Here are cool mosses deep,
And through the moss the ivies creep,
10 And in the stream the long-leaved flowers weep,
And from the craggy ledge the poppy hangs in sleep.

2

Why are we weighed upon with heaviness,
And utterly consumed with sharp distress,
While all things else have rest from weariness?
15 All things have rest: why should we toil alone,
We only toil, who are the first things,
And make perpetual moan,
Still from one sorrow to another thrown;
Nor ever fold our wings,
20 And cease from wanderings,
Nor steep our brows in slumber's holy balm;
Nor harken what the inner spirit sings,
"There is no joy but calm!"
Why should we only toil, the roof and crown of things?

1832

Break, Break, Break

Break, break, break,
   On thy cold gray stones, O Sea!
And I would that my tongue could utter
   The thoughts that arise in me.

5 O well for the fisherman's boy,
   That he shouts with his sister at play!
O well for the sailor lad,
   That he sings in his boat on the bay!

And the stately ships go on
10   To their haven under the hill;
But O for the touch of a vanished hand,
   And the sound of a voice that is still!

Break, break, break
   At the foot of thy crags, O Sea!
15 But the tender grace of a day that is dead
   Will never come back to me.

1834

The Splendor Falls on Castle Walls

The splendor falls on castle walls
   And snowy summits old in story:
The long light shakes across the lakes,
   And the wild cataract leaps in glory.
5 Blow, bugle, blow, set the wild echoes flying.
Blow, bugle; answer, echoes, dying, dying, dying.

O hark, O hear! how thin and clear,
   And thinner, clearer, farther going!
O sweet and far from cliff and scar
10   The horns of Elfland faintly blowing!
Blow, let us hear the purple glens replying:
Blow, bugle; answer, echoes, dying, dying, dying.

O love, they die in yon rich sky,
   They faint on hill or field or river;
15   Our echoes roll from soul to soul,
   And grow for ever and for ever.
Blow, bugle, blow, set the wild echoes flying,
And answer, echoes, answer, dying, dying, dying.

1850

From **In Memoriam A. H. H.**

OBIIT, MDCCCXXXIII

1

I held it truth, with him who sings
    To one clear harp in divers tones,
    That men may rise on stepping-stones
Of their dead selves to higher things.

5 But who shall so forecast the years
    And find in loss a gain to match?
    Or reach a hand through time to catch
The far-off interest of tears?

Let Love clasp Grief lest both be drowned,
10   Let darkness keep her raven gloss.
    Ah, sweeter to be drunk with loss,
To dance with Death, to beat the ground,

Than that the victor Hours should scorn
    The long result of love, and boast,
15   "Behold the man that loved and lost,
But all he was is overworn,"

7

Dark house, by which once more I stand
    Here in the long unlovely street,
    Doors, where my heart was used to beat
20 So quickly, waiting for a hand,

A hand that can be clasped no more—
    Behold me, for I cannot sleep,
    And like a guilty thing I creep
At earliest morning to the door.

25 He is not here; but far away
    The noise of life begins again,
    And ghastly through the drizzling rain
On the bald street breaks the blank day.

11

Calm is the morn without a sound,
30   Calm as to suit a calmer grief,
    And only through the faded leaf
The chestnut pattering to the ground;

Calm and deep peace on this high wold,[1]
   And on these dews that drench and furze,
35   And all the silvery gossamers
That twinkle into green and gold;

Calm and still light on yon great plain
   That sweeps with all its autumn bowers,
   And crowded farms and lessening towers,
40 To mingle with the bounding main;

Calm and deep peace in this wide air,
   These leaves that redden to the fall,
   And in my heart, if calm at all,
If any calm, a calm despair;

45 Calm on the seas, and silver sleep,
   And waves that sway themselves in rest,
   And dead calm in the noble breast
Which heaves but with the heaving deep.

50

Be near me when my light is low,
50   When the blood creeps, and the nerves prick
   And tingle; and the heart is sick,
And all the wheels of being slow.

Be near me when the sensuous frame
   Is racked with pangs that conquer trust;
55   And Time, a maniac scattering dust,
And Life, a Fury slinging flame.

Be near me when my faith is dry,
   And men the flies of latter spring,
   That lay their eggs, and sting and sing
60 And weave their petty cells and die.

Be near me when I fade away,
   To point the term of human strife,
   And on the low dark verge of life
The twilight of eternal day.

130

65 Thy voice is on the rolling air;
   I hear thee where the waters run;
   Thou standest in the rising sun,
And in the setting thou art fair.

___
[1]upland plain

What are thou then? I cannot guess;
70   But though I seem in star and flower
    To feel thee some diffusive power,
I do not therefore love thee less.

My love involves the love before;
    My love is vaster passion now;
75   Though mixed with God and Nature thou,
I seem to love thee more and more.

Far off thou art, but ever nigh;
    I have thee still, and I rejoice;
    I prosper, circled with thy voice;
80 I shall not lose thee though I die.

                                      1850

The Eagle

Fragment

He clasps the crag with crooked hands;
Close to the sun in lonely lands,
Ringed with the azure world, he stands.

The wrinkled sea beneath him crawls;
5 He watches from his mountain walls,
And like a thunderbolt he falls.

                                      1851

Crossing the Bar

Sunset and evening star,
    And one clear call for me!
And may there be no moaning of the bar,
    When I put out to sea,

5 But such a tide as moving seems asleep,
    Too full for sound and foam,
When that which drew from out the boundless deep
    Turns again home.

Twilight and evening bell,
10   And after that the dark!
And may there be no sadness of farewell,
    When I embark;

For though from out our bourne of Time and Place
    The flood may bear me far,

15 I hope to see my Pilot face to face
    When I have crossed the bar.

1889

The Lady of Shalott

PART I

On either side the river lie
Long fields of barley and of rye,
That clothe the wold and meet the sky;
And thro' the field the road runs by
5   To many-tower'd Camelot;
And up and down the people go,
Gazing where the lilies blow
Round an island there below,
    The island of Shalott.

10 Willows whiten, aspens quiver,
Little breezes dusk and shiver
Thro' the wave that runs for ever
By the island in the river
    Flowing down to Camelot.
15 Four gray walls, and four gray towers,
Overlook a space of flowers,
And the silent isle imbowers
    The Lady of Shalott.

By the margin, willow-veil'd,
20 Slide the heavy barges trail'd
By slow horses; and unhail'd
The shallop flitteth silken-sail'd
    Skimming down to Camelot:
But who hath seen her wave her hand?
25 Or at the casement seen her stand?
Or is she known in all the land,
    The Lady of Shalott?

Only reapers, reaping early
In among the bearded barley,
30 Hear a song that echoes cheerly
From the river winding clearly,
    Down to tower'd Camelot:
And by the moon the reaper weary,
Piling sheaves in uplands airy,
35 Listening, whispers "Tis the fairy
    Lady of Shalott."

PART II

There she weaves by night and day
A magic web with colours gay.
She has heard a whisper say,
40 A curse is on her if she stay
        To look down to Camelot.
She knows not what the curse may be,
And so she weaveth steadily,
And little other care hath she,
45   The Lady of Shalott.

And moving thro' a mirror clear
That hangs before her all the year,
Shadows of the world appear.
There she sees the highway near
50   Winding down to Camelot:
There the river eddy whirls,
And there the surly village-churls,
And the red cloaks of market girls,
        Pass onward from Shalott.

55 Sometimes a troop of damsels glad,
An abbot on an ambling pad,
Sometimes a curly shepherd-lad,
Or long-hair'd page in crimson clad,
        Goes by to tower'd Camelot;
60 And sometimes thro' the mirror blue
The knights come riding two and two:
She hath no loyal knight and true,
        The Lady of Shalott.

But in her web she still delights
65 To weave the mirror's magic sights,
For often thro' the silent nights
A funeral, with plumes and lights
        And music, went to Camelot:
Or when the moon was overhead,
70 Came two young lovers lately wed;
"I am half sick of shadows," said
        The Lady of Shalott.

PART III

A bow-shot from her bower-eaves,
He rode between the barley-sheaves,
75 The sun came dazzling thro' the leaves,

And flamed upon the brazen greaves
      Of bold Sir Lancelot.
A red-cross knight for ever kneel'd
To a lady in his shield,
80 That sparkled on the yellow field,
      Beside remote Shalott.

The gemmy bridle glitter'd free,
Like to some branch of stars we see
Hung in the golden Galaxy.
85 The bridle bells rang merrily
      As he rode down to Camelot:
And from his blazon'd baldric slung
A mighty silver bugle hung,
And as he rode his armour rung,
90   Beside remote Shalott.

All in the blue unclouded weather
Thick-jewell'd shone the saddle-leather,
The helmet and the helmet-feather
Burn'd like one burning flame together,
95   As he rode down to Camelot.
As often thro' the purple night,
Below the starry clusters bright,
Some bearded meteor, trailing light,
      Moves over still Shalott.

100 His broad clear brow in sunlight glow'd;
On burnish'd hooves his war-horse trode;
From underneath his helmet flow'd
His coal-black curls as on he rode,
      As he rode down to Camelot.
105 From the bank and from the river
he flash'd into the crystal mirror,
"Tirra lirra," by the river
      Sang Sir Lancelot.

She left the web, she left the loom,
110 She made three paces thro' the room,
She saw the water-lily bloom,
She saw the helmet and the plume,
      She look'd down to Camelot.
Out flew the web and floated wide;
115 The mirror crack'd from side to side;
"The curse is come upon me," cried
      The Lady of Shalott.

PART IV

In the stormy east-wind straining,
The pale yellow woods were waning,
120 The broad stream in his banks complaining,
Heavily the low sky raining
      Over tower'd Camelot;
Down she came and found a boat
Beneath a willow left afloat,
125 And round about the prow she wrote
      The Lady of Shalott.

And down the river's dim expanse
Like some bold seër in a trance,
Seeing all his own mischance —
130 With a glassy countenance
      Did she look to Camelot.
And at the closing of the day
She loosed the chain, and down she lay;
The broad stream bore her far away,
135   The Lady of Shalott.

Lying, robed in snowy white
That loosely flew to left and right —
The leaves upon her falling light —
Thro' the noises of the night
140   She floated down to Camelot:
And as the boat-head wound along
The willowy hills and fields among,
They heard her singing her last song,
      The Lady of Shalott.

145 Heard a carol, mournful, holy,
Chanted loudly, chanted lowly,
Till her blood was frozen slowly,
And her eyes were darken'd wholly,
      Turn'd to tower'd Camelot.
150 For ere she reach'd upon the tide
The first house by the water-side,
Singing in her song she died,
      The Lady of Shalott.

Under tower and balcony,
155 By garden-wall and gallery,
A gleaming shape she floated by,
Dead-pale between the houses high,
      Silent into Camelot.

Out upon the wharfs they came,
160 Knight and burgher, lord and dame,
And round the prow they read her name,
　　　The Lady of Shalott.

Who is this? and what is here?
And in the lighted palace near
165 Died the sound of royal cheer;
And they cross'd themselves for fear,
　　　All the knights at Camelot:
But Lancelot mused a little space;
He said, "She has a lovely face;
170 God in his mercy lend her grace,
　　　The Lady of Shalott."

　　　　　　　　　　　　　　　　　1832

Robert Browning

(1812–1889)

My Last Duchess

Ferrara

That's my last duchess painted on the wall,
Looking as if she were alive. I call
That piece a wonder, now: Frà Pandolf's[1] hands
Worked busily a day, and there she stands.
5 Will't please you sit and look at her? I said
"Frà Pandolf" by design, for never read
Strangers like you that pictured countenance,
The depth and passion of its earnest glance,
But to myself they turned (since none puts by
10 The curtain I have drawn for you, but I)
And seemed as they would ask me, if they durst,
How such a glance came there; so, not the first
Are you to turn and ask thus. Sir, 'twas not
Her husband's presence only, called the spot
15 Of joy into the Duchess' cheek: perhaps
Frà Pandolf chanced to say "Her mantle laps
"Over my lady's wrist too much," or "Paint
"Must never hope to reproduce the faint
"Half-flush that dies along her throat": such stuff
20 Was courtesy, she thought, and cause enough

---

[1]a fictitious artist, as is Claus of Innsbruck in the last line

For calling up that spot of joy. She had
A heart—how shall I say?—too soon made glad,
Too easily impressed; she liked whate'er
She looked on, and her looks went everywhere.
25 Sir, 'twas all one! My favor at her breast,
The dropping of the daylight in the West,
The bough of cherries some officious fool
Brook in the orchard for her, the white mule
She rode with round the terrace—all and each
30 Would draw from her alike the approving speech,
Or blush, at least. She thanked men—good! but thanked
Somehow—I know not how—as if she ranked
My gift of a nine-hundred-years-old name
With anybody's gift. Who'd stoop to blame
35 This sort of trifling? Even had you skill
In speech—which I have not—to make your will
Quite clear to such an one, and say, "Just this
"Or that in you disgusts me; here you miss,
"Or there exceed the mark"—and if she let
40 Herself be lessoned so, nor plainly set
Her wits to yours, forsooth, and made excuse,
—E'en then would be some stooping; and I choose
Never to stoop. Oh sir, she smiled, no doubt,
Whene'er I passed her; but who passed without
45 Much the same smile? This grew; I gave commands;
Then all smiles stopped together. There she stands
As if alive. Will 't please you rise? We'll meet
The company below, then. I repeat,
The Count your master's known munificence
50 Is ample warrant that no just pretense
Of mine for dowry will be disallowed;
Though his fair daughter's self, as I avowed
At starting, is my object. Nay, we'll go
Together down, sir. Notice Neptune, though,
55 Taming a sea-horse, thought a rarity,
Which Claus of Innsbruck cast in bronze for me!

1842

Home-Thoughts, from Abroad

1

Oh, to be in England
Now that April's there,
And whoever wakes in England

Sees, some morning, unaware,
5   That the lowest boughs and the brushwood sheaf
Round the elm-tree bole are in tiny leaf,
While the chaffinch sings on the orchard bough
In England—now!

2

And after April, when May follows,
10   And the whitethroat builds, and all the swallows!
Hark, where my blossomed pear-tree in the hedge
Leans to the field and scatters on the clover
Blossoms and dewdrops—at the bent spray's edge—
That's the wise thrush; he sings each song twice over,
15   Lest you should think he never could recapture
The first fine careless rapture!
And though the fields look rough with hoary dew,
All will be gay when noontide wakes anew
The buttercups, the little children's dower
20   —Far brighter than this gaudy melon-flower!

1845

Meeting at Night

1

The gray sea and the long black land;
And the yellow half-moon large and low;
And the startled little waves that leap
In fiery ringlets from their sleep,
5   As I gain the cove with pushing prow,
And quench its speed i' the slushy sand.

2

Then a mile of warm sea-scented beach;
Three fields to cross till a farm appears;
A tap at the pane, the quick sharp scratch
10   And blue spurt of a lighted match,
And a voice less loud, through its joys and fears,
Than the two hearts beating each to each!

1845

Parting at Morning

Round the cape of a sudden came the sea,
And the sun looked over the mountain's rim:

And straight was a path of gold for him,
And the need of a world of men for me.

1845

Walt Whitman

(1819–1892)

Song of Myself[1]

I celebrate myself,
And what I assume you shall assume,
For every atom belonging to me as good belongs to you.

I loafe and invite my soul,
5   I lean and loafe at my ease . . . . observing a spear of summer grass.

Houses and rooms are full of perfumes . . . . the shelves are crowded with
     perfumes,
I breathe the fragrance myself, and know it and like it,
The distillation would intoxicate me also, but I shall not let it.

The atmosphere is not a perfume . . . . it has no taste of the distillation . . . . it is
     odorless,
10   It is for my mouth forever . . . . I am in love with it,
I will go to the bank by the wood and become undisguised and naked,
I am mad for it to be in contact with me.

The smoke of my own breath,
Echoes, ripples, and buzzed whispers . . . . loveroot, silkthread, crotch and vine,
15   My respiration and inspiration . . . . the beating of my heart . . . .the passing of
     blood and air through my lungs,
The sniff of green leaves and dry leaves, and of the shore and darkcolored
     sea-rocks, and of hay in the barn,
The sound of the belched words of my voice . . . . words loosed to the eddies of
     the wind,

A few light kisses . . . . a few embraces . . . . a reaching around of arms,
The play of shine and shade on the trees as the supple boughs wag,
20   The delight alone or in the rush of the streets, or along the fields and hillsides,

---

[1]"Song of Myself" was the first of the twelve untitled poems that followed the Preface in the first edition of *Leaves of Grass* (1855). In the 1856 *Leaves* it was titled "Poem of Walt Whitman, An American." It was not until the final edition of *Leaves of Grass* in 1881 that the poem was titled "Song of Myself." We have used the 1855 version of "Song of Myself" because in later editions of the poem, Whitman toned down some of the more radical stylistic, linguistic, and thematic features of the original edition of *Leaves of Grass*.

The feeling of health . . . . the full-noon trill . . . . the song of me rising from bed
  and meeting the sun.

Have you reckoned a thousand acres much? Have you reckoned the earth
  much?
Have you practiced so long to learn to read?
Have you felt so proud to get at the meaning of poems?

25 Stop this day and night with me and you shall possess the origin of all poems,
  You shall possess the good of the earth and sun . . . . there are millions of suns
    left,
  You shall no longer take things at second or third hand . . . . nor look through
    the eyes of the dead . . . nor feed on the spectres in books,
  You shall not look through my eyes either, nor take things from me,
  You shall listen to all sides and filter them from yourself.

30 I have heard what the talkers were talking . . . . the talk of the beginning and the
    end,
  But I do not talk of the beginning or the end.

There was never any more inception than there is now,
Nor any more youth or age than there is now;
And will never be any more perfection than there is now,
35 Nor any more heaven or hell than there is now.

Urge and urge and urge,
Always the procreant urge of the world.

Out of the dimness opposite equals advance . . . . Always substance and
  increase,
Always a knit of identity . . . . always distinction . . . . always a breed of life.
40 To elaborate is no avail . . . . Learned and unlearned feel that it is so.

Sure as the most certain sure . . . . plumb in the uprights, well entretied, braced
  in the beams,
Stout as a horse, affectionate, haughty, electrical,
I and this mystery here we stand.

Clear and sweet is my soul . . . . and clear and sweet is all that is not my soul.

45 Lack one lacks both . . . . and the unseen is proved by the seen,
Till that becomes unseen and receives proof in its turn.

Showing the best and dividing it from the worst, age vexes age,
Knowing the perfect fitness and equanimity of things, while they discuss I am
  silent, and go bathe and admire myself.

Welcome is every organ and attribute of me, and of any man hearty and clean,
50 Not an inch nor a particle of an inch is vile, and none shall be less familiar than
  the rest.

I am satisfied . . . . I see, dance, laugh, sing;
As God comes a loving bedfellow and sleeps at my side all night and close on
    the peep of the day,
And leaves for me baskets covered with white towels bulging the house with
    their plenty,
Shall I postpone my acceptation and realization and scream at my eyes,
55 That they turn from gazing after and down the road,
And forthwith cipher and show me to a cent,
Exactly the contents of one, and exactly the contents of two, and which is
    ahead?

Trippers and askers surround me,
People I meet . . . . the effect upon me of my early life . . . . of the ward and city I
    live in . . . of the nation,
60 The latest news . . . . discoveries, inventions, societies . . . . authors old and new,
My dinner, dress, associates, looks, business, compliments, dues,
The real or fancied indifference of some man or woman I love,
The sickness of one of my folks—or of myself . . . . or illdoing . . . . or loss or
    lack of money . . . . or depressions or exaltations,
They come to me days and nights and go from me again,
65 But they are not the Me myself.

Apart from the pulling and hauling stands what I am,
Stands amused, complacent, compassionating, idle, unitary,
Looks down, is erect, bends an arm on an impalpable certain rest,
Looks with its sidecurved head curious what will come next,
70 Both in and out of the game, and watching and wondering at it.

Backward I see in my own days where I sweated through fog with linguists and
    contenders,
I have no mockings or arguments . . . . I witness and wait.

I believe in you my soul . . . . the other I am must not abase itself to you,
And you must not be abased to the other.

75 Loafe with me on the grass . . . . loose the stop from your throat,
Not words, not music or rhyme I want . . . . not custom or lecture, not even the
    best,
Only the lull I like, the hum of your valved voice.

I mind how we lay in June, such a transparent summer morning;
You settled your head athwart my hips and gently turned over upon me,
80 And parted the shirt from my bosom-bone, and plunged your tongue to my
    barestript heart,
And reached till you felt my beard, and reached till you held my feet.

Swiftly arose and spread around me the peace and joy and knowledge that pass
    all the art and argument of the earth;

And I know that the hand of God is the elderhand of my own,
And I know that the spirit of God is the eldest brother of my own,
85 And that all the men ever born are also my brothers . . . . and the women my
        sisters and lovers,

And that a kelson[2] of the creation is love;
And limitless are leaves stiff or drooping in the fields,
And brown ants in the little wells beneath them,
And mossy scabs of the wormfence, and heaped stones, and elder and mullen
        and pokeweed.

90 A child said, What is the grass? fetching it to me with full hands;
How could I answer the child? . . . . I do not know what it is any more than he.

I guess it must be the flag of my disposition, out of hopeful green stuff woven.

Or I guess it is the handkerchief of the Lord,
A scented gift and remembrancer designedly dropped,
95 Bearing the owner's name someway in the corners, that we may see and remark,
        and say Whose?

Or I guess the grass is itself a child . . . . the produced babe of the vegetation.

Or I guess it is a uniform hieroglyphic,
And it means, Sprouting alike in broad zones and narrow zones,
Growing among black folks as among white,
100 Kanuck, Tuckahoe, Congressman, Cuff,[3] I give them the same, I
        receive them the same.

And now it seems to me the beautiful uncut hair of graves.

Tenderly will I use you curling grass,
It may be you transpire from the breasts of young men,
It may be if I had known them I would have loved them;
105 It may be you are from old people and from women, and from offspring taken
        soon out of their mothers' laps,
And here you are the mothers' laps.

This grass is very dark to be from the white heads of old mothers,
Darker than the colorless beards of old men,
Dark to come from under the faint red roofs of mouths.

110 O I perceive after all so many uttering tongues!
And I perceive they do not come from the roofs of mouths for nothing.

I wish I could translate the hints about the dead young men and women,
And the hints about old men and mothers, and the offspring taken soon out of
        their laps.

---

[2]a structural unit that connects or reinforces, like the keelson that braces the keel of a ship
[3]Kanuck, a French Canadian; Tuckahoe, a Virginian; Cuff, a black person

What do you think has become of the young and old men?
115 And what do you think has become of the women and children?

They are alive and well somewhere;
The smallest sprout shows there is really no death,
And if ever there was it led forward life, and does not wait at the end to arrest it,
And ceased the moment life appeared.

120 All goes onward and outward . . . . and nothing collapses,
And to die is different from what any one supposed, and luckier.

Has any one supposed it lucky to be born?
I hasten to inform him or her it is just as lucky to die, and I know it.

I pass death with the dying, and birth with the new-washed babe . . . . and am
    not contained between my hat and boots,
125 And peruse manifold objects, no two alike, and every one good,
The earth good, and the stars good, and their adjuncts all good.

I am not an earth nor an adjunct of an earth,
I am the mate and companion of people, all just as immortal and fathomless as
    myself;
They do not know how immortal, but I know.

130 Every kind for itself and its own . . . . for me mine male and female,

For me all that have been boys and that love women,
For me the man that is proud and feels how it stings to be slighted,
For me the sweetheart and the old maid . . . . for me mothers and the mothers
    of mothers,
For me lips that have smiled, eyes that have shed tears,
135 For me children and the begetters of children.

Who need be afraid of the merge?
Undrape . . . . you are not guilty to me, nor stale nor discarded,
I see through the broadcloth and gingham whether or no,
And am around, tenacious, acquisitive, tireless . . . . and can never be shaken
    away.

140 The little one sleeps in its cradle,
I lift the gauze and look a long time, and silently brush away flies with my hand.

The youngster and the redfaced girl turn aside up the bushy hill,
I peeringly view them from the top.

The suicide sprawls on the bloody floor of the bedroom.
145 It is so . . . . I witnessed the corpse . . . . there the pistol had fallen.

The blab of the pave . . . . the tires of carts and sluff of bootsoles and talk of the
    promenaders,

The heavy omnibus, the driver with his interrogating thumb, the clank of the
    shod horses on the granite floor,
The carnival of sleighs, the clinking and shouted jokes and pelts of snowballs;
The hurrahs for popular favorites . . . . the fury of roused mobs,
150 The flap of the curtained litter—the sick man inside, borne to the hospital,
The meeting of enemies, the sudden oath, the blows and fall,
The excited crowd—the policeman with his star quickly working his passage to
    the centre of the crowd;
The impassive stones that receive and return so many echoes,
The souls moving along . . . . are they invisible while the least atom of the stones
    is visible?

155 What groans of overfed or half-starved who fall on the flags[4] sunstruck or in
    fits,
What exclamations of women taken suddenly, who hurry home and give birth
    to babes,
What living and buried speech is always vibrating here . . . . what howls
    restrained by decorum,
Arrests of criminals, slights, adulterous offers made, acceptances, rejections
    with convex lips,
I mind them or the resonance of them . . . . I come again and again.

160 The big doors of the country-barn stand open and ready,
The dried grass of the harvest-time loads the slow-drawn wagon,
The clear light plays on the brown gray and green intertinged,
The armfuls are packed to the sagging mow:
I am there . . . . I help . . . . I came stretched atop of the load,
165 I felt its soft jolts . . . . one leg reclined on the other,
I jump from the crossbeams, and seize the clover and timothy,
And roll head over heels, and tangle my hair full of wisps.

Alone far in the wilds and mountains I hunt,
Wandering amazed at my own lightness and glee,
170 In the late afternoon choosing a safe spot to pass the night,
Kindling a fire and broiling the freshkilled game,
Soundly falling asleep on the gathered leaves, my dog and gun by my side.

The Yankee clipper is under her three skysails . . . . she cuts the sparkle and
    scud,
My eyes settle the land . . . . I bend at her prow or shout joyously from the deck.

175 The boatmen and clamdiggers arose early and stopped for me,
I tucked my trowser-ends in my boots and went and had a good time,
You should have been with us that day round the chowder-kettle.

---

[4]slabs of flagstone used for paving

I saw the marriage of the trapper in the open air in the farwest . . . . the bride
    was a red girl,
Her father and his friends sat near by crosslegged and dumbly smoking . . . .
    they had moccasins to their feet and large thick blankets hanging from
    their shoulders;
180 On a bank lounged the trapper . . . . he was dressed mostly in skins . . . . his
    luxuriant beard and curls protected his neck,
One hand rested on his rifle . . . . the other hand held firmly the wrist of the
    red girl,
She had long eyelashes . . . . her head was bare . . . . her coarse straight locks
    descended upon her voluptuous limbs and reached to her feet.

The runaway slave[5] came to my house and stopped outside,
I heard his motions crackling the twigs of the woodpile,
185 Through the swung half-door of the kitchen I saw him limpsey and weak,
And went where he sat on a log, and led him in and assured him,
And brought water and filled a tub for his sweated body and bruised feet,
And gave him a room that entered from my own, and gave him some coarse
    clean clothes,
And remember perfectly well his revolving eyes and his awkwardness,
190 And remember putting plasters on the galls of his neck and ankles;
He staid with me a week before he was recuperated and passed north,
I had him sit next me at table . . . . my firelock leaned in the corner.

Twenty-eight young men bathe by the shore,
Twenty-eight young men, and all so friendly,
195 Twenty-eight years of womanly life, and all so lonesome.

She owns the fine house by the rise of the bank,
She hides handsome and richly drest aft the blinds of the window.

Which of the young men does she like the best?
Ah the homeliest of them is beautiful to her.
200 Where are you off to, lady? for I see you,
You splash in the water there, yet stay stock still in your room.

Dancing and laughing along the beach came the twenty-ninth bather,
The rest did not see her, but she saw them and loved them.

The beards of the young men glistened with wet, it ran from their long hair,
205 Little streams passed all over their bodies.

An unseen hand also passed over their bodies,
It descended tremblingly from their temples and ribs.

---

[5]A new and more rigorous Fugitive Slave Act, which required that inhabitants of the free states assist
  in the capture and return of runaway slaves, was adopted as part of the politically controversial
  Compromise of 1850.

The young men float on their backs, their white bellies swell to the sun . . . .
    they do not ask who seizes fast to them,
They do not know who puffs and declines with pendant and bending arch,
210 They do not think whom they souse with spray.

The butcher-boy puts off his killing-clothes, or sharpens his knife at the stall in
    the market,
I loiter enjoying his repartee and his shuffle and breakdown.[6]
Blacksmiths with grimed and hairy chests environ the anvil,
Each has his main-sledge . . . . they are all out . . . . there is a great heat in the
    fire.

215 From the cinder-strewed threshold I follow their movements,
The lithe sheer of their waists plays even with their massive arms,
Overhand the hammers roll—overhead so slow—overhand so sure,
They do not hasten, each man hits in his place.

The negro holds firmly the reins of his four horses . . . . the block swags
    underneath on its tied-over chain,
220 The negro that drives the huge dray of the stoneyard . . . . steady and tall he
    stands poised on one leg on the stringpiece,
His blue shirt exposes his ample neck and breast and loosens over his hipband,
His glance is calm and commanding . . . . he tosses the slouch of his hat away
    from his forehead,
The sun falls on his crispy hair and moustache . . . . falls on the black of his
    polish'd and perfect limbs.

I behold the picturesque giant and love him . . . . and I do not stop there,
225 I go with the team also.

In me the caresser of life wherever moving . . . . backward as well as forward
    slueing,
To niches aside and junior bending.

Oxen that rattle the yoke or halt in the shade, what is that you express in your
    eyes?
It seems to me more than all the print I have read in my life.

230 My tread scares the wood-drake and wood-duck on my distant and daylong
    ramble,
They rise together, they slowly circle around.
. . . . I believe in those winged purposes,
And acknowledge the red yellow and white playing within me,
And consider the green and violet and the tufted crown intentional;

---

[6]dances popularized by minstrel shows

235 And do not call the tortoise unworthy because she is not something else,
And the mockingbird in the swamp never studied the gamut, yet trills pretty
    well to me,
And the look of the bay mare shames silliness out of me.

The wild gander leads his flock through the cool night,
Ya-honk! he says, and sounds it down to me like an invitation;
240 The pert may suppose its meaningless, but I listen closer,
I find its purpose and place up there toward the November sky.

The sharphoofed moose of the north, the cat on the housesill, the chickadee,
    the prairie-dog,
The litter of the grunting sow as they tug at her teats,
The brood of the turkeyhen, and she with her halfspread wings,
245 I see in them and myself the same old law.
The press of my foot to the earth springs a hundred affections,
They scorn the best I can do to relate them.

I am enamoured of growing outdoors,
Of men that live among cattle or taste of the ocean or woods,
250 Of the builders and steerers of ships, of the wielders of axes and mauls, of the
    drivers of horses,
I can eat and sleep with them week in and week out.

What is commonest and cheapest and nearest and easiest is Me,
Me going in for my chances, spending for vast returns,
Adorning myself to bestow myself on the first that will take me,
255 Not asking the sky to come down to my goodwill,
Scattering it freely forever.

The pure contralto sings in the organloft,
The carpenter dresses his plank . . . . the tongue of his foreplane whistles its
    wild ascending lisp,
The married and unmarried children ride home to their thanksgiving dinner,
260 The pilot seizes the king-pin, he heaves down with a strong arm,
The mate stands braced in the whaleboat, lance and harpoon are ready,
The duck-shooter walks by silent and cautious stretches,
The deacons are ordained with crossed hands at the altar,
The spinning-girl retreats and advances to the hum of the big wheel,
265 The farmer stops by the bars of a Sunday and looks at the oats and rye,
The lunatic is carried at last to the asylum a confirmed case,
He will never sleep any more as he did in the cot in his mother's bedroom;
The jour printer with gray head and gaunt jaws works at his case,
He turns his quid of tobacco, his eyes get blurred with the manuscript;
270 The malformed limbs are tied to the anatomist's table,
What is removed drops horribly in a pail;

The quadroon girl is sold at the stand . . . . the drunkard nods by the barroom stove,
The machinist rolls up his sleeves . . . . the policeman travels his beat . . . . the gate-keeper marks who pass,
The young fellow drives the express-wagon . . . . I love him though I do not know him;
275   The half-breed straps on his light boots to compete in the race,
The western turkey-shooting draws old and young . . . . some lean on their rifles, some sit on logs,
Out from the crowd steps the marksman and takes his position and levels his piece;
The groups of newly-come immigrants cover the wharf or levee,
The woollypates hoe in the sugarfield, the overseer views them from his saddle;
280   The bugle calls in the ballroom, the gentlemen run for their partners, the dancers bow to each other;
The youth lies awake in the cedar-roofed garret and harks to the musical rain,
The Wolverine[7] sets traps on the creek that helps fill the Huron,
The reformer ascends the platform, he spouts with his mouth and nose,
The company returns from its excursion, the darkey brings up the rear and bears the well-riddled target,
285   The squaw wrapt in her yellow-hemmed cloth is offering moccasins and beadbags for sale,
The connoisseur peers along the exhibition-gallery with halfshut eyes bent sideways,
The deckhands make fast the steamboat, the plank is thrown for the shoregoing passengers,
The young sister holds out the skein, the elder sister winds it off in a ball and stops now and then for the knots,
The one-year wife is recovering and happy, a week ago she bore her first child,
290   The cleanhaired Yankee girl works with her sewing-machine or in the factory or mill,
The nine months' gone is in the parturition chamber, her faintness and pains are advancing;
The pavingman leans on his twohanded rammer—the reporter's lead flies swiftly over the notebook—the signpainter is lettering with red and gold,
The canal-boy trots on the towpath—the bookkeeper counts at his desk—the shoemaker waxes his thread,
The conductor beats time for the band and all the performers follow him,
295   The child is baptised—the convert is making the first professions,
The regatta is spread on the bay . . . . how the white sails sparkle!
The drover watches his drove, he sings out to them that would stray,

---

[7]inhabitant of Michigan

The pedlar sweats with his pack on his back—the purchaser higgles about the
   odd cent,
The camera and plate are prepared, the lady must sit for her daguerreotype,
300 The bride unrumples her white dress, the minutehand of the clock moves
   slowly,
The opium eater reclines with rigid head and just-opened lips,
The prostitute draggles her shawl, her bonnet bobs on her tipsy and pimpled
   neck,
The crowd laugh at her blackguard oaths, the men jeer and wink to each other,
(Miserable! I do not laugh at your oaths nor jeer you,)
305 The President holds a cabinet council, he is surrounded by the great secretaries,
On the piazza walk five friendly matrons with twined arms;
The crew of the fish-smack pack repeated layers of halibut in the hold,
The Missourian crosses the plains toting his wares and his cattle,
The fare-collector goes through the train—he gives notice by the jingling of
   loose change,
310 The floormen are laying the floor—the tinners are tinning the roof—the
   masons are calling for mortar,
In single file each shouldering his hod pass onward the laborers;
Seasons pursuing each other the indescribable crowd is gathered . . . . it is the
   Fourth of July . . . . what salutes of cannon and small arms!
Seasons pursuing each other the plougher ploughs and the mower mows and
   the wintergrain falls in the ground;
Off on the lakes the pikefisher watches and waits by the hole in the frozen
   surface,
315 The stumps stand thick round the clearing, the squatter strikes deep with his
   axe,
The flatboatmen make fast toward dusk near the cottonwood or pekantrees,
The coon-seekers go now through the regions of the Red river, or through those
   drained by the Tennessee, or through those of the Arkansas,
The torches shine in the dark that hangs on the Chattahoochee or Altamahaw;
Patriarchs sit at supper with sons and grandsons and great grandsons around
   them,
320 In walls of adobe, in canvass tents, rest hunters and trappers after their day's
   sport.
The city sleeps and the country sleeps,
The living sleep for their time . . . . the dead sleep for their time,
The old husband sleeps by his wife and the young husband sleeps by his wife;
And these one and all tend inward to me, and I tend outward to them,
325 And such as it is to be of these more or less I am.

I am of old and young, of the foolish as much as the wise,
Regardless of others, ever regardful of others,
Maternal as well as paternal, a child as well as a man,

Stuffed with the stuff that is coarse, and stuffed with the stuff that is fine,
330 One of the great nation, the nation of many nations—the smallest the same and
    the largest the same,
A southerner soon as a northerner, a planter nonchalant and hospitable,
A Yankee bound my own way . . . . ready for trade . . . . my joints the limberest
    joints on earth and the sternest joints on earth,
A Kentuckian walking the vale of the Elkhorn in my deerskin leggings,
A boatman over the lakes or bays or along coasts . . . . a Hoosier, a Badger, a
    Buckeye,[8]
335 A Lousianian or Georgian, a poke-easy from sandhills and pines,
At home on Canadian snowshoes or up in the bush, or with fishermen off
    Newfoundland,
At home in the fleet of iceboats, sailing with the rest and tacking,
At home on the hills of Vermont or in the woods of Maine or the Texan ranch,
Comrade of Californians . . . . comrade of free northwesterners, loving their big
    proportions,
340 Comrade of raftsmen and coalmen—comrade of all who shake hands and
    welcome to drink and meat;
A learner with the simplest, a teacher of the thoughtfulest,
A novice beginning experient of myriads of seasons,
Of every hue and trade and rank, of every caste and religion,
Not merely of the New World but of Africa Europe or Asia . . . . a wandering
    savage,
345 A farmer, mechanic, or artist . . . . a gentleman, sailor, lover or quaker,
A prisoner, fancy-man, rowdy, lawyer, physician or priest.

I resist anything better than my own diversity,
And breathe the air and leave plenty after me,
And am not stuck up, and am in my place.

350 The moth and the fisheggs are in their place,
The suns I see and the suns I cannot see are in their place,
The palpable is in its place and the impalpable is in its place.

These are the thoughts of all men in all ages and lands, they are not original
    with me,
If they are not yours as much as mine they are nothing or next to nothing,
355 If they do not enclose everything they are next to nothing,
If they are not the riddle and the untying of the riddle they are nothing,
If they are not just as close as they are distant they are nothing.

This is the grass that grows wherever the land is and the water is,
This is the common air that bathes the globe.

---

[8]inhabitants of Indiana, Wisconsin, and Ohio, respectively

360 This is the breath of laws and songs and behaviour,
This is the tasteless water of souls . . . . this is the true sustenance,
It is for the illiterate . . . . it is for the judges of the supreme court . . . . it is for
the federal capitol and the state capitols,
It is for the admirable communes of literary men and composers and singers
and lecturers and engineers and savans,
It is for the endless races or working people and farmers and seamen.

365 This is the trill of a thousand clear cornets and scream of the octave flute and
strike of triangles.

I play not a march for victors only . . . . I play great marches for conquered and
slain persons.

Have you heard that it was good to gain the day?
I also say it is good to fall . . . . battles are lost in the same spirit in which they
are won.

I sound triumphal drums for the dead . . . . I fling through my embouchures[9]
the loudest and gayest music to them,
370 Vivas to those who have failed, and to those whose war-vessels sank in the sea,
and those themselves who sank in the sea,
And to all generals that lost engagements, and all overcome heroes, and the
numberless unknown heroes equal to the greatest heroes known.

This is the meal pleasantly set . . . . this is the meat and drink for natural
hunger,
It is for the wicked just the same as the righteous . . . . I make appointments
with all,
I will not have a single person slighted or left away,
375 The keptwoman and sponger and thief are hereby invited . . . . the heavy-lipped
slave is invited . . . . the venerealee is invited,
There shall be no difference between them and the rest.

This is the press of a bashful hand . . . . this is the float and odor of hair,
This is the touch of my lips to yours . . . . this is the murmur of yearning,
This is the far-off depth and height reflecting my own face,
380 This is the thoughtful merge of myself and the outlet again.

Do you guess I have some intricate purpose?
Well I have . . . . for the April rain has, and the mica on the side of a rock has.

Do you take it I would astonish?
Does the daylight astonish? or the early redstart twittering through the woods?
385 Do I astonish more than they?

---

[9]another borrowing from the French, suggesting an opening, or a mouthpiece of a musical instrument

This hour I tell things in confidence,
I might not tell everybody but I will tell you.

Who goes there! hankering, gross, mystical, nude?
How is it I extract strength from the beef I eat?

390 What is a man anyhow? What am I? and what are you?
All I mark as my own you shall offset it with your own,
Else it were time lost listening to me.

I do not snivel that snivel the world over,
That months are vacuums and the ground but wallow and filth,
395 That life is a suck and a sell, and nothing remains at the end but threadbare
    crape and tears.

Whimpering and truckling fold with powders for invalids . . . . conformity goes
    to the fourth-removed,
I cock my hat as I please indoors or out.

Shall I pray? Shall I venerate and be ceremonious?
I have pried through the strata and analyzed to a hair,
400 And counselled with doctors and calculated close and found no sweeter fat than
    sticks to my own bones.

In all people I see myself, none more and not one a barleycorn less,
And the good or bad I say of myself I say of them.

And I know I am solid and sound,
To me the converging objects of the universe perpetually flow,
405 All are written to me, and I must get what the writing means.

And I know I am deathless,
I know this orbit of mine cannot be swept by a carpenter's compass,
I know I shall not pass like a child's carlacue cut with a burnt stick at night.

I know I am august,
410 I do not trouble my spirit to vindicate itself or be understood,
I see that the elementary laws never apologize,
I reckon I behave no prouder than the level I plant my house by after all.

I exist as I am, that is enough,
If no other in the world be aware I sit content,
415 And if each and all be aware I sit content.

One world is aware, and by far the largest to me, and that is myself,
And whether I come to my own today or in ten thousand or ten million years,
I can cheerfully take it now, or with equal cheerfulness I can wait.

My foothold is tenoned and mortised in granite,
420 I laugh at what you call dissolution,
And I know the amplitude of time.

I am the poet of the body,
And I am the poet of the soul.

The pleasures of heaven are with me, and the pains of hell are with me,
425 The first I graft and increase upon myself . . . . the latter I translate into a new
    tongue.

I am the poet of the woman the same as the man,
And I say it is as great to be a woman as to be a man,
And I say there is nothing greater than the mother of men.

I chant a new chant of dilation or pride,
430 We have had ducking and deprecating about enough,
I show that size is only development.

Have you outstript the rest? Are you the President?
It is a trifle . . . . they will more than arrive there every one, and still pass on.

I am he that walks with the tender and growing night;
435 I call to the earth and sea half-held by the night.

Press close barebosomed night! Press close magnetic nourishing night!
Night of south winds! Night of the large few stars!
Still nodding night! Mad naked summer night!

Smile O voluptuous coolbreathed earth!
440 Earth of the slumbering and liquid trees!
Earth of departed sunset! Earth of the mountains misty-topt!
Earth of the vitreous pour of the full moon just tinged with blue!
Earth of shine and dark mottling the tide of the river!
Earth of the limpid gray of clouds brighter and clearer for my sake!
445 Far-swooping elbowed earth! Rich apple-blossomed earth!
Smile, for your lover comes!

Prodigal! you have given me love! . . . . therefore I to you give love!
O unspeakable passionate love!

Thruster holding me tight and that I hold tight!
450 We hurt each other as the bridegroom and the bride hurt each other.

You sea! I resign myself to you also . . . . I guess what you mean,
I behold from the beach your crooked inviting fingers,
I believe you refuse to go back without feeling of me;
We must have a turn together . . . . I undress . . . . hurry me out of sight of the
    land,
455 Cushion me soft . . . . rock me in billowy drowse,
Dash me with amorous wet . . . . I can repay you.

Sea of stretched ground swells!
Sea breathing broad and convulsive breaths!

Sea of the brine of life! Sea of unshovelled and always-ready graves!
460   Howler and scooper of storms! Capricious and dainty sea!
I am integral with you . . . . I too am of one phase and of all phases.

Partaker of influx and efflux . . . . extoler of hate and conciliation,
Extoler of amies[10] and those that sleep in each others' arms.

I am he attesting sympathy;
465   Shall I make my list of things in the house and skip the house that supports
        them?

I am the poet of commonsense and of the demonstrable and of immortality;
And am not the poet of goodness only . . . . I do not decline to be the poet of
        wickedness also.

Washes and razors for foofoos . . . . for me freckles and a bristling beard.

What blurt is it about virtue and about vice?
470   Evil propels me, and reform of evil propels me . . . . I stand indifferent,
My gait is no faultfinder's or rejecter's gait,
I moisten the roots of all that has grown.

Did you fear some scrofula out of the unflagging pregnancy?
Did you guess the celestial laws are yet to be worked over and rectified?

475   I step up to say that what we do is right and what we affirm is right . . . . and
        some is only the ore of right,
Witnesses of us . . . . one side a balance and the antipodal side a balance,
Soft doctrine as steady help as stable doctrine,
Thoughts and deeds of the present our rouse and early start.

This minute that comes to me over the past decillions,
480   There is no better than it now.

What behaved well in the past or behaves well today is not such a wonder,
The wonder is always and always how there can be a mean man or an infidel.

Endless unfolding of words of ages!
And mine a word of the modern . . . . a word en masse.

485   A word of the faith that never balks,
One time as good as another time . . . . here or henceforward it is all the same
        to me.

A world of reality . . . . materialism first and last imbueing.

Hurrah for positive science! Long live exact demonstration!
Fetch stonecrop and mix it with cedar and branches of lilac;

---

[10]French for girlfriend; Whitman probably intended to suggest comrades and lovers of either sex.

490   This is the lexicographer or chemist . . . . this made a grammar of the old
            cartouches,[11]
These mariners put the ship through dangerous unknown seas,
This is the geologist, and this works with the scalpel, and this is a mathematician.

Gentlemen I receive you, and attach and clasp hands with you,
The facts are useful and real . . . . they are not my dwelling . . . . I enter by them
            to an area of the dwelling.

495   I am less the reminder of property or qualities, and more the reminder of life,
And go on the square for my own sake and for others' sakes,
And make short account of neuters and geldings, and favor men and women
            fully equipped,
And beat the gong of revolt, and stop with fugitives and them that plot and
            conspire.

Walt Whitman an American, one of the roughs, a kosmos,
500   Disorderly fleshy and sensual . . . . eating drinking and breeding,
No sentimentalist . . . . no stander above men and women or apart
            from them . . . . no more modest than immodest.

Unscrew the locks from the doors!
Unscrew the doors themselves from their jambs!

Whoever degrades another degrades me . . . . and whatever is done or said
            returns at last to me,
505   And whatever I do or say I also return.

Through me the afflatus[12] surging and surging . . . . through me the current and
            index.

I speak the password primeval . . . . I give the sign of democracy;
By God! I will accept nothing which all cannot have their counterpart of on the
            same terms.

Through me many long dumb voices,
510   Voices of the interminable generations of slaves,
Voices of prostitutes and of deformed persons,
Voices of the diseased and despairing, and of thieves and dwarfs,
Voices of cycles of preparation and accretion,
And of the threads that connect the stars—and of wombs, and of the
            fatherstuff,
515   And of the rights of them the others are down upon,
Of the trivial and flat and foolish and despised,
Of fog in the air and beetles rolling balls of dung.

---

[11]scroll-like tablets used for the inscription of Egyptian hieroglyphics
[12]creative spirit or divine breath

Through me forbidden voices,
Voices of sexes and lusts . . . . voices veiled, and I remove the veil,
520 Voices indecent by me clarified and transfigured.

I do not press my finger across my mouth,
I keep as delicate around the bowels as around the head and heart,
Copulation is no more rank to me than death is.

I believe in the flesh and the appetites,
525 Seeing hearing and feeling are miracles, and each part and tag of me is a
    miracle.

Divine am I inside and out, and I make holy whatever I touch or am touched
    from;
The scent of these arm-pits is aroma finer than prayer,
This head is more than churches or bibles or creeds.

If I worship any particular thing it shall be some of the spread of my body;
530 Translucent mould of me it shall be you,
Shaded ledges and rests, firm masculine coulter,[13] it shall be you,
Whatever goes to the tilth of me it shall be you,
You my rich blood, your milky stream pale strippings of my life;
Breast that presses against other breasts it shall be you,
535 My brain it shall be your occult convolutions,
Root of washed sweet-flag, timorous pond-snipe, nest of guarded duplicate
    eggs, it shall be you,
Mixed tussled hay of head and beard and brawn it shall be you,
Trickling sap of maple, fibre of manly wheat, it shall be you;
Sun so generous it shall be you,
540 Vapors lighting and shading my face it shall be you,
You sweaty brooks and dews it shall be you,
Winds whose soft-tickling genitals rub against me it shall be you,
Broad muscular fields, branches of liveoak, loving lounger in my winding paths,
    it shall be you,
Hands I have taken, face I have kissed, mortal I have ever touched, it shall be
    you.

545 I dote on myself . . . . there is that lot of me, and all so luscious,
Each moment and whatever happens thrills me with joy.
I cannot tell how my ankles bend . . . . nor whence the cause of my faintest wish,
Nor the cause of the friendship I emit . . . . nor the cause of the friendship I take
    again.

To walk up my stoop is unaccountable . . . . I pause to consider if it really be,
550 That I eat and drink is spectacle enough for the great authors and schools,

---

[13]the iron blade of a plow

A morning-glory at my window satisfies me more than the metaphysics of
    books.

To behold the daybreak!
The little light fades the immense and diaphanous shadows,
The air tastes good to my palate.

555 Hefts of the moving world at innocent gambols, silently rising, freshly exuding,
Scooting obliquely high and low.

Something I cannot see puts upward libidinous[14] prongs,
Seas of bright juice suffuse heaven.

The earth by the sky staid with . . . . the daily close of their junction,
560 The heaved challenge from the east that moment over my head,
The mocking taunt, See then whether you shall be master!

Dazzling and tremendous how quick the sunrise would kill me,
If I could not now and always send sunrise out of me.

We also ascend dazzling and tremendous as the sun,
565 We found our own my soul in the calm and cool of the daybreak.

My voice goes after what my eyes cannot reach,
With the twirl of my tongue I encompass worlds and volumes of worlds.
Speech is the twin of my vision . . . . it is unequal to measure itself.

It provokes me forever,
570 It says sarcastically, Walt, you understand enough . . . . why don't you let it out
    then?

Come now I will not be tantalized . . . . you conceive too much of articulation.

Do you not know how the buds beneath are folded?
Waiting in gloom protected by frost,
The dirt receding before my prophetical screams,
575 I underlying causes to balance them at last,
My knowledge my live parts . . . . it keeping tally with the meaning of things,
Happiness . . . . which whoever hears me let him or her set out in search of this
    day.

My final merit I refuse you . . . . I refuse putting from me the best I am.

Encompass worlds but never try to encompass me,
580 I crowd your noisiest talk by looking toward you.

Writing and talk do not prove me,
I carry the plenum of proof and every thing else in my face,
With the hush of my lips I confound the topmost skeptic.

---

[14]full of sexual energy, desire

I think I will do nothing for a long time but listen,
585 And accrue what I hear into myself . . . . and let sounds contribute toward me.

I hear the bravuras of birds . . . . the bustle of growing wheat . . . . gossip of
    flames . . . . clack of sticks cooking my meals.

I hear the sound of the human voice . . . . a sound I love,
I hear all sounds as they are tuned to their uses . . . . sounds of the city and
    sounds out of the city . . . . sounds of the day and night;
Talkative young ones to those that like them . . . . the recitative of fish-pedlars
    and fruit-pedlars . . . . the loud laugh of workpeople at their meals,
590 The angry base of disjointed friendship . . . . the faint tones of the sick,
The judge with hands tight to the desk, his shaky lips pronouncing
    a death-sentence,
The heave'e'yo of stevedores unlading ships by the wharves . . . . the refrain of
    the anchor-lifters;
The ring of alarm-bells . . . . the cry of fire . . . . the whirr of swift-streaking
    engines and hose-carts with premonitory tinkles and colored lights,
The steam-whistle . . . . the solid roll of the train of approaching cars;
595 The slow-march played at night at the head of the association,
They go to guard some corpse . . . . the flag-tops are draped with black muslin.

I hear the violincello or man's heart's complaint,
And hear the keyed cornet or else the echo of sunset.

I hear the chorus . . . . it is a grand-opera . . . . this indeed is music!

600 A tenor large and fresh as the creation fills me,
The orbic flex of his mouth is pouring and filling me full.

I hear the trained soprano . . . . she convulses me like the climax of my
    love-grip;
The orchestra whirls me wider than Uranus flies,
It wrenches unnamable ardors from my breast,
605 It throbs me to gulps of the farthest down horror,
It sails me . . . . I dab with bare feet . . . . they are licked by the indolent waves,
I am exposed . . . . cut by bitter and poisoned hail,
Steeped amid honeyed morphine . . . . my windpipe squeezed in the fakes[15] of
    death,
Let up again to feel the puzzle of puzzles,
610 And that we call Being.

To be in any form, what is that?
If nothing lay more developed the quahaug and its callous shell were enough.

---

[15]coils of rope

Mine is no callous shell,
I have instant conductors all over me whether I pass or stop,
615 They seize every object and lead it harmlessly through me.

I merely stir, press, feel with my fingers, and am happy,
To touch my person to some one else's is about as much as I can stand.

Is this then a touch? . . . . quivering me to a new identity,
Flames and ether making a rush for my veins,
620 Treacherous tip of me reaching and crowding to help them,
My flesh and blood playing out lightning, to strike what is hardly different from
      myself,
On all sides prurient provokers stiffening my limbs,
Straining the udder of my heart for its withheld drip,
Behaving licentious toward me, taking no denial,
625 Depriving me of my best as for a purpose,
Unbottoning my clothes and holding me by the bare waist,
Deluding my confusion with the calm of the sunlight and pasture fields,
Immodestly sliding the fellow-senses away,
They bribed to swap off with touch, and go and graze at the edges of me,
630 No consideration, no regard for my draining strength or my anger,
Fetching the rest of the herd around to enjoy them awhile,
Then all uniting to stand on a headland and worry me.

The sentries desert every other part of me,
They have left me helpless to a red marauder,
635 They all come to the headland to witness and assist against me.

I am given up by traitors;
I talk wildly . . . . I have lost my wits . . . . I and nobody else am the greatest
      traitor,
I went myself first to the headland . . . . my own hands carried me there.

You villain touch! what are you doing? . . . . my breath is tight in its throat;
640 Unclench your floodgates! you are too much for me.

Blind loving wrestling touch! Sheathed hooded sharptoothed touch!
Did it make you ache so leaving me?

Parting tracked by arriving . . . . perpetual payment of the perpetual loan,
Rich showering rain, and recompense richer afterward.

645 Sprouts take and accumulate . . . . stand by the curb prolific and vital,
Landscapes projected masculine full-sized and golden.

All truths wait in all things,
They neither hasten their own delivery nor resist it,
They do not need the obstetric forceps of the surgeon,

650 The insignificant is as big to me as any,
What is less or more than a touch?

Logic and sermons never convince,
The damp of the night drives deeper into my soul.

Only what proves itself to every man and woman is so,
655 Only what nobody denies is so.

A minute and a drop of me settle my brain;
I believe the soggy clods shall become lovers and lamps,
And a compend of compends is the meat of a man or woman,
And a summit and flower there is the feeling they have for each other,
660 And they are to branch boundlessly out of that lesson until it becomes omnific,
And until every one shall delight us, and we them.

I believe a leaf of grass is no less than the journeywork of the stars,
And the pismire is equally perfect, and a grain of sand, and the egg of the wren,
And the tree-toad is a chef-d'ouvre[16] for the highest,
665 And the running blackberry would adorn the parlors of heaven,
And the narrowest hinge in my hand puts to scorn all machinery,
And the cow crunching with depressed head surpasses any statue,
And a mouse is miracle enough to stagger sextillions of infidels,
And I could come every afternoon of my life to look at the farmer's girl boiling
   her iron tea-kettle and baking shortcake.

670 I find I incorporate gneiss and coal and long-threaded moss and
      fruits and grains and esculent roots,
And am stucco'd with quadrupeds and birds all over,
And have distanced what is behind me for good reasons,
And call any thing close again when I desire it.

In vain the speeding or shyness,
675 In vain the plutonic rocks send their old heat against my approach,
In vain the mastadon retreats beneath its own powdered bones,
In vain objects stand leagues off and assume manifold shapes,
In vain the ocean settling in hollows and the great monsters lying low,
In vain the buzzard houses herself with the sky,
680 In vain the snake slides through the creepers and logs,
In vain the elk takes to the inner passes of the woods,
In vain the razorbilled auk sails far north to Labrador,
I follow quickly . . . . I ascend to the nest in the fissure of the cliff.

I think I could turn and live awhile with the animals . . . . they are so placid and
      self-contained,
685 I stand and look at them sometimes half the day long.

---

[16]masterpiece

They do not sweat and whine about their condition,
They do not lie awake in the dark and weep for their sins,
They do not make me sick discussing their duty to God,
Not one is dissatisfied . . . . not one is demented with the mania of owning
    things,
690 Not one kneels to another nor to his kind that lived thousands of years ago,
Not one is respectable or industrious over the whole earth.

So they show their relations to me and I accept them;
They bring me tokens of myself . . . . they evince them plainly in their
    possession.

I do not know where they got those tokens,
695 I must have passed that way untold times ago and negligently dropt them,
Myself moving forward then and now forever,
Gathering and showing more always and with velocity,
Infinite and omnigenous and the like of these among them;
Not too exclusive toward the reachers of my remembrancers,
700 Picking out here one that shall be my amie,
Choosing to go with him on brotherly terms.

A gigantic beauty of a stallion, fresh and responsive to my caresses,
Head high in the forehead and wide between the ears,
Limbs glossy and supple, tail dusting the ground,
705 Eyes well apart and full of sparkling wickedness . . . . ears finely cut and flexibly
    moving.

His nostrils dilate . . . . my heels embrace him . . . . his well built limbs tremble
    with pleasure . . . . we speed around and return.
I but use you a moment and then I resign you stallion . . . . and do not need
    your paces, and outgallop them,
And myself as I stand or sit pass faster than you.

Swift wind! Space! My Soul! Now I know it is true what I guessed at;
710 What I guessed when I loafed on the grass,
What I guessed while I lay alone in my bed . . . . and again as I walked the beach
    under the paling stars of the morning.

My ties and ballasts[17] leave me . . . . I travel . . . . I sail . . . . my elbows rest in the
    sea-gaps,
I skirt the sierras . . . . my palms cover continents,
I am afoot with my vision.

715 By the city's quadrangular houses . . . . in log-huts, or camping with
    lumbermen,
Along the ruts of the turnpike . . . . along the dry gulch and rivulet bed,

---

[17]as of a hot-air balloon

Hoeing my onion-patch, and rows of carrots and parsnips . . . . crossing
    savannas . . . trailing in forests,
Prospecting . . . . gold-digging . . . . girdling the trees of a new purchase,
Scorched ankle-deep by the hot sand . . . . hauling my boat down the shallow
    river;
720 Where the panther walks to and fro on a limb overhead . . . . where the buck
    turns furiously at the hunter,
Where the rattlesnake suns his flabby length on a rock . . . . where the otter is
    feeding on fish,
Where the alligator in his tough pimples sleeps by the bayou,
Where the black bear is searching for roots or honey . . . . where the beaver pats
    the mud with his paddle-tail;
Over the growing sugar . . . . over the cottonplant . . . . over the rice in its low
    moist field;
725 Over the sharp-peaked farmhouse with its scalloped scum and slender shoots
    from the gutters;
Over the western persimmon . . . . over the longleaved corn and the delicate
    blueflowered flax;
Over the white and brown buckwheat, a hummer and a buzzer there with the
    rest,
Over the dusky green of the rye as it ripples and shades in the breeze;
Scaling mountains . . . . pulling myself cautiously up . . . . holding on by low
    scragged limbs,
730 Walking the path worn in the grass and beat through the leaves of the brush;
Where the quail is whistling betwixt the woods and the wheatlot,
Where the bat flies in the July eve . . . . where the great goldbug drops through
    the dark;
Where the flails keep time on the barn floor,
Where the brook puts out of the roots of the old tree and flows to the meadow,
735 Where cattle stand and shake away flies with the tremulous shuddering of their
    hides,
Where the cheese-cloth hangs in the kitchen, and andirons straddle
    the hearth-slab, and cobwebs fall in festoons from the rafters;
Where triphammers crash . . . . where the press is whirling its cylinders;
Wherever the human heart beats with terrible throes out of its ribs:
Where the pear-shaped balloon is floating aloft . . . . floating in it myself and
    looking composedly down:
740 Where the life-car[18] is drawn on the slipnoose . . . . where the heat hatches
    pale-green eggs in the dented sand,
Where the she-whale swims with her calves and never forsakes them,
Where the steamship trails hindways its long pennant of smoke,
Where the ground-shark's fin cuts like a black chip out of the water,

---

[18] a water-tight rescue vessel used to save passengers at sea

Where the half-burned brig is riding on unknown currents,
745 Where the shells grow to her slimy deck, and the dead are corrupting below;
Where the striped and starred flag is borne at the head of the regiments;
Approaching Manhattan, up by the long-stretching island,
Under Niagara, the cataract falling like a veil over my countenance;
Upon a door-step . . . . upon the horse-block of hard wood outside,
750 Upon the race-course, or enjoying pic-nics or jigs or a good game of base-ball,
At he-festivals with blackguard jibes and ironical license and bull-dances
      and drinking and laughter,
At the cider-mill, tasting the sweet of the brown sqush[19]. . . . sucking the juice
      through a straw,
At apple-pealings, wanting kisses for all the red fruit I find,
At musters[20] and beach-parties and friendly bees and huskings and house-raisings;
755 Where the mockingbird sounds his delicious gurgles, and cackles and screams
      and weeps,
Where the hay-rick stands in the barnyard, and the dry-stalks are scattered, and
      the brood cow waits in the hovel,
Where the bull advances to do his masculine work, and the stud to the mare,
      and the cock is treading the hen,
Where the heifers browse, and the geese nip their food with short jerks;
Where the sundown shadows lengthen over the limitless and lonesome prairie,
760 Where the herds of buffalo make a crawling spread of the square miles far and
      near;
Where the hummingbird shimmers . . . . where the neck of the longlived swan is
      curving and winding;
Where the laughing-gull scoots by the slappy shore and laughs her near-human
      laugh;
Where beehives range on a gray bench in the garden half-hid by the high weeds;
Where the band-necked partridges roost in a ring on the ground with their
      heads out;
765 Where burial coaches enter the arched gates of a cemetery;
Where winter wolves bark amid wastes of snow and icicled trees;
Where the yellow-crowned heron comes to the edge of the marsh at night and
      feeds upon small crabs;
Where the splash of swimmers and divers cools the warm noon;
Where the katydid works her chromatic reed on the walnut-tree over the well;
770 Through patches of citrons and cucumbers with silver-wired leaves,
Through the salt-lick or orange glade . . . . or under conical firs;
Through the gymnasium . . . . through the curtained saloon . . . . through the
      office or public hall;
Pleased with the native and pleased with the foreign . . . . pleased with the new
      and old,

---

[19]mush
[20]gatherings of people

Pleased with women, the homely as well as the handsome,
775 Pleased with the quakeress as she puts off her bonnet and talks melodiously,
Pleased with the primitive tunes of the choir of the whitewashed church,
Pleased with the earnest words of the sweating Methodist preacher, or any
     preacher . . . . looking seriously at the camp-meeting;
Looking in at the shop-windows in Broadway the whole forenoon . . . . pressing
     the flesh of my nose to the thick plate-glass,
Wandering the same afternoon with my face turned up to the clouds;
780 My right and left arms round the side of two friends and I in the middle;
Coming home with the bearded and dark-cheeked bush-boy . . . . riding behind
     him at the drape of the day;
Far from the settlements studying the print of animals' feet, or the moccasin
     print;
By the cot in the hospital reaching lemonade to a feverish patient,
By the coffined corpse when all is still, examining with a candle;
785 Voyaging to every port to dicker and adventure;
Hurrying with the modern crowd, as eager and fickle as any,
Hot toward one I hate, ready in my madness to knife him;
Solitary at midnight in my back yard, my thoughts gone from me a long while,
Walking the old hills of Judea with the beautiful gentle god by my side;
790 Speeding through space . . . . speeding through heaven and the stars,
Speeding amid the seven satellites and the broad ring and the diameter of
     eighty thousand miles,
Speeding with tailed meteors . . . . throwing fire-balls like the rest,
Carrying the crescent child that carries its own full mother in its belly;
Storming enjoying planning loving cautioning,
795 Backing and filling, appearing and disappearing,
I tread day and night such roads.

I visit the orchards of God and look at the spheric product,
And look at quintillions ripened, and look at quintillions green.

I fly the flight of the fluid and swallowing soul,
800 My course runs below the soundings of plummets.

I help myself to material and immaterial,
No guard can shut me off, no law can prevent me.

I anchor my ship for a little while only,
My messengers continually cruise away or bring their returns to me.

805 I go hunting polar furs and the seal . . . . leaping chasms with a pike-pointed
     staff . . . . clinging to topples[21] of brittle and blue.

---

[21]pieces of ice

I ascend to the foretruck . . . . I take my place late at night in the crow's nest . . . .
    we sail through the arctic sea . . . . it is plenty light enough,
Through the clear atmosphere I stretch around on the wonderful beauty,
The enormous masses of ice pass me and I pass them . . . . the scenery is plain in
    all directions,
The white-topped mountains point up in the distance . . . . I fling out my
    fancies toward them;
810 We are about approaching some great battlefield in which we are soon to be
    engaged,
We pass the colossal outposts of the encampments . . . . we pass with still feet
    and caution;
Or we are entering by the suburbs some vast and ruined city . . . . the blocks
    and fallen architecture more than all the living cities of the globe.

I am a free companion . . . . I bivouac by invading watchfires.

I turn the bridegroom out of bed and stay with the bride myself,
815 And tighten her all night to my thighs and lips.

My voice is the wife's voice, the screech by the rail of the stairs,
They fetch my man's body up dripping and drowned.

I understand the large hearts of heroes,
The courage of present times and all times;
820 How the skipper[22] saw the crowded and rudderless wreck of the steamship, and
    death chasing it up and down the storm,
How he knuckled tight and gave not back one inch, and was faithful of days and
    faithful of nights,
And chalked in large letters on a board, Be of good cheer, We will not desert you;
How he saved the drifting company at last,
How the lank loose-gowned women looked when boated from the side of their
    prepared graves,
825 How the silent old-faced infants, and the lifted sick, and the sharp-lipped
    unshaved men;
All this I swallow and it tastes good . . . . I like it well, and it becomes mine,
I am the man . . . . I suffered . . . . I was there.

The disdain and calmness of martyrs,
The mother condemned for a witch and burnt with dry wood, and her children
    gazing on;
830 The hounded slave that flags in the race and leans by the fence, blowing and
    covered with sweat,
The twinges that sting like needles his legs and neck,

---

[22]Whitman describes the shipwreck of the *San Francisco*, which was reported in the New York *Weekly Tribune* on January 21, 1854; he kept a copy of this article among his belongings.

The murderous buckshot and the bullets,
All these I feel or am.

I am the hounded slave . . . . I wince at the bite of the dogs,
835   Hell and despair are upon me . . . . crack and again crack the marksmen,
I clutch the rails of the fence . . . . my gore dribs[23] thinned with the ooze of my
     skin,
I fall on the weeds and stones,
The riders spur their unwilling horses and haul close,
They taunt my dizzy ears . . . . they beat me violently over the head with their
     whip-stocks.

840   Agonies are one of my changes of garments;
I do not ask the wounded person how he feels . . . . I myself become the
     wounded person,
My hurt turns livid upon me as I lean on a cane and observe.

I am the mashed fireman with breastbone broken . . . . tumbling walls buried
     me in their debris,
Heat and smoke I inspired . . . . I heard the yelling shouts of my comrades,
845   I heard the distant click of their picks and shovels;
They have cleared the beams away . . . . they tenderly lift me forth.

I lie in the night air in my red shirt . . . . the pervading hush is for my sake,
Painless after all I lie, exhausted but not so unhappy,
White and beautiful are the faces around me . . . . the heads are bared of their
     fire-caps,
850   The kneeling crowd fades with the light of the torches.

Distant and dead resuscitate,
They show as the dial or move as the hands of me . . . . and I am the clock
     myself.
I am an old artillerist, and tell of some fort's bombardment . . . . and am there
     again.

Again the reveille of drummers . . . . again the attacking cannon and mortars
     and howitzers,
855   Again the attacked send their cannon responsive.

I take part . . . . I see and hear the whole,
The cries and curses and roar . . . . the plaudits for well aimed shots,
The ambulanza slowly passing and trailing its red drip,
Workmen searching after damages and to make indispensable repairs,
860   The fall of grenades through the rent roof . . . . the fan-shaped explosion,
The whizz of limbs heads stone wood and iron high in the air.

---

[23]short for dribbles

Again gurgles the mouth of my dying general . . . . he furiously waves with his
    hand,
He gasps through the clot . . . . Mind not me . . . . mind . . . . the entrenchments.

I tell not the fall of Alamo . . . . not one escaped to tell the fall of Alamo,
865 The hundred and fifty are dumb yet at Alamo.

Hear now the tale of a jetblack sunrise,
Hear of the murder in cold blood of four hundred and twelve young men.[24]

Retreating they had formed in a hollow square with their baggage
    for breastworks,
Nine hundred lives out of the surrounding enemy's nine times their number
    was the price they took in advance,
870 Their colonel was wounded and their ammunition gone,
They treated for an honorable capitulation, received writing and seal, gave up
    their arms, and marched back prisoners of war.

They were the glory of the race of rangers,
Matchless with a horse, a rifle, a song, a supper, or a courtship,
Large, turbulent, brave, handsome, generous, proud, and affectionate,
875 Bearded, sunburnt, dressed in the free costume of hunters,
Not a single one over thirty years of age.

The second Sunday morning they were brought out in squads and
    massacred . . . . it was beautiful early summer,
The work commenced about five o'clock and was over by eight.

None obeyed the command to kneel,
880 Some made a mad and helpless rush . . . . some stood stark and straight,
A few fell at once, shot in the temple or heart . . . . the living and dead lay
    together,
The maimed and mangled dug in the dirt . . . . the new-comers saw them there;
Some half-killed attempted to crawl away,
These were dispatched with bayonets or battered with the blunts of muskets;
885 A youth not seventeen years old seized his assassin till two more came to release
    him,
The three were all torn, and covered with the boy's blood.

At eleven o'clock began the burning of the bodies;
And that is the tale of the murder of the four hundred and twelve young men,
And that was a jetblack sunrise.

---

[24]Whitman tells the story of the deaths of Captain Fannin and his company of 371 Texans at the
hands of the Mexicans after their surrender at Goliad on March 27, 1836; unlike Emerson and
Thoreau, Whitman supported the Mexican War (1846–1848).

890 Did you read in the seabooks of the oldfashioned frigate-fight?[25]
Did you learn who won by the light of the moon and stars?

Our foe was no skulk in his ship, I tell you,
His was the English pluck, and there is no tougher or truer, and never was, and
    never will be;
Along the lowered eve he came, horribly raking us.

895 We closed with him . . . . the yard entangled . . . . the cannon touched,
My captain lashed fast with his own hands.

We had received some eighteen-pound shots under the water,
On our lower-gun-deck two large pieces had burst at the first fire, killing all
    around and blowing up overhead.

Ten o'clock at night, and the full moon shining and the leaks on the gain, and
    five feet of water reported,
900 The master-at-arms loosing the prisoners confined in the after-hold to give
    them a chance for themselves.

The transit to and from the magazine was now stopped by the sentinels,
They saw so many strange faces they did not know whom to trust.

Our frigate was afire . . . . the other asked if we demanded quarters? if our
    colors were struck and the fighting done?

I laughed content when I heard the voice of my little captain,
905 We have not struck, he composedly cried, We have just begun our part of the
    fighting.

Only three guns were in use,
One was directed by the captain himself against the enemy's mainmast,
Two well-served with grape and canister silenced his musketry and cleared his
    decks.

The tops alone seconded the fire of this little battery, especially the maintop,
910 They all held out bravely during the whole of the action.

Not a moment's cease,
The leaks gained fast on the pumps . . . . the fire eat toward the powder-magazine,
One of the pumps was shot away . . . . it was generally thought we were sinking.

Serene stood the little captain,
915 He was not hurried . . . . his voice was neither high nor low,
His eyes gave more light to us than our battle-lanterns.

Toward twelve at night, there in the beams of the moon they surrendered to us.

---

[25]Whitman tells the story of the Revolutionary sea battle on September 23, 1779 between the *Bon-homme Richard,* commanded by John Paul Jones, and the British *Serapis.*

Stretched and still lay the midnight,
Two great hulls motionless on the breast of the darkness,
920 Our vessel riddled and slowly sinking . . . . preparations to pass to the one we
      had conquered,
The captain on the quarter deck coldly giving his orders through a countenance
      white as a sheet,
Near by the corpse of the child that served in the cabin,
The dead face of an old salt with long white hair and carefully curled whiskers,
The flames spite of all that could be done flickering aloft and below,
925 The husky voices of the two or three officers yet fit for duty,
Formless stacks of bodies and bodies by themselves . . . . dabs of flesh upon the
      masts and spars,
The cut of cordage and the dangle of rigging . . . . the slight shock of the soothe
      of waves,
Black and impassive guns, and litter of powder-parcels, and the strong scent,
Delicate sniffs of the seabreeze . . . . smells of sedgy grass and fields by the
      shore . . . . death-messages given in charge to survivors,
930 The hiss of the surgeon's knife and the gnawing teeth of his saw,
The wheeze, the cluck, the swash of falling blood : . . . . the short
      wild scream, the long dull tapering groan,
These so . . . . these irretrievable.

O Christ! My fit is mastering me!
What the rebel said gaily adjusting his throat to the rope-noose,
935 What the savage at the stump, his eye-sockets empty, his mouth spirting
      whoops and defiance,
What stills the traveler come to the vault at Mount Vernon,
What sobers the Brooklyn boy as he looks down the shores of the Wallabout
      and remembers the prison ships,[26]
What burnt the gums of the redcoat at Saratoga[27] when he surrendered his
      brigades,
These become mine and me every one, and they are but little,
940 I become as much more as I like.

I become any presence or truth of humanity here,
And see myself in prison shaped like another man,
And feel the dull unintermitted pain.

For me the keepers of convicts shoulder their carbines and keep watch,
945 It is I let out in the morning and barred at night.

---

[26]British prison ships along Wallabout Bay, where American rebels were held captive during the Revolutionary War
[27]On October 17, 1777, the British General Burgoyne surrendered to American forces at Saratoga;
the battle was a turning point because it enlisted French assistance for the American cause.

Not a mutineer walks handcuffed to the jail, but I am handcuffed to him and
    walk by his side,
I am less the jolly one there, and more the silent one with sweat on my
    twitching lips.

Not a youngster is taken for larceny, but I go up too and am tried and sentenced.

Not a cholera patient lies at the last gasp, but I also lie at the last gasp,
950 My face is ash-colored, my sinews . . . . away from me people retreat.

Askers embody themselves in me, and I am embodied in them,
I project my hat and sit shamefaced and beg.

I rise extatic through all, and sweep with the true gravitation,
The whirling and whirling is elemental within me.

955 Somehow I have been stunned. Stand back!
Give me a little time beyond my cuffed head and slumbers and dreams and
    gaping,
I discover myself on a verge of the usual mistake.

That I could forget the mockers and insults!
That I could forget the trickling tears and the blows of the bludgeons and
    hammers!
960 That I could look with a separate look on my own crucifixion and
    bloody crowning!

I remember . . . . I resume the overstaid fraction,[28]
The grave of rock multiplies what has been confided to it . . . . or to any graves,
The corpses rise . . . . the gashes heal . . . . the fastenings roll away.

I troop forth replenished with supreme power, one of an average unending
    procession,
965 We walk the roads of Ohio and Massachusetts and Virginia and Wisconsin and
    New York and New Orleans and Texas and Montreal and San Francisco and
    Charleston and Savannah and Mexico,
Inland and by the seacoast and boundary lines . . . . and we pass the boundary
    lines.

Our swift ordinances are on their way over the whole earth,
The blossoms we wear in our hats are the growth of two thousand years.

Eleves[29] I salute you,
970 I see the approach of your numberless gangs . . . . I see you understand
    yourselves and me,

---

[28]Whitman's meaning is unclear. The reference may be temporal, alluding to the poet's having stayed
    too long among scenes of suffering and pain. But the words may also allude to Christ as the "over-
    staid fraction" that the poet "resumes" as a living power within himself.
[29]French for students

And know that they who have eyes are divine, and the blind and lame are
    equally divine,
And that my steps drag behind yours yet go before them,
And are aware how I am with you no more than I am with everybody.

The friendly and flowing savage . . . . Who is he?
975 Is he waiting for civilization or past it and mastering it?

Is he some southwesterner raised outdoors? Is he Canadian?
Is he from the Mississippi country? or from Iowa, Oregon or California? or
    from the mountains? or prairie life or bush-life? or from the sea?

Wherever he goes men and women accept and desire him,
They desire he should like them and touch them and speak to them and stay
    with them.

980 Behaviour lawless as snow-flakes . . . . words simple as grass . . . . uncombed
    head and laughter and naivete;
Slowstepping feet and the common features, and the common modes and
    emanations,
They descend in new forms from the tips of his fingers,
They are wafted with the odor of his body or breath . . . . they fly out of the
    glance of his eyes.

Flaunt of the sunshine I need not your bask . . . . lie over,
985 You light surfaces only . . . . I force the surfaces and the depths also.

Earth! you seem to look for something at my hands,
Say old topknot! what do you want?

Man or woman! I might tell how I like you, but cannot,
And might tell what it is in me and what it is in you, but cannot,
990 And might tell the pinings I have . . . . the pulse of my nights and days.

Behold I do not give lectures or a little charity,
What I give I give out of myself.

You there, impotent, loose in the knees, open your scarfed chops till I blow grit
    within you,
Spread your palms and lift the flaps of your pockets,
995 I am not to be denied . . . . I compel . . . . I have stores plenty and to spare,
And any thing I have I bestow.

I do not ask who you are . . . . that is not important to me,
You can do nothing and be nothing but what I will infold you.

To a drudge of the cottonfields or emptier of privies I lean . . . . on his right
    cheek I put the family kiss,
1000 And in my soul I swear I never will deny him.

On women fit for conception I start bigger and nimbler babes,
This day I am jetting the stuff of far more arrogant republics.

To any one dying . . . . thither I speed and twist the knob of the door,
Turn the bedclothes toward the foot of the bed,
1005 Let the physician and the priest go home.

I seize the descending man . . . . I raise him with resistless will.

O despairer, here is my neck,
By God! you shall not go down! Hang your whole weight upon me.

I dilate you with tremendous breath . . . . I buoy you up;
1010 Every room of the house do I fill with an armed force . . . . lovers of me, bafflers
      of graves:
Sleep! I and they keep guard all night;
Not doubt, not decease shall dare to lay finger upon you,
I have embraced you, and henceforth possess you to myself,
And when you rise in the morning you will find what I tell you is so.

1015 I am he bringing help for the sick as they pant on their backs,
And for strong upright men I bring yet more needed help.

I heard what was said of the universe,
Heard it and heard of several thousand years;
It is a middling well as far as it goes . . . . but is that all?

1020 Magnifying and applying come I,
Outbidding at the start the old cautious hucksters,
The most they offer for mankind and eternity less than a spirt of
      my own seminal wet,
Taking myself the exact dimensions of Jehovah and laying them away,
Lithographing Kronos and Zeus his son, and Hercules his grandson,
1025 Buying drafts of Osiris and Isis and Belus and Brahma and Adonai,
In my portfolio placing Manito loose, and Allah on a leaf, and the
      crucifix engraved,
With Odin, and the hideous-faced Mexitli, and all idols and images,[30]
Honestly taking them all for what they are worth, and not a cent more,
Admitting they were alive and did the work of their day,
1030 Admitting they bore mites as for unfledged birds who have now to rise and fly
      and sing for themselves,
Accepting the rough deific sketches to fill out better in myself . . . . bestowing
      them freely on each man and woman I see,

---

[30]Whitman's list of gods includes sacred figures from several different religions: Jehovah (the Jewish
and Christian God); Kronos, Zeus, and Hercules (Greek gods); Osiris and Isis (Egyptian fertility
gods); Belus (a legendary Assyrian king); Brahma (the supreme Hindu spirit); Adonai (Lord, in
Judaism); Manito (an Algonquian Indian spirit); Allah (Moslem god); Odin (a Norwegian god of
war); Mexitli (an Aztec Indian god of war).

Discovering as much or more in a framer framing a house,
Putting higher claims for him there with his rolled-up sleeves, driving the mallet
    and chisel;
Not objecting to special revelations . . . . considering a curl of smoke or a hair
    on the back of my hand as curious as any revelation;
1035 Those ahold of fire-engines and hook-and-ladder ropes more to me than the
    gods of the antique wars,
Minding their voices peal through the crash of destruction,
Their brawny limbs passing safe over charred laths . . . . their white foreheads
    whole and unhurt out of the flames;
By the mechanic's wife with her babe at her nipple interceding for every person
    born;
Three scythes at harvest whizzing in a row from three lusty angels with shirts
    bagged out at their waists;
1040 The snag-toothed hostler with red hair redeeming sins past and to come,
Selling all he possesses and traveling on foot to fee lawyers for his brother and
    sit by him while he is tried for forgery:
What was strewn in the amplest strewing the square rod about me, and not
    filling the square rod then;
The bull and the bug never worshipped half enough,
Dung and dirt more admirable than was dreamed,
1045 The supernatural of no account . . . . myself waiting my time to be one of the
    supremes,
The day getting ready for me when I shall do as much good as the best, and be
    as prodigious,
Guessing when I am it will not tickle me much to receive puffs out of pulpit or
    print;
By my life-lumps! becoming already a creator!
Putting myself here and now to the ambushed womb of the shadows!
1050 . . . . A call in the midst of the crowd,
My own voice, orotund sweeping the final.

Come my children,
Come my boys and girls, and my women and household and intimates,
Now the performer launches his nerve . . . . he has passed his prelude on the
    reeds within.

1055 Easily written loosefingered chords! I feel the thrum of their climax and close.

My head evolves on my neck,
Music rolls, but not from the organ . . . . folks are around me, but they are no
    household of mine.

Ever the hard and unsunk ground,
Ever the eaters and drinkers . . . . ever the upward and downward sun . . . . ever
    the air and the ceaseless tides,
1060 Ever myself and my neighbors, refreshing and wicked and real,

Ever the old inexplicable query . . . . ever that thorned thumb—that breath of
    itches and thirsts,
Ever the vexer's hoot! hoot! till we find where the sly one hides and bring him
    forth;
Ever love . . . . ever the sobbing liquid of life,
Ever the bandage under the chin . . . . ever the tressels of death.

1065 Here and there with dimes on the eyes walking,
To feed the greed of the belly the brains liberally spooning,
Tickets buying or taking or selling, but in to the feast never once going;
Many sweating and ploughing and thrashing, and then the chaff for payment
    receiving,
A few idly owning, and they the wheat continually claiming.

1070 This is the city . . . . and I am one of the citizens;
Whatever interests the rest interests me . . . . politics, churches, newspapers,
    schools,
Benevolent societies, improvements, banks, tariffs, steamships, factories,
    markets,
Stocks and stores and real estate and personal estate.

They who piddle and patter here in collars and tailed coats . . . . I am aware who
    they are . . . . and that they are not worms or fleas,
1075 I acknowledge the duplicates of myself under all the scrape-lipped and
    pipe-legged concealments.

The weakest and shallowest is deathless with me,
What I do and say the same waits for them,
Every thought that flounders in me the same flounders in them.

I know perfectly well my own egotism,
1080 And know my omniverous words, and cannot say any less,
And would fetch you whoever you are flush with myself.

My words are words of a questioning, and to indicate reality;
This printed and bound book . . . . but the printer and the printing-office boy?
The marriage estate and settlement . . . . but the body and mind of the
    bridegroom? also those of the bride?
1085 The panorama of the sea . . . . but the sea itself?
The well-taken photographs . . . . but your wife or friend close and solid in your
    arms?
The fleet of ships of the line and all the modern improvements . . . . but the
    craft and pluck of the admiral?
The dishes and fare and furniture . . . . but the host and hostess, and the look
    out of their eyes?
The sky up there . . . . yet here or next door or across the way?
1090 The saints and sages in history . . . . but you yourself?

Sermons and creeds and theology . . . . but the human brain, and what is called
    reason, and what is called love and what is called life?

I do not despise you priests;
My faith is the greatest of faiths and the least of faiths,
Enclosing all worship ancient and modern, and all between ancient and
    modern,
1095   Believing I shall come again upon the earth after five thousand years,
Waiting responses from oracles . . . . honoring the gods . . . . saluting the sun,
Making a fetish of the first rock or stump . . . . powowing with sticks in the
    circle of obis,[31]
Helping the lama[32] or brahmin as he trims the lamps of the idols,
Dancing yet through the streets in a phallic procession . . . . rapt and austere in
    the woods, a gymnosophist,[33]
1100   Drinking mead from the skull-cup . . . . to shasta and vedas admirant . . . .
    minding the koran,[34]
Walking the teokallis,[35] spotted with gore from the stone and knife—beating the
    serpent-skin drum;
Accepting the gospels, accepting him that was crucified, knowing assuredly that
    he is divine,
To the mass kneeling—to the puritan's prayer rising—sitting patiently in a pew,
Ranting and frothing in my insane crisis—waiting dead-like till my spirit
    arouses me;
1105   Looking forth on pavement and land, and outside of pavement and land,
Belonging to the winders of the circuit of circuits.

One of that centripetal and centrifugal gang,
I turn and talk like a man leaving charges before a journey.

Down-hearted doubters, dull and excluded,
1110   Frivolous sullen moping angry affected disheartened atheistical,
I know every one of you, and know the unspoken interrogatories,
By experience I know them.

How the flukes splash!
How they contort rapid as lightning, with spasms and spouts of blood!

1115   Be at peace bloody flukes of doubters and sullen mopers,
I take my place among you as much as among any;
The past is the push of you and me and all precisely the same,

---

[31]sorcery, of African origin, practiced by blacks in the British West Indies and in the American south
[32]Tibetan high priest; brahmin, Hindu high priest
[33]member of an ancient sect of naked Hindu ascetics
[34]shasta and vedas, Hindu sacred texts; the Koran, the sacred text of Islam
[35]an Aztec temple

And the night is for you and me and all,
And what is yet untried and afterward is for you and me and all.

1120 I do not know what is untried and afterward,
But I know it is sure and alive, and sufficient.

Each who passes is considered, and each who stops is considered, and not a
single one can it fail.

It cannot fail the young man who died and was buried,
Nor the young woman who died and was put by his side,
1125 Nor the little child that peeped in at the door and then drew back and was never
seen again,
Nor the old man who has lived without purpose, and feels it with bitterness
worse than gall,
Nor him in the poorhouse tubercled by rum and the bad disorder,
Nor the numberless slaughtered and wrecked . . . . nor the brutish koboo,[36]
called the ordure of humanity,
Nor the sacs merely floating with open mouths for food to slip in,
1130 Nor any thing in the earth, or down in the oldest graves of the earth,
Nor any thing in the myriads of spheres, nor one of the myriads of myriads that
inhabit them,
Nor the present, nor the least wisp that is known.

It is time to explain myself . . . . let us stand up.

What is known I strip away . . . . I launch all men and women forward with me
into the unknown.

1135 The clock indicates the moment . . . . but what does eternity indicate?

Eternity lies in bottomless reservoirs . . . . its buckets are rising forever and ever,
They pour and they pour and they exhale away.

We have thus far exhausted trillions of winters and summers;
There are trillions ahead, and trillions ahead of them.

1140 Births have brought us richness and variety,
And other births will bring us richness and variety.

I do not call one greater and one smaller,
That which fills its period and place is equal to any.

Were mankind murderous or jealous upon you my brother or my sister?
1145 I am sorry for you . . . . they are not murderous or jealous upon me;
All has been gentle with me . . . . I keep no account with lamentation;
What have I to do with lamentation?

---

[36]native of Sumatra

I am an acme of things accomplished, and I an encloser of things to be.

My feet strike an apex of the apices of the stairs,
1150　On every step bunches of ages, and larger bunches between the steps,
All below duly traveled—and still I mount and mount.

Rise after rise bow the phantoms behind me,
Afar down I see the huge first Nothing, the vapor from the nostrils of death,
I know I was even there . . . . I waited unseen and always,
1155　And slept while God carried me through the lethargic mist,
And took my time . . . . and took no hurt from the foetid carbon.

Long I was hugged close . . . . long and long.

Immense have been the preparations for me,
Faithful and friendly the arms that have helped me.

1160　Cycles ferried my cradle, rowing and rowing like cheerful boatmen;
For room to me stars kept aside in their own rings,
They sent influences to look after what was to hold me.

Before I was born out of my mother generations guided me,
My embryo has never been torpid . . . . nothing could overlay it;
1165　For it the nebula cohered to an orb . . . . the long slow strata piled to rest it
　　　　on . . . . vast vegetables gave it sustenance,
Monstrous sauroids[37] transported it in their mouths and deposited it with care.

All forces have been steadily employed to complete and delight me,
Now I stand on this stop with my soul.

Span of youth! Ever-pushed elasticity! Manhood balanced and florid and full!

1170　My lovers suffocate me!
Crowding my lips, and thick in the pores of my skin,
Jostling me through streets and public halls . . . . coming naked to me at night,
Crying by day Ahoy from the rocks of the river . . . . swinging and chirping over
　　　　my head,
Calling my name from flowerbeds or vines or tangled underbrush,
1175　Or while I swim in the bath . . . . or drink from the pump at the corner . . . . or
　　　　the curtain is down at the opera . . . . or I glimpse at a woman's face in the
　　　　railroad car;
Lighting on every moment of my life,
Bussing[38] my body with soft and balsamic busses,
Noiselessly passing handfuls out of their hearts and giving them to be mine.

Old age superbly rising! Ineffable grace of dying days!

---

[37]prehistoric reptiles
[38]kissing

1180 Every condition promulges not only itself . . . . it promulges what grows after
        and out of itself,
    And the dark hush promulges as much as any.

    I open my scuttle at night and see the far-sprinkled systems,
    And all I see, multiplied as high as I can cipher, edge but the rim of the farther
        systems.

    Wider and wider they spread, expanding and always expanding,
1185 Outward and outward and forever outward.

    My sun has his sun, and round him obediently wheels,
    He joins with his partners a group of superior circuit,
    And greater sets follow, making specks of the greatest inside them.

    There is no stoppage, and never can be stoppage;
1190 If I and you and the worlds and all beneath or upon their surfaces, and all the
        palpable life, were this moment reduced back to a pallid float, it would not
        avail in the long run,
    We should surely bring up again where we now stand,
    And as surely go as much farther, and then farther and farther.

    A few quadrillions of eras, a few octillions of cubic leagues, do not hazard the
        span, or make it impatient,
    They are but parts . . . . any thing is but a part.

1195 See ever so far . . . . there is limitless space outside of that,
    Count ever so much . . . . there is limitless time around that.

    Our rendezvous is fitly appointed . . . . God will be there and wait till we come.

    I know I have the best of time and space—and that I was never measured, and
        never will be measured.

    I tramp a perpetual journey,
1200 My signs are a rain-proof coat and good shoes and a staff cut from the woods;
    No friend of mine takes his ease in my chair,
    I have no chair, nor church nor philosophy;
    I lead no man to a dinner-table or library or exchange,
    But each man and each woman of you I lead upon a knoll,
1205 My left hand hooks you round the waist,
    My right hand points to landscapes of continents, and a plain public road.

    Not I, not any one else can travel that road for you,
    You must travel it for yourself.

    It is not far . . . . it is within reach,
1210 Perhaps you have been on it since you were born, and did not know,
    Perhaps it is every where on water and on land.

Shoulder your duds, and I will mine, and let us hasten forth;
Wonderful cities and free nations we shall fetch as we go.

If you tire, give me both burdens, and rest the chuff of your hand on my hip,
1215 And in due time you shall repay the same service to me;
For after we start we never lie by again.

This day before dawn I ascended a hill and looked at the crowded heaven,
And I said to my spirit, When we become the enfolders of those orbs and the
     pleasure and knowledge of every thing in them, shall we be filled and
     satisfied then?
And my spirit said No, we level that lift to pass and continue beyond.
1220 You are also asking me questions, and I hear you;
I answer that I cannot answer . . . . you must find out for yourself.

Sit awhile wayfarer,
Here are biscuits to eat and here is milk to drink,
But as soon as you sleep and renew yourself in sweet clothes I will certainly kiss
     you with my goodbye kiss and open the gate for your egress hence.

1225 Long enough have you dreamed contemptible dreams,
Now I wash the gum from your eyes,
You must habit yourself to the dazzle of the light and of every moment of your
     life.

Long have you timidly waded, holding a plank by the shore,
Now I will you to be a bold swimmer,
1230 To jump off in the midst of the sea, and rise again and nod to me and shout,
     and laughingly dash with your hair.

I am the teacher of athletes,
He that by me spreads a wider breast than my own proves the width of my own,
He most honors my style who learns under it to destroy the teacher.

The boy I love, the same becomes a man not through derived power but in his
     own right,
1235 Wicked, rather than virtuous out of conformity or fear,
Fond of his sweetheart, relishing well his steak,
Unrequited love or a slight cutting him worse than a wound cuts,
First rate to ride, to fight, to hit the bull's eye, to sail a skiff, to sing a song or
     play on the banjo,
Preferring scars and faces pitted with smallpox over all latherers and those that
     keep out of the sun.

1240 I teach straying from me, yet who can stray from me?
I follow you whoever you are from the present hour;
My words itch at your ears till you understand them.

I do not say these things for a dollar, or to fill up the time while I wait for a boat;
It is you talking just as much myself . . . . I act as the tongue of you,
1245 It was tied in your mouth . . . . in mine it begins to be loosened.

I swear I will never mention love or death inside a house,
And I swear I never will translate myself at all, only to him or her who privately
    stays with me in the open air.

If you would understand me go to the heights or water-shore,
The nearest gnat is an explanation and a drop or the motion of waves a key,
1250 The maul the oar and the handsaw second my words.

No shuttered room or school can commune with me,
But roughs and little children better than they.

The young mechanic is closest to me . . . . he knows me pretty well,
The woodman that takes his axe and jug with him shall take me with him all
    day,
1255 The farmboy ploughing in the field feels good at the sound of my voice,
In vessels that sail my words must sail . . . . I go with fishermen and seamen, and
    love them,
My face rubs to the hunter's face when he lies down alone in his blanket,
The driver thinking of me does not mind the jolt of his wagon,
The young mother and old mother shall comprehend me,
1260 The girl and the wife rest the needle a moment and forget where they are,
They and all would resume what I have told them.

I have said that the soul is not more than the body,
And I have said that the body is not more than the soul,
And nothing, not God, is greater to one than one's self is,
1265 And whoever walks a furlong without sympathy walks to his own funeral,
    dressed in his shroud,
And I or you pocketless of a dime may purchase the pick of the earth,
And to glance with an eye or show a bean in its pod confounds the learning of
    all times,
And there is no trade or employment but the young man following it may
    become a hero,
And there is no object so soft but it makes a hub for the wheeled universe,
1270 And any man or woman shall stand cool and supercilious before a
    million universes.

And I call to mankind, Be not curious about God,
For I who am curious about each am not curious about God,
No array of terms can say how much I am at peace about God and about
    death.

I hear and behold God in every object, yet I understand God not in the least,
1275 Nor do I understand who there can be more wonderful than myself.

Why should I wish to see God better than this day?
I see something of God each hour of the twenty-four, and each moment then,
In the faces of men and women I see God, and in my own face in the glass;
I find letters from God dropped in the street, and every one is signed by God's
  name,
1280 And I leave them where they are, for I know that others will punctually come
  forever and ever.

And as to you death, and you bitter hug of mortality . . . . it is idle to try to
  alarm me.

To his work without flinching the accoucheur[39] comes,
I see the elderhand pressing receiving supporting,
I recline by the sills of the exquisite flexible doors . . . . and mark the outlet, and
  mark the relief and escape.
1285 And as to you corpse I think you are good manure, but that does not offend me,
I smell the white roses sweetscented and growing,
I reach to the leafy lips . . . . I reach to the polished breasts of melons.

And as to you life, I reckon you are the leavings of many deaths,
No doubt I have died myself ten thousand times before.

1290 I hear you whispering there O stars of heaven,
O suns . . . . O grass of graves . . . . O perpetual transfers and promotions . . . . if
  you do not say anything how can I say anything?

Of the turbid pool that lies in the autumn forest,
Of the moon that descends the steeps of the soughing twilight,
Toss, sparkles of day and dusk . . . . toss on the black stems that decay in the
  muck,
1295 Toss to the moaning gibberish of the dry limbs.

I ascend from the moon . . . . I ascend from the night,
And perceive of the ghastly glitter the sunbeams reflected,
And debouch[40] to the steady and central from the offspring great or small.

There is that in me . . . . I do not know what it is . . . . but I know it is in me.

1300 Wrenched and sweaty . . . . calm and cool then my body becomes;
I sleep . . . . I sleep long.

I do not know it . . . . it is without name . . . . it is a word unsaid,
It is not in any dictionary or utterance or symbol.

Something it swings on more than the earth I swing on,
1305 To it the creation is the friend whose embracing awakes me.

---

[39]French for midwife
[40]from the French word *deboucher,* to issue forth

Perhaps I might tell more . . . . Outlines! I plead for my brothers and sisters.

Do you see O my brothers and sisters?
It is not chaos or death . . . . it is form and union and plan . . . . it is eternal
    life . . . . it is happiness.

The past and present wilt . . . . I have filled them and emptied them,
1310 And proceed to fill my next fold of the future.

Listener up there! Here you . . . . what have you to confide to me?
Look in my face while I snuff the sidle of evening,
Talk honestly, for no one else hears you, and I stay only a minute longer.

Do I contradict myself?
1315 Very well then . . . . I contradict myself;
I am large . . . . I contain multitudes.

I concentrate toward them that are nigh . . . . I wait on the door-slab.

Who has done his day's work and will soonest be through with his supper?
Who wishes to walk with me?

1320 Will you speak before I am gone? Will you prove already too late?

The spotted hawk swoops by and accuses me . . . . he complains of my gab and
    my loitering.

I too am not a bit tamed . . . . I too am untranslatable,
I sound my barbaric yawp over the roofs of the world.

The last scud of day holds back for me,
1325 It flings my likeness after the rest and true as any on the shadowed wilds,
It coaxes me to the vapor and the dusk.

I depart as air . . . . I shake my white locks at the runaway sun,
I effuse my flesh in eddies and drift it in lacy jags.

I bequeath myself to the dirt to grow from the grass I love,
1330 If you want me again look for me under your bootsoles.

You will hardly know who I am or what I mean,
But I shall be good health to you nevertheless,
And filter and fibre your blood.

Failing to fetch me at first keep encouraged,
1335 Missing me one place search another
I stop some where waiting for you[41]

1855

---

[41]There is no period at the end of the original version of "Song of Myself," an omission that Whitman
    as scrupulous editor of his poems surely intended.

When I Heard the Learn'd Astronomer

When I heard the learn'd astronomer,
When the proofs, the figures, were ranged in columns before me,
When I was shown the charts and diagrams, to add, divide, and measure them,
When I sitting heard the astronomer where he lectured with much applause in
      the lecture-room,
5 How soon unaccountable I became tired and sick,
Till rising and gliding out I wander'd off by myself,
In the mystical moist night-air, and from time to time,
Look'd up in perfect silence at the stars.

1865

When Lilacs Last in the Dooryard Bloom'd[1]

1

When lilacs last in the dooryard bloom'd,
And the great star early dropp'd in the western sky in the night,
I mourn'd, and yet shall mourn with ever-returning spring.

Ever-returning spring, trinity sure to me you bring,
5 Lilac blooming perennial and drooping star in the west,
And thought of him I love.

2

O powerful western fallen star!
O shades of night—O moody, tearful night!
O great star disappear'd—O the black murk that hides the star!
10 O cruel hands that hold me powerless—O helpless soul of me!
O harsh surrounding cloud that will not free my soul.

3

In the dooryard fronting an old farm-house near the white-wash'd palings,
Stands the lilac-bush tall-growing with heart-shaped leaves of rich green,
With many a pointed blossom rising delicate, with the perfume strong I love,
15 With every leaf a miracle—and from this bush in the dooryard,
With delicate-color'd blossoms and heart-shaped leaves of rich green,
A sprig with its flower I break.

4

In the swamp in secluded recesses,
A shy and hidden bird is warbling a song,

---

[1]This poem is an elegy to Abraham Lincoln.

20 Solitary the thrush,
  The hermit withdrawn to himself, avoiding the settlements,
  Sings by himself a song.

  Song of the bleeding throat,
  Death's outlet song of life, (for well dear brother I know,
25 If thou wast not granted to sing thou would'st surely die.)

5

  Over the breast of the spring, the land, amid cities,
  Amid lanes and through old woods, where lately the violets peep'd from the
      ground, spotting the gray debris,
  Amid the grass in the fields each side of the lanes, passing the endless grass,
  Passing the yellow-spear'd wheat, every grain from its shroud in the
      dark-brown fields uprisen,
30 Passing the apple-tree blows of white and pink in the orchards,
  Carrying a corpse to where it shall rest in the grave,
  Night and day journeys a coffin.

6

  Coffin that passes through lanes and streets,
  Through day and night with the great cloud darkening the land,
35 With the pomp of the inloop'd flags with the cities draped in black,
  With the show of the States themselves as of crape-veil'd women standing,
  With processions long and winding and the flambeaus of the night,
  With the countless torches lit, with the silent sea of faces and the unbared
      heads,
  With the waiting depot, the arriving coffin, and the sombre faces,
40 With dirges through the night, with the thousand voices rising strong
      and solemn,
  With all the mournful voices of the dirges pour'd around the coffin,
  The dim-lit churches and the shuddering organs—where amid these you
      journey,
  With the tolling tolling bells' perpetual clang,
  Here, coffin that slowly passes,
45 I give you my sprig of lilac.

7

  (Nor for you, for one alone,
  Blossoms and branches green to coffins all I bring,
  For fresh as the morning, thus would I chant a song for you O sane and sacred
      death.

  All over bouquets of roses,
50 O death, I cover you over with roses and early lilies,

But mostly and now the lilac that blooms the first,
Copious I break, I break the sprigs from the bushes,
With loaded arms I come, pouring for you,
For you and the coffins all of you O death.)

8

55 O western orb sailing the heaven,
Now I know what you must have meant as a month since I walk'd,
As I walk'd in silence the transparent shadowy night,
As I saw you had something to tell as you bent to me night after night,
As you droop'd from the sky low down as if to my side, (while the other star's all
    look'd on,)
60 As we wander'd together the solemn night, (for something I know not what
    kept me from sleep,)
As the night advanced, and I saw on the rim of the west how full you were of
    woe,
As I stood on the rising ground in the breeze in the cool transparent night,
As I watch'd where you pass'd and was lost in the netherward black of the night,
As my soul in its trouble dissatisfied sank, as where you sad orb,
65 Concluded, dropt in the night, and was gone.

9

Sing on there in the swamp,
O singer bashful and tender, I hear your notes, I hear your call,
I hear, I come presently, I understand you,
But a moment I linger, for the lustrous star has detain'd me,
70 The star my departing comrade holds and detains me.

10

O how shall I warble myself for the dead one there I loved?
And how shall I deck my song for the large sweet soul that has gone?
And what shall my perfume be for the grave of him I love?

Sea-winds blown from east and west,
75 Blown from the Eastern sea and blown from the Western sea, till there on the
    prairies meeting,
These and with these and the breath of my chant,
I'll perfume the grave of him I love.

11

O what shall I hang on the chamber walls?
And what shall the pictures be that I hang on the walls,
80 To adorn the burial-house of him I love?

Pictures of growing spring and farms and homes,
With the Fourth-month eve at sundown, and the gray smoke lucid and bright,
With floods of the yellow gold of the gorgeous, indolent, sinking sun, burning,
    expanding the air,
With the fresh sweet herbage under foot, and the pale green leaves of the trees
    prolific,
85 In the distance the flowing glaze, the breast of the river, with a wind-dapple
    here and there,
With ranging hills on the banks, with many a line against the sky, and shadows,
And the city at hand with dwellings so dense, and stacks of chimneys,
And all the scenes of life and the workshops, and the workmen homeward
    returning.

12

Lo, body and soul—this land,
90 My own Manhattan with spires, and the sparkling and hurrying tides, and the
    ships,
The varied and ample land, the South and the North in the light, Ohio's shores
    and flashing Missouri,
And ever the far-spreading prairies cover'd with grass and corn.

Lo, the most excellent sun so calm and haughty,
The violet and purple morn with just-felt breezes,
95 The gentle soft-born measureless light,
The miracle spreading bathing all, the fulfill'd noon,
The coming eve delicious, the welcome night and the stars,
Over my cities shining all, enveloping man and land.

13

Sing on, sing on you gray-brown bird,
100 Sing from the swamps, the recesses, pour your chant from the bushes,
Limitless out of the dusk, out of the cedars and pines.

Sing on dearest brother, warble your reedy song,
Loud human song, with voice of uttermost woe.

O liquid and free and tender!
105 O wild and loose to my soul—O wondrous singer!
You only I hear—yet the star holds me, (but will soon depart,)
Yet the lilac with mastering odor holds me.

14

Now while I sat in the day and look'd forth,
In the close of the day with its light and the fields of spring, and the farmers
    preparing their crops,

110 In the large unconscious scenery of my land with its lakes and forests,
In the heavenly aerial beauty, (after the perturb'd winds and the storms,)
Under the arching heavens of the afternoon swift passing, and the voices of
    children and women.
The many-moving sea-tides, and I saw the ships how they sail'd,
And the summer approaching with richness, and the fields all busy with
    labor,
115 And the infinite separate houses, how they all went on, each with its
    meals and minutia of daily usages,
And the streets how their throbbings throbb'd, and the cities pent—lo, then and
    there,
Falling upon them all and among them all, enveloping me with the rest,
Appear'd the cloud, appear'd the long black trail,
And I knew death, its thought, and the sacred knowledge of death.

120 Then with the knowledge of death as walking one side of me,
And the thought of death close-walking the other side of me,
And I in the middle as with companions, and as holding the hands of
    companions,
I fled forth to the hiding receiving night that talks not,
Down to the shores of the water, the path by the swamp in the dimness,
125 To the solemn shadowy cedars and ghostly pines so still.

And the singer so shy to the rest receiv'd me,
The gray-brown bird I know receiv'd us comrades three,
And he sang the carol of death, and a verse for him I love.

From deep secluded recesses,
130 From the fragrant cedars and the ghostly pines so still,
Came the carol of the bird.

And the charm of the carol rapt me,
As I held as if by their hands my comrades in the night,
And the voice of my spirit tallied the song of the bird.

135 *Come lovely and soothing death,*
Undulate round the world, serenely arriving, arriving,
In the day, in the night, to all, to each,
Sooner or later delicate death.

Prais'd be the fathomless universe,
140 *For life and joy, and for objects and knowledge curious,*
And for love, sweet love—but praise! praise! praise!
For the sure-enwinding arms of cool-enfolding death.

Dark mother always gliding near with soft feet,
Have none chanted for thee a chant of fullest welcome?

145 *Then I chant it for thee, I glorify thee above all,*
   I bring thee a song that when thou must indeed come, come unfalteringly.

   Approach strong deliveress,
   When it is so, when thou hast taken them I joyously sing the dead,
   Lost in the loving floating ocean of thee,
150 *Laved in the flood of thy bliss O death.*

   From me to thee glad serenades,
   Dances for thee I propose saluting thee, adornments, and feastings for thee,
   And the sights of the open landscape and the high-spread sky are fitting,
   And life and the fields, and the huge and thoughtful night.

155 *The night in silence under many a star,*
   The ocean shore and the husky whispering wave whose voice I know,
   And the soul turning to thee O vast and well-veil'd death,
   And the body gratefully nestling close to thee.

   Over the tree-tops I float thee a song,
160 *Over the rising and sinking waves, over the myriad fields and the prairies wide,*
   Over the dense-pack'd cities all and the teeming wharves and ways,
   I float this carol with joy, with joy to thee O death.

15

   To the tally of my soul,
   Loud and strong kept up the gray-brown bird,
165 With pure deliberate notes spreading filling the night.

   Loud in the pines and cedars dim,
   Clear in the freshness moist and the swamp-perfume,
   And I with my comrades there in the night.

   While my sight that was bound in my eyes unclosed,
170 As to long panoramas of visions.

   And I saw askant the armies,
   I saw as in noiseless dreams hundreds of battle-flags,
   Borne through the smoke of the battles and pierc'd with missiles I saw them,
   And carried hither and yon through the smoke, and torn and bloody,
175 And at last but a few shreds left on the staffs, (and all in silence,)
   And the staffs all splinter'd and broken.

   I saw battle-corpses, myriads of them,
   And the white skeletons of young men, I saw them,
   I saw the debris and debris of all the slain soldiers of the war,
180 But I saw they were not as was thought,
   They themselves were fully at rest, they suffer'd not,

The living remain'd and suffer'd, the mother suffer'd,
And the wife and the child and the musing comrade suffer'd,
And the armies that remain'd suffer'd.

16

185 Passing the visions, passing the night,
Passing, unloosing the hold of my comrade's hands,
Passing the song of the hermit bird and the tallying song of my soul,
Victorious song, death's outlet song, yet varying ever-altering song,
As low and wailing, yet clear the notes, rising and falling, flooding the night,
190 Sadly sinking and fainting, as warning and warning, and yet again bursting with
    joy,
Covering the earth and filling the spread of the heaven,
As that powerful psalm in the night I heard from recesses,
Passing, I leave thee lilac with heart-shaped leaves,
I leave thee there in the door-yard, blooming, returning with spring.

195 I cease from my song for thee,
From my gaze on thee in the west, fronting the west, communing with thee,
O comrade lustrous with silver face in the night.

Yet each to keep and all, retrievements out of the night,
The song, the wondrous chant of the gray-brown bird,
200 And the tallying chant, the echo arous'd in my soul,
With the lustrous and drooping star with the countenance full of woe,
With the holders holding my hand nearing the call of the bird,
Comrades mine and I in the midst, and their memory ever to keep, for the dead
    I loved so well,
For the sweetest, wisest soul of all my days and lands—and this for his dear
    sake,
205 Lilac and star and bird twined with the chant of my soul,
There in the fragrant pines and the cedars dusk and dim.

                                                              1865

A Noiseless Patient Spider

A noiseless patient spider,
I mark'd where on a little promontory it stood isolated,
Mark'd how to explore the vacant vast surrounding,
It launch'd forth filament, filament, filament, out of itself,
 5 Ever unreeling down, ever tirelessly speeding them.

And you O my soul where you stand,
Surrounded, detached, in measureless oceans of space,

Ceaselessly musing, venturing, throwing, seeking the spheres to connect them,
Till the bridge you will need be form'd, till the ductile anchor hold,
10 Till the gossamer thread you fling catch somewhere, O my soul.

1868

Alice Cary

(1820–1871)

The Bridal Veil

We're married, they say, and you think you have won me,—
Well, take this white veil from my head, and look on me;
Here's matter to vex you, and matter to grieve you,
Here's doubt to distrust you, and faith to believe you,—
5 I am all as you see, common earth, common dew;
Be wary, and mould me to roses, not rue!

Ah! shake out the filmy thing, fold after fold,
And see if you have me to keep and to hold,—
Look close on my heart—see the worst of its sinning,—
10 It is not yours to-day for the yesterday's winning—
The past is not mine—I am too proud to borrow—
You must grow to new heights if I love you to-morrow.

I have wings flattened down and hid under my veil:
They are subtle as light—you can never undo them,
15 And swift in their flight—you can never pursue them,
And spite of all clasping, and spite of all bands,
I can slip like a shadow, a dream, from your hands.

Nay, call me not cruel, and fear not to take me,
I am yours for my life-time, to be what you make me,—
20 To wear my white veil for a sign, or a cover,
As you shall be proven my lord, or my lover;
A cover for peace that is dead, or a token
Of bliss that can never be written or spoken.

The West Country

Have you been in our wild west country? then
   You have often had to pass
Its cabins lying like bird's nests in
   The wild green prairie grass.

5 Have you seen the women forget their wheels
    As they sat at the door to spin—
Have you seen the darning fall away
    From their fingers worn and thin,

As they asked you news of the villages
10   Where they were used to be,
Gay girls at work in the factories
    With their lovers gone to sea!

Ah, have you thought of the bravery
    That no loud praise provokes—
15 Of the tragedies acted in the lives
    Or poor, hard-working folks!

Of the little more, and the little more
    Of hardship which they press
Upon their own tired hands to make
20   The toil for the children less:

And not in vain; for many a lad
    Born to rough work and ways,
Strips off his ragged coat, and makes
    Men clothe him with their praise.

Matthew Arnold

(1822–1888)

Shakespeare

Others abide our question. Thou art free.
We ask and ask—thou smilest and art still,
Out-topping knowledge. For the loftiest hill,
Who to the stars uncrowns his majesty,

5 Planting his stedfast footsteps in the sea,
Making the heaven of heavens his dwelling-place,
Spares but the cloudy border of his base
To the foiled searching of mortality;

And thou, who didst the stars and sunbeams know,
10 Self-schooled, self-scanned, self-honored, self-secure,
Didst tread on earth unguessed at—better so!

All pains the immortal spirit must endure,
All weakness which impairs, all griefs which bow,
Find their sole speech in that victorious brow.

1849

Dover Beach

The sea is calm tonight.
The tide is full, the moon lies fair
Upon the straits;—on the French coast the light
Gleams and is gone; the cliffs of England stand,
5 Glimmering and vast, out in the tranquil bay.
Come to the window, sweet is the night-air!
Only, from the long line of spray
Where the sea meets the moon-blanched land,
Listen! you hear the grating roar
10 Of pebbles which the waves draw back, and fling,
At their return, up the high strand,
Begin, and cease, and then again begin,
With tremulous cadence slow, and bring
The eternal note of sadness in.

15 Sophocles long ago
Heard it on the Aegean, and it brought
Into his mind the turbid ebb and flow
Of human misery; we
Find also in the sound a thought,
20 Hearing it by this distant northern sea.

The Sea of Faith
Was once, too, at the full, and round earth's shore
Lay like the folds of a bright girdle furled.
But now I only hear
25 Its melancholy, long, withdrawing road,
Retreating, to the breath
Of the night-wind, down the vast edges drear
And naked shingles of the world.

Ah, love, let us be true
30 To one another! for the world, which seems
To lie before us like a land of dreams,
So various, so beautiful, so new,
Hath really neither joy, nor love, nor light,
Nor certitude, nor peace, nor help for pain;
35 And we are here as on a darkling plain

Swept with confused alarms of struggle and flight,
Where ignorant armies clash by night.

1867

Emily Dickinson

(1830–1886)

Success is counted sweetest (#67)

Success is counted sweetest
By those who ne'er succeed.
To comprehend a nectar[1]
Requires sorest need.

5 Not one of all the purple Host
Who took the Flag[2] today
Can tell the definition
So clear of Victory

As he defeated—dying—
10 On whose forbidden ear
The distant strains of triumph
Burst agonized and clear!

1890

I taste a liquor never brewed (#214)

I taste a liquor never brewed—
From Tankards scooped in Pearl—
Not all the Vats upon the Rhine
Yield such an Alcohol!

5 Inebriate of Air—am I—
And Debauchee of Dew—
Reeling—thro endless summer days—
From inns of Molten Blue—

When "Landlords" turn the drunken Bee
10 Out of the Foxglove's door—

---

[1]drink of Greek and Roman gods
[2]vanquished the enemy

When Butterflies—renounce their "drams"—
I shall but drink the more!

Till Seraphs swing their snowy Hats—
And Saints—to windows run—
15 To see the little Tippler
Leaning against the—Sun—

                                                                    1860

I like a look of Agony (#241)

I like a look of Agony,
Because I know it's true—
Men do not sham Convulsion,
Nor simulate, a Throe—

5 The Eyes glaze once—and that is Death—
Impossible to feign
The Beads upon the Forehead
By homely Anguish Strung.

                                                                    1890

Wild Nights—Wild Nights! (#249)

Wild Nights—Wild Nights!
Were I with thee
Wild Nights should be
Our luxury!

5 Futile—the Winds—
To a Heart in port—
Done with the Compass—
Done with the Chart!

Rowing in Eden—
10 Ah, the Sea!
Might I but moor—Tonight—
In Thee![1]

                                                                    1891

I can wade Grief (#252)

I can wade Grief—
Whole Pools of it—
I'm used to that—

---

[1]Dickinson juxtaposes stormy nights with lovers' sheltered ports and moorings.

But the least push of Joy
5 Breaks up my feet—
And I tip—drunken—
Let no Pebble—smile—
'Twas the New Liquor—
That was all!
10 Power is only Pain—
Stranded, thro' Discipline,
Till Weights—will hang—
Give Balm—to Giants—
And they'll wilt, like Men—
15 Give Himmaleh—[1]
They'll Carry—Him!

                                        1891

There's a certain Slant of light (#258)

There's a certain Slant of light,
Winter Afternoons—
That oppresses, like the Heft
Of Cathedral Tunes—

5 Heavenly Hurt, it gives us—
We can find no scar,
But internal difference,
Where the Meanings, are—

None may teach it—Any—
10 'Tis the Seal Despair—
An imperial affliction
Sent us of the Air—

When it comes, the Landscape listens—
Shadows—hold their breath—
15 When it goes, 'tis like the Distance
On the look of Death—

                                        1860

I felt a Funeral, in my Brain (#280)

I felt a Funeral, in my Brain
And Mourners to and fro
Kept treading—treading—till it seemed
That Sense was breaking through—[1]

---

[1]a personification of the Himalayan Mountains

---

[1]Sense was giving way.

5 And when they all were seated,
   A Service, like a Drum—
   Kept beating—beating—till I thought
   My Mind was going numb—

   And then I heard them lift a Box
10 And creak across my Soul
   With those same Boots of Lead, again,
   The Space—began to toll,

   As[2] all the Heavens were a Bell,
   And Being, but an Ear,
15 And I, and Silence, some strange Race
   Wrecked, solitary, here—

   And then a Plank in Reason, broke,
   And I dropped down, and down—
   And hit a World, at every plunge,
20 And Finished knowing—then—

                                                        1896

I'm Nobody! Who are you? (#288)

   I'm Nobody! Who are you?
   Are you—Nobody—too?
   Then there's a pair of us!
   Don't tell! they'd banish us—you know!

5 How dreary—to be—Somebody!
   How public—like a Frog—
   To tell your name—the livelong June—
   To an admiring Bog!

                                                        1891

The Soul selects her own Society (#303)

   The Soul selects her own Society—
   Then—shuts the Door—
   To her divine Majority—
   Present no more—

5 Unmoved—she notes the Chariots—pausing—
   At her low Gate—
   Unmoved—an Emperor be kneeling
   Upon her Mat—

---

[2]As if; Dickinson often uses "as" in this way.

I've known her—from an ample nation—
10 Choose One—
Then—close the Valves of her attention—
Like Stone—

                                                        1890

A Bird came down the Walk (#328)

A Bird came down the Walk—
He did not know I saw—
He bit an Angleworm in halves
And ate the fellow, raw,

5 And then he drank a Dew
From a convenient Grass—
And then hopped sidewise to the Wall
To let a Beetle pass—

He glanced with rapid eyes
10 That hurried all around—
They looked like frightened Beads, I thought—
He stirred his Velvet Head

Like one in danger, Cautious,
I offered him a Crumb
15 And he unrolled his feathers
And rowed him softer home—

Than Oars divide the Ocean,
Too silver for a seam—
Or Butterflies, off Banks of Noon
20 Leap, plashless[1] as they swim.

                                                        1891

After great pain, a formal feeling comes (#341)

After great pain, a formal feeling comes—
The Nerves sit ceremonious, like Tombs—
The stiff Heart questions was it He, that bore,
And Yesterday, or Centuries before?

5 The Feet, mechanical, go round—
Of Ground, or Air, or Ought—[1]

---
[1]splashless
---
[1]Dickinson's spelling of *aught;* anything

A Wooden way
Regardless grown,[2]
A Quartz contentment, like a stone—

10 This is the Hour of Lead—
Remembered, if outlived,
As Freezing persons, recollect the Snow—
First—Chill—then Stupor—then the letting go—

1929

Much Madness is divinest Sense (#435)

Much Madness is divinest Sense—
To a discerning Eye—
Much Sense—the starkest Madness—
'Tis the Majority
5 In this, as All, prevail—
Assent—and you are sane—
Demur—you're straightway dangerous—
And handled with a Chain—

1861

This is my letter to the World (#441)[1]

This is my letter to the World
That never wrote to Me—
The simple News that Nature told—
With tender Majesty

5 Her Message is committed
To Hands I cannot see—
For love of Her—Sweet—countrymen—
Judge tenderly—of Me

1890

I heard a Fly buzz—when I died (#465)

I heard a Fly buzz—when I died—
The Stillness in the Room
Was like the Stillness in the Air—
Between the Heaves of Storm—

---

[2]having stopped noticing

[1]This poem was placed by Higginson and Todd just after the table of contents and before the first
page of selections in the first edition of Dickinson's poetry, published in 1890. There is no indica-
tion that she intended it as an introduction to all of the fascicles; it is lodged in fascicle 24 where it
shares a page with part of another poem.

5 The Eyes around—had wrung them dry—
And Breaths were gathering firm
For the last Onset—when the King
Be witnessed—in the Room—

I willed my Keepsakes—Signed away
10 What portion of me be
Assignable—and then it was
There interposed a Fly—

With Blue—uncertain—stumbling Buzz—
Between the light—and me—
15 And then the Windows failed—and then
I could not see to see—

1896

Pain—has an Element of Blank (#650)

Pain—has an Element of Blank—
It cannot recollect
When it begun—or if there were
A time when it was not—

5 It has no Future—but itself—
It's[1] Infinite contain
It's Past—enlightened to perceive
New Periods—of Pain.

1890

Because I could not stop for Death (#712)

Because I could not stop for Death—
He kindly stopped for me—
The Carriage held but just Ourselves—
And Immortality.

5 We slowly drove—He knew no haste
And I had put away
My labor and my leisure too,
For His Civility—

We passed the School, where Children strove
10 At Recess—in the Ring—
We passed the Fields of Gazing Grain—
We passed the Setting Sun—

---

[1]Use of the possessive *its* with an apostrophe is an error that Dickinson made consistently.

Or rather—He passed Us—
The Dews drew quivering and chill—
15 For only Gossamer, my Gown—
My Tippet¹—only Tulle—

We paused before a House that seemed
A Swelling of the Ground—
The Roof was scarcely visible—
20 The Cornice—in the Ground—

Since then—'tis Centuries—and yet
Feels shorter than the Day
I first surmised the Horses' Heads
Were toward Eternity—

1862

My Life had stood—a Loaded Gun (#754)

My Life had stood—a Loaded Gun—
In Corners—till a Day
The Owner passed—identified—
And carried Me away—

5 And now We roam in Sovreign Woods—
And now We hunt the Doe—
And every time I speak for Him—
The Mountains straight reply—

And do I smile, such cordial light
10 Upon the Valley glow—
It is as a Vesuvian¹ face
Had let it's pleasure through—

And when at Night—Our good Day done—
I guard My Master's Head—
15 'Tis better than the Eider-Duck's²
Deep Pillow—to have shared—

To foe of His—I'm deadly foe—
None stir the second time—
On whom I lay a Yellow Eye—
20 Or an Emphatic Thumb—

---

¹a short cape

---

¹volcanic, like Mt. Vesuvius in Italy; capable of breathing fire, light, and destruction
²downy (with duck down)

Though I than He—may longer live
He longer must—than I—
For I have but the power to kill,
Without—the power to die—

1863

The Poets light but Lamps (#883)

The Poets light but Lamps—
Themselves—go out—
The Wicks they stimulate—
If vital Light

5 Inhere as do the Suns—
Each Age a Lens
Disseminating their
Circumference—

1863

A narrow Fellow in the Grass (#986)

A narrow Fellow in the Grass
Occasionally rides—
You may have met Him—did you not
His notice sudden is—

5 The Grass divides as with a Comb—
A spotted Shaft is seen—
And then it closes at your feet
And opens further on—

He likes a Boggy Acre
10 A Floor too cool for Corn—
Yet when a Boy, and Barefoot—
I more than once at Noon
Have passed, I thought, a Whip lash
Unbraiding in the Sun
15 When stooping to secure it
It wrinkled, and was gone—

Several of Nature's People
I know, and they know me—
I feel for them a transport
20 Of Cordiality—

But never met this Fellow
Attended, or alone

Without a tighter breathing
And Zero at the Bone—

1865

I never saw a Moor (#1052)

I never saw a Moor—
I never saw the Sea—
Yet know I how the Heather looks
And what a Billow be.

5 I never spoke with God
Nor visited in Heaven—
Yet certain am I of the spot
As if the Checks were given—

1864

The Bustle in a House (#1078)

The Bustle in a House
The Morning after Death
Is solemnest of industries
Enacted upon Earth—

5 The Sweeping up the Heart
And putting Love away
We shall not want to use again
Until Eternity.

1865

Tell all the Truth but tell it slant (#1129)

Tell all the Truth but tell it slant—
Success in Circuit lies
Too bright for our infirm Delight
The Truth's superb surprise
5 As Lightning to the Children eased
With explanation kind
The Truth must dazzle gradually
Or every man be blind—

1866

A Route of Evanescence (#1463)

A Route of Evanescence
With a revolving Wheel—
A Resonance of Emerald—

A Rush of Cochineal—[1]
5 And every Blossom on the Bush
Adjusts it's tumbled Head—
The mail from Tunis,[2] probably,
An easy Morning's Ride—[3]

1879

My life closed twice before its close (#1732)

My life closed twice before its close—
It yet remains to see
If Immortality unveil
A third event to me

5 So huge, so hopeless to conceive
As these that twice befell.
Parting is all we know of heaven,
And all we need of hell.

1868

To make a prairie it takes a clover and one bee (#1755)

To make a prairie it takes a clover and one bee,
One clover, and a bee,
And revery.
The revery alone will do,
5 If bees are few.

1896

Helen Hunt Jackson

(1830–1885)

Her Eyes

That they are brown, no man will dare to say
He knows. And yet I think that no man's look
Ever those depths of light and shade forsook,
Until their gentle pain warned him away.

---

[1]brilliant red dye
[2]an African city in Tunisia, near the ancient site of Carthage
[3]Dickinson sent copies of this poem in several letters to friends and referred to it as "A Humming Bird."

5 Of all sweet things I know but one which may
   Be likened to her eyes.
                     When, in deep nook
   Of some green field, the water of a brook
   Makes lingering, whirling eddy in its way,
   Round soft drowned leaves; and in a flash of sun
10 They turn to gold, until the ripples run
   Now brown, now yellow, changing as by some
   Swift spell.
               I know not with what body come
   The saints. But this I know, my Paradise
15 Will mean the resurrection of her eyes.

                                       1873

Found Frozen

She died, as many travellers have died,
O'ertaken on an Alpine road by night;
Numbed and bewildered by the falling snow,
Striving, in spite of falling pulse, and limbs
5 Which faltered and grew feeble at each step,
To toil up the icy steep, and bear
Patient and faithful to the last, the load
Which, in the sunny morn seemed light!
                       And yet
'T was in the place she called her home, she died;
10 And they who loved her with the all of love
Their wintry natures had to give, stood by
And wept some tears, and wrote above her grave
Some common record which they thought was true;
But I, who loved her first, and last, and best,—*I* knew.

                                       1873

Danger

With what a childish and short-sighted sense
Fear seeks for safety; reckons up the days
Of danger and escape, the hours and ways
Of death; it breathless flies the pestilence;
5 It walls itself in towers of defence;
By land, by sea, against the storm it lays
Down barriers; then, comforted, it says:
"This spot, this hour is safe." Oh, vain pretence!
Man born of man knows nothing when he goes;

10 The winds blow where they list, and will disclose
To no man which brings safety, which brings risk.
The mighty are brought low by many a thing
Too small to name. Beneath the daisy's disk
Lies hid the pebble for the fatal sling.

1873

Lewis Carroll

(1832–1898)

Jabberwocky

'Twas brillig, and the slithy toves
   Did gyre and gimble in the wabe;
All mimsy were the borogoves,
   And the mome raths outgrabe.

5 "Beware the Jabberwock, my son!
   The jaws that bite, the claws that catch!
Beware the Jubjub bird, and shun
   The frumious Bandersnatch!"

He took his vorpal sword in hand
10   Long time the manxome foe he sought—
So rested he by the Tumtum tree,
   And stood awhile in thought.

And, as in uffish thought he stood,
   The Jabberwock, with eyes of flame,
15 Came whiffling through the tulgey wood,
   And burbled as it came!

One, two! One, two! And through and through
   The vorpal blade went snicker-snack!
He left it dead, and with its head
20   He went galumphing back.

"And hast thou slain the Jabberwock?
   Come to my arms, my beamish boy!
O frabjous day! Callooh! Callay!"
   He chortled in his joy.

25 'Twas brillig, and the slithy toves
   Did gyre and gimble in the wabe;

All mimsy were the borogoves,
   And the mome raths outgrabe.

1871

Thomas Hardy

(1840–1928)

The Ruined Maid

"O 'Melia, my dear, this does everything crown!
Who could have supposed I should meet you in Town?
And whence such fair garments, such prosperi-ty?"—
"O didn't you know I'd been ruined?" said she.

5 —"You left us in tatters, without shoes or socks,
Tired of digging potatoes, and spudding up docks;[1]
And now you've gay bracelets and bright feathers three!"—
"Yes: that's how we dress when we're ruined," said she.

—"At home in the barton[2] you said 'thee' and 'thou,'
10 And 'thik oon,' and 'theäs oon,' and 't'other'; but now
Your talking quite fits 'ee for high compa-ny!"—
"Some polish is gained with one's ruin," said she.

—"Your hands were like paws then, your face blue and bleak
But now I'm bewitched by your delicate cheek,
15 And your little gloves fit as on any la-dy!"—
"We never do work when we're ruined," said she.

—"You used to call home-life a hag-ridden dream,
And you'd sign, and you'd sock; but at present you seem
To know not of megrims[3] or melancho-ly!"—
20 "True. One's pretty lively when ruined," said she.

—"I wish I had feathers, a fine sweeping gown,
And a delicate face, and could strut about Town!"—
"My dear—a raw country girl, such as you be,
Cannot quite expect that. You ain't ruined," said she.

1866

---

[1]digging up weeds
[2]farmyard
[3]low spirits

Neutral Tones

We stood by a pond that winter day,
And the sun was white, as though chidden of God,
And a few leaves lay on the starving sod;
    —They had fallen from an ash, and were gray.

5 Your eyes on me were as eyes that rove
Over tedious riddles of years ago;
And some words played between us to and fro
    On which lost the more by our love.

The smile on your mouth was the deadest thing
10 Alive enough to have strength to die;
And a grin of bitterness swept thereby
    Like an ominous bird a-wing. . . .

Since then, keen lessons that love deceives,
And wrings with wrong, have shaped to me
15 Your face, and the God-curst sun, and a tree,
    And a pond edged with grayish leaves.

1867

The Man He Killed

   "Had he and I but met
    By some old ancient inn,
We should have sat us down to wet
    Right many a nipperkin![1]

5   "But ranged as infantry,
    And staring face to face,
I shot at him as he at me,
    And killed him in his place.

   "I shot him dead because—
10   Because he was my foe,
Just so: my foe of course he was;
    That's clear enough; although

   "He thought he'd 'list, perhaps,
    Off-hand like—just as I—
15 Was out of work—had sold his traps—
    No other reason why.

---

[1] about a half-pint

"Yes; quaint and curious war is!
  You shoot a fellow down
You'd treat if met where any bar is,
20   Or help to half-a-crown."

1902

The Convergence of the Twain

(Lines on the loss of the "Titanic")

1

In a solitude of the sea
  Deep from human vanity,
And the Pride of Life that planned her, stilly couches she.

2

Steel chambers, late the pyres
5   Of her salamandrine fires,
Cold currents third, and turn to rhythmic tidal lyres.

3

Over the mirrors meant
  To glass the opulent
The sea-worm crawls—grotesque, slimed, dumb, indifferent.

4

10   Jewels in joy designed
  To ravish the sensuous mind
Lie lightless, all their sparkles bleared and black and blind.

5

Dim moon-eyed fishes near
  Gaze at the gilded gear
15 And query: "What does this vaingloriousness down here?" . . .

6

Well: while was fashioning
  This creature of cleaving wing,
The Immanent Will that stirs and urges everything

7

Prepared a sinister mate
20   For her—so gaily great—
A Shape of Ice, for the time far and dissociate.

8

And as the smart ship grew
In stature, grace, and hue,
In shadowy silent distance grew the Iceberg too.

9

25   Alien they seemed to be:
No mortal eye could see
The intimate welding of their later history.

10

Or sign that they were bent
By paths coincident
30 On being anon twin halves of one august event,

11

Till the Spinner of the Years
Said "Now!" And each one hears,
And consummation comes, and jars two hemispheres.

1912

Channel Firing

That night your great guns, unawares,
Shook all our coffins as we lay,
And broke the chancel window-squares,
We thought it was the Judgment-day

5 And sat upright. While drearisome
Arose the howl of wakened hounds:
The mouse let fall the altar-crumb,
The worms drew back into the mounds,

The glebe cow[1] drooled. Till God called "No;
10 It's gunnery practice out at sea
Just as before you went below;
The world is as it used to be:

"All nations striving strong to make
Red war yet redder. Mad as hatters
15 They do no more for Christès sake
Than you who are helpless in such matters.

_____
[1]cow pastured in the parson's meadow

"That this is not the judgment-hour
For some of them's a blessed thing,
For if it were they'd have to scour
20 Hell's floor for so much threatening . . .

"Ha, ha. It will be warmer when
I blow the trumpet (if indeed
I ever do; for you are men,
And rest eternal sorely need)."

25 So down we lay again. "I wonder,
Will the world ever saner be,"
Said, one "than when He sent us under
In our indifferent century!"

And many a skeleton shook his head.
30 "Instead of preaching forty year,"
My neighbor Parson Thirdly said,
"I wish I had stuck to pipes and beer."

Again the guns disturbed the hour,
Roaring their readiness to avenge,
35 As far inland as Stourton Tower,
And Camelot, and starlit Stonehenge.[2]

1914

Ina Coolbrith

(1841–1928)

Withheld

Therein is sunlight, and sweet sound:
    Cool flow of waters, musical,
    Soft stir of insect-wings, and fall
Of blossom-snow upon the ground.

5 The birds flit in and out the trees,
    Their bright, sweet throats strained full with song.

---

[2]Stourton Tower commemorates King Alfred's ninth-century victory over the Danes; Camelot is the legendary site of King Arthur's court; Stonehenge is the mysterious, pre-Celtic monument on Salisbury Plain.

The flower-beds, the summer long,
  Are black and murmurous with bees.

Th' unrippled leaved hang faint with dew
10   In hushes of the breezeless morn.
    At eventide the stars, new born,
And the white moonlight, glimmer through.

Therein are all glad things whereof
    Life holdeth need through changing years;
15   Therein sweet rest, sweet end of tears,
Therein sweet labors, born of love.

This is my heritage, mine own,
    That alien hands from me withhold.
    From barrëd windows, dark and cold,
20 I view, with heart that maketh moan.

They fetter feet and hands; they give
    Me bitter, thankless tasks to do;
    And, cruel wise, still feed anew
My one small hope, that I may live.

25 And, that no single pang I miss,
    Lo! this one little window-space
    Is left, where through my eyes may trace
How sweeter than all sweet it is.

I Cannot Count My Life a Loss

I cannot count my life a loss,
    With all its length of evil days.
I hold them only as the dross
    About its gold, whose worth outweighs:
5   For each and all I give Him praise.

For, drawing nearer to the brink
    That leadeth down to final rest,
I see with clearer eyes, I think,
    And much that vexed me and oppressed,
10   Have learned was right, and just, and best.

So though I may but dimly guess
    Its far intent, this gift of His
I honor; nor would know the less
    One sorrow, or in pain or bliss
15   Have other than it was and is.

Gerard Manley Hopkins

(1844–1889)

Heaven—Haven

A Nun Takes the Veil

    I have desired to go
        Where springs not fail,
To fields where flies no sharp and sided hail
    And a few lilies blow.

5   And I have asked to be
        Where no storms come,
Where the green swell is in the havens dumb,
      And out of the swing of the sea.

                  1918

Pied Beauty

Glory be to God for dappled things—
    For skies of couple-color as a brinded cow;
      For rose-moles all in stipple upon trout that swim;
Fresh-firecoal chestnut-falls; finches' wings;
5   Landscape plotted and pieced—fold, fallow, and plough;
      And áll trádes, their gear and tackle and trim.
All things counter, original, spare, strange;
    Whatever is fickle, freckled (who knows how?)
      With swift, slow; sweet, sour; adazzle, dim;
10 He fathers-forth whose beauty is past change:
          Praise him.

                  1877

Spring and Fall

To a young child

    Márgarét, are you gríeving
Over Goldengrove unleaving?
Leáves, líke the things of man, you
With your fresh thoughts care for, can you?
5 Áh! ás the heart grows older
It will come to such sights colder
By and by, nor spare a sigh
Though worlds of wanwood leafmeal lie;
And yet you wíll weep and know why.

10   Now no matter, child, the name:
    Sórrow's spríngs áre the same.
    Nor mouth had, no nor mind, expressed
    What heart heard of, ghost guessed:
    It ís the blight man was born for,
15   It is Margaret you mourn for.

1880

(Carrion Comfort[1])

Not, I'll not, carrion comfort, Despair, not feast on thee;
Not untwist—slack they may be—these last strands of man
In me ór, most weary, cry *I can no more.* I can;
Can something, hope, wish day come, not choose not to be.

5   But ah, but O thou terrible, why wouldst thou rude on me
    Thy wring-world right foot rock? lay a lionlimb against me? scan
    With darksome devouring eyes my bruisèd bones? and fan,
    O in turns of tempest, me heaped there; me frantic to avoid thee and flee?

Why? That my chaff might fly; my grain lie, sheer and clear.
10   Nay in all that toil, that coil, since (seems) I kissed the rod,
    Hand rather, my heart lo! lapped strength, stole joy, would laugh, chéer.
    Cheer whom though? the hero whose heaven-handling flung me, fóot tród
    Me? or me that fought him? O which one? is it each one? That night, that year
    Of now done darkness I wretch lay wrestling with (my God!) my God.

1885

No Worst, There Is None

No worst, there is none. Pitched past pitch of grief,
More pangs will, schooled at forepangs, wilder wring.
Comforter, where, where is your comforting?
Mary, mother of us, where is your relief?
5   My cries heave, herds-long,[1] huddle in a main, a chief
    woe, world-sorrow; on an age-old anvil wince and sing—
    Then lull, then leave off. Fury had shrieked "No ling-
    ering! Let me be fell: force I must be brief."
    O the mind, mind has mountains; cliffs of fall
10   Frightful, sheer, no-man-fathomed. Hold them cheap
    May who ne'er hung there. Nor does long our small

---

[1] The title was added by Robert Bridges.

---

[1] like the successive cries of a herd of lost sheep

Durance deal with that steep or deep. Here! creep,
Wretch, under a comfort serves in a whirlwind: all
Life death does end and each day dies with sleep.

1885

A. E. Housman

(1859–1936)

From **A Shropshire Lad**

Loveliest of Trees, the Cherry Now

Loveliest of trees, the cherry now
Is hung with bloom along the bough,
And stands about the woodland ride
Wearing white for Eastertide.

5 Now, of my threescore years and ten,
Twenty will not come again,
And take from seventy springs a score,
It only leaves me fifty more.

And since to look at things in bloom
10 Fifty springs are little room,
About the woodlands I will go
To see the cherry hung with snow.

1896

When I Was One-and-Twenty

When I was one-and-twenty
   I heard a wise man say,
"Give crowns and pounds and guineas
   But not your heart away;
5 Give pearls away and rubies
   But keep you fancy free."
But I was one-and-twenty,
   No use to talk to me.

When I was one-and-twenty
10   I heard him say again,
"The heart out of the bosom
   Was never given in vain;
'Tis paid with sighs a plenty

And sold for endless rue."
15 And I am two-and-twenty,
And oh, 'tis true, 'tis true.

1896

To an Athlete Dying Young

The time you won your town the race
We chaired you through the market-place;
Man and boy stood cheering by,
And home we brought you shoulder-high.

5 To-day, the road all runners come,
Shoulder-high we bring you home,
And set you at your threshold down,
Townsman of a stiller town.

Smart lad, to slip betimes away
10 From fields where glory does not stay
And early though the laurel grows
It withers quicker than the rose.

Eyes the shady night has shut
Cannot see the record cut,
15 And silence sounds no worse than cheers
After earth has stopped the ears:

Now you will not swell the rout
Of lads that wore their honors out,
Runners whom renown outran
20 And the name died before the man.

So set, before its echoes fade,
The fleet foot on the sill of shade,
And hold to the low lintel up
The still-defended challenge-cup.

25 And round that early-laurelled head
Will flock to gaze the strengthless dead,
And find unwithered on its curls
The garland briefer than a girl's.

1896

From Far, from Eve and Morning

From far, from eve and morning
And yon twelve-winded sky,

The stuff of life to knit me
    Blew hither: here am I.

5 Now—for a breath I tarry
    Nor yet disperse apart—
Take my hand quick and tell me,
    What have you in your heart.

Speak now, and I will answer;
10   How shall I help you, say;
Ere to the wind's twelve quarters
    I take my endless way.

1896

With Rue My Heart Is Laden

With rue my heart is laden
    For golden friends I had,
For many a rose-lipt maiden
    And many a lightfoot lad.

5 By brooks too broad for leaping
    The lightfoot boys are laid;
The rose-lipt girls are sleeping
    In fields where roses fade.

1896

"Terence, This Is Stupid Stuff . . ."

    "Terence, this is stupid stuff:
You eat your victuals fast enough;
There can't be much amiss, 'tis clear,
To see the rate you drink your beer.
5 But oh, good Lord, the verse you make,
It gives a chap the belly-ache.
The cow, the old cow, she is dead;
It sleeps well, the hornèd head:
We poor lads, 'tis our turn now
10 To hear such tunes as killed the cow.
Pretty friendship 'tis to rhyme
Your friends to death before their time
Moping melancholy mad:
Come, pipe a tune to dance to, lad."

15   Why, if 'tis dancing you would be,
There's brisker pipes than poetry.
Say, for what were hop-yards meant,

Or why was Burton built on Trent?[1]
Oh many a peer of England brews
20 Livelier liquor than the Muse,
And malt does more than Milton can
To justify God's ways to man.
Ale, man, ale's the stuff to drink
For fellows whom it hurts to think:
25 Look into the pewter pot
To see the world as the world's not.
And faith, 'tis pleasant till 'tis past:
The mischief is that 'twill not last.
Oh I have been to Ludlow fair
30 And left my necktie God knows where,
And carried half-way home, or near,
Pints and quarts of Ludlow beer:
Then the world seemed none so bad,
And I myself a sterling lad;
35 And down in lovely muck I've lain,
Happy till I woke again.
Then I saw the morning sky:
Heigho, the tale was all a lie;
The world, it was the old world yet,
40 I was I, my things were wet,
And nothing now remained to do
But begin the game anew.

Therefore, since the world has still
Much good, but much less good than ill,
45 And while the sun and moon endure
Luck's a chance, but trouble's sure,
I'd face it as a wise man would,
And train for ill and not for good.
'Tis true, the stuff I bring for sale
50 Is not so brisk a brew as ale:
Out of a stem that scored the hand
I wrung it in a weary land.
But take it: if the smack is sour,
The better for the embittered hour;
55 It should do good to heart and head
When your soul is in my soul's stead;
And I will friend you, if I may,
In the dark and cloudy day.

_____

[1] a town noted for its breweries

There was a king reigned in the East:
60 There, when kings will sit to feast,
They get their fill before they think
With poisoned meat and poisoned drink.
He gathered all that springs to birth
From the many-venomed earth;
65 First a little, thence to more,
He sampled all her killing store;
An easy, smiling, seasoned sound,
Sate the king when healths went round.
They put arsenic in his meat
70 And stared aghast to watch him eat;
They poured strychnine in his cup
And shook to see him drink it up:
They shook, they stared as white's their shirt:
Them it was their poison hurt.
75 —I tell the tale that I heard told.
Mithridates,[2] he died old.

1896

Rudyard Kipling

(1865–1936)

Gunga Din

You may talk o' gin and beer
When you're quartered safe out 'ere,
An' you're sent to penny-fights an' Aldershot it;
But when it comes to slaughter
5 You will do your work on water,
An' you'll lick the bloomin' boots of 'im that's got it.
Now in Injia's sunny clime,
Where I used to spend my time
A-servin' of 'Er Majesty the Queen,
10 Of all them blackfaced crew
The finest man I knew
Was our regimental bhisti, Gunga Din.
      He was "Din! Din! Din!
   "You limpin' lump o' brick-dust, Gunga Din!

---

[2]king of Pontus in the first century B.C., who made himself immune to certain poisons by taking
  them frequently in small doses

15   "Hi! Slippy *hitherao!*
      "Water, get it! *Panee lao,*[1]
   "You squidgy-nosed old idol, Gunga Din."

The uniform 'e wore
Was nothin' much before,
20 An' rather less than 'arf o' that be'ind,
For a piece o' twisty rag
An' a goatskin water-bag
Was all the field-equipment 'e could find.
When the sweatin' troop-train lay
25 In a sidin' through the day,
Where the 'eat would make your bloomin' eyebrows crawl,
We shouted "Harry By!"[2]
Till our throats were bricky-dry,
Then we wopped 'im 'cause 'e couldn't serve us all.
30   It was "Din! Din! Din!
   "You 'eathen, where the mischief 'ave you been?
      "You put some *juldee*[3] in it
      "Or I'll *marrow*[4] you this minute
   "If you don't fill up my helmet, Gunga Din!"

35 'E would dot an' carry one
Till the longest day was done;
An' 'e didn't seem to know the use o' fear.
If we charged or broke or cut,
You could bet your bloomin' nut,
40 'E'd be waitin' fifty paces right flank rear.
With 'is mussick[5] on 'is back,
'E would skip with our attack,
An' watch us till the bugles made "Retire,"
An' for all 'is dirty 'ide
45 'E was white, clear white, inside
When 'e went to tend the wounded under fire!
    It was "Din! Din! Din!"
  With the bullets kickin' dust-spots on the green.
    When the cartridges ran out,
50   You could hear the front-ranks shout,
   "Hi! ammunition-mules an' Gunga Din!"

---

[1] Bring water swiftly.
[2] O brother.
[3] Be quick.
[4] hit you
[5] water-skin

I shan't forgit the night
When I dropped be'ind the fight
With a bullet where my belt-plate should 'a' been.
55 I was chokin' mad with thirst,
An' the man that spied me first
Was our good old grinnin', gruntin' Gunga Din.
'E lifted up my 'ead,
An' he plugged me where I bled,
60 An' 'e guv me 'arf-a-pint o' water green.
It was crawlin' and it stunk,
But of all the drinks I've drunk,
I'm gratefullest to one from Gunga Din.
　　　It was "Din! Din! Din!
65 　"'Ere's a beggar with a bullet through 'is spleen;
　　　"'E's chawin' up the ground,
　　　"An' 'e's kickin' all around:
　　"For Gawd's sake git the water, Gunga Din!"

'E carried me away
70 To where a dooli lay,
An' a bullet come an' drilled the beggar clean.
'E put me safe inside,
An' just before 'e died,
"I 'ope you liked your drink," sez Gunga Din.
75 So I'll meet 'im later on
At the place where 'e is gone—
Where it's always double drill and no canteen.
'E'll be squattin' on the coals
Givin' drink to poor damned souls,
80 An' I'll get a swig in hell from Gunga Din!
　　　Yes, Din! Din! Din!
　You Lazarushian-leather Gunga Din!
　　　Though I've belted you and flayed you,
　　　By the livin' Gawd that made you,
85 　You're a better man than I am, Gunga Din!

1890

If

If you can keep your head when all about you
　　Are losing theirs and blaming it on you,
If you can trust yourself when all men doubt you.
　　But make allowance for their doubting too;
5 If you can wait and not be tired by waiting,
　　Or being lied about, don't deal in lies,

Or being hated, don't give way to hating,
    And yet don't look too good, nor talk too wise:

If you can dream—and not make dreams your master
10   If you can think—and not make thoughts your aim
If you can meet with Triumph and Disaster
    And treat those two impostors just the same;
If you can bear to hear the truth you've spoken
    Twisted by knaves to make a trap for fools,
15 Or watch the things you gave your life to, broken,
    And stoop and build 'em up with worn-out tools:

If you can make one heap of all your winnings
    And risk it on one turn of pitch-and-toss,
And lose, and start again at your beginnings
20   And never breathe a word about your loss;
If you can force your heart and nerve and sinew
    To serve your turn long after they are gone,
And so hold on when there is nothing in you
    Except the Will which says to them: "Hold on!"

25 If you can talk with crowds and keep your virtue,
    Or walk with Kings—nor lose the common touch,
If neither foes nor loving friends can hurt you,
    If all men count with you, but none too much;
If you can fill the unforgiving minute
30   With sixty seconds' worth of distance run,
Yours is the Earth and everything that's in it,
    And—which is more—you'll be a Man, my son!

1910

5

A BRIEF HISTORY

The beginning of World War I in 1914 signaled the collapse of the old world order. The certainties of the nineteenth century collapsed into the anxiety and confusion of the beginning of the twentieth century. Established dynasties crumbled, national alliances failed, communism overwhelmed the Russian empire. The United States began to become a true world power, striding into the vacuum created by the war and its aftermath. World War I, the War to End All Wars, proved after a short recess to be the prelude to World War II. All of this was reflected in the poetry of the era.

William Butler Yeats's poetry chronicled the Irish Rebellion and a world whose "center would not hold." "The best," he wrote in *The Second Coming,* "lack all conviction/While the worst are full of passionate intensity." A poet who began writing in the Romantic tradition, Yeats allowed realism to enter into his poems while holding on to traditional form and structure.

Two soon-to-be-famous American poets, Eliot and Pound, however, expatriated themselves to England to escape what they believed to be an American resistance to change and to revitalized traditional ideas. Their poems combined a respect for tradition with the need to reinvigorate old ways with the fragmentation and vision of a new century. Pound, especially, led the movement from a poetry of the past to a new poetic vision. Imagism demanded that the poem focus on the subject itself, allow no unnecessary words, and make a break with traditional rigid metrical patterns. Pound and Eliot experimented and absorbed into their poems the successful, established innovations of the European literary movements, especially Realism and Symbolism, while Gertrude Stein, another expatriate, created a poetry of startling eccentricity, private symbolism, and an explosive verbal virtuosity so personal and particular as to seemingly defy (like Eliot) anything but pale imitations.

In America, William Carlos Williams's and E. E. Cummings's free-verse poems, and Wallace Stevens's traditional structures imploding with exotic language, contrasted with Robert Frost's carefully crafted traditional poetry. Frost captured the reassuring sound of New England dialects while ironically layering into his poems a darkness and skepticism often overlooked when he reigned as America's most popular poet. Socially and politically, the world reflected revolution, innovation, and reaction. So, too, the poets reflected change, experimentation, and pessimistic nostalgia. Art, as ever, reflected life. In contrast to what had prevailed in the past, however, conflicting views of art and poetry coexisted simultaneously as schools of thought. Increasingly, as no single view prevailed, a cold war began in poetry, as adamant as the cold war in politics. The fierceness of dogma and the shrill sound of partisanship filled the air.

Ireland's Yeats is an example of a poet trained in conventional Romantic verse who evolves into a modern poet. Keeping his sense of form and structure, Yeats modernized his verse in part by changing his imagery. In contrast to the mythological *Leda and the Swan,* for instance, his *Irish Airman* flies and dies in a sky of war and machinery. In *The Second Coming,* Yeats created a modern beast slouching toward a symbolic Bethlehem to compete with the traditional Christian message of hope and redemption. In America, Edwin Arlington Robinson used conventional verse forms to write about a changing American character. Robert Frost also wrote in conventional verse forms, but his diction sounds distinctly American. Many of his rural New England poems—for instance, *Stopping by Woods*—raise familiar country images to the level of symbolism. A new-world American character comes through in poems as traditional as the sonnet (*Once by the Pacific*) and as elaborate as the conceit (*Design*). Another American poet, Wallace Stevens, attached dazzling tropical imagery and exotic language to established conventional blank verse. William Carlos Williams created a poetry of clean flashing imagery and free-verse rhythms. Ezra Pound and H. D. demanded that concise images replace the sometimes drawn-out metrics and language of accentual-syllabic verse. Their poetry often appeals to direct visual experience and relies on the reader to draw the subtle comparisons that give such poems meaning. T. S. Eliot combined a striking imagery with historical and mythological allusions. He experimented with combinations of traditional verse and modern experience. His tired, middle-aged Prufrock, for instance, yearns in a free-verse poem—sometimes rhymed, sometimes not—after the grace and elegance of a bygone civilization.

William Butler Yeats

(1865–1939)

The Lake Isle of Innisfree

I will arise and go now, and go to Innisfree,
And a small cabin built there, of clay and wattles[1] made:
Nine bean-rows will I have there, a hive for the honey-bee,
And live alone in the bee-loud glade.

5 And I shall have some peace there, for peace comes dropping slow,
Dropping from the veils of the morning to where the cricket sings;
There midnight's all a glimmer, and noon a purple glow,
And evening full of linnet's wings.

I will arise and go now, for always night and day
10 I hear lake water lapping with low sounds by the shore;
While I stand on the roadway, or on the pavements gray,
I hear it in the deep heart's core.

                                    1893

When You Are Old

When you are old and gray and full of sleep,
And nodding by the fire, take down this book,
And slowly read, and dream of the soft look
Your eyes had once, and of their shadows deep;

5 How many loved your moments of glad grace,
And loved your beauty with love false or true,
But one man loved the pilgrim soul in you,
And loved the sorrows of your changing face;

And bending down beside the glowing bars,
10 Murmur, a little sadly, how Love fled
And paced upon the mountains overhead
And hid his face amid a crowd of stars.

                                    1892

The Folly of Being Comforted

One that is ever kind said yesterday:
"Your well-belovèd's hair has threads of gray,
And little shadows come about her eyes;
Time can but make it easier to be wise

---

[1]rods woven with twigs to form a wall or roof

5 Though now it seem impossible, and so
  All that you need is patience."
                        Heart cries, "No,
  I have not a crumb of comfort, not a grain.
  Time can but make her beauty over again:
10 Because of that great nobleness of hers
  The fire that stirs about her, when she stirs,
  Burns but more clearly. O she had not these ways
  When all the wild summer was in her gaze."

  O heart! O heart! if she'd but turn her head,
15 You'd know the folly of being comforted.

                                     1904

Easter 1916[1]

I have met them at close of day
Coming with vivid faces
From counter or desk among gray
Eighteenth-century houses.
5 I have passed with a nod of the head
Or polite meaningless words,
Or have lingered awhile and said
Polite meaningless words,
And thought before I had done
10 Of a mocking tale or a gibe
To please a companion
Around the fire at the club,
Being certain that they and I
But lived where motley is worn:
15 All changed, changed utterly:
A terrible beauty is born.

That woman's days were spent
In ignorant good will,
Her nights in argument
20 Until her voice grew shrill.
What voice more sweet than hers
When, young and beautiful,
She rode to harriers?
This man had kept a school
25 And rode our wingéd horse;
This other his helper and friend
Was coming into his force;
He might have won fame in the end,

---

[1]date of Irish Nationalist uprising

So sensitive his nature seemed,
30 So daring and sweet his thought.
This other man I had dreamed
A drunken, vainglorious lout.
He had done most bitter wrong
To some who are near my heart,
35 Yet I number him in the song;
He, too, has resigned his part
In the casual comedy;
He, too, has been changed in his turn,
Transformed utterly:
40 A terrible beauty is born.

Hearts with one purpose alone
Through summer and winter seem
Enchanted to a stone
To trouble the living stream.
45 The horse that comes from the road,
The rider, the birds that range
From cloud to tumbling cloud,
Minute by minute they change;
A shadow of cloud on the stream
50 Changes minute by minute;
A horse-hoof slides on the brim,
And a horse plashes within it;
The long-legged moor-hens dive,
And hens to moor-cocks call;
55 Minute by minute they live:
The stone's in the midst of all.

Too long a sacrifice
Can make a stone of the heart.
O when may it suffice?
60 That is Heaven's part, our part
To murmur name upon name,
As a mother names her child
When sleep at last has come
On limbs that had run wild.
65 What is it but nightfall?
No, no, not night but death;
Was it needless death after all?
For England may keep faith
For all that is done and said.
70 We know their dream; enough
To know they dreamed and are dead;
And what if excess of love

Bewildered them till they died?
I write it out in a verse—
75 MacDonagh and MacBride
And Connolly and Pearse
Now and in time to be,
Wherever green is worn,
Are changed, changed utterly:
80 A terrible beauty is born.

1916

The Wild Swans at Coole

The trees are in their autumn beauty,
The woodland paths are dry,
Under the October twilight the water
Mirrors a still sky;
5 Upon the brimming water among the stones
Are nine-and-fifty swans.

The nineteenth autumn has come upon me
Since I first made my count;
I saw, before I had well finished,
10 All suddenly mount
And scatter wheeling in great broken rings
Upon their clamorous wings.

I have looked upon those brilliant creatures,
And now my heart is sore.
15 All's changed since I, hearing at twilight,
The first time on this shore,
The bell-beat of their wings above my head,
Trod with a lighter tread.

Unwearied still, lover by lover,
20 They paddle in the cold
Companionable streams or climb the air;
Their hearts have not grown old;
Passion or conquest, wander where they will,
Attend upon them still.

25 But now they drift on the still water,
Mysterious, beautiful;
Among what rushes will they build,
By what lake's edge or pool
Delight men's eyes when I awake some day
30 To find they have flown away?

1917

An Irish Airman Foresees His Death[1]

I know that I shall meet my fate
Somewhere among the clouds above;
Those that I fight I do not hate,
Those that I guard I do not love;
5 My country is Kiltartan Cross,[2]
My countrymen Kiltartan's poor,
No likely end could bring them loss
Or leave them happier than before.
Nor law, nor duty bade me fight,
10 Nor public men, nor cheering crowds,
A lonely impulse of delight
Drove to this tumult in the clouds;
I balanced all, brought all to mind,
The years to come seemed waste of breath,
15 A waste of breath the years behind
In balance with this life, this death.

1919

The Second Coming

Turning and turning in the widening gyre
The falcon cannot hear the falconer;
Things fall apart; the centre cannot hold;
Mere anarchy is loosed upon the world,
5 The blood-dimmed tide is loosed, and everywhere
The ceremony of innocence is drowned;
The best lack all conviction, while the worst
Are full of passionate intensity.

Surely some revelation is at hand;
10 Surely the Second Coming is at hand.
The Second Coming! Hardly are those words out
When a vast image out of *Spiritus Mundi*[1]
Troubles my sight: somewhere in sands of the desert
A shape with lion body and the head of a man,
15 A gaze blank and pitiless as the sun,
Is moving its slow thighs, while all about it
Reel shadows of the indignant desert birds.
The darkness drops again; but now I know
That twenty centuries of stony sleep

---

[1]Major Robert Gregory, son of Yeat's friend and patroness Lady Augusta Gregory, was killed in action
 in 1918.
[2]Kiltartan is an Irish village near Coole Park, the estate of the Gregorys.

---

[1]soul of the universe

20 Were vexed to nightmare by a rocking cradle,
   And what rough beast, its hour come round at last,
   Slouches toward Bethlehem to be born?

1921

Leda and the Swan[1]

A sudden blow: the great wings beating still
Above the staggering girl, her thighs caressed
By the dark webs, her nape caught in his bill,
He holds her helpless breast upon his breast.

5 How can those terrified vague fingers push
  The feathered glory from her loosening thighs?
  And how can body, laid in that white rush,
  But feel the strange heart beating where it lies?

A shudder in the loins engenders there
10 The broken wall, the burning roof and tower[2]
   And Agamemnon dead.
                          Being so caught up,
   So mastered by the brute blood of the air,
   Did she put on his knowledge with his power
15 Before the indifferent beak could let her drop?

1928

Sailing to Byzantium

1

That is no country for old men. The young
In one another's arms, birds in the trees
—Those dying generations—at their song,
The salmon-falls, the mackerel-crowded seas,
5 Fish, flesh, or fowl, commend all summer long
  Whatever is begotten, born, and dies.
  Caught in that sensual music all neglect
  Monuments of unageing intellect.

2

An aged man is but a paltry thing,
10 A tattered coat upon a stick, unless
   Soul clap its hands and sing, and louder sing

---

[1]In Greek mythology, Leda was ravished by Zeus, in the form of a swan.
[2]The fall of Troy; Agamemnon was murdered by his wife Clytemnestra upon his return home from Troy.

For every tatter in its mortal dress,
Nor is there singing school but studying
Monuments of its own magnificence;
15 And therefore I have sailed the seas and come
To the holy city of Byzantium.

3

O sages standing in God's holy fire
As in the gold mosaic of a wall,
Come from the holy fire, perne in a gyre,
20 And be the singing masters of my soul.
Consume my heart away; sick with desire
And fastened to a dying animal
It knows not what it is; and gather me
Into the artifice of eternity.

4

25 Once out of nature I shall never take
My bodily form from any natural thing,
But such a form as Grecian goldsmiths make
Of hammered gold and gold enamelling
To keep a drowsy Emperor awake;
30 Or set upon a golden bough to sing
To lords and ladies of Byzantium
Of what is past, or passing, or to come.

1928

Among School Children

1

I walk through the long schoolroom questioning;
A kind old nun in a white hood replies;
The children learn to cipher and to sing,
To study reading-books and histories,
5 To cut and sew, be neat in everything
In the best modern way—the children's eyes
In momentary wonder stare upon
A sixty-year-old smiling public man.

2

I dream of a Ledaean body,[1] bent
10 Above a sinking fire, a tale that she

---

[1]like Leda, the daughter of Helen of Troy

Told of a harsh reproof, or trivial event
That changed some childish day to tragedy—
Told, and it seemed that our two natures blent
Into a sphere from youthful sympathy,
15 Or else, to alter Plato's parable,
Into the yolk and white of the one shell.

3

And thinking of that fit of grief or rage
I look upon one child or t'other there
And wonder if she stood so at that age—
20 For even daughters of the swan can share
Something of every paddler's heritage—
And had that color upon cheek or hair,
And thereupon my heart is driven wild:
She stands before me as a living child.

4

25 Her present image floats into the mind—
Did Quattrocento finger fashion it
Hollow of cheek as though it drank the wind
And took a mess of shadows for its meat?
And I though never of Ledaean kind
30 Had pretty plumage once—enough of that,
Better to smile on all that smile, and show
There is a comfortable kind of old scarecrow.

5

What youthful mother, a shape upon her lap
Honey of generation had betrayed,
35 And that must sleep, shriek, struggle to escape
As recollection or the drug decide,
Would think her son, did she but see that shape
With sixty or more winters on its head,
A compensation for the pang of his birth,
40 Or the uncertainty of his setting forth?

6

Plato thought nature but a spume that plays
Upon a ghostly paradigm of things;
Solider Aristotle played the taws
Upon the bottom of a king of kings;
45 World-famous golden-thighed Pythagoras
Fingered upon a fiddle-stick or strings

What a star sang and careless Muses heard:
Old clothes upon old sticks to scare a bird.

7

Both nuns and mothers worship images,
50 But those the candles light are not as those
That animate a mother's reveries,
But keep a marble or a bronze repose.
And yet they too break hearts—O Presences
That passion, piety or affection knows,
55 And that all heavenly glory symbolize—
O self-born mockers of man's enterprise;

8

Labor is blossoming or dancing where
The body is not bruised to pleasure soul,
Nor beauty born out of its own despair,
60 Nor blear-eyed wisdom out of midnight oil.
O chestnut-tree, great-rooted blossomer,
Are you the leaf, the blossom or the bole?
O body swayed to music, O brightening glance,
How can we know the dancer from the dance?

1933

After Long Silence

Speech after long silence; it is right,
All other lovers being estranged or dead,
Unfriendly lamplight hid under its shade,
The curtains drawn upon unfriendly night,
5 That we descant and yet again descant
Upon the supreme theme of Art and Song:
Bodily decrepitude is wisdom; young
We loved each other and were ignorant.

Lapis Lazuli[1]

(For Harry Clifton)

I have heard that hysterical women say
They are sick of the palette and fiddle-bow,
Of poets that are always gay,
For everybody knows or else should know
5 That if nothing drastic is done

---

[1] a deep-blue semi-precious stone

Aeroplane and Zeppelin will come out,
Pitch like King Billy bomb-balls in
Until the town lie beaten flat.

All perform their tragic play,
10 There struts Hamlet, there is Lear,
That's Ophelia, that Cordelia;
Yet they, should the last scene be there,
The great stage curtain about to drop,
If worthy their prominent part in the play,
15 Do not break up their lines to weep.
They know that Hamlet and Lear are gay;
Gaiety transfiguring all that dread.
All men have aimed at, found and lost;
Black out; Heaven blazing into the head:
20 Tragedy wrought to its uttermost.
Though Hamlet rambles and Lear rages,
And all the drop-scenes drop at once
Upon a hundred thousand stages,
It cannot grow by an inch or an ounce.

25 On their own feet they came, or on shipboard,
Camelback, horseback, ass-back, mule-back,
Old civilizations put to the sword.
Then they and their wisdom went to rack:
No handiwork of Callimachus,[2]
30 Who handled marble as if it were bronze,
Made draperies that seemed to rise
When sea-wind swept the corner, stands;
His long lamp-chimney shaped like the stem
Of a slender palm, stood but a day;
35 All things fall and are built again,
And those that build them again are gay.

Two Chinamen, behind them a third,
Are carved in lapis lazuli,
Over them flies a long-legged bird,
40 A symbol of longevity;
The third, doubtless a serving-man,
Carries a musical instrument.

Every discoloration of the stone,
Every accidental crack or dent,
45 Seems a water-course or an avalanche,

---

[2]Greek sculptor of the fifth century B.C.

Or lofty slope where it still snows
Though doubtless plum or cherry-branch
Sweetens the little half-way house
Those Chinamen climb towards, and I
50 Delight to imagine them seated there;
There, on the mountain and the sky,
On all the tragic scene they stare.
One asks for mournful melodies;
Accomplished fingers begin to play.
55 Their eyes mid many wrinkles, their eyes,
Their ancient, glittering eyes, are gay.

1938

Politics

"In our time the destiny of man presents its meaning in political terms."—

THOMAS MANN

How can I, that girl standing there,
My attention fix
On Roman or on Russian
Or on Spanish politics?
5 Yet here's a travelled man that knows
What he talks about,
And there's a politician
That has read and thought,
And maybe what they say is true
10 Of war and war's alarms,
But O that I were young again
And held her in my arms!

1938

Adam's Curse

We sat together at one summer's end,
That beautiful mild woman, your close friend,
And you and I, and talked of poetry.
I said, "A line will take us hours maybe;
5 Yet if it does not seem a moment's thought,
Our stitching and unstitching has been naught.
Better go down upon your marrow-bones
And scrub a kitchen pavement, or break stones
Like an old pauper, in all kinds of weather;
10 For to articulate sweet sounds together
Is to work harder than all these, and yet

Be thought an idler by the noisy set
Of bankers, schoolmasters, and clergymen
The martyrs call the world."

                            And thereupon
15 That beautiful mild woman for whose sake
There's many a one shall find out all heartache
On finding that her voice is sweet and low
Replied, "To be born woman is to know—
Although they do not talk of it at school—
20 That we must labour to be beautiful."

I said, "It's certain there is no fine thing
Since Adam's fall but needs much labouring.
There have been lovers who thought love should be
So much compounded of high courtesy
25 That they would sigh and quote with learned looks
Precedents out of beautiful old books;
Yet now it seems an idle trade enough."

We sat grown quiet at the name of love;
We saw the last embers of daylight die,
30 And in the trembling blue-green of the sky
A moon, worn as if it had been a shell
Washed by time's waters as they rose and fell
About the stars and broke in days and years.

I had a thought for no one's but your ears:
35 That you were beautiful, and that I strove
To love you in the old high way of love;
That it had all seemed happy, and yet we'd grown
As weary-hearted as that hollow moon.

                                          1904

From **Oedipus at Colonus**

Endure what life God gives and ask no longer span;
Cease to remember the delights of youth, travel-wearied aged man;
Delight becomes death-longing if all longing else be vain.

Even from that delight memory treasures so,
5 Death, despair, division of families, all entanglements of mankind grow,
As that old wandering beggar and these God-hated children know.

In the long echoing street the laughing dancers throng,
The bride is carried to the bridegroom's chamber through torchlight and
    tumultuous song;
I celebrate the silent kiss that ends short life or long.

10 Never to have lived is best, ancient writers say;
Never to have drawn the breath of life, never to have looked into the
     eye of day;
The second best's a gay goodnight and quickly turn away.

1928

Crazy Jane Talks with the Bishop

I met the Bishop on the road
And much said he and I.
"Those breasts are flat and fallen now
those veins must soon be dry;
5 Live in a heavenly mansion,
Not in some foul sty."

"Fair and foul are near of kin,
And fair needs foul," I cried.
"My friends are gone, but that's a truth
10 Nor grave nor bed denied,
Learned in bodily lowliness
And in the heart's pride.

"A woman can be proud and stiff
When on love intent;
15 But Love has pitched his mansion in
The place of excrement;
For nothing can be sole or whole
That has not been rent."

1933

Ernest Dowson

(1867–1900)

Non sum qualis eram bonae sub regno Cynarae[1]

Last night, ah, yesternight, betwixt her lips and mine
There fell thy shadow, Cynara! thy breath was shed
Upon my soul between the kisses and the wine;
And I was desolate and sick of an old passion,
5   Yea, I was desolate and bowed my head:
I have been faithful to thee, Cynara! in my fashion.

-----

[1]I am not what I was under the reign of the good Cynara" (Horace, *Odes* IV.i).

All night upon mine heart I felt her warm heart beat,
Night-long within mine arms in love and sleep she lay;
Surely the kisses of her bought red mouth were sweet;
10 But I was desolate and sick of an old passion,
    When I awoke and found the dawn was gray:
I have been faithful to thee, Cynara! in my fashion.

I have forgot much, Cynara! gone with the wind,
Flung roses, roses riotously with the throng,
15 Dancing, to put thy pale, lost lilies out of mind;
But I was desolate and sick of an old passion,
    Yea, all the time, because the dance was long:
I have been faithful to thee, Cynara! in my fashion.

I cried for madder music and for stronger wine,
20 But when the feast is finished and the lamps expire,
Then falls thy shadow, Cynara! the night is thine;
And I am desolate and sick of an old passion,
    Yea hungry for the lips of my desire:
I have been faithful to thee, Cynara! in my fashion.

1896

Edwin Arlington Robinson

(1869–1935)

Miniver Cheevy

Miniver Cheevy, child of scorn,
    Grew lean while he assailed the seasons;
He wept that he was ever born,
    And he had reasons.

5 Miniver loved the days of old
    When swords were bright and steeds were prancing;
The vision of a warrior bold
    Would set him dancing.

Miniver sighed for what was not,
10   And dreamed, and rested from his labors;
He dreamed of Thebes and Camelot,
    And Priam's neighbors.

Miniver mourned the ripe renown
    That made so many a name so fragrant;

15 He mourned Romance, now on the town,
    And Art, a vagrant.

Miniver loved the Medici,
    Albeit he had never seen one;
He would have sinned incessantly
20   Could he have been one.

Miniver cursed the commonplace
    And eyed a khaki suit with loathing;
He missed the medieval grace
    Of iron clothing.

25 Miniver scorned the gold he sought,
    But sore annoyed was he without it;
Miniver thought, and thought, and thought,
    And thought about it.

Miniver Cheevy, born too late,
30   Scratched his head and kept on thinking;
Miniver coughed, and called it fate,
    And kept on drinking.

1910

For a Dead Lady

No more with overflowing light
Shall fill the eyes that now are faded,
Nor shall another's fringe with night
Their woman-hidden world as they did.
5 No more shall quiver down the days
The flowing wonder of her ways,
Whereof no language may requite
The shifting and the many-shaded.

The grace, divine definitive,
10 Clings only as a faint forestalling;
The laugh that love could not forgive
Is hushed, and answers to no calling;
The forehead and the little ears
Have gone where Saturn keeps the years;
15 The breast where roses could not live
Has done with rising and with falling.

The beauty, shattered by the laws
That have creation in their keeping,
No longer trembles at applause,

20 Or over children that are sleeping;
And we who delve in beauty's lore
Know all that we have known before
Of what inexorable cause
Makes Time so vicious in his reaping.

1910

Eros Turannos[1]

She fears him, and will always ask
    What fated her to choose him;
She meets in his engaging mask
    All reasons to refuse him;
5 But what she meets and what she fears
Are less than are the downward years,
Drawn slowly to the foamless weirs
    Of age, were she to lose him.

Between a blurred sagacity
10   That once had power to sound him,
And Love, that will not let him be
    The Judas[2] that she found him,
Her pride assuages her almost,
As if it were alone the cost.
15 He sees that he will not be lost,
    And waits and looks around him.

A sense of ocean and old trees
    Envelopes and allures him;
Tradition, touching all he sees,
20   Beguiles and reassures him;
And all her doubts of what he says
Are dimmed with what she knows of days—
Till even prejudice delays
    And fades, and she secures him.

25 The falling leaf inaugurates
    The reign of her confusion;
The pounding wave reverberates
    The dirge of her illusion;
And home, where passion lived and died,
30 Becomes a place where she can hide,

---

[1]tyrannical Love
[2]the disciple who betrayed Christ

While all the town and harbor side
   Vibrate with her seclusion.

We tell you, tapping on our brows,
   The story as it should be,
35 As if the story of a house
    Were told, or ever could be;
We'll have no kindly veil between
Her visions and those we have seen,
As if we guessed what hers have been,
40   Or what they are or would be.

Meanwhile we do no harm; for they
   That with a god have striven,
Not hearing much of what we say,
   Take what the god has given;
45 Though like waves breaking it may be,
Or like a changed familiar tree,
Or like a stairway to the sea
   Where down the blind are driven.

                                1916

Mr. Flood's Party

Old Eben Flood, climbing alone one night
Over the hill between the town below
And the forsaken upland hermitage
That held as much as he should ever know
5 On earth again of home, paused warily.
The road was his with not a native near;
And Eben, having leisure, said aloud,
For no man else in Tilbury Town to hear:

"Well, Mr. Flood, we have the harvest moon
10 Again, and we may not have many more;
The bird is on the wing, the poet says,
And you and I have said it here before.
Drink to the bird." He raised up to the light
The jug that he had gone so far to fill,
15 And answered huskily: "Well, Mr. Flood,
Since you propose it, I believe I will."

Alone, as if enduring to the end
A valiant armor of scarred hopes outworn,
He stood there in the middle of the road

20 Like Roland's ghost winding a silent horn.[1]
   Below him, in the town among the trees,
   Where friends of other days had honored him,
   A phantom salutation of the dead
   Rang thinly till old Eben's eyes were dim.

25 Then, as a mother lays her sleeping child
   Down tenderly, fearing it may awake,
   He set the jug down slowly at his feet
   With trembling care, knowing that most things break,
   And only when assured that on firm earth
30 It stood, as the uncertain lives of men
   Assuredly did not, he paced away,
   And with his hand extended paused again:

   "Well, Mr. Flood, we have not met like this
   In a long time; and many a change has come
35 To both of us, I fear, since last it was
   We had a drop together. Welcome home!"
   Convivially returning with himself,
   Again he raised the jug up to the light;
   And with an acquiescent quaver said:
40 "Well, Mr. Flood, if you insist, I might.

   "Only a very little, Mr. Flood—
   For auld lang syne. No more, sir; that will do."
   So, for the time, apparently it did,
   And Eben evidently thought so too;
45 For soon amid the silver loneliness
   Of night he lifted up his voice and sang,
   Secure, with only two moons listening,
   Until the whole harmonious landscape rang—

   "For auld lang syne." The weary throat gave out,
50 The last word wavered; and the song being done,
   He raised again the jug regretfully
   And shook his head, and was again alone.
   There was not much that was ahead of him,
   And there was nothing in the town below—
55 Where strangers would have shut the many doors
   That many friends had opened long ago.

                                                    1920

   ——————
   [1]In the medieval *Song of Roland*, the hero refuses to blow his horn for help at the Battle of Roncevaux
    and loses his life.

Karma[1]

Christmas was in the air and all was well
With him, but for a few confusing flaws
In divers of God's images. Because
A friend of his would neither buy nor sell,
5 Was he to answer for the axe that fell?
He pondered; and the reason for it was,
Partly, a slowly freezing Santa Claus
Upon the corner, with his beard and bell.

Acknowledging an improvident surprise,
10 He magnified a fancy that he wished
The friend whom he had wrecked were here again.
Not sure of that, he found a compromise;
And from the fulness of his heart he fished
A dime for Jesus who had died for men.

1925

New England

Here where the wind is always north-north-east
And children learn to walk on frozen toes,
Wonder begets an envy of all those
Who boil elsewhere with such a lyric yeast
5 Of love that you will hear them at a feast
Where demons would appeal for some repose,
Still clamoring where the chalice overflows
And crying wildest who have drunk the least.

Passion is here a soilure of the wits,
10 We're told, and Love a cross for them to bear;
Joy shivers in the corner where she knits
And Conscience always has the rocking-chair,
Cheerful as when she tortured into fits
The first cat that was ever killed by Care.

1925

---

[1]In Buddhist philosophy, the cumulative results of a person's deeds in one stage of his existence, controlling his fate in the next.

Walter de la Mare

(1873–1956)

The Listeners

"Is there anybody there?" said the Traveller,
    Knocking on the moonlit door;
And his horse in the silence champed the grasses
    Of the forest's ferny floor:
5 And a bird flew up out of the turret,
    Above the Traveller's head:
And he smote upon the door again a second time;
    "Is there anybody there?" he said.
But no one descended to the Traveller;
10   No head from the leaf-fringed sill
Leaned over and looked into his grey eyes,
    Where he stood perplexed and still.
But only a host of phantom listeners
    That dwelt in the lone house then
15 Stood listening in the quiet of the moonlight
    To that voice from the world of men:
Stood thronging the faint moonbeams on the dark stair,
    That goes down to the empty hall,
Hearkening in an air stirred and shaken
20   By the lonely Traveller's call.
And he felt in his heart their strangeness,
    Their stillness answering his cry,
While his horse moved, cropping the dark turf,
    'Neath the starred and leafy sky;
25 For he suddenly smote on the door, even
    Louder, and lifted his head:—
"Tell them I came, and no one answered,
    That I kept my word," he said.
Never the least stir made the listeners,
30   Though every word he spake
Fell echoing through the shadowiness of the still house
    From the one man left awake:
Ay, they heard his foot upon the stirrup,
    And the sound of iron on stone,
35 And how the silence surged softly backward,
    When the plunging hoofs were gone.

1912

Robert Frost

(1874–1963)

Mending Wall

Something there is that doesn't love a wall,
That sends the frozen-ground-swell under it
And spills the upper boulders in the sun,
And makes gaps even two can pass abreast.
5 The work of hunters is another thing:
I have come after them and made repair
Where they have left not one stone on a stone,
But they would have the rabbit out of hiding,
To please the yelping dogs. The gaps I mean,
10 No one has seen them made or heard them made,
But at spring mending-time we find them there.
I let my neighbor know beyond the hill;
And on a day we meet to walk the line
And set the wall between us once again.
15 We keep the wall between us as we go.
To each the boulders that have fallen to each.
And some are loaves and some so nearly balls
We have to use a spell to make them balance:
'Stay where you are until our backs are turned!'
20 We wear our fingers rough with handling them.
Oh, just another kind of outdoor game,
One on a side. It comes to little more:
There where it is we do not need the wall:
He is all pine and I am apple orchard.
25 My apple trees will never get across
And eat the cones under his pines, I tell him.
He only says, 'Good fences make good neighbors.'
Spring is the mischief in me, and I wonder
If I could put a notion in his head:
30 '*Why* do they make good neighbors? Isn't it
Where there are cows? But here there are no cows,
Before I built a wall I'd ask to know
What I was walling in or walling out,
And to whom I was like to give offense.
35 Something there is that doesn't love a wall,
That wants it down.' I could say 'Elves' to him,
But it's not elves exactly, and I'd rather
He said it for himself. I see him there,

Bringing a stone grasped firmly by the top
40 In each hand, like an old-stone savage armed.
He moves in darkness as it seems to me,
Not of woods only and the shade of trees.
He will not go behind his father's saying,
And he likes having thought of it so well
45 He says again, 'Good fences make good neighbors.'

1914

The Road Not Taken

Two roads diverged in a yellow wood,
And sorry I could not travel both
And be one traveler, long I stood
And looked down one as far as I could
5 To where it bent in the undergrowth;

Then took the other, as just as fair,
And having perhaps the better claim,
Because it was grassy and wanted wear;
Though as for that, the passing there
10 Had worn them really about the same,

And both that morning equally lay
In leaves no step had trodden black.
Oh, I kept the first for another day!
Yet knowing how way leads on to way,
15 I doubted if I should ever come back.

I shall be telling this with a sigh
Somewhere ages and ages hence:
Two roads diverged in a wood, and I—
I took the one less traveled by,
20 And that has made all the difference.

1916

Birches

When I see birches bend to left and right
Across the lines of straighter darker trees,
I like to think some boy's been swinging them.
But swinging doesn't bend them down to stay
5 As ice-storms do. Often you must have seen them

Loaded with ice a sunny winter morning
After a rain. They click upon themselves
As the breeze rises, and turn many-colored
As the stir cracks and crazes their enamel.
10 Soon the sun's warmth makes them shed crystal shells
Shattering and avalanching on the snowcrust—
Such heaps of broken glass to sweep away
You'd think the inner dome of heaven had fallen.
They are dragged to the withered bracken by the load,
15 And they seem not to break; though once they are bowed
So low for long, they never right themselves:
You may see their trunks arching in the woods
Years afterwards, trailing their leaves on the ground
Like girls on hands and knees that throw their hair
20 Before them over their heads to dry in the sun.
But I was going to say when Truth broke in
With all her matter-of-fact about the ice-storm,
I should prefer to have some boy bend them
As he went out and in to fetch the cows—
25 Some boy too far from town to learn baseball,
Whose only play was what he found himself,
Summer or winter, and could play alone.
One by one he subdued his father's trees
By riding them down over and over again
30 Until he took the stiffness out of them,
And not one but hung limp, not one was left
For him to conquer. He learned all there was
To learn about not launching out too soon
And so not carrying the tree away
35 Clear to the ground. He always kept his poise
To the top branches, climbing carefully
With the same pains you use to fill a cup
Up to the brim, and even above the brim.
Then he flung outward, feet first, with a swish,
40 Kicking his way down through the air to the ground.
So was I once myself a swinger of birches.
And so I dream of going back to be.
It's when I'm weary of considerations,
And life is too much like a pathless wood
45 Where your face burns and tickles with the cobwebs
Broken across it, and one eye is weeping
From a twig's having lashed across it open.
I'd like to get away from earth awhile

And then come back to it and begin over.
50   May no fate willfully misunderstand me
And half grant what I wish and snatch me away
Not to return. Earth's the right place for love:
I don't know where it's likely to go better.
I'd like to go by climbing a birch tree,
55   And climb black branches up a snow-white trunk,
Toward heaven, till the tree could bear no more,
But dipped its top and set me down again.
That would be good both going and coming back.
One could do worse than be a swinger of birches.

1916

Fire and Ice

Some say the world will end in fire,
Some say in ice.
From what I've tasted of desire
I hold with those who favor fire.
5   But if it had to perish twice,
I think I know enough of hate
To say that for destruction ice
Is also great
And would suffice

1923

Stopping by Woods on a Snowy Evening

Whose woods these are I think I know.
His house is in the village, though;
He will not see me stopping here
To watch his woods fill up with snow.

5   My little horse must think it queer
To stop without a farmhouse near
Between the woods and frozen lake
The darkest evening of the year.

He gives his harness bells a shake
10   To ask if there is some mistake.
The only other sound's the sweep
Of easy wind and downy flake.

The woods are lovely, dark, and deep,
But I have promises to keep,

15 And miles to go before I sleep,
    And miles to go before I sleep.

1923

Once by the Pacific

The shattered water made a misty din.
Great waves looked over others coming in,
And thought of doing something to the shore
That water never did to land before.
5 The clouds were low and hairy in the skies,
Like locks blown forward in the gleam of eyes.
You could not tell, and yet it looked as if
The shore was lucky in being backed by cliff,
The cliff in being backed by continent;
10 It looked as if a night of dark intent
Was coming, and not only a night, an age.
Someone had better be prepared for rage.
There would be more than ocean-water broken
Before God's last *Put out the Light* was spoken.

1928

Departmental

An ant on the tablecloth
Ran into a dormant moth
Of many times his size.
He showed not the least surprise.
5 His business wasn't with such.
He gave it scarcely a touch,
And was off on his duty run.
Yet if he encountered one
Of the hive's enquiry squad
10 Whose work is to find out God
And the nature of time and space,
He would put him onto the case.
Ants are a curious race;
One crossing with hurried tread
15 The body of one of their dead
Isn't given a moment's arrest—
Seems not even impressed.
But he no doubt reports to any
With whom he crosses antennae,
20 And they no doubt report

To the higher-up at court.
Then word goes forth in Formic:
'Death's come to Jerry McCormic,
Our selfless forager Jerry.
25 Will the special Janizary
Whose office it is to bury
The dead of the commissary
Go bring him home to his people.
Lay him in a state on a sepal.
30 Wrap him for shroud in a petal.
Embalm him with ichor of nettle.
This is the word of your Queen.'
And presently on the scene
Appears a solemn mortician;
35 And taking formal position
With feelers calmly atwiddle,
Seizes the dead by the middle,
And heaving him high in air,
Carries him out of there.
40 No one stands round to stare.
It is nobody else's affair.

It couldn't be called ungentle.
But how thoroughly departmental.

1936

Design

I found a dimpled spider, fat and white,
On a white heal-all, holding up a moth
Like a white piece of rigid satin cloth—
Assorted characters of death and blight
5 Mixed ready to begin the morning right,
Like the ingredients of a witches' broth—
A snow-drop spider, a flower like a froth,
And dead wings carried like a paper kite.

What had that flower to do with being white,
10 The wayside blue and innocent heal-all?
What brought the kindred spider to that height,
Then steered the white moth thither in the night?
What but design of darkness to appall?—
If design govern in a thing so small.

1936

The Draft Horse

With a lantern that wouldn't burn
In too frail a buggy we drove
Behind too heavy a horse
Through a pitch-dark limitless grove.

5 And a man came out of the trees
And took our horse by the head
And reaching back to his ribs
Deliberately stabbed him dead.

The ponderous beast went down
10 With a crack of a broken shaft.
And the night drew through the trees
In one long invidious draft.

The most unquestioning pair
That ever accepted fate
15 And the least disposed to ascribe
Any more than we had to to hate,

We assumed that the man himself
Or someone he had to obey
Wanted us to get down
20 And walk the rest of the way.

1962

In Winter in the Woods Alone

In winter in the woods alone
Against the trees I go.
I mark a maple for my own
And lay the maple low.

5 At four o'clock I shoulder ax,
And in the afterglow
I link a line of shadowy tracks
Across the tinted snow.

I see for Nature no defeat
10 In one tree's overthrow
Or for myself in my retreat
For yet another blow.

1962

Robert Service

(1874–1958)

The Cremation of Sam McGee

> *There are strange things done in the midnight sun*
> > *By the men who moil for gold;*
> *The Artic trails have their secret tales*
> > *That would make your blood run cold;*
5 > *The Northern Lights have seen queer sights,*
> > *But the queerest they ever did see*
> *Was that night on the marge of Lake Lebarge*
> > *I cremated Sam McGee.*

Now Sam McGee was from Tennessee, where the cotton blooms and blows.
10 Why he left his home in the South to roam 'round the Pole, God only knows.
He was always cold, but the land of gold seemed to hold him like a spell;
Though he'd often say in his homely way that "he'd sooner live in hell."

On a Christmas Day we were mushing our way over the Dawson trail.
Talk of your cold! through the parka's fold it stabbed like a driven nail.
15 If our eyes we'd close, then the lashes froze till sometimes we couldn't see;
It wasn't much fun, but the only one to whimper was Sam McGee.

And that very night, as we lay packed tight in our robes beneath the snow,
And the dogs were fed, and the stars o'erhead were dancing heel and toe,
He turned to me, and "Cap," says he, "I'll cash in this trip, I guess;
20 And if I do, I'm asking that you won't refuse my last request."

Well, he seemed so low that I couldn't say no; then he says with a sort
    of moan:
"It's the cursèd cold, and it's got right hold till I'm chilled clean through to
    the bone.
Yet 'tain't being dead—it's my awful dread of the icy grave that pains;
So I want you to swear that, foul or fair, you'll cremate my last remains."

25 A pal's last need is a thing to heed, so I swore I would not fail;
And we started on at the streak of dawn; but God! he looked ghastly pale.
He crouched on the sleigh, and he raved all day of his home in Tennessee;
And before nightfall a corpse was all that was left of Sam McGee.

There wasn't a breath in that land of death, and I hurried, horror-driven,
30 With a corpse half hid that I couldn't get rid, because of a promise given;
It was lashed to the sleigh, and it seemed to say: "You may tax your brawn
    and brains,
But you promised true, and it's up to you to cremate those last remains."

Now a promise made is a debt unpaid, and the trail has its own stern code.
In the days to come, though my lips were dumb, in my heart how I cursed
    that load.
35 In the long, long night, by the lone firelight, while the huskies, round in a ring,
Howled out their woes to the homeless snows— O God! how I loathed
    the thing.

And every day that quiet clay seemd to heavy and heavier grow;
And on I went, though the dogs were spent and the grub was getting low;
The trail was bad, and I felt half mad, but I swore I would not give in;
40 And I'd often sing to the hateful thing, and it hearkened with a grin.

Till I came to the marge of Lake Lebarge, and derelict there lay;
It was jammed in the ice, but I saw in a trice it was called the "Alice May."
And I looked at it, and I thought a bit, and I looked at my frozen chum;
Then "Here," said I, with a sudden cry, "is my cre-ma-tor-eum."

45 Some planks I tore from the cabin floor, and I lit the boiler fire;
Some coal I found that was lying around, and I heaped the fuel higher;
The flames just soared, and the furnace roared—such a blaze you seldom see;
And I burrowed a hole in the glowing coal, and I stuffed in Sam McGee.

Then I made a hike, for I didn't like to hear him sizzle so;
50 And the heavens scowled, and the huskies howled, and the wind began to blow.
It was icy cold, but the hot sweat rolled down my cheeks, and I don't know why;
And the greasy smoke in an inky cloak went streaking down the sky.

I do not know how long in the snow I wrestled with grisly fear;
But the stars came out and they danced about ere again I ventured near;
55 I was sick with dread, but I bravely said: "I'll just take a peep inside.
I guess he's cooked, and it's time I looked"; . . . then the door I opend wide.

And there sat Sam, looking cool and calm, in the heart of the furnace roar;
And he wore a smile you could see a mile, and he said "Please close that door.
It's fine in here, but I greatly fear you'll let in the cold and storm—
60 Since I left Plumtree, down in Tennessee, it's the first time I've been warm."

    There are strange things done in the midnight sun
      By the men who moil for gold;
    The Artic trails have their secret tales
      That would make your blood run cold;
65   *The Northern Lights have seen queer sights,*
      But the queerest they ever did see
    Was that night on the marge of Lake Lebarge
      I cremated Sam McGee.

1907

Gertrude Stein

(1874–1945)

A Petticoat

A light white, a disgrace, an ink spot, a rosy charm.

1914

A Waist

A star glide, a single frantic sullenness, a single financial grass greediness.

Object that is in wood. Hold the pine, hold the dark, hold in the rush, make the bottom.

A piece of crystal. A change, in a change that is remarkable there is no reason to say that there was a time.

A woolen object gilded. A country climb is the best disgrace, a couple of practices any of them in order is so left.

1914

A Time to Eat

A pleasant simple habitual and tyrannical and authorised and educated and resumed and articulate separation. This is not tardy.

1914

From Before the Flowers of Friendship Faded Friendship Faded

29

I love my love with a v
Because it is like that
I love myself with a b
Because I am beside that
5 A king.
I love my love with an a
Because she is a queen
I love my love and a a is the best of then
Think well and be a king,
10 Think more and think again
I love my love with a dress and a hat
I love my love and not with this or with that
I love my love with a y because she is my bride
I love her with a d because she is my love beside
15 Thank you for being there
Nobody has to care

Thank you for being here
Because you are not there.
    And with and without me which is and without she she can be
late and then and how and all around we think and found that it is
time to cry she and I.

1931

Carl Sandburg

(1878–1967)

Early Copper

A slim and singing copper girl,
They lived next to the earth for her sake
And the yellow corn was in their faces
And the cooper curve of prairie sunset.

5   In her April eyes bringing
Corn tassels shining from Duluth and Itasca,
From La Crosse to Keokuk and St. Louis, to the Big Muddy,
The yellow-hoofed Big Muddy meeting the Father of Waters,
In her eyes corn rows running to the prairie ends,
10 In her eyes copper men living next to the earth for her sake.

1960

Fog

The fog comes
on little cat feet.

It sits looking
over harbor and city
5 on silent haunches
and then moves on.

1916

Cool Tombs

When Abraham Lincoln was shoveled into the tombs, he forgot the copperheads
    and the assassin . . . in the dust, in the cool tombs.
And Ulysses Grant lost all thought of con men and Wall Street, cash and collat-
    eral turned ashes . . . in the dust, in the cool tombs.

Pocahontas' body, lovely as a poplar, sweet as a red haw in November or a paw-
    paw in May, did she wonder? does she remember? . . . in the dust, in the cool
    tombs?
Take any streetful of people buying clothes and groceries, cheering a hero or
    throwing confetti and blowing tin horns . . . tell me if the lovers are losers
    . . . tell me if any get more than the lovers . . . in the dust . . . in the cool
    tombs.

1918

Wallace Stevens

(1879–1955)

Sunday Morning

1

Complacencies of the peignoir, and late
Coffee and oranges in a sunny chair,
And the green freedom of a cockatoo
Upon a rug mingle to dissipate
5 The holy hush of ancient sacrifice.
She dreams a little, and she feels the dark
Encroachment of that old catastrophe,
As a calm darkens among water-lights.
The pungent oranges and bright, green wings
10 Seem things in some procession of the dead,
Winding across wide water, without sound.
The day is like wide water, without sound,
Stilled for the passing of her dreaming feet
Over the seas, to silent Palestine,
15 Dominion of the blood and sepulchre.

2

Why should she give her bounty to the dead?
What is divinity if it can come
Only in silent shadows and in dreams?
Shall she not find in comforts of the sun,
20 In pungent fruit and bright, green wings, or else
In any balm or beauty of the earth,
Things to be cherished like the thought of heaven?
Divinity must live within herself:
Passions of rain, or moods in falling snow;
25 Grievings in loneliness, or unsubdued

Elations when the forest blooms; gusty
Emotions on wet roads on autumn nights;
All pleasures and all pains, remembering
The bough of summer and the winter branch.
30 These are the measures destined for her soul.

3

Jove in the clouds had his inhuman birth.
No mother suckled him, no sweet land gave
Large-mannered motions to his mythy mind
He moved among us, as a muttering king,
35 Magnificent, would move among his hinds
Until our blood, commingling, virginal,
With heaven, brought such requital to desire
The very hinds discerned it, in a star.
Shall our blood fail? Or shall it come to be
40 The blood of paradise? And shall the earth
Seem all of paradise that we shall know?
The sky will be much friendlier then than now,
A part of labor and a part of pain,
And next in glory to enduring love,
45 Not this dividing and indifferent blue.

4

She says, "I am content when wakened birds,
Before they fly, test the reality
Of misty fields, by their sweet questionings;
But when the birds are gone, and their warm fields
50 Return no more, where, then, is paradise?"
There is not any haunt of prophecy,
Nor any old chimera of the grave,
Neither the golden underground, nor isle
Melodious, where spirits gat them home,
55 Nor visionary south, nor cloudy palm
Remote on heaven's hill, that has endured
As April's green endures; or will endure
Like her remembrance of awakened birds,
Or her desire for June and evening, tipped
60 By the consummation of the swallow's wings.

5

She says, "But in contentment I still feel
The need of some imperishable bliss."
Death is the mother of beauty; hence from her,

Alone, shall come fulfilment to our dreams
65 And our desires. Although she strews the leaves
Of sure obliteration on our paths,
The path sick sorrow took, the many paths
Where triumph rang its brassy phrase, or love
Whispered a little out of tenderness,
70 She makes a willow shiver in the sun
For maidens who were wont to sit and gaze
Upon the grass, relinquished to their feet.
She causes boys to pile new plums and pears
On disregarded plate. The maidens taste
75 And stray impassioned in the littering leaves.

6

Is there no change of death in paradise?
Does ripe fruit never fall? Or do the boughs
Hang always heavy in that perfect sky,
Unchanging, yet so like our perishing earth,
80 With rivers like our own that seek for seas
They never find, the same receding shores
That never touch with inarticulate pang?
Why set the pear upon those river-banks
Or spice the shores with odors of the plum?
85 Alas, that they should wear our colors there,
The silken weavings of our afternoons,
And pick the strings of our insipid lutes!
Death is the mother of beauty, mystical,
Within whose burning bosom we devise
90 Our earthly mothers waiting, sleeplessly.

7

Supple and turbulent, a ring of men
Shall chant in orgy on a summer morn
Their boisterous devotion to the sun,
Not as a god, but as a god might be,
95 Naked among them, like a savage source.
Their chant shall be a chant of paradise,
Out of their blood, returning to the sky;
And in their chant shall enter, voice by voice,
The windy lake wherein their lord delights,
100 The trees, like serafin, and echoing hills,
That choir among themselves long afterward.
They shall know well the heavenly fellowship
Of men that perish and of summer morn.

And whence they came and whither they shall go
105 The dew upon their feet shall manifest.

8

She hears, upon that water without sound,
A voice that cries, "The tomb in Palestine
Is not the porch of spirits lingering.
It is the grave of Jesus, where he lay."
110 We live in an old chaos of the sun,
Or old dependency of day and night,
Or island solitude, unsponsored, free,
Of that wide water, inescapable.
Deer walk upon our mountains, and the quail
115 Whistle about us their spontaneous cries;
Sweet berries ripen in the wilderness;
And, in the isolation of the sky,
At evening, casual flocks of pigeons make
Ambiguous undulations as they sink,
120 Downward to darkness, on extended wings.

1937

Anecdote of the Jar

I placed a jar in Tennessee,
And round it was, upon a hill.
It made the slovenly wilderness
Surround that hill.

5 The wilderness rose up to it,
And sprawled around, no longer wild.
The jar was round upon the ground
And tall and of a port in air.

It took dominion everywhere.
10 The jar was gray and bare.
It did not give of bird or bush,
Like nothing else in Tennessee.

1937

Thirteen Ways of Looking at a Blackbird

I

Among the twenty snowy mountains,
The only moving thing
Was the eye of the blackbird.

II

I was of three minds,
5   Like a tree
In which there are three blackbirds.

III

The blackbird whirled in the autumn winds.
It was a small part of the pantomime.

IV

A man and a woman
10   Are one.
A man and a woman and a blackbird
Are one.

V

I do not know which to prefer,
The beauty of inflections,
15   Or the beauty of innuendoes,
The blackbird whistling
Or just after.

VI

Icicles filled the long window
With barbaric glass.
20   The shadow of the blackbird
Crossed it, to and fro.
The mood
Traced in the shadow
An indecipherable cause.

VII

25   O thin men of Haddam[1]
Why do you imagine golden birds?
Do you not see how the blackbird
Walks around the feet
Of the women about you?

VIII

30   I know noble accents
And lucid, inescapable rhythms;

----

[1]A town in Connecticut; Stevens liked its name.

But I know, too,
That the blackbird is involved
In what I know.

IX

35 When the blackbird flew out of sight,
It marked the edge
Of one of many circles.

X

At the sight of blackbirds
Flying in a green light,
40 Even the bawds of euphony
Would cry out sharply.

XI

He rode over Connecticut
In a glass coach.
Once, a fear pierced him,
45 In that he mistook
The shadow of his equipage
For blackbirds.

XII

The river is moving.
The blackbird must be flying.

XIII

50 It was evening all afternoon.
It was snowing
And it was going to snow.
The blackbird sat
In the cedar-limbs.

1923

The Snow Man

One must have a mind of winter
To regard the frost and the boughs
Of the pine-trees crusted with snow;

And have been cold a long time
5 To behold the junipers shagged with ice,
The spruces rough in the distant glitter

Of the January sun; and not to think
Of any misery in the sound of the wind,
In the sound of a few leaves,

10 Which is the sound of the land
Full of the same wind
That is blowing in the same bare place

For the listener, who listens in the snow,
And, nothing himself, beholds
15 Nothing that is not there and the nothing that is.

1937

The Emperor of Ice-Cream

Call the roller of big cigars,
The muscular one, and bid him whip
In kitchen cups concupiscent curds.
Let the wenches dawdle in such dress
5 As they are used to wear, and let the boys
Bring flowers in last month's newspapers.
Let be be finale of seem.
The only emperor is the emperor of ice-cream.

Take from the dresser of deal,
10 Lacking the three glass knobs, that sheet
On which she embroidered fantails once
And spread it so as to cover her face.
If her horny feet protrude, they come
To show how cold she is, and dumb.
15 Let the lamp affix its beam.
The only emperor is the emperor of ice-cream.

1937

The Idea of Order at Key West

She sang beyond the genius of the sea.
The water never formed to mind or voice,
Like a body wholly body, fluttering
Its empty sleeves; and yet its mimic motion
5 Made constant cry, caused constantly a cry,
That was not ours although we understood,
Inhuman, of the veritable ocean.

The sea was not a mask. No more was she.
The song and water were not medleyed sound

10 Even if what she sang was what she heard,
Since what she sang was uttered word by word.
It may be that in all her phrases stirred
The grinding water and the gasping wind;
But it was she and not the sea we heard.

15 For she was the maker of the song she sang.
The ever-hooded, tragic-gestured sea
Was merely a place by which she walked to sing.
Whose spirit is this? we said, because we knew
It was the spirit that we sought and knew
20 That we should ask this often as she sang.
If it was only the dark voice of the sea
That rose, or even colored by many waves;
If it was only the outer voice of sky
And cloud, of the sunken coral water-walled,
25 However clear, it would have been deep air,
The heaving speech of air, a summer sound
Repeated in a summer without end
And sound alone. But it was more than that,
More even than her voice, and ours, among
30 The meaningless plungings of water and the wind,
Theatrical distances, bronze shadows heaped
On high horizons, mountainous atmospheres
Of sky and sea.
                        It was her voice that made
35 The sky acutest at its vanishing.
She measured to the hour its solitude.
She was the single artificer of the world
In which she sang. And when she sang, the sea,
Whatever self it had, became the self
40 That was her song, for she was the maker. Then we,
As we beheld her striding there alone,
Knew that there never was a world for her
Except the one she sang and, singing, made.

Ramon Fernandez,[1] tell me, if you know,
45 Why, when the singing ended and we turned
Toward the town, tell why the glassy lights,
The lights in the fishing boats at anchor there,
As the night descended, tilting in the air,
Mastered the night and portioned out the sea,

---

[1]does not refer to an actual person

50 Fixing emblazoned zones and fiery poles,
   Arranging, deepening, enchanting night.

Oh! Blessed rage for order, pale Ramon,
The maker's rage to order words of the sea,
Words of the fragrant portals, dimly-starred,
55 And of ourselves and of our origins,
   In ghostlier demarcations, keener sounds.

                                                      1934

Peter Quince at the Clavier

I

Just as my fingers on these keys
Make music, so the selfsame sounds
On my spirit make a music, too.

Music is feeling, then, not sound;
5 And thus it is that what I feel,
Here in this room, desiring you,

Thinking of your blue-shadowed silk,
Is music. It is like the strain
Waked in the elders by Susanna.

10 Of a green evening, clear and warm,
   She bathed in her still garden, while
   The red-eyed elders watching, felt

The basses of their beings throb
In witching chords, and their thin blood
15 Pulse pizzicati of Hosanna.

II

In the green water, clear and warm,
Susanna lay.
She searched
   The touch of springs,
20 And found
   Concealed imaginings,
   She sighed,
   For so much melody.

Upon the bank, she stood
25 In the cool
   Of spent emotions.

She felt, among the leaves,
The dew
Of old devotions.

30   She walked upon the grass,
Still quavering.
The winds were like her maids,
On timid feet,
Fetching her woven scarves,
35   Yet wavering.

A breath upon her hand
Muted the night.
She turned—
A cymbal crashed,
40   And roaring horns.

III

Soon, with a noise like tambourines,
Came her attendant Byzantines.

They wondered why Susanna cried
Against the elders by her side;

45   And as they whispered, the refrain
Was like a willow swept by rain.

Anon, their lamps' uplifted flame
Revealed Susanna and her shame.

And then, the simpering Byzantines
50 . Fled, with a noise like tambourines.

IV

Beauty is momentary in the mind—
The fitful tracing of a portal;
But in the flesh it is immortal.

The body dies; the body's beauty lives.
55   So evenings die, in their green going,
A wave, interminably flowing.
So gardens die, their meek breath scenting
The cowl of winter, done repenting.
So maidens die, to the auroral
60   Celebration of a maiden's choral.
Susanna's music touched the bawdy strings
Of those white elders; but, escaping,

Left only Death's ironic scraping.
Now, in its immortality, it plays
65 On the clear viol of her memory,
And makes a constant sacrament of praise.

1937

Bantams in Pine-Woods

Chieftain Iffucan of Azcan in caftan
Of tan with henna hackles, halt!

Damned universal cock, as if the sun
Was blackamoor to bear your blazing tail.

5 Fat! Fat! Fat! Fat! I am the personal.
Your world is you. I am my world.

You ten-foot poet among inchlings. Fat!
Begone! An inchling bristles in these pines,

Bristles, and points their Appalachian tangs,
10 And fears not portly Azcan nor his hoos.

1937

William Carlos Williams

(1883–1963)

The Young Housewife

At ten A.M. the young housewife
moves about in negligee behind
the wooden walls of her husband's house.
I pass solitary in my car.

5 Then again she comes to the curb
to call the ice-man, fish-man, and stands
shy, uncorseted, tucking in
stray ends of hair, and I compare her
to a fallen leaf.

10 The noiseless wheels of my car
rush with a crackling sound over
dried leaves as I bow and pass smiling.

1917

The Red Wheelbarrow

so much depends
upon

a red wheel
barrow

5 glazed with rain
water

beside the white
chickens.

1923

The Yachts

contend in a sea which the land partly encloses
shielding them from the too heavy blows
of an ungoverned ocean which when it chooses

tortures the biggest hulls, the best man knows
5 to pit against its beatings, and sinks them pitilessly.
Mothlike in mists, scintillant in the minute

brilliance of cloudless days, with broad bellying sails
they glide to the wind tossing green water
from their sharp prows while over them the crew crawls

10 ant like, solicitously grooming them, releasing,
making fast as they turn, lean far over and having
caught the wind again, side by side, head for the mark.

In a well guarded arena of open water surrounded by
lesser and greater craft which, sycophant, lumbering
15 and flittering follow them, they appear youthful, rare

as the light of a happy eye, live with the grace
of all that in the mind is fleckless, free and
naturally to be desired. Now the sea which holds them

is moody, lapping their glossy sides, as if feeling
20 for some slightest flaw but fails completely.
Today no race. Then the wind comes again. The yachts

move, jockeying for a start, the signal is set and they
are off. Now the waves strike at them but they are too
well made, they slip through, though they take in canvas.

25 Arms with hands grasping seek to clutch at the prows.
Bodies thrown recklessly in the way are cut aside.
It is a sea of faces about them in agony, in despair

until the horror of the race dawns staggering the mind,
the whole sea become an entanglement of water bodies
30 lost to the world bearing what they cannot hold. Broken,

beaten, desolate, reaching from the dead to be taken up
they cry out, failing, failing! their cries rising
in waves still as the skillful yachts pass over.

1935

The Dance

In Breughel's great picture, The Kermess,[1]
the dancers go round, they go round and
around, the squeal and the blare and the
tweedle of bagpipes, a bugle and fiddles
5 tipping their bellies (round as the thick-
sided glasses whose wash they impound)
their hips and their bellies off balance
to turn them. Kicking and rolling about
the Fair Grounds, swinging their butts, those
10 shanks must be sound to bear up under such
rollicking measures, prance as they dance
in Breughel's great picture, The Kermess.

1944

The Great Figure

Among the rain
and lights
I saw the figure 5
in gold
5 on a red
firetruck
moving
tense
unheeded
10 to gong clangs
siren howls
and wheels rumbling
through the dark city.

1921

---

[1]Pieter Breughel (1525?–1569), Flemish painter. "Kermess" means "fair."

This Is Just to Say

I have eaten
the plums
that were in
the icebox

5 and which
you were probably
saving
for breakfast

Forgive me
10 they were delicious
so sweet
and so cold

1934

Tract

I will teach you my townspeople
how to perform a funeral—
for you have it over a troop
of artists—
5 unless one should scour the world—
you have the ground sense necessary.
See! the hearse leads.
I begin with a design for a hearse.
For Christ's sake not black—
10 nor white either—and not polished!
Let it be weathered—like a farm wagon—
with gilt wheels (this could be
applied fresh at small expense)
or no wheels at all:
15 a rough dray to drag over the ground.

Knock the glass out!
My God—glass, my townspeople!
For what purpose? Is it for the dead
to look out or for us to see
20 how well he is housed or to see
the flowers or the lack of them—
or what?
To keep the rain and snow from him?
He will have a heavier rain soon:

25 pebbles and dirt and what not.
Let there be no glass—
and no upholstery, phew!
and no little brass rollers
and small easy wheels on the bottom—
30 my townspeople what are you thinking of?

A rough plain hearse then
with gilt wheels and no top at all.
On this the coffin lies
by its own weight.

35   No wreaths please—
especially no hot house flowers.
Some common memento is better,
something he prized and is known by:
his old clothes—a few books perhaps—
40 God knows what! You realize
how we are about these things
my townspeople—
something will be found—anything
even flowers if he had come to that.
45 So much for the hearse.

For heaven's sake though see to the driver!
Take off the silk hat! In fact
that's no place at all for him—
up there unceremoniously
50 dragging our friend out to his own dignity!
Bring him down—bring him down!
Low and inconspicuous! I'd not have him ride
on the wagon at all—damn him—
the undertaker's understrapper!
55 Let him hold the reins
and walk at the side
and inconspicuously too!

Then briefly as to yourselves:
Walk behind—as they do in France,
60 seventh class, or if you ride
Hell take curtains! Go with some show
of inconvenience; sit openly—
to the weather as to grief.
Or do you think you can shut grief in?
65 What—from us? We who have perhaps

nothing to lose? Share with us
share with us—it will be money
in your pockets.
                          Go now
I think you are ready.

1917

To Elsie

The pure products of America
go crazy—
mountain folk from Kentucky

or the ribbed north end of
5 Jersey
with its isolate lakes and

valleys, its deaf-mutes, thieves
old names
and promiscuity between

10 devil-may-care men who have taken
to railroading
out of sheer lust of adventure—

and young slatterns, bathed
in filth
15 from Monday to Saturday

to be tricked out that night
with gauds
from imaginations which have no

peasant traditions to give them
20 character
but flutter and flaunt

sheer rags—succumbing without
emotion
save numbed terror

25 under some hedge of choke-cherry
or viburnum—
which they cannot express—

Unless it be that marriage
perhaps
30 with a dash of Indian blood

will throw up a girl so desolate
so hemmed round
with disease or murder

that she'll be rescued by an
35 agent—
reared by the state and

sent out at fifteen to work in
some hard-pressed
house in the suburbs—

40 some doctor's family, some Elsie-
voluptuous water
expressing with broken

brain the truth about us—
her great
45 ungainly hips and flopping breasts

addressed to cheap
jewelry
and rich young men with fine eyes

as if the earth under our feet
50 were
an excrement of some sky

and we degraded prisoners
destined
to hunger until we eat filth

55 while the imagination strains
after deer
going by fields of goldenrod in

the stifling heat of September
Somehow
60 it seems to destroy us

It is only in isolate flecks that
something
is given off

No one
65 to witness
and adjust, no one to drive the car

1923

D. H. Lawrence

(1885–1930)

Piano

Softly, in the dusk, a woman is singing to me;
Taking me back down the vista of years, till I see
A child sitting under the piano, in the boom of the tingling strings
And pressing the small, poised feet of a mother who smiles as she sings.

5 In spite of myself, the insidious mastery of song
Betrays me back, till the heart of me weeps to belong
To the old Sunday evenings at home, with winter outside
And hymns in the cozy parlor, the tinkling piano our guide.

So now it is vain for the singer to burst into clamor
10 With the great black piano appassionato. The glamour
Of childish days is upon me, my manhood is cast
Down in the flood of remembrance, I weep like a child for the past.

1914

Snake

A snake came to my water-trough
On a hot, hot day, and I in pajamas for the heat,
To drink there.

In the deep, strange-scented shade of the great dark carob-tree
5 I came down the steps with my pitcher
And must wait, must stand and wait, for there he was at the trough before
    me.

He reached down from a fissure in the earth-wall in the gloom
And trailed his yellow-brown slackness soft-bellied down, over the edge of the
    stone trough
And rested his throat upon the stone bottom,
10 And where the water had dripped from the tap, in a small clearness,
He sipped with his straight mouth,
Softly drank through his straight gums, into his slack long body,
Silently.

Someone was before me at my water-trough,
15 And I, like a second comer, waiting.

He lifted his head from his drinking, as cattle do,
And looked at me vaguely, as drinking cattle do,
And flickered his two-forked tongue from his lips, and mused a moment,

And stooped and drank a little more,
20 Being earth-brown, earth-golden from the burning bowels of the earth
On the day of Sicilian July, with Etna smoking.
The voice of my education said to me
He must be killed,
For in Sicily the black, black snakes are innocent, the gold are venomous.

25 And voices in me said, If you were a man
You would take a stick and break him now, and finish him off.

But must I confess how I liked him,
How glad I was he had come like a guest in quiet, to drink at my water-trough
And depart peaceful, pacified, and thankless,
30 Into the burning bowels of this earth?

Was it cowardice, that I dared not kill him?
Was it perversity, that I longed to talk to him?
Was it humility, to feel so honored?
I felt so honored.

35 And yet those voices:
If you were not afraid, you would kill him!

And truly I was afraid, I was most afraid,
But even so, honored still more
That he should seek my hospitality
40 From out the dark door of the secret earth.

He drank enough
And lifted his head, dreamily, as one who has drunken,
And flickered his tongue like a forked night on the air, so black,
Seeming to lick his lips,
45 And looked around like a god, unseeing, into the air,
And slowly turned his head,
And slowly, very slowly, as if thrice adream,
Proceeded to draw his slow length curving round
And climb again the broken bank of my wall-face.

50 And as he put his head into that dreadful hole,
And as he slowly drew up, snake-easing his shoulders, and entered farther,
A sort of horror, a sort of protest against his withdrawing into that horrid black
    hole,
Deliberately going into the blackness, and slowly drawing himself after,
Overcame me now his back was turned.

55 I looked round, I put down my pitcher,
I picked up a clumsy log
And threw it at the water-trough with a clatter.

I think it did not hit him,
But suddenly that part of him that was left behind convulsed in undignified
    haste
60 Writhed like lightning, and was gone
Into the black hole, the earth-lipped fissure in the wall-front,
At which, in the intense still noon, I stared with fascination.

And immediately I regretted it.
I thought how paltry, how vulgar, what a mean act!
65 I despised myself and the voices of my accursed human education.

And I thought of the albatross
And I wished he would come back, my snake.

For he seemed to me again like a king,
Like a king in exile, uncrowned in the underworld,
70 Now due to be crowned again.

And so, I missed my chance with one of the lords
Of life.
And I have something to expiate;
A pettiness.

1921

Ezra Pound

(1885–1972)

The Garden

En Robe de Parade.

    SAMAIN[1]

Like a skein of loose silk blown against a wall
She walks by the railing of a path in Kensington Gardens,
And she is dying piece-meal
    of a sort of emotional anaemia.

5 And round about there is a rabble
Of the filthy, sturdy, unkillable infants of the very poor.
They shall inherit the earth.

---

[1]"Dressed for state"; Albert Samain (1858–1900) was a French symbolist.

In her is the end of breeding.
Her boredom is exquisite and excessive.
10 She would like some one to speak to her,
And is almost afraid that I
    will commit that indiscretion

                                                      1916

Salutation

O generation of the thoroughly smug
    and thoroughly uncomfortable,
I have seen fishermen picnicking in the sun,
I have seen them with untidy families,
5 I have seen their smiles full of teeth
    and heard ungainly laughter.
And I am happier than you are,
And they were happier than I am;
And the fish swim in the lake
10   and do not even own clothing.

                                                      1914

In a Station of the Metro

The apparition of these faces in the crowd;
Petals on a wet, black bough.

                                                      1916

Dance Figure

For the Marriage in Cana of Galilee

Dark eyed,
O woman of my dreams,
Ivory sandalled,
There is none like thee among the dancers,
5 None with swift feet.
I have not found thee in the tents,
In the broken darkness.
I have not found thee at the well-head
Among the women with pitchers.
10 Thine arms are as a young sapling under the bark;
Thy face as a river with lights.

White as an almond are thy shoulders;
As new almonds stripped from the husk.

.They guard thee not with eunuchs;
15 Not with bars of copper.

Gilt turquoise and silver are in the place of thy rest.
A brown robe, with threads of gold woven in
          patterns, hast thou gathered about thee,
O Nathat-Ikanaie, 'Tree-at-the-river.'

As a rillet among the sedge are thy hands upon me;
20 Thy fingers a frosted stream.

Thy maidens are white like pebbles;
Their music about thee!

There is none like thee among the dancers;
None with swift feet.

L'Art, 1910

Green arsenic smeared on an egg-white cloth,
Crushed strawberries! Come, let us feast our eyes.

                                        1916

The Tea Shop

The girl in the tea shop
              Is not so beautiful as she was,
The August has worn against her.
She does not get up the stairs so eagerly;
5 Yes, she also will turn middle-aged,
And the glow of youth that she spread about us
              As she brought us our muffins
Will be spread about us no longer.
              She also will turn middle-aged.

Ancient Music

Winter is icumen in,
Lhude sing Goddamm,
Raineth drop and staineth slop,
And how the wind doth ramm!
5   Sing : Goddamm.
Skiddeth bus and sloppeth us,
An ague hath my ham.
Freezeth river, turneth liver,
          Damn you, sing : Goddamm.

10 Goddamm, Goddamm, 'tis why I am, Goddamm,
        So 'gainst the winter's balm.
    Sing goddamm, damm, sing Goddamm,
    Sing goddamm, sing goddamm, DAMM.

The River-Merchant's Wife: A Letter

While my hair was still cut straight across my forehead
I played about the front gate, pulling flowers.
You came by on bamboo stilts, playing horse,
You walked about my seat, playing with blue plums.
5 And we went on living in the village of Chokan:
Two small people, without dislike or suspicion.

At fourteen I married My Lord you.
I never laughed, being bashful.
Lowering my head, I looked at the wall.
10 Called to, a thousand times, I never looked back.

At fifteen I stopped scowling,
I desired my dust to be mingled with yours
Forever and forever and forever.
Why should I climb the look out?

15 At sixteen you departed,
You went into far Ku-to-yen, by the river of swirling eddies,
And you have been gone five months.
The monkeys make sorrowful noise overhead.

You dragged your feet when you went out.
20 By the gate now, the moss is grown, the different mosses,
Too deep to clear them away!
The leaves fall early this autumn, in wind.
The paired butterflies are already yellow with August
Over the grass in the West garden;
25 They hurt me. I grow older.
If you are coming down through the narrows of the river Kiang,
Please let me know beforehand,
And I will come out to meet you
                As far as Cho-fu-Sa.

                                By *Rihaku*[1]

                                1915

---

[1]*Rihaku* is a transcription of the Japanese form of the name of the great Chinese poet Li Po (701–762).

These Fought in Any Case[1]

These fought in any case,
and some believing,
> pro domo,[2] in any case . . .

Some quick to arm,
5 some for adventure,
some from fear of weakness,
some from fear of censure,
some for love of slaughter, in imagination,
learning later . . .
10 some in fear, learning love of slaughter;

Died some, pro patria,
> non "dulce" non "et decor"[3] . . .
walked eye-deep in hell
believing in old men's lies, then unbelieving
15 came home, home to a lie,
home to many deceits,
home to old lies and new infamy;
usury age-old and age-thick
and liars in public places.

20 Daring as never before, wastage as never before.
Young blood and high blood,
fair cheeks, and fine bodies;

fortitude as never before
frankness as never before,
25 disillusions as never told in the old days,
hysterias, trench confessions,
laughter out of dead bellies.

From **The Cantos**

Canto LXXXI

libretto

Yet
95 Ere the season died a-cold
Borne upon a zephyr's shoulder

---

[1]Section IV from "E. P. Ode pour L'Election de Son Sépulcre" ("E. P. Ode on the Selection of His Tomb").
[2]"for homeland"
[3]An ironic allusion to Horace's famous line "Dulce et decorum est pro patria mori" ("It is sweet and fitting to die for one's country").

I rose through the aureate sky
        Lawes and Jenkins guard thy rest
        Dolmetsch ever be thy guest,
100 Has he tempered the viol's wood
To enforce both   the grave   and the acute?
Has he curved us the bowl of the lute?
        Lawes and Jenkins guard thy rest
        Dolmetsch ever be thy guest,
105 Hast 'ou fashioned so airy a mood
    To draw up leaf from the root?
Hast 'ou found   a cloud   so light
    As seemed neither mist nor shade?

        Then resolve me, tell me aright
110   If Waller sang or Dowland played.

     Your eyen two wol sleye me sodenly
     I may the beauté of hem nat susteyne

And for 180 years almost nothing.

Ed ascoltando il leggier mormorio
115   there came new subtlety of eyes into my tent,
whether of spirit or hypostasis,
    but what the blindfold hides
or at carneval
             nor any pair showed anger
120   Saw but the eyes and stance between the eyes,
colour, diastasis,
    careless or unaware it had not the
  whole tent's room
nor was place for the full Ειδώς[1]
125 interpass, penetrate
    casting but shade beyond the other lights
     sky's clear
     night's sea
     green of the mountain pool
130   shone from the unmasked eyes in half-mask's space.
What thou lovest well remains,
             the rest is dross

---

[1] *Eidos* (Greek): knowing

What thou lov'st well shall not be reft from thee
What thou lov'st well is thy true heritage
135 Whose world, or mine or theirs
                    or is it of none?
First came the seen, then thus the palpable
        Elysium, though it were in the halls of hell,
What thou lovest well is thy true heritage
140 What thou lov'st well shall not be reft from thee

The ant's a centaur in his dragon world.
Pull down thy vanity, it is not man
Made courage, or made order, or made grace,
        Pull down thy vanity, I say pull down.
145 Learn of the green world what can be thy place
In scaled invention or true artistry,
Pull down thy vanity,
                    Paquin pull down!
The green casque has outdone your elegance.

150 "Master thyself, then others shall thee beare"
        Pull down thy vanity
Thou art a beaten dog beneath the hail,
A swollen magpie in a fitful sun,
Half black half white
155 Nor knowst'ou wing from tail
Pull down thy vanity
                    How mean thy hates
Fostered in falsity,
                    Pull down thy vanity,
160 Rathe to destroy, niggard in charity,
Pull down they vanity,
                    I say pull down.

But to have done instead of not doing
            this is not vanity
165 To have, with decency, knocked
That a Blunt should open
            To have gathered from the air a live tradition
or from a fine old eye the unconquered flame
This is not vanity.
170   Here error is all in the not done,
all in the diffidence that faltered . . .

1948

From **Hugh Selwyn Mauberley**

<u>LIFE AND CONTACTS</u>

"Vocat aestus in umbram."[1]

NEMESIANUS EC. IV.

E. P. Ode pour L'Election de Son Sepulchre[2]

I

For three years, out of key with his time,
He strove to resuscitate the dead art
Of poetry; to maintain "the sublime"
In the old sense. Wrong from the start—

5   No, hardly, but seeing he had been born
In a half savage country, out of date;
Bent resolutely on wringing lilies from the acorn;
Capaneus; trout for factitious bait;

Ἴδμεν γάρ τοι πάνθ᾽, ὅσ᾽ ἐνὶ Τροίῃ[3]
10   Caught in the unstopped ear;
Giving the rocks small lee-way
The chopped seas held him, therefore, that year.

His true Penelope was Flaubert,
He fished by obstinate isles;
15   Observed the elegance of Circe's hair
Rather than the mottoes on sun-dials.

Unaffected by "The march of events,"
He passed from men's memory in *l'an trentuniesme
De son eage;*[4] the case presents
20   No adjunct to the Muses' diadem.

II

The age demanded an image
Of its accelerated grimace,
Something for the modern stage,
Not, at any rate, an Attic grace;

25   Not, not certainly, the obscure reveries
Of the inward gaze;

---

[1]Latin: "Summer heat calls us into the shade."
[2]French: Ode on the choice of His Tomb
[3]*Idmen gár toi pánth hos eni Troíe* (Greek): for we know all the things that are in Troy
[4]Old French: in the thirty-first year of his life

Better mendacities
Than the classics in paraphrase!

The "age demanded" chiefly a mould in plaster,
30 Made with no loss of time,
A prose kinema,[5] not, not assuredly, alabaster
Or the "sculpture" of rhyme.

1920

H. D. (Hilda Doolittle)

(1886–1961)

Heat

O wind, rend open the heat,
cut apart the heat,
rend it to tatters.

Fruit cannot drop
5 through this thick air—
fruit cannot fall into heat
that presses up and blunts
the points of pears
and rounds the grapes.

10 Cut the heat—
plough through it,
turning it on either side
of your path.

1916

Sea Rose

Rose, harsh rose,
marred and with stint of petals,
meagre flower, thin,
sparse of leaf,

5 more precious
than a wet rose,
single on a stem—
you are caught in the drift.

---

[5]Greek: movement

Stunted, with small leaf,
10   you are flung on the sand,
you are lifted
in the crisp sand
that drives in the wind.

Can the spice-rose
15   drip such acrid fragrance
hardened in a leaf?

1916

Oread

Whirl up, sea—
whirl your pointed pines,
splash your great pines
on our rocks,
5   hurl your green over us,
cover us with your pools of fir.

1924

Robinson Jeffers

(1887–1962)

Divinely Superfluous Beauty

The storm-dances of gulls, the barking game of seals,
Over and under the ocean . . .
Divinely superfluous beauty
Rules the games, presides over destinies, makes trees grow
5   And hills tower, waves fall.
The incredible beauty of joy
Stars with fire the joining of lips, O let our loves too
Be joined, there is not a maiden
Burns and thirsts for love
10   More than my blood for you, by the shore of seals while the wings
Weave like a web in the air
Divinely superfluous beauty.

Love the Wild Swan

"I hate my verses, every line, every word.
Oh pale and brittle pencils ever to try
One grass-blade's curve, or the throat of one bird
That clings to twig, ruffled against white sky.

5 Oh cracked and twilight mirrors ever to catch
One color, one glinting flash, of the splendor of things.
Unlucky hunter, Oh bullets of wax,
The lion beauty, the wild-swan wings, the storm of the wings."
—This wild swan of a world is no hunter's game.
10 Better bullets than yours would miss the white breast,
Better mirrors than yours would crack in the flame.
Does it matter whether you hate your . . . self? At least
Love your eyes that can see, your mind that can
Hear the music, the thunder of the wings. Love the wild swan.

Cassandra[1]

The mad girl with the staring eyes and long white fingers
Hooked in the stones of the wall,
The storm-wrack hair and the screeching mouth: does it matter, Cassandra,
Whether the people believe
5 Your bitter fountain? Truly men hate the truth; they'd liefer
Meet a tiger on the road.
Therefore the poets honey their truth with lying; but religion-
Venders and political men
Pour from the barrel, new lies on the old, and are praised for kindly
10 Wisdom. Poor bitch, be wise.
No: you'll still mumble in a corner a crust of truth, to men
And gods disgusting.—You and I, Cassandra.

Marianne Moore

(1887–1972)

Poetry

I, too, dislike it: there are things that are important beyond all this fiddle.
　　Reading it, however, with a perfect contempt for it, one discovers in
　　it after all, a place for the genuine.
　　　　Hands that can grasp, eyes
5　　　　that can dilate, hair that can rise
　　　　　　if it must, these things are important not because a

high-sounding interpretation can be put upon them but because they are
　　useful. When they become so derivative as to become unintelligible,
　　the same thing may be said for all of us, that we
10　　　　do not admire what

---

[1]princess of Troy, gifted with the power of prophecy but doomed never to be believed

we cannot understand: the bat
    holding on upside down or in quest of something to

eat, elephants pushing, a wild horse taking a roll, a tireless wolf under
    a tree, the immovable critic twitching his skin like a horse that feels a flea, the
        base-
15   ball fan, the statistician—
    nor is it valid
        to discriminate against "business documents and

school-books";[1] all these phenomena are important. One must make
        a distinction
    however: when dragged into prominence by half poets, the result
        is not poetry,
20   nor till the poets among us can be
      "literalists of
    the imagination"[2]—above
       insolence and triviality and can present

for inspection, "imaginary gardens with real toads in them," shall we have
25   it. In the meantime, if you demand on the one hand,
    the raw material of poetry in
      all its rawness and
      that which is on the other hand
        genuine, you are interested in poetry.

                                          1921

A Grave

Man looking into the sea,
taking the view from those who have as much right to it as you have to yourself,
it is human nature to stand in the middle of a thing,
but you cannot stand in the middle of this;
5 the sea has nothing to give but a well excavated grave.
The firs stand in a procession, each with an emerald turkey-foot at the top,
reserved as their contours, saying nothing;
repression, however, is not the most obvious characteristic of the sea;
the sea is a collector, quick to return a rapacious look.
10 There are others besides you who have worn that look—
whose expression is no longer a protest; the fish no longer investigate them
for their bones have not lasted:
men lower nets, unconscious of the fact that they are desecrating a grave,

---

[1]Moore's note cites Tolstoy's diary: "Poetry is everything with the exception of business documents
  and school books."
[2]from Yeats, *Ideas of Good and Evil*

and row quickly away—the blades of the oars
15   moving together like the feet of water-spiders as if there were no such
      thing as death.
The wrinkles progress among themselves in a phalanx—beautiful under
      networks of foam,
and fade breathlessly while the sea rustles in and out of the seaweed;
the birds swim through the air at top speed, emitting catcalls as heretofore—
the tortoise-shell scourges about the feet of the cliffs, in motion beneath them;
20   and the ocean, under the pulsation of lighthouses and noise of bell-buoys,
    advances as usual, looking as if it were not that ocean in which dropped things
      are bound to sink—
in which if they turn and twist, it is neither with volition nor consciousness.

                                                1924

The Mind Is an Enchanting Thing

is an enchanted thing
    like the glaze on a
katydid-wing
      subdivided by sun
5   till the nettings are legion.
Like Gieseking[1] playing Scarlatti;[2]

like the apteryx-awl[3]
    as a beak, or the
kiwi's rain-shawl
10   of haired feathers, the mind
      feeling its way as though blind,
walks along with its eyes on the ground.

It has memory's ear
    that can hear without
15 having to hear.
      Like the gyroscope's fall,
      truly unequivocal
because trued by regnant certainty,

it is a power of
20   strong enchantment. It
is like the dove-
      neck animated by
      sun; it is memory's eye;
it's conscientious inconsistency.

---

[1]Walter Gieseking (1895–1956), eminent German pianist
[2]Domenico Scarlatti (1685–1757), Italian composer of brilliant keyboard sonatas
[3]An apteryx is a flightless bird with a long, slender beak resembling the shape of an awl.

25 It tears off the veil; tears
      the temptation, the
mist the heart wears,
        from its eyes,—if the heart
        has a face; it takes apart
30 dejection. It's fire in the dove-neck's

iridescence; in the
      inconsistencies
of Scarlatti.
        Unconfusion submits
35   its confusion to proof; it's
not a Herod's oath[4] that cannot change.

                    1944

Edwin Muir

(1887–1959)

Childhood

Long time he lay upon the sunny hill,
    To his father's house below securely bound.
Far off the silent, changing sound was still,
    With the black islands lying thick around.

5 He saw each separate height, each vaguer hue,
    Where the massed islands rolled in mist away,
And though all ran together in his view
    He knew that unseen straits between them lay.

Often he wondered what new shores were there.
10   In thought he saw the still light on the sand,
The shallow water clear in tranquil air,
    And walked through it in joy from strand to strand.

Over the sound a ship so slow would pass
    That in the black hill's gloom it seemed to lie.
15 The evening sound was smooth like sunken glass,
    And time seemed finished ere the ship passed by.

Grey tiny rocks slept round him where he lay,
    Moveless as they, more still as evening came,

---

[4]See Matthew 2:1–16.

The grasses threw straight shadows far away,
20   And from the house his mother called his name.

1925

The Animals

They do not live in the world,
Are not in time and space.
From birth to death hurled
No word do they have, not one
5 To plant a foot upon,
Were never in any place.

For with names the world was called
Out of the empty air,
With names was built and walled,
10 Line and circle and square,
Dust and emerald;
Snatched from deceiving death
By the articulate breath.

But these have never trod
15 Twice the familiar track,
Never never turned back
Into the memoried day.
All is new and near
In the unchanging Here
20 Of the fifth great day of God,
That shall remain the same,
Never shall pass away.

On the sixth day we came.

1952

The Brothers

Last night I watched my brothers play,
The gentle and the reckless one,
In a field two yards away.
For half a century they were gone
5 Beyond the other side of care
To be among the peaceful dead.
Even in a dream how could I dare
Interrogate that happiness
So wildly spent yet never less?
10 For still they raced about the green

And were like two revolving suns;
A brightness poured from head to head,
So strong I could not see their eyes
Or look into their paradise.
15 What were they doing, the happy ones?
Yet where I was they once had been.

I thought, How could I be so dull,
Twenty thousand days ago,
Not to see they were beautiful?
20 I asked them, Were you really so
As you are now, that other day?
And the dream was soon away.

For then we played for victory
And not to make each other glad.
25 A darkness covered every head,
Frowns twisted the original face,
And through that mask we could not see
The beauty and the buried grace.

I have observed in foolish awe
30 The dateless mid-days of the law
And seen indifferent justice done
By everyone on everyone.
And in a vision I have seen
My brothers playing on the green.

1956

T. S. Eliot

(1888–1965)

The Love Song of J. Alfred Prufrock

S'io credesse che mia risposta fosse
A persona che mai tornasse al mondo,
Questa fiamma staria senza piu scosse.
Ma perciocche giammai di questo fondo
Non torno vivo alcun, s'i'odo il vero,
Senza tema d'infamia ti rispondo.[1]

---

[1]"If I thought that my response were given to one who would ever return to the world, this flame would move no more. But since never from this depth has man returned alive, if what I hear is true, without fear of infamy I answer thee." In Dante's *Inferno* these words are addressed to the poet by the spirit of Guida da Montefeltro.

Let us go then, you and I,
When the evening is spread out against the sky
Like a patient etherized upon a table;
Let us go, through certain half-deserted streets,
5 The muttering retreats
Of restless nights in one-night cheap hotels
And sawdust restaurants with oyster-shells:
Streets that follow like a tedious argument
Of insidious intent
10 To lead you to an overwhelming question . . .
Oh, do not ask, "What is it?"
Let us go and make our visit.

In the room the women come and go
Talking of Michelangelo.

15 The yellow fog that rubs its back upon the window-panes
The yellow smoke that rubs its muzzle on the window panes
Licked its tongue into the corners of the evening,
Lingered upon the pools that stand in drains,
Let fall upon its back the soot that falls from chimneys,
20 Slipped by the terrace, made a sudden leap,
And seeing that it was a soft October night,
Curled once about the house, and fell asleep.

And indeed there will be time
For the yellow smoke that slides along the street,
25 Rubbing its back upon the window-panes;
There will be time, there will be time
To prepare a face to meet the faces that you meet;
There will be time to murder and create,
And time for all the works and days of hands
30 That lift and drop a question on your plate;
Time for you and time for me,
And time yet for a hundred indecisions,
And for a hundred visions and revisions,
Before the taking of a toast and tea.

35 In the room the women come and go
Talking of Michelangelo.

And indeed there will be time
To wonder, "Do I dare?" and, "Do I dare?"
Time to turn back and descend the stair,
40 With a bald spot in the middle of my hair—
[They will say: "How his hair is growing thin!"]
My morning coat, my collar mounting firmly to the chin,

My necktie rich and modest, but asserted by a simple pin—
[They will say: "But how his arms and legs are thin!"]
45 Do I dare
Disturb the universe?
In a minute there is time
For decisions and revisions which a minute will reverse.

For I have known them all already, known them all:
50 Have known the evenings, mornings, afternoons,
I have measured out my life with coffee spoons;
I know the voices dying with a dying fall
Beneath the music from a farther room.
    So how should I presume?

55 And I have known the eyes already, known them all—
The eyes that fix you in a formulated phrase,
And when I am formulated, sprawling on a pin,
When I am pinned and wriggling on the wall,
Then how should I begin
60 To spit out all the butt-ends of my days and ways?
    And how should I presume?

And I have known the arms already, known them all—
Arms that are braceleted and white and bare
[But in the lamplight, downed with light brown hair!]
65 Is it perfume from a dress
That makes me so digress?
Arms that lie along a table, or wrap about a shawl.
    And should I then presume?
    And how should I begin?

70 Shall I say, I have gone at dusk through narrow streets
And watched the smoke that rises from the pipes
Of lonely men in shirt-sleeves, leaning out of windows? . . .

I should have been a pair of ragged claws
Scuttling across the floors of silent seas.

75 And the afternoon, the evening, sleeps so peacefully!
Smoothed by long fingers,
Asleep . . . tired . . . or it malingers,
Stretched on the floor, here beside you and me.

Should I, after tea and cakes and ices,
80 Have the strength to force the moment to its crisis?
But though I have wept and fasted, wept and prayed,
Though I have seen my head [grown slightly bald] brought in upon a
    platter,
I am no prophet—and here's no great matter;
I have seen the moment of my greatness flicker,
85 And I have seen the eternal Footman hold my coat, and snicker,
And in short, I was afraid.

And would it have been worth it, after all,
After the cups, the marmalade, the tea,
Among the porcelain, among some talk of you and me,
90 Would it have been worth while,
To have bitten off the matter with a smile,
To have squeezed the universe into a ball
To roll it toward some overwhelming question,

To say: "I am Lazarus, come from the dead,
95 Come back to tell you all, I shall tell you all"—
If one, settling a pillow by her head,
      Should say: "That is not what I meant at all.
      That is not it, at all."

And would it have been worth it, after all,
100 Would it have been worth while,
After the sunsets and the dooryards and the sprinkled streets,
After the novels, after the teacups, after the skirts that trail along the floor—
And this, and so much more?—
It is impossible to say just what I mean!
105 But as if a magic lantern threw the nerves in patterns on a screen:
Would it have been worth while
If one, settling a pillow or throwing off a shawl,
And turning toward the window, should say:
      "That is not it at all,
110   That is not what I meant, at all."

No! I am not Prince Hamlet, nor was meant to be;
Am an attendant lord, one that will do
To swell a progress, start a scene or two,
Advise the prince; no doubt, an easy tool,
115 Deferential, glad to be of use,
Politic, cautious, and meticulous;

Full of high sentence, but a bit obtuse;
At times, indeed, almost ridiculous—
Almost, at times, the Fool.

120   I grow old . . . I grow old . . .
I shall wear the bottoms of my trousers rolled.

Shall I part my hair behind? Do I dare to eat a peach?
I shall wear white flannel trousers, and walk upon the beach.
I have heard the mermaids singing, each to each.

125   I do not think that they will sing to me.
I have seen them riding seaward on the waves
Combing the white hair of the waves blown back
When the wind blows the water white and black.

We have lingered in the chambers of the sea
130   By sea-girls wreathed with seaweed red and brown
Till human voices wake us, and we drown.

1917

The Waste Land[1]

"*Nam Sibyllam quidem Cumis ego ipse oculis meis vidi in ampulla pendere, et cum illi
pueri dicerent: Σίβνλλα τί θέλεις, respondebat illa: ἀποθανεῖν θέλω.*"[2]

—FOR EZRA POUND
il miglior fabbro.[3]

I. The Burial of the Dead[4]

April is the cruellest month, breeding
Lilacs out of the dead land, mixing
Memory and desire, stirring
Dull roots with spring rain.

---

[1]In the first hard-cover edition of *The Waste Land,* Eliot included several pages of "Notes," acknowledging his indebtedness to Miss Jessie L. Weston's book on the Grail Legend, *From Ritual to Romance,* as suggesting "the title . . . the plan and a good deal of the incidental symbolism of the poem." He also cited as a source the volumes of James G. Frazer's *The Golden Bough* which deal with "vegetation ceremonies." As deemed particularly helpful, Eliot's notes are summarized in these footnotes.

[2]Petronius's *Satyricon* (first century A.D.) recounts the story of the Sibyl of Cumae, given eternal life but thus doomed to perpetual old age: "For once I myself saw with my own eyes, the Sibyl at Cumae hanging in a cage, and when the children said to her, 'Sibyl, what do you want?' she replied, 'I want to die.'"

[3]"The better maker," Eliot's recognition of Pound for his extensive, sensitive help in shaping the poem. The quotation, from Dante's *Purgatorio* XXVI, 117, was a tribute to the Provençal poet Arnaut Daniel.

[4]The phrase is from the burial service of the Anglican Church.

5 Winter kept us warm, covering
Earth in forgetful snow, feeding
A little life with dried tubers.
Summer surprised us, coming over the Starnbergersee[5]
With a shower of rain; we stopped in the colonnade,
10 And went on in sunlight, into the Hofgarten,[6]
And drank coffee, and talked for an hour.
Bin gar keine Russin, stamm' aus Litauen, echt deutsch.[7]
And when we were children, staying at the archduke's,
My cousin's, he took me out on a sled,
15 And I was frightened. He said, Marie,
Marie, hold on tight. And down we went.
In the mountains, there you feel free.
I read, much of the night, and go south in the winter.

What are the roots that clutch, what branches grow
20 Out of this stony rubbish? Son of man,[8]
You cannot say, or guess, for you know only
A heap of broken images, where the sun beats,
And the dead tree gives no shelter, the cricket no relief,[9]
And the dry stone no sound of water. Only
25 There is shadow under this red rock,[10]
(Come in under the shadow of this red rock),
And I will show you something different from either
Your shadow at morning striding behind you
Or your shadow at evening rising to meet you;
30 I will show you fear in a handful of dust.

> *Frisch weht der Wind*
> *Der Heimat zu*
> *Mein irisch Kind,*
> *Wo weilest du?*[11]

---

[5]A lake near Munich. Lines 8–16 echo passages in Countess Marie Larisch's *My Past* (1913).

[6]Munich public park with cafés, formerly the grounds of a palace

[7]"I am no Russian, I come from Lithuania, a real German."

[8]Eliot's note: "Cf. Ezekiel II, i." God addresses Ezekiel as "Son of man," and calls upon him to "stand upon thy feet, and I will speak unto thee."

[9]Eliot's note: "Cf. Ecclesiastes XII." The Preacher points to old age when "the grasshopper shall be a burden and desire shall fail."

[10]Isaiah 32:1–2 prophesies that when the Messiah comes it "shall be . . . as rivers of water in a dry place, as the shadow of a great rock in a weary land."

[11]Eliot's note: "*Tristan und Isolde*, I, verses 5–8." In Wagner's opera, the lines are sung by a sailor aboard Tristan's ship, thinking of his beloved in Ireland: "Fresh blows the wind homeward; my Irish child, where are you waiting?"

35 "You gave me hyacinths first a year ago;
"They called me the hyacinth girl."[12]
—Yet when we came back, late, from the Hyacinth garden,
Your arms full, and your hair wet, I could not
Speak, and my eyes failed, I was neither
40 Living nor dead, and I knew nothing,
Looking into the heart of light, the silence.
Oed' und leer das Meer.[13]

Madame Sosostris,[14] famous clairvoyante,
Had a bad cold, nevertheless
45 Is known to be the wisest woman in Europe,
With a wicked pack of cards.[15] Here, said she,
Is your card, the drowned Phoenician Sailor,[16]
(Those are pearls that were his eyes.[17] Look!)
Here is Belladonna, the Lady of the Rocks,[18]

50 The lady of situations.
Here is the man with three staves, and here the Wheel,[19]
And here is the one-eyed merchant,[20] and this card,
Which is blank, is something he carries on his back,
Which I am forbidden to see. I do not find
55 The Hanged Man. Fear death by water.

---

[12]In Ovid's *Metamorphoses*, X, Hyacinth is a young boy slain by a rival for Apollo's love.

[13]"wide and empty the sea," the message given the dying Tristan, waiting for the ship bringing Isolde

[14]The name alludes to Sesotris, a 12th-dynasty Egyptian king, adapted by Aldous Huxley in *Chrome Yello* (1921) to Sesostris, the Sorceress of Ectabana, a woman fortune-teller.

[15]The reference is to the Tarot deck once, but no longer, significant in Eastern magic. Its four suits, cup, dish, lance, and sword, are life symbols in the Grail Legend. Eliot's note: "I am not familiar with the exact constitution of the Tarot pack of cards, from which I have obviously departed to suit my own convenience. The Hanged man, a member of the traditional pack, fits my purpose in two ways: because he is associated in my mind with the Hanged God of Frazer, and because I associate him with the hooded figure in the passage of the disciples to Emmaus in Part V. The Phoenician Sailor and the Merchant appear later; also the 'crowds of people,' and Death by Water is executed in Part IV. The Man with Three Staves (an authentic member of the Tarot pack) I associate, quite arbitrarily, with the Fisher King himself." Eliot's disclaimer should be attended, since the Phoenician Sailor, for example, is not a member of the pack.

[16]According to Eliot's note, the Smyrna merchant (1. 209) "melts into the Phoenician Sailor." The Phoenicians were seagoing merchants who spread Egyptian fertility cults throughout the Mediterranean. He is a type of the fertility god annually "drowned" as a symbol of the death of winter.

[17]From Ariel's song in Shakespeare's *The Tempest*, I. ii. 398; Ariel sings of the transformation from supposed death to "something rich and strange." See also "A Game of Chess," 1. 125.

[18]Suggestive of several "situations": literally, beautiful lady, the name ambiguously expands into the names of the poisonous nightshade, of a cosmetic and of the Madonna, or Virgin Mary, painted by Leonardo da Vinci as *Madonna of the Rocks*.

[19]The Wheel on one of the Tarot cards is the Wheel of Fortune.

[20]Cf. Mr. Eugenides, 1.209; on the Tarot card he is shown in profile, thus "one-eyed."

I see crowds of people, walking round in a ring.
Thank you. If you see dear Mrs. Equitone,
Tell her I bring the horoscope myself:
One must be so careful these days.

60 Unreal City,[21]
Under the brown fog of a winter dawn,
A crowd flowed over London Bridge, so many,
I had not thought death had undone so many.[22]
Sighs, short and infrequent, were exhaled,[23]
65 And each man fixed his eyes before his feet.
Flowed up the hill and down King William Street,
To where Saint Mary Woolnoth kept the hours
With a dead sound on the final stroke of nine.[24]
There I saw one I knew, and stopped him, crying: "Stetson!
70 "You who were with me in the ships at Mylae![25]
"That corpse you planted last year in your garden,
"Has it begun to sprout? Will it bloom this year?
"Or has the sudden frost disturbed its bed?
"Oh keep the Dog far hence, that's friend to men,
75 "Or with his nails he'll dig it up again![26]
"You! hypocrite lecteur!—mon semblable,—mon frère!"[27]

---

[21]Eliot's note: "Cf. Baudelaire: 'Fourmillante cité, cité pleine de rêves,/ Où le spectre en plein jour raccroche le passant.'" In translation: "Swarming city, city full of dreams,/Where the specter in full day accosts the passerby." *Les Fleurs du Mal (The Flowers of Evil)*.

[22]A rendering of *Inferno*, III, 55–57, quoted in Eliot's note. Canto III deals with those living without praise or blame.

[23]A rendering of *Inferno* IV, 25–27, quoted in Eliot's note. Canto IV deals with those in Limbo who had lived virtuously but died before Christ, and were thus excluded from Christian salvation.

[24]Eliot's note wryly comments, "A Phenomenon which I have often noticed." Indeed he had, for it was partly the route Eliot took for many years to his desk at Lloyd's. If he passed under the clock of the "Bankers Church" at nine, he would have been on time at the office, a few steps down the street. The church is also possibly an allusion to the Chapel Perilous in the Grail Legend. See also Lines 388–9.

[25]Rome won a naval battle at Mylae (260 B.C.) in a commercial war against Carthage.

[26]Lines 71–75 constitute a parody of the anticipation of the resurrection of the fertility god. Eliot's note refers to Webster's *The White Devil*. A Roman woman fears her murdered relatives will be disinterred: "But keep the wolf far thence, that's foe to men,/For with his nails he'll dig them up again." In welding his "theft,"—Eliot's term for such literary "borrowing"—into something "new" he made two significant changes" "foe" to "friend" and "wolf" to "Dog," thus alluding to the "Dog Star"—the bright star Sirius whose annual positioning coincided with the flooding of the Nile in consonance with the fertility ceremonies. The passage has occasioned a great deal of speculative comment with reference to naturalistic and humanistic suggestions that seem at odds with the rebirth of the god.

[27]Eliot's note refers to Baudelaire's *Fleurs du Mal*. The apposite lines in the introductory poem to the volume may be rendered, "Hypocrite reader!—my likeness—my brother!"

II. A Game of Chess[28]

The Chair she sat in, like a burnished throne,
Glowed on the marble,[29] where the glass
Held up by standards wrought with fruited vines
80 From which a golden Cupidon peeped out
(Another hid his eyes behind his wing)
Doubled the flames of sevenbranched candelabra
Reflecting light upon the table as
The glitter of her jewels rose to meet it,
85 From satin cases poured in rich profusion;
In vials of ivory and coloured glass
Unstoppered, lurked her strange synthetic perfumes,
Unguent, powdered, or liquid—troubled, confused
And drowned the sense in odours; stirred by the air
90 That freshened from the window, these ascended
In fattening the prolonged candle-flames,
Flung their smoke into the laquearia,[30]
Stirring the pattern on the coffered ceiling.
Huge sea-wood fed with copper
95 Burned green and orange, framed by the coloured stone,
In which sad light a carvèd dolphin swam.
Above the antique mantel was displayed
As though a window gave upon the sylvan scene[31]
The change of Philomel, by the barbarous king
100 So rudely forced; yet there the nightingale
Filled all the desert with inviolable voice
And still she cried, and still the world pursues,
"Jug Jug"[32] to dirty ears.
And other withered stumps of time

---

[28]The title alludes to Thomas Middleton's *A Game of Chess* (1627), about a marriage for political purposes, and *Woman Beware Women* (1657), in which a chess game is used as a means of keeping a woman occupied while her daughter-in-law is being seduced, the seduction being described in terms of chess. See also 1. 137.

[29]Shakespeare's *Anthony and Cleopatra*, II. ii. 190–1: "The barge she sat in, like a burnished throne,/Burn'd on the water."

[30]An echo of the "paneled ceiling" of the banquet hall in which Queen Dido of Carthage received Aeneas, *Aeneid*, I, 726; she commits suicide after Aeneas leaves her to found Rome.

[31]Eliot's note for line 98 refers to *Paradise Lost*, IV, 140 for "sylvan scene," the phrase used in Satan's first visit to the Garden. The actual scene, however, is that of the "change of Philomel"; and Eliot for line 99 refers to "Ovid *Metamorphoses*, VI, Philomela." Thus the two failures of love are conjoined—and added to the two previous failures figured in the opulent furnishing of the lady's boudoir. Eve's temptation by Satan will lead to carnal debauchery and expulsion from the Garden. Ovid recounts the rape of Philomela by Tereus, her sister's husband. Eventually, to escape his wrath, she is transformed into a nightingale. The motif of the transformation of suffering into art continues through line 103 and, pointed to by Eliot's note, in lines 203–6.

[32]The stylized representation of the song of the nightingale in Elizabethan poetry

105 Were told upon the walls; staring forms
Leaned out, leaning, hushing the room enclosed.
Footsteps shuffled on the stair.
Under the firelight, under the brush, her hair
Spread out in fiery points
110 Glowed into words, then would be savagely still.

     "My nerves are bad to-night. Yes, bad. Stay with me.
"Speak to me. Why do you never speak. Speak.
     "What are you thinking of? What thinking? What?
"I never know what you are thinking. Think."

115   I think we are in rats' alley
Where the dead men lost their bones.

     "What is that noise?"
                    The wind under the door.
"What is that noise now? What is the wind doing?"
120   Nothing again nothing.
                                "Do
"You know nothing? Do you see nothing? Do you remember
"Nothing?"

     I remember
125 Those are pearls that were his eyes.
"Are you alive, or not? Is there nothing in your head?"
                               But

O O O O that Shakespeherian Rag—
It's so elegant
130 So intelligent
"What shall I do now? What shall I do?"
"I shall rush out as I am, and walk the street
"With my hair down, so. What shall we do to-morrow?
"What shall we ever do"
135   The hot water at ten.
And if it rains, a closed car at four.
And we shall play a game of chess,
Pressing lidless eyes and waiting for a knock upon the door.

When Lil's husband got demobbed,[33] I said—
140 I didn't mince my words, I said to her myself,
HURRY UP PLEASE ITS TIME [34]
Now Albert's coming back, make yourself a bit smart.
He'll want to know what you done with that money he gave you

---

[33]slang for "demobilized" from the army after WWI
[34]announcement by the "pub" bartender that it is closing time

To get yourself some teeth. He did, I was there.
145 You have them all out, Lil, and get a nice set,
He said, I swear, I can't bear to look at you.
And no more can't I, I said, and think of poor Albert,
He's been in the army four years, he wants a good time,
And if you don't give it him, there's others will, I said.
150 Oh is there, she said. Something o' that, I said.
Then I'll know who to thank, she said, and give me a straight look.
Hurry up please its time
If you don't like it you can get on with it, I said.
Others can pick and choose if you can't.
155 But if Albert makes off, it won't be for lack of telling.
You ought to be ashamed, I said, to look so antique.
(And her only thirty-one.)
I can't help it, she said, pulling a long face,
It's them pills I took, to bring it off, she said.
160 (She's had five already, and nearly died of young George.)
The chemist[35] said it would be all right, but I've never been the same.
You are a proper fool, I said.
Well, if Albert won't leave you alone, there it is, I said,
What you get married for if you don't want children?
165 Hurry up please its time
Well, that Sunday Albert was home, they had a hot gammon,[36]
And they asked me in to dinner, to get the beauty of it hot—
Hurry up please its time
Hurry up please its time
170 Goonight Bill. Goonight Lou. Goonight May. Goonight.
Ta ta. Goonight. Goonight.
Good night, ladies, good night, sweet ladies, good night, good night.[37]

III. The Fire Sermon[38]

The river's tent is broken: the last fingers of leaf
Clutch and sink into the wet bank. The wind
175 Crosses the brown land, unheard. The nymphs are departed.

---

[35]druggist

[36]ham or the lower end of a side of bacon; suggestively, thigh

[37]alludes to both Ophelia's words before drowning herself, *Hamlet,* iv.v. 72, and to a popular song "Good night ladies, we're going to leave you now"

[38]The title of this section is especially evocative. It serves as a kind of rubric for the various scenes of lust, past and present, which follow, and it anticipates the express references to Buddha's *Fire Sermon* and St. Augustine's *Confessions* in the concluding lines and in Eliot's notes to those lines (307–9). Given the accurate London geography of the poem and the fact that *The Waste Land* began as, and to some extent remains, a poem about London in the Dryden vein, it is worth noting that overlooking the scenes mentioned, especially in lines 259–65, is the imposing Monument to the Great Fire of London of 1666.

Sweet Thames, run softly, till I end my song.[39]
The river bears no empty bottles, sandwich papers,
Silk handkerchiefs, cardboard boxes, cigarette ends
Or other testimony of summer nights. The nymphs are departed.
180 And their friends, the loitering heirs of city directors;
Departed, have left no addresses.
By the waters of Leman I sat down and wept . . .[40]
Sweet Thames, run softly till I end my song,
Sweet Thames, run softly, for I speak not loud or long.
185 But at my back in a cold blast I hear[41]
The rattle of the bones, and chuckle spread from ear to ear.
A rat crept softly through the vegetation
Dragging its slimy belly on the bank
While I was fishing in the dull canal
190 On a winter evening round behind the gashouse
Musing upon the king my brother's wreck[42]
And on the king my father's death before him.
White bodies naked on the low damp ground
And bones cast in a little low dry garret,
195 Rattled by the rat's foot only, year to year.
But at my back from time to time I hear
The sound of horns and motors, which shall bring
Sweeney to Mrs. Porter in the spring.[43]
O the moon shone bright on Mrs. Porter
200 And on her daughter
They wash their feet in soda water[44]
Et O ces voix d'enfants, chantant dans la coupole![45]

Twit twit twit
Jug jug jug jug jug jug

---

[39]The refrain of Edmund Spenser's *Prothalamion,* a late-sixteenth-century celebration of marriage in the then-pastoral setting along the Thames River near London.

[40]In Psalms 137:1 the exiled Jews express their longing for home: "By the rivers of Babylon, there we sat down, yea, we wept, when we remembered Zion." Eliot largely finished the poem at Lake Leman, as Lake Geneva is also called, at a sanatorium where he had gone for care.

[41]Lines 185 and 196 allude to Andrew Marvell's "To His Coy Mistress," lines 21–24.

[42]An allusion again, to *The Tempest.* Ferdinand, believing his father dead, is "Sitting on a bank,/Weeping again the King my father's wreck," I., ii. 389–90.

[43]Eliot's note quotes the relevant lines from John Day's *Parliament of Bees:* "When of a sudden, listening, you shall hear, A noise of horns and hunting, which shall bring/Actaeon to Diana in the spring/Where all shall see her naked skin. . . ." As a punishment of thus seeing the goddess of chastity naked, Actaeon was changed into a stag, hunted, and killed.

[44]Eliot here uses some sanitized lines from a bawdy song of World War I, which actually was a parody of the popular ballad, "Little Redwing."

[45]Eliot's note calls attention to Paul Verlaine's sonnet, "Parsifal," the last line of which goes, "And O those children singing in the choir." The feet of Parsifal, in Wagner's opera, are washed before he enters the sanctuary. The children are singing at the ceremony. In Verlaine's poem, there are sexual implications.

205 So rudely forc'd.
     Tereu[46]

     Unreal City
     Under the brown fog of a winter noon
     Mr. Eugenides, the Smyrna merchant
210 Unshaven, with a pocket full of currants
     C.i.f.[47] London: documents at sight,
     Asked me in demotic French
     To luncheon at the Cannon Street Hotel
     Followed by a weekend at the Metropole.[48]

215 At the violet hour, when the eyes and back
     Turn upward from the desk, when the human engine waits
     Like a taxi throbbing waiting,
     I Tiresias,[49] though blind, throbbing between two lives.
     Old man with wrinkled female breasts, can see
220 At the violet hour, the evening hour that strives
     Homeward, and brings the sailor home from sea,
     The typist home at teatime, clears her breakfast, lights
     Her stove, and lays out food in tins.
     Out of the window perilously spread
225 Her drying combinations touched by the sun's last rays,
     On the divan are piled (at night her bed)
     Stockings, slippers, camisoles, and stays.
     I Tiresias, old man with wrinkled dugs
     Perceived the scene, and foretold the rest—
230 I to awaited the expected guest.
     He, the young man carbuncular, arrives,
     A small house agent's clerk, with one bold stare,

---

[46]See Notes 6 and 7 (p. 339).

[47]Eliot's explanation, "carriage and insurance free to London," has been corrected by Mrs. Valerie Eliot to "cost, insurance and freight."

[48]The Cannon Street Hotel is a commercial hotel in that area of the City, the Metropole a hotel in Brighton popular for assignations.

[49]Eliot's note: "Tiresias, although a mere spectator and not indeed a 'character,' is yet the most important personage in the poem, uniting all the rest. Just as the one-eyed merchant, seller of currants, melts into the Phoenician sailor, and the latter is not wholly distinct from Ferdinand Prince of Naples, so all the women are one woman, and the two sexes meet in Tiresias. What Tiresias *sees*, in fact is the substance of the poem. The whole passage from Ovid is of great anthropological interest." The Latin passage that is quoted may be summarized as follows: Tiresias saw two snakes copulating, separated them and became a woman; after seven years he saw the same sight, again separated them, became a man again. When Jove and Juno disputed whether more pleasure in love was enjoyed by male or female, they referred the question to Tiresias, who said women. Juno in her anger blinded him, but Jove, unable to undo her action, gave him the power of infallible divination.

One of the low on whom assurance sits
As a silk hat on a Bradford[50] millionaire.
235 The time is now propitious, as he guesses,
The meal is ended, she is bored and tired,
Endeavours to engage her in caresses
Which still are unreproved, if undesired.
Flushed and decided, he assaults at once;
240 Exploring hands encounter no defence;
His vanity requires no response,
And makes a welcome of indifference.
(And I Tiresias have foresuffered all
Enacted on this same divan or bed;
245 I who have sat by Thebes below the wall
And walked among the lowest of the dead.)[51]
Bestows one final patronizing kiss,
And gropes his way, finding the stairs unlit . . .

She turns and looks a moment in the glass,
250 Hardly aware of her departed lover;
Her brain allows one half-formed thought to pass:
"Well now that's done: and I'm glad it's over."
When lovely woman stoops to folly and
Paces about her room again, alone,
255 She smoothes her hair with automatic hand,
And puts a record on the gramophone.[52]
"This music crept by me upon the waters"[53]
And along the Strand, up Queen Victoria Street.
O City city, I can sometimes hear
260 Beside a public bar in Lower Thames Street,
The pleasant whining of a mandoline
And a clatter and a chatter from within
Where fishmen lounge at noon: where the walls
Of Magnus Martyr hold
265 Inexplicable splendour of Ionian white and gold.[54]

---

[50]a manufacturing town in Yorkshire, England, noted for the rapid fortunes made during WWI

[51]the site of Tiresias' prophecies and of his witnessing the fate of Oedipus and Creon

[52]Eliot's note refers to the song in Goldsmith's *The Vicar of Wakefield:* "When lovely woman stoops to folly/ And finds too late that men betray/ What charm can soothe her melancholy,/ What art can wash her guilt away?/ The only art her guilt to cover,/ To hide her shame from every eye,/ To give repentance to her lover/ And wring his bosom—is to die."

[53]an exact quotation from Ariel's song of transformation in *The Tempest,* I. ii. 391

[54]Eliot's note: "The interior of St Magnus Martyr is to my mind one of the finest among Wren's interiors." Nearby the Billingsgate Fishmarket and across the street from "The Cock," "where fishmen lounge at noon," it was known as the "Fishmen's Church."

The river sweats[55]
Oil and tar
The barges drift
With the turning tide
270 Red sails
Wide
To leeward, swing on the heavy spar.
The barges wash
Drifting logs
275 Down Greenwich reach
Past the Isle of Dogs.
   Weialala leia
   Wallala leialala

Elizabeth and Leicester[56]
280 Beating oars
The stern was formed
A gilded shell
Red and gold
The brisk swell
285 Rippled both shores
Southwest wind
Carried down stream
The peal of bells
White towers
290   Weialala leia
   Wallala leialala

"Trams and dusty trees.
Highbury bore me. Richmond and Kew
Undid me. By Richmond I raised my knees
295 Supine on the floor of a narrow canoe."

"My feet are at Moorgate,[57] and my heart
Under my feet. After the event
He wept. He promised 'a new start.'
I made no comment. What should I resent?"

300 "On Margate Sands.[58]
I can connect

---

[55]Eliot's note: "The Song of the (three) Thames-daughters begins here. From line 292 to 306 inclusive they speak in turn. V. *Götterdämmerung,* III, i: the Rhine-daughters."

[56]a reference to the fruitless love affair of Queen Elizabeth and the Earl of Leicester, referred to in Eliot's note

[57]Highbury, Richmond, Kew, and Moorgate are all areas in or around London.

[58]a resort on the sea where Eliot, suffering from stress, spent a short period before going to the sanatorium on Lake Geneva

Nothing with nothing.
The broken fingernails of dirty hands.
My people humble people who expect
305 Nothing."
          la la

To Carthage then I came[59]

Burning burning burning burning
O Lord Thou pluckest me out
310 O Lord Thou pluckest

burning

IV. Death by Water[60]

Phlebas the Phoenician, a fortnight dead,
Forgot the cry of gulls, and the deep sea swell
And the profit and loss.
315   A current under sea
Picked his bones in whispers. As he rose and fell
He passed the stages of his age and youth
Entering the whirlpool.
          Gentile or Jew
320 O you who turn the wheel and look to windward,
Consider Phlebas, who was once handsome and tall as you.

V. What the Thunder Said[61]

After the torchlight red on sweaty faces
After the frosty silence in the gardens
After the agony in stony places
325 The shouting and the crying
Prison and palace and reverberation
Of thunder of spring over distant mountains
He who was living is now dead

---

[59]Eliot virtually instructs the reader to consider together the last five lines of "The Fire Sermon." Of line 307 he quotes St. Augustine's *Confessions*, "to Carthage then I came, where a cauldron of unholy love sang all about my ears." Of line 308, he points to "The complete text of the Buddha's Fire Sermon (which corresponds in importance to the Sermon on the Mount) from which these words are taken. . . ." Of line 309, after citing *Confessions* again, "The collocation of these two representatives of eastern and western asceticism, as the culmination of this part of the poem, is not an accident."

[60]There is no consensus as to whether this short section, drastically cut by Ezra Pound, is in anticipation of rebirth or annihilation. Interestingly, it is translated from the concluding lines of Eliot's "Dans le Restaurant," written in French.

[61]Eliot's note: "In the first part of Part V three themes are employed: the journey to Emmaus, the approach to the Chapel Perilous (see Miss Weston's book) and the present decay of eastern Europe." See lines 360, 388, 369, respectively.

We who were living are now dying
330 With a little patience[62]

Here is no water but only rock
Rock and no water and the sandy road
The road winding above among the mountains
Which are mountains of rock without water
335 If there were water we should stop and drink
Amongst the rock one cannot stop or think
Sweat is dry and feet are in the sand
If there were only water amongst the rock
Dead mountain mouth of carious teeth that cannot spit
340 Here one can neither stand nor lie nor sit
There is not even silence in the mountains
But dry sterile thunder without rain
There is not even solitude in the mountains
But red sullen faces sneer and snarl
345 From doors of mudcracked houses
                              If there were water
And no rock
If there were rock
And also water
350 And water
A spring
A pool among the rock
If there were the sound of water only
Not the cicada
355 And dry grass singing
But sound of water over a rock
Where the hermit-thrush sings in the pine trees
Drip drop drip drop drop drop drop
But there is no water

360 Who is the third who walks always beside you?
When I count, there are only you and I together
But when I look ahead up the white road
There is always another one walking beside you
Gliding wrapt in a brown mantle, hooded
365 I do not know whether a man or a woman
—But who is that on the other side of you?

What is that sound high in the air
Murmur of maternal lamentation

---

[62]Lines 322–330 allude to Christ's travail in the gardens of Gethsemane and Golgotha—but also to
   that of the other slain gods of anthropology through whom new life was invoked.

Who are those hooded hordes swarming
370 Over endless plains, stumbling in cracked earth
Ringed by the flat horizon only
What is the city over the mountains
Cracks and reforms and bursts in the violet air
Falling towers
375   Jerusalem Athens Alexandria
Vienna London
Unreal

A woman drew her long black hair out tight
And fiddled whisper music on those strings
380 And bats with baby faces in the violet light
Whistled, and beat their wings
And crawled head downward down a blackened wall
And upside down in air were towers
Tolling reminiscent bells, that kept the hours
385 And voices singing out of empty cisterns and exhausted wells.

In this decayed hole among the mountains
In the faint moonlight, the grass is singing
Over the tumbled graves, about the chapel
There is the empty chapel, only the wind's home.
390 It has no windows, and the door swings,
Dry bones can harm no one.
Only a cock stood on the rooftree
Co co rico co co rico[63]
In a flash of lightning. Then a damp gust
395 Bringing rain
Ganga[64] was sunken, and the limp leaves
Waited for rain, while the black clouds
Gathered far distant, over Himavant.[65]
The jungle crouched, humped in silence.
400 Then spoke the thunder
DA[66]
Datta: what have we given?
My friend, blood shaking my heart
The awful daring of a moment's surrender

---

[63]In folklore, the cock's crow was thought to indicate the departure of ghosts. In Matthew, as Christ predicted, Peter denies him three times before the cock crows.

[64]The Ganges River in India is sacred to Hindus, a place of purification.

[65]a Himalayan mountain

[66]Eliot's note: "DaTa, dayadhvam, damyata' (Give, sympathise, control)." With this introduction of the onomatopoetic Sanskrit, the density of allusion, only partially accommodated in these footnotes for reasons of space and clarity of progression, seems to intensify.

405 Which an age of prudence can never retract
By this, and this only, we have existed
Which is not to be found in our obituaries
Or in memories draped by the beneficent spider[67]
Or under seals broken by the lean solicitor
410 In our empty rooms
Da
Dayadhvam: I have heard the key[68]
Turn in the door once and turn once only
We think of the key, each in his prison
415 Thinking of the key, each confirms a prison
Only at nightfall, aethereal rumours
Revive for a moment a broken Coriolanus[69]
Da
Damyata: The boat responded
420 Gaily, to the hand expert with sail and oar
The sea was calm, your heart would have responded
Gaily, when invited, beating obedient
To controlling hands

I sat upon the shore
425 Fishing,[70] with the arid plain behind me
Shall I at least set my lands in order?
London Bridge is falling down falling down falling down
Poi s'ascose nel foco che gli affina[71]
Quando fiam uti chelidon[72]—O swallow swallow
430 *Le Prince d'Aquitaine à la tour abolie*[73]

---

[67]Eliot's note refers to Webster's *The White Devil:* "they'll remarry/ Ere the worm pierce your winding-sheet, ere the spider/ Make a thin curtain for your epitaphs."

[68]Eliot's note refers to Dante's Ugolino in *Inferno,* XXXIII, 46, starved to death in the locked tower and to F.H. Bradley's postulation that "my experience falls within my own circle. . . . the whole world for each is peculiar and private to that soul."

[69]Coriolanus, threatened with banishment from Rome, chose exile, and, although he tried to return, was eventually "broken." Shakespeare's *Coriolanus* deals with his tragedy.

[70]Eliot's note directs the reader to Weston's "chapter on the Fisher King." The King in the Grail Legends typically lived on a river or seashore. Fish is a fertility or life symbol. This meaning was often forgotten, however, and the title of the Fisher King in medieval romances was accounted for by describing him as fishing.

[71]"Then he hid himself in the fire that refines them." Eliot's note refers to *Purgatorio,* XXVI, 145–48, where the poet Arnaut Daniel, remembering his lechery, speaks this line.

[72]"When shall I be like the swallow?" Eliot's note refers to the Latin poem, *Pervigilium Veneris,* with its echo of Philomela, recalling the idea of finding a voice through suffering. In this anonymous poem, the myth is imaged in the swallow. "O Swallow, Swallow" appears in one of the songs in Tennyson's "The Princess."

[73]"The Prince of Aquitaine in the ruined tower" is from Gérard de Nerval's sonnet "*El Desdichado*" ("The Disinherited One").

These fragments I have shored against my ruins
Why then Ile fit you. Hieronymo's mad againe.[74]
Datta, Dayadhvam. Damyata.
    Shantih   shantih   shantih[75]

1922

Sweeney Among the Nightingales

ὤμοι, πέπληγμαι καιρί αν πληγὴν ἔσω[1]

Apeneck Sweeney spreads his knees
Letting his arms hang down to laugh,
The zebra stripes along his jaw
Swelling to maculate giraffe.

5   The circles of the stormy moon
Slide westward toward the River Plate,[2]
Death and the Raven[3] drift above
And Sweeney guards the hornèd gate.[4]

Gloomy Orion[5] and the Dog[6]
10 Are veiled; and hushed and shrunken seas;
The person in the Spanish cape
Tries to sit on Sweeney's knees

Slips and pulls the table cloth
Overturns a coffee-cup,
15 Reorganized upon the floor
She yawns and draws a stocking up;

The silent man in mocha brown
Sprawls at the window-sill and gapes;
The waiter brings in oranges
20 Bananas figs and hothouse grapes;

---

[74]When Hieronymo in Thomas Kyd's play, *The Spanish Tragedy, Hieronymo's Mad Againe* (1594), is
  asked to write a court play, he replies, "I'll fit [supply] you." Through the play, despite his madness,
  he is able to revenge himself on the murderers of his son in a pattern similar to that of *Hamlet*.
[75]Eliot's note: "Shantih. Repeated as here, a formal ending to an Upanishad [sacred Hindu text]. 'The
  Peace which passeth understanding' is our equivalent to this word."

---

[1]From Aeschylus' Agamemnon: "Oh, I have been struck deep with a deadly blow."
[2]Rio de la Plata in South America
[3]the constellation Corvus
[4]Through the gates of ivory, in Greek mythology, come dreams that are pleasant but untrue;
  through the gates of horn, dreams that are unpleasant but true.
[5]an equatorial constellation
[6]the dog-star Sirius, near Orion

The silent vertebrate in brown
Contracts and concentrates, withdraws;
Rachel *née* Rabinovitch
Tears at the grapes with murderous paws;

25   She and the lady in the cape
Are suspect, thought to be in league;
Therefore the man with heavy eyes
Declines the gambit, shows fatigue,

Leaves the room and reappears
30   Outside the window, leaning in,
Branches of wistaria
Circumscribe a golden grin;

The host with someone indistinct
Converses at the door apart,
35   The nightingales are singing near
The Convent of the Sacred Heart,

And sang within the bloody wood
When Agamemnon cried aloud,
And let their liquid siftings fall
40   To stain the stiff dishonored shroud.

1919

Journey of the Magi

"A cold coming we had of it,
Just the worst time of the year
For a journey, and such a long journey:
The ways deep and the weather sharp,
5   The very dead of winter."[1]
And the camels galled, sore-footed, refractory,
Lying down in the melting snow.
There were times we regretted
The summer palaces on slopes, the terraces,
10   And the silken girls bringing sherbet.
Then the camel men cursing and grumbling
And running away, and wanting their liquor and women,
And the night-fires going out, and the lack of shelters,
And the cities hostile and the towns unfriendly

---

[1]adapted from a seventeenth-century sermon of Lancelot Andrewes

15 And the villages dirty and charging high prices:
A hard time we had of it.
At the end we preferred to travel all night,
Sleeping in snatches,
With the voices singing in our ears, saying
20 That this was all folly.

Then at dawn we came down to a temperate valley,
Wet, below the snow line, smelling of vegetation;
With a running stream and a water-mill beating the darkness,
And three trees on the low sky,
25 And an old white horse galloped away in the meadow.
Then we came to a tavern with vine-leaves over the lintel,
Six hands at an open door dicing for pieces of silver,
And feet kicking the empty wine-skins.
But there was no information, and so we continued
30 And arrived at evening, not a moment too soon
Finding the place; it was (you may say) satisfactory.
All this was a long time ago, I remember,
And I would do it again, but set down
This set down
35 This: were we led all that way for
Birth or Death? There was a Birth, certainly,
We had evidence and no doubt. I had seen birth and death,
But had thought they were different; this Birth was
Hard and bitter agony for us, like Death, our death.
40 We returned to our places, these Kingdoms,
But no longer at ease here, in the old dispensation,
With an alien people clutching their gods.
I should be glad of another death.

1927

6

A BRIEF HISTORY

By the time the twentieth century was drawing to a close, an uneasy political peace, wrapped in a pitched battle, prevailed. After a series of limited but agonizingly protracted wars in Korea, Vietnam, and elsewhere, Communism collapsed in Europe. The English-speaking nations, led by Britain and the United States, were dynamically consolidating and learning to live with new national poetic voices. New critical theories arose to explain what modern and postmodern poetry had become, or to direct poetry toward one or another school of thought. In the English-speaking world, as elsewhere, the forces of action, reaction, and inaction battled across the social and artistic landscape.

Before the 1950s, new critical theory had established the criteria of examining a poem as a self-contained object, relatively free of the distractions of a poet's biography and private personal struggles. Following the poetry of Whitman, Williams, Ferlinghetti, and Olson (among others), the Beat poets, represented by Allen Ginsberg, insisted on a poetry that was based on the personal and controversial. This poetry elevated the countercultural and trusted the spontaneous. Whatever else may have happened to the short-lived Flower Power movement of peace and paper, versus struggle and metal, or the music of the Beatles versus Heavy Metal, almost single-handedly the Beat poets wrenched poetry from the often self-absorbed mandarin atmosphere of the classroom and tried to return it unmediated to the people and the streets, to a spontaneous and uninitiated audience. The Civil Rights movement helped to validate African-American liberties and to consolidate the work of pioneer literary poets of the Harlem Renaissance like Langston Hughes. Foreshadowed by poets like Anne Sexton and Sylvia Plath, the feminist movement, as well as Deconstructionism, now began to question the historically prevailing view of a patriarchal, male-oriented society and create an alternative view that questions and finds new tools for examining traditional poetry and its historical assumptions. Gay and lesbian poetry also began to rise out of the "closet" of Whitman, Housman, and Auden, as well as the intimate symbolism of Gertrude Stein. Allen Ginsberg, Thom Gunn, and Adrienne Rich bring directly, defiantly, unembarrassedly, and naturally into poetry what Oscar Wilde once called the "love that dared not speak its name." Performance poets, like slammers and rap poets, create a revived dimension of poetry as theater and personal exchange.

As a result of this complexity, contemporary poetry offers a kind of upside-down return to Eden, a curious version of an original state of innocence. This is not the innocence of those who have not been touched by grown-up realities.

Legends and scriptures tell us that there is no return to an original Eden. In the Book of Genesis in the Bible, an angel stands guard with a flaming sword before that door, barring any return.

Sometimes the poet, disguised but as much a guide as was Virgil in Dante's *Divine Comedy,* can bring us to a new, or perhaps corrective, place, where readers can name anew, like latter-day Adams and Eves, the world they have come to know by habit and by custom.

Poets' visions and their worlds are not absolute truths, obviously. A reader's favorite poem today will be a sudden, visionary view. That poem and view may be the recollection of a past and lost moment, or perhaps the hope of some future, anticipated dream. Poems cut a way through the thickets of the present world. For a moment, careful or transported readers can use a poem to break through to a world uncluttered or redefined by definition; a world brilliant with, or broken by, possibility; a world rearranged by the elegance, music, bluster, and "yawp" of language.

When Archibald MacLeish wrote in *Ars Poetica* that a poem "must not mean/but be," he was asserting in one more way the canon of the imagist movement. e. e. cummings added to direct imagery an easy, offhanded American diction and a lyrical typographical play: lower-casing all words, dividing lines in unexpected places. Dylan Thomas, like Marianne Moore before him, explored the possibilities of syllabic verse; others, like Philip Larkin and Yvor Winters, maintained a commitment to traditional verse. W. H. Auden enriched traditional forms with ingenious modern variations. The spontaneity and technical iconoclasm of Whitman's verse resurfaced in the lines of Ferlinghetti and Ginsberg. Both composed poems seemingly out of the raw experience of the street, offering little if any acknowledgment to the tradition of formal verse—although in *A Supermarket in California,* Ginsberg makes allusions to classical mythology as easily as any classical poet would. Many poets have experimented at various times with accentual, syllabic, or accentual-syllabic verse. Poets like Richard Wilbur and Thom Gunn remain basically formal, serious about traditional demands. Robert Lowell and Theodore Roethke at various periods explored formal verse and the looser free-verse forms. John Berryman raised diction and syntax almost to the level of a new rhetoric. An amalgam of many styles exists simultaneously. Two of the usual characteristics of modern poetry are a concern for clarity of image— in both formal and informal verse—and sometimes a confessional lyricism in which the poet becomes obsessed with self-exploration. The social concerns of some writers create a verse in which the message or the sincerity of the experience is expected to take precedence over any technical apparatus, such as the brilliance of a metaphor or the deliberate control of language. Meanwhile, modern poetry is being fed from new sources and strengths: the vision and vocabulary of a rising generation of African-American poets, a surge of poetry by women questioning conventional wisdom.

John Crowe Ransom

(1888–1974)

Bells for John Whiteside's Daughter

There was such speed in her little body,
And such lightness in her footfall,
It is no wonder her brown study
Astonishes us all.

5 Her wars were bruited in our high window.
We looked among orchard trees and beyond
Where she took arms against her shadow,
Or harried unto the pond

The lazy geese, like a snow cloud
10 Dripping their snow on the green grass,
Tricking and stopping, sleepy and proud,
Who cried in goose, Alas,

For the tireless heart within the little
Lady with rod that made them rise
15 From their noon apple-dreams and scuttle
Goose-fashion under the skies!

But now go the bells, and we are ready,
In one house we are sternly stopped
To say we are vexed at her brown study,
20 Lying so primly propped.

1924

Old Mansion

As an intruder I trudged with careful innocence
To mask in decency a meddlesome stare,
Passing the old house often on its eminence,
Exhaling my foreign weed on its weighted air.

5 Here age seemed newly imaged for the historian
After his monstrous châteaux on the Loire,
A beauty not for depicting by old vulgarian
Reiterations which gentle readers abhor.

Each time of seeing I absorbed some other feature
10 Of a house whose legend could in no wise be brief

Nor ignoble, for it expired as sweetly as Nature,
With her tinge of oxidation on autumn leaf.

It was a Southern manor. One need hardly imagine
Towers, white monoliths, or even ivied walls;
15   But sufficient state if its peacock *was* a pigeon;
Where no courts held, but grave rites and funerals.

Indeed, not distant, possibly not external
To the property, were tombstones, where the catafalque
Had carried their dead; and projected a note too charnel
20   But for the honeysuckle on its intricate stalk.

Stability was the character of its rectangle
Whose line was seen in part and guessed in part
Through trees. Decay was the tone of old brick and shingle.
Green blinds dragging frightened the watchful heart

25   To assert: "Your mansion, long and richly inhabited,
Its exits and entrances suiting the children of man,
Will not forever be thus, O man, exhibited,
And one had best hurry to enter it if one can."

And at last with my happier angel's own temerity,
30   Did I clang their brazen knocker against the door,
To beg their dole of a look, in simple charity,
Or crumbs of history dropping from their great store.

But it came to nothing—and may so gross denial,
Which has been deplored duly with a beating of the breast,
35   Never shorten the tired historian, loyal
To acknowledge defeat and discover a new quest—

The old mistress was ill, and sent my dismissal
By one even more wrappered and lean and dark
Than that warped concierge and imperturbable vassal
40   Who bids you begone from her master's Gothic park.

Emphatically, the old house crumbled; the ruins
Would litter, as already the leaves, this petted sward;
And no annalist went in to the lord or the peons;
The antiquary would finger the bits of shard.

45   But on retreating I saw myself in the token,
How loving from my foreign weed the feather curled
On the languid air; and I went with courage shaken
To dip, alas, into some unseemlier world.

Piazza Piece

—I am a gentleman in a dustcoat trying
To make you hear. Your ears are soft and small
And listen to an old man not at all,
They want the young men's whispering and sighing.
5 But see the roses on your trellis dying
And hear the spectral singing of the moon;
For I must have my lovely lady soon,
I am a gentleman in a dustcoat trying.

—I am a lady young in beauty waiting
10 Until my truelove comes, and then we kiss.
But what grey man among the vines is this
Whose words are dry and faint as in a dream?
Back from my trellis, Sir, before I scream!
I am a lady young in beauty waiting.

1925

Spectral Lovers

By night they haunted a thicket of April mist,
Out of that black ground suddenly come to birth,
Else angels lost in each other and fallen on earth.
Lovers they knew they were, but why unclasped, unkissed?
5 Why should two lovers be frozen apart in fear?
And yet they were, they were.

Over the shredding of an April blossom
Scarcely her fingers touched him, quick with care,
Yet of evasions even she made a snare.
10 The heart was bold that clanged within her bosom,
The moment perfect, the time stopped for them,
Still her face turned from him.

Strong were the batteries of the April night
And the stealthy emanations of the field;
15 Should the walls of her prison undefended yield
And open her treasure to the first clamorous knight?
"This is the mad moon, and shall I surrender all?
If he but ask it I shall."

And gesturing largely to the moon of Easter,
20 Mincing his steps and swishing the jubilant grass,
Beheading some field-flowers that had come to pass,
He had reduced his tributaries faster
Had not considerations pinched his heart
Unfitly for his art.

25 "Do I reel with the sap of April like a drunkard?
   Blessed is he that taketh this richest of cities:
   But it is so stainless the sack were a thousand pities.
   This is that marble fortress not to be conquered,
   Lest its white peace in the black flame turn to tinder
30 And an unutterable cinder."

   They passed me once in April, in the mist,
   No other season is it when one walks and discovers
   Two tall and wandering, like spectral lovers,
   White in the season's moon-gold and amethyst,
35 Who touch quick fingers fluttering like a bird
   Whose songs shall never be heard.

                                                        1925

Archibald MacLeish

(1892–1982)

Ars Poetica

A poem should be palpable and mute
As a globed fruit,

Dumb
As old medallions to the thumb,

5 Silent as the sleeve-worn stone
Of casement ledges where the moss has grown—

A poem should be wordless
As the flight of birds.

A poem should be motionless in time
10 As the moon climbs,

Leaving, as the moon releases
Twig by twig the night-entangled trees,

Leaving, as the moon behind the winter leaves
Memory by memory the mind—

15 A poem should be motionless in time
As the moon climbs.

A poem should be equal to:
Not true.

For all the history of grief
20 An empty doorway and a maple leaf.

For love
The leaning grasses and two lights above the sea—

A poem should not mean
But be.

1926

You, Andrew Marvell[1]

And here face down beneath the sun
And here upon earth's noonward height
To feel the always coming on
The always rising of the night:

5 To feel creep up the curving east
The earthy chill of dusk and slow
Upon those under lands the vast
And ever climbing shadow grow

And strange at Ecbatan[2] the trees
10 Take leaf by leaf the evening strange
The flooding dark about their knees
The mountains over Persia change

And now at Kermanshah[3] the gate
Dark empty and the withered grass
15 And through the twilight now the late
Few travelers in the westward pass

And Baghdad darken and the bridge
Across the silent river gone
And through Arabia the edge
20 Of evening widen and steal on

And deepen on Palmyra's[4] street
The wheel rut in the ruined stone
And Lebanon fade out and Crete
High through the clouds and overblown

25 And over Sicily the air
Still flashing with the landward gulls
And loom and slowly disappear
The sails above the shadowy hulls

---

[1]The allusion is to Marvell's "To His Coy Mistress."
[2]Ecbatana, ancient Persian city, modern Hamadan
[3]city in western Iran
[4]ancient city in Syria

And Spain go under and the shore
30 Of Africa the gilded sand
And evening vanish and no more
The low pale light across that land

Nor now the long light on the sea:

And here face downward in the sun
35 To feel how swift how secretly
The shadow of the night comes on . . .

1930

Edna St. Vincent Millay

(1892–1950)

First Fig

My candle burns at both ends;
    It will not last the night;
But ah, my foes, and oh, my friends—
    It gives a lovely light!

1920

Sonnet 2

Time does not bring relief; you all have lied
Who told me time would ease me of my pain!
I miss him in the weeping of the rain;
I want him at the shrinking of the tide;
5 The old snows melt from every mountain-side,
And last year's leaves are smoke in every lane;
But last year's bitter loving must remain
Heaped on my heart, and my old thoughts abide.
There are a hundred places where I fear
10 To go,—so with his memory they brim.
And entering with relief some quiet place
Where never fell his foot or shone his face
I say, "There is no memory of him here!"
And so stand stricken, so remembering him.

1917

Sonnet 11

I shall forget you presently, my dear,
So make the most of this, your little day,
Your little month, your little half a year,
Ere I forget, or die, or move away,
5 And we are done forever; by and by
I shall forget you, as I said, but now,
If you entreat me with your loveliest lie
I will protest you with my favorite vow.
I would indeed that love were longer-lived,
10 And oaths were not so brittle as they are,
But so it is, and nature has contrived
To struggle on without a break thus far,—
Whether or not we find what we are seeking
Is idle, biologically speaking.

1920

Sonnet 15

Only until this cigarette is ended.
A little moment at the end of all,
While on the floor the quiet ashes fall,
And in the firelight to a lance extended,
5 Bizarrely with the jazzing music blended,
The broken shadow dances on the wall,
I will permit my memory to recall
The vision of you, by all my dreams attended.
And then adieu,—farewell!—the dream is done.
10 Yours is a face of which I can forget
The color and the features, every one,
The words not ever, and the smiles not yet;
But in your day this moment is the sun
Upon a hill, after the sun has set.

1921

Sonnet 27

I know I am but summer to your heart,
And not the full four seasons of the year;
And you must welcome from another part
Such noble moods as are not mine, my dear.
5 No gracious weight of golden fruits to sell
Have I, nor any wise and wintry thing;
And I have loved you all too long and well

To carry still the high sweet breast of Spring.
Wherefore I say: O love, as summer goes,
10 I must be gone, steal forth with silent drums,
That you may hail anew the bird and rose
When I come back to you, as summer comes.
Else will you seek, at some not distant time,
Even your summer in another clime.

1923

Sonnet 42

What lips my lips have kissed, and where, and why,
I have forgotten, and what arms have lain
Under my head till morning; but the rain
Is full of ghosts tonight, that tap and sigh
5 Upon the glass and listen for reply,
And in my heart there stirs a quiet pain
For unremembered lads that not again
Will turn to me at midnight with a cry.
Thus in the winter stands the lonely tree,
10 Nor knows what birds have vanished one by one,
Yet knows its boughs more silent than before:
I cannot say what loves have come and gone,
I only know that summer sang in me
A little while, that in me sings no more.

1922

Sonnet 95

Women have loved before as I love now;
At least, in lively chronicles of the past—
Of Irish waters by a Cornish prow
Or Trojan waters by a Spartan mast
5 Much to their cost invaded—here and there,
Hunting the amorous line, skimming the rest,
I find some woman bearing as I bear
Love like a burning city in the breast.
I think however that of all alive
10 I only in such utter, ancient way
Do suffer love; in me alone survive
The unregenerate passions of a day
When treacherous queens, with death upon the tread,
Heedless and willful, took their knights to bed.

1931

Sonnet 99

Love is not all; it is not meat nor drink
Nor slumber nor a roof against the rain;
Nor yet a floating spar to men that sink
And rise and sink and rise and sink again;
5 Love can not fill the thickened lung with breath,
Nor clean the blood, nor set the fractured bone;
Yet many a man is making friends with death
Even as I speak, for lack of love alone.
It well may be that in a difficult hour,
10 Pinned down by pain and moaning for release,
Or nagged by want past resolution's power,
I might be driven to sell your love for peace,
Or trade the memory of this night for food.
It well may be. I do not think I would.

1931

Sonnet 115

Even in the moment of our earliest kiss,
When sighed the straitened bud into the flower,
Sat the dry seed of most unwelcome this;
And that I knew, though not the day and hour.
5 Too season-wise am I, being country-bred,
To tilt at autumn or defy the frost:
Snuffing the chill even as my fathers did,
I say with them, "What's out tonight is lost."
I only hoped, with the mild hope of all
10 Who watch the leaf take shape upon the tree,
A fairer summer and a later fall
Than in these parts a man is apt to see,
And sunny clusters ripened for the wine:
I tell you this across the blackened vine.

1931

Sonnet 116

Well, I have lost you; and I lost you fairly;
In my own way, and with my full consent.
Say what you will, kings in a tumbrel rarely
Went to their deaths more proud than this one went.
5 Some nights of apprehension and hot weeping
I will confess; but that's permitted me;
Day dried my eyes; I was not one for keeping

Rubbed in a cage a wing that would be free.
If I had loved you less or played you slyly
10 I might have held you for a summer more,
But at the cost of words I value highly,
And no such summer as the one before.
Should I outlive this anguish—and men do—
I shall have only good to say of you.

1931

Sonnet 120

If in the years to come you should recall,
When faint at heart or fallen on hungry days,
Or full of griefs and little if at all
From them distracted by delights or praise;
5 When failing powers or good opinion lost
Have bowed your neck, should you recall to mind
How of all men I honored you the most,
Holding you noblest among mortal-kind:
Might not my love—although the curving blade
10 From whose wide mowing none may hope to hide,
Me long ago below the frost had laid—
Restore you somewhat to your former pride?
Indeed I think this memory, even then,
Must raise you high among the run of men.

1931

Wilfred Owen

(1893–1918)

Strange Meeting

It seemed that out of battle I escaped
Down some profound dull tunnel, long since scooped
Through granites which titanic wars had groined.
Yet also there encumbered sleepers groaned,
5 Too fast in thought or death to be bestirred.
Then, as I probed them, one sprang up, and stared
With piteous recognition in fixed eyes,
Lifting distressful hands as if to bless.
And by his smile, I knew that sullen hall,
10 By his dead smile I knew we stood in Hell.
With a thousand pains that vision's face was grained;

Yet no blood reached there from the upper ground,
And no guns thumped, or down the flues made moan.
"Strange friend," I said, "here is no cause to mourn."
15 "None," said the other, "save the undone years,
The hopelessness. Whatever hope is yours,
Was my life also; I went hunting wild
After the wildest beauty in the world,
Which lies not calm in eyes, or braided hair,
20 But mocks the steady running of the hour,
And if it grieves, grieves richlier than here.
For of my glee might many men have laughed,
And of my weeping something had been left,
Which must die now. I mean the truth untold,
25 The pity of war, the pity war distilled.
Now men will go content with what we spoiled,
Or, discontent, boil bloody, and be spilled.
They will be swift with swiftness of the tigress.
None will break ranks, though nations trek from progress.
30 Courage was mine, and I had mystery,
Wisdom was mine, and I had mastery:
To miss the march of this retreating world
Into vain citadels that are not walled.
Then, when much blood had clogged their chariot-wheels,
35 I would go up and wash them from sweet wells,
Even with truths that lie too deep for taint.
I would have poured my spirit without stint
But not through wounds; not on the cess of war.
Foreheads of men have bled where no wounds were.
40 I am the enemy you killed, my friend.
I knew you in this dark: for so you frowned
Yesterday through me as you jabbed and killed.
I parried; but my hands were loath and cold.
Let us sleep now. . . ."

1919

Dulce et Decorum Est[1]

Bent double, like old beggars under sacks,
Knock-kneed, coughing like hags, we cursed through sludge,
Till on the haunting flares we turned our backs
And towards our distant rest began to trudge.
5 Men marched asleep. Many had lost their boots
But limped on, blood-shod. All went lame; all blind;

---

[1]Horace: "Dulce et decorum est pro patria mori" ("It is sweet and fitting to die for one's country").

Drunk with fatigue; deaf even to the hoots
Of tired, outstripped Five-Nines that dropped behind.

Gas! Gas! Quick, boys!—An ecstasy of fumbling,
10 Fitting the clumsy helmets just in time;
But someone still was yelling out and stumbling
And flound'ring like a man in fire or lime . . .
Dim, through the misty panes and thick green light,
As under a green sea, I saw him drowning.

15 In all my dreams, before my helpless sight,
He plunges at me, guttering, choking, drowning.

If in some smothering dreams you too could pace
Behind the wagon that we flung him in,
And watch the white eyes writhing in his face,
20 His hanging face, like a devil's sick of sin;
If you could hear, at every jolt, the blood
Come gargling from the froth-corrupted lungs,
Obscene as cancer, bitter as the cud
Of vile, incurable sores on innocent tongues,—
25 My friend, you would not tell with such high zest
To children ardent for some desperate glory,
The old Lie: Dulce et decorum est
Pro patria mori.

1920

Anthem for Doomed Youth

What passing-bells for these who die as cattle?
    Only the monstrous anger of the guns.
    Only the stuttering rifles' rapid rattle
Can patter out their hasty orisons.
5 No mockeries now for them; no prayers nor bells,
    Nor any voice of mourning save the choirs—
The shrill, demented choirs of wailing shells;
    And bugles calling for them from sad shires.

What candles may be held to speed them all?
10   Not in the hands of boys, but in their eyes
Shall shine the holy glimmers of good-byes.
    The pallor of girls' brows shall be their pall;
Their flowers the tenderness of patient minds,
And each slow dusk a drawing-down of blinds.

1917

Dorothy Parker

(1893–1967)

Résumé

Razors pain you;
Rivers are damp;
Acids stain you;
And drugs cause cramp.
5 Guns aren't lawful;
Nooses give;
Gas smells awful;
You might as well live.

1926

Unfortunate Coincidence

By the time you swear you're his,
    Shivering and sighing,
And he vows his passion is
    Infinite, undying —
5 Lady, make a note of this:
    One of you is lying.

1929

Indian Summer

In youth, it was a way I had
    To do my best to please,
And change, with every passing lad,
    To suit his theories.

5 But now I know the things I know,
    And do the things I do;
And if you do not like me so,
    To hell, my love, with you!

1931

One Perfect Rose

A single flow'r he sent me, since we met.
    All tenderly his messenger he chose;
Deep-hearted, pure, with scented dew still wet —
    One perfect rose.

5 I knew the language of the floweret;
    "My fragile leaves," it said, "his heart enclose."
Love long has taken for his amulet
    One perfect rose.

Why is it no one ever sent me yet
10   One perfect limousine, do you suppose?
Ah no, it's always just my luck to get
    One perfect rose.

                                                1930

E. E. Cummings

(1894–1963)

the Cambridge ladies who live in furnished souls

the Cambridge ladies who live in furnished souls
are unbeautiful and have comfortable minds
(also, with the church's protestant blessings
daughters, unscented shapeless spirited)
5 they believe in Christ and Longfellow, both dead,
are invariably interested in so many things—
at the present writing one still finds
delighted fingers knitting for the is it Poles?
perhaps. While permanent faces coyly bandy
10 scandal of Mrs. N and Professor D
. . . . the Cambridge ladies do not care, above
Cambridge if sometimes in its box of
sky lavender and cornerless, the
moon rattles like a fragment of angry candy

                                              1923

may i feel said he

may i feel said he
(i'll squeal said she
just once said he)
it's fun said she

5 (may i touch said he
how much said she

a lot said he)
why not said she

(let's go said he
10 not too far said she
what's too far said he
where you are said she)

may i stay said he
(which way said she
15 like this said he
if you kiss said she

may i move said he
is it love said she)
if you're willing said he
20 (but you're killing said she

but it's life said he
but your wife said she
now said he)
ow said she

25 (tiptop said he
don't stop said she
oh no said he)
go slow said she

(cccome? said he
30 ummm said she)
you're divine! said he
(you are Mine said she)

1935

All in green went my love riding

All in green went my love riding
on a great horse of gold
into the silver dawn.

four lean hounds crouched low and smiling
5 the merry deer ran before.

Fleeter be they than dappled dreams
the swift sweet deer
the red rare deer.

Four red roebuck at a white water
10 the cruel bugle sang before.

Horn at hip went my love riding
riding the echo down
into the silver dawn.

four lean hounds crouched low and smiling
15 the level meadows ran before.

Softer be they than slippered sleep
the lean lithe deer
the fleet flown deer.

Four fleet does at a gold valley
20 the famished arrow sang before.

Bow at belt went my love riding
riding the mountain down
into the silver dawn.

four lean hounds crouched low and smiling
25 the sheer peaks ran before.

Paler be they than daunting death
the sleek slim deer
the tall tense deer.

Four tall stags at a green mountain
30 the lucky hunter sang before.

All in green went my love riding
on a great horse of gold
into the silver dawn.

four lean hounds crouched low and smiling
35 my heart fell dead before.

1923

in Just-

in Just-
spring   when the world is mud-
luscious the little
lame balloonman

5 whistles   far   and wee

and eddieandbill come
running from marbles and
piracies and it's
spring

10 when the world is puddle-wonderful

the queer
old balloonman whistles
far   and   wee
and bettyandisbel come dancing

15 from hop-scotch and jump-rope and

it's
spring
and
        the

20   goat-footed
balloonMan   whistles
far
and
wee

                                        1923

Buffalo Bill's

Buffalo Bill's
defunct
        who used to
        ride a watersmooth-silver
5   stallion
and break onetwothreefourfive pigeonsjustlikethat
                                        Jesus

he was a handsome man
                and what i want to know is
10 how do you like your blueeyed boy
Mister Death

                                        1923

my sweet old etcetera

my sweet old etcetera
aunt lucy during the recent

war could and what
is more did tell you just
5 what everybody was fighting

for,
my sister

isabel created hundreds
(and
10 hundreds) of socks not to
mention shirts fleaproof earwarmers

etcetera wristers etcetera, my
mother hoped that

i would die etcetera
15 bravely of course my father used
to become hoarse talking about how it was
a privilege and if only he
could meanwhile my

self etcetera lay quietly
20 in the deep mud et

cetera
(dreaming,
et
    cetera, of
25 Your smile
eyes knees and of your Etcetera)

i sing of Olaf glad and big

i sing of Olaf glad and big
whose warmest heart recoiled at war:
a conscientious object-or

his wellbelovèd colonel (trig
5 westpointer most succinctly bred)
took erring Olaf soon in hand;
but—though an host of overjoyed
noncoms (first knocking on the head
him) do through icy waters roll
10 that helplessness which others stroke
with brushes recently employed
anent this muddy toiletbowl,
while kindred intellects evoke
allegiance per blunt instruments—
15 Olaf (being to all intents
a corpse and wanting any rag
upon what God unto him gave)
responds, without getting annoyed
"I will not kiss your f.ing flag"

20 straightway the silver bird looked grave
(departing hurriedly to shave)

but—though all kinds of officers
(a yearning nation's blueeyed pride)
their passive prey did kick and curse
25 until for wear their clarion
voices and boots were much the worse,
and egged the firstclassprivates on
his rectum wickedly to tease
by means of skilfully applied
30 bayonets roasted hot with heat—
Olaf (upon what were once knees)
does almost ceaselessly repeat
"there is some s. I will not eat."

our president,being of which
35 assertions duly notified
threw the yellowsonofabitch
into a dungeon,where he died

Christ (of His mercy infinite)
i pray to see;and Olaf,too

40 preponderatingly because
unless statistics lie he was
more brave than me:more blond than you.

1931

l(a

l(a

le
af
fa

5 ll

s)
one
l

iness

1959

Louise Bogan

(1897–1970)

The Crossed Apple

I've come to give you fruit from out my orchard,
Of wide report.
I have trees there that bear me many apples
Of every sort:

5 Clear, streakèd; red and russet; green and golden;
Sour and sweet.
This apple's from a tree yet unbeholden,
Where two kinds meet,—

So that this side is red without a dapple,
10 And this side's hue
Is clear and snowy. It's a lovely apple.
It is for you.

Within are five black pips as big as peas,
As you will find,
15 Potent to breed you five great apple trees
Of varying kind:

To breed you wood for fire, leaves for shade,
Apples for sauce.
Oh, this is a good apple for a maid,
20 It is a cross,

Fine on the finer, so the flesh is tight,
And grained like silk.
Sweet Burning gave the red side, and the white
Is Meadow Milk.

25 Eat it; and you will taste more than the fruit:
The blossom, too,
The sun, the air, the darkness at the root,
The rain, the dew,

The earth we came to, and the time we flee,
30 The fire and the breast.
I claim the white part, maiden, that's for me.
You take the rest.

Medusa

I had come to the house, in a cave of trees,
Facing a sheer sky.

Everything moved,—a bell hung ready to strike,
Sun and reflection wheeled by.

5 When the bare eyes were before me
And the hissing hair,
Held up at a window, seen through a door.
The stiff bald eyes, the serpents on the forehead
Formed in the air.

10 This is a dead scene forever now.
Nothing will ever stir.
The end will never brighten it more than this,
Nor the rain blur.

The water will always fall, and will not fall,
15 And the tipped bell make no sound.
The grass will always be growing for hay
Deep on the ground.

And I shall stand here like a shadow
Under the great balanced day,
20 My eyes on the yellow dust, that was lifting in the wind,
And does not drift away.

                                                    1921

Hart Crane

(1899–1932)

Proem: To Brooklyn Bridge

How many dawns, chill from his rippling rest
The seagull's wings shall dip and pivot him,
Shedding white rings of tumult, building high
Over the chained bay waters Liberty—

5 Then, with inviolate curve, forsake our eyes
As apparitional as sails that cross
Some page of figures to be filed away;
—Till elevators drop us from our day . . .

I think of cinemas, panoramic sleights
10 With multitudes bent toward some flashing scene
Never disclosed, but hastened to again,
Foretold to other eyes on the same screen;

And Thee, across the harbor, silver-paced
As though the sun took steps of thee, yet left
15 Some motion ever unspent in thy stride,—
Implicitly thy freedom staying thee!

Out of some subway scuttle, cell or loft
A bedlamite speeds to thy parapets,
Tilting there momently, shrill shirt ballooning,
20 A jest falls from the speechless caravan.

Down Wall, from girder into street noon leaks,
A rip-tooth of the sky's acetylene;
All afternoon the cloud-flown derricks turn . . .
Thy cables breathe the North Atlantic still.

25 And obscure as that heaven of the Jews,
Thy guerdon . . . Accolade thou dost bestow
Of anonymity time cannot raise;
Vibrant reprieve and pardon thou dost show.

O harp and altar, of the fury fused,
30 (How could mere toil align thy choiring strings!)
Terrific threshold of the prophet's pledge,
Prayer of pariah, and the lover's cry,—

Again the traffic lights that skim thy swift
Unfractioned idiom, immaculate sigh of stars,
35 Beading thy path—condense eternity:
And we have seen night lifted in thine arms.

Under thy shadow by the piers I waited;
Only in darkness is thy shadow clear.
The City's fiery parcels all undone,
40 Already snow submerges an iron year . . .

O Sleepless as the river under thee,
Vaulting the sea, the prairies' dreaming sod,
Unto us lowliest sometime sweep, descend
And of the curveship lend a myth to God.

1930

Chaplinesque

We make our meek adjustments,
Contented with such random consolations

As the wind deposits
In slithered and too ample pockets.

5 For we can still love the world, who find
   A famished kitten on the step, and know
   Recesses for it from the fury of the street,
   Or warm torn elbow coverts.

   We will sidestep, and to the final smirk
10 Dally the doom of that inevitable thumb
   That slowly chafes its puckered index toward us,
   Facing the dull squint with what innocence
   And what surprise!

   And yet these fine collapses are not lies
15 More than the pirouettes of any pliant cane;
   Our obsequies are, in a way, no enterprise.
   We can evade you, and all else but the heart:
   What blame to us if the heart live on.

   The game enforces smirks; but we have seen
20 The moon in lonely alleys make
   A grail of laughter of an empty ash can,
   And through all sound of gaiety and quest
   Have heard a kitten in the wilderness.

                                             1926

Janet Lewis

(1899–   )

Girl Help

Mild and slow and young,
She moves about the room,
And stirs the summer dust
With her wide broom.

5 In the warm, lofted air,
   Soft lips together pressed,
   Soft wispy hair,
   She stops to rest.

   And stops to breathe,
10 Amid the summer hum,
   The great white lilac bloom
   Scented with days to come.

Allen Tate

(1899–1979)

Ode to the Confederate Dead

Row after row with strict impunity
The headstones yield their names to the element,
The wind whirrs without recollection;
In the riven troughs the splayed leaves
5 Pile up, of nature the casual sacrament
To the seasonal eternity of death;
Then driven by the fierce scrutiny
Of heaven to their election in the vast breath,
They sough the rumor of mortality.

10 Autumn is desolation in the plot
Of a thousand acres where these memories grow
From the inexhaustible bodies that are not
Dead, but feed the grass row after rich row.
Think of the autumns that have come and gone!
15 Ambitious November with the humors of the year,
With a particular zeal for every slab,
Staining the uncomfortable angels that rot
On the slabs, a wing chipped here, an arm there:
The brute curiosity of an angel's stare
20 Turns you, like them, to stone,
Transforms the heaving air
Till plunged to a heavier world below
You shift your sea-space blindly
Heaving, turning like the blind crab.

25   Dazed by the wind, only the wind
        The leaves flying, plunge

You know who have waited by the wall
The twilight certainty of an animal,
Those midnight restitutions of the blood
30 You know—the immitigable pines, the smoky frieze
Of the sky, the sudden call: you know the rage,
The cold pool left by the mounting flood,
Of muted Zeno and Parmenides.[1]
You who have waited for the angry resolution
35 Of those desires that should be yours tomorrow,

---

[1]Greek philosophers of the Eleatic School, who held that change is illusion

You know the unimportant shrift of death
And praise the vision
And praise the arrogant circumstance
Of those who fall
40 Rank upon rank, hurried beyond decision—
Here by the sagging gate, stopped by the wall.

     Seeing, seeing only the leaves
     Flying, plunge and expire

Turn your eyes to the immoderate past,
45 Turn to the inscrutable infantry rising
Demons out of the earth—they will not last.
Stonewall, Stonewall, and the sunken fields of hemp,
Shiloh, Antietam, Malvern Hill, Bull Run.
Lost in that orient of the thick and fast
50 You will curse the setting sun.

     Cursing only the leaves crying
     Like an old man in a storm

You hear the shout, the crazy hemlocks point
With troubled fingers to the silence which
55 Smothers you, a mummy, in time.

       The hound bitch
Toothless and dying, in a musty cellar
Hears the wind only.

       Now that the salt of their blood
60 Stiffens the saltier oblivion of the sea,
Seals the malignant purity of the flood,
What shall we who count our days and bow
Our heads with a commemorial woe
In the ribboned coats of grim felicity,
65 What shall we say of the bones, unclean,
Whose verdurous anonymity will grow?
The ragged arms, the ragged heads and eyes
Lost in these acres of the insane green?
The gray lean spiders come, they come and go;
70 In a tangle of willows without light
The singular screech-owl's tight
Invisible lyric seeds the mind
With the furious murmur of their chivalry.

     We shall say only the leaves
75   Flying, plunge and expire

We shall say only the leaves whispering
In the improbable mist of nightfall
That flies on multiple wing:
Night is the beginning and the end
80 And in between the ends of distraction
Waits mute speculation, the patient curse
That stones the eyes, or like the jaguar leaps
For his own image in a jungle pool, his victim.

What shall we say who have knowledge
85 Carried to the heart? Shall we take the act
To the grave? Shall we, more hopeful, set up the grave
In the house? The ravenous grave?

        Leave now
The shut gate and the decomposing wall:
90 The gentle serpent, green in the mulberry bush,
Riots with his tongue through the hush—
Sentinel of the grave who counts us all!

                                      1928

Yvor Winters

(1900–1968)

At the San Francisco Airport

To my Daughter, 1954

This is the terminal: the light
Gives perfect vision, false and hard;
The metal glitters, deep and bright.
Great planes are waiting in the yard—
5 They are already in the night.

And you are here beside me, small,
Contained and fragile, and intent
On things that I but half recall—
Yet going whither you are bent.
10 I am the past, and that is all.

But you and I in part are one:
The frightened brain, the nervous will,
The knowledge of what must be done,

The passion to acquire the skill
15 To face that which you dare not shun.

The rain of matter upon sense
Destroys me momently. The score:
There comes what will come. The expense
Is what one thought, and something more—
20 One's being and intelligence.

This is the terminal, the break.
Beyond this point, on lines of air,
You take the way that you must take;
And I remain in light and stare—
25 In light, and nothing else, awake.

1954

Langston Hughes

(1902–1967)

The Negro Speaks of Rivers

I've known rivers:
I've known rivers ancient as the world and older than the flow of human blood
    in human veins.

My soul has grown deep like the rivers.

I bathed in the Euphrates when dawns were young.
5 I built my hut near the Congo and it lulled me to sleep.

I looked upon the Nile and raised the pyramids above it.
I heard the singing of the Mississippi when Abe Lincoln went down to
    New Orleans, and I've seen its muddy bosom turn all golden in the sunset.

I've known rivers:
Ancient, dusky rivers.

10 My soul has grown deep like the rivers.

1926

I, Too

I, too, sing America.

I am the darker brother.
They send me to eat in the kitchen

When company comes,
5   But I laugh,
And eat well,
And grow strong.

Tomorrow,
I'll be at the table
10   When company comes.
Nobody'll dare
Say to me,
"Eat in the kitchen,"
Then.

15   Besides,
They'll see how beautiful I am
And be ashamed—

I, too, am America.

Old Walt

Old Walt Whitman
Went finding and seeking,
Finding less than sought
Seeking more than found,
5   Every detail minding
Of the seeking or the finding.

Pleasured equally
In seeking as in finding,
Each detail minding,
10   Old Walt went seeking
And finding.

Harlem

What happens to a dream deferred?

Does it dry up
like a raisin in the sun?
Or fester like a sore—
5   And then run?

Does it stink like rotten meat?
Or crust and sugar over—
like a syrupy sweet?

Maybe it just sags
10 like a heavy load.

Or does it explode?

1951

Stevie Smith

(1902–1972)

Not Waving but Drowning

Nobody heard him, the dead man,
But still he lay moaning:
I was much further out than you thought
And not waving but drowning.

5 Poor chap, he always loved larking
And now he's dead
It must have been too cold for him his heart gave way,
They said.

Oh, no no no, it was too cold always
10 (Still the dead one lay moaning)
I was much too far out all my life
And not waving but drowning.

1957

Countee Cullen

(1903–1946)

For a Lady I Know

She even thinks that up in heaven
Her class lies late and snores,
While poor black cherubs rise at seven
To do celestial chores.

Heritage

(For Harold Jackman)

What is Africa to me:
Copper sun or scarlet sea,

Jungle star or jungle track,
Strong bronzed men, or regal black
5 Women from whose loins I sprang
When the birds of Eden sang?
One three centuries removed
From the scenes his fathers loved,
Spicy grove, cinnamon tree,
10 *What is Africa to me?*

So I lie, who all day long
Want no sound except the song
Sung by wild barbaric birds
Goading massive jungle herds,
15 Juggernauts of flesh that pass
Trampling tall defiant grass
Where young forest lovers lie,
Plighting troth beneath the sky.
So I lie, who always hear,
20 Though I cram against my ear
Both my thumbs, and keep them there,
Great drums throbbing through the air.
So I lie, whose fount of pride,
Dear distress, and joy allied,
25 Is my somber flesh and skin,
With the dark blood dammed within
Like great pulsing tides of wine
That, I fear, must burst the fine
Channels of the chafing net
30 Where they surge and foam and fret.

Africa? A book one thumbs
Listlessly, till slumber comes.
Unremembered are her bats
Circling through the night, her cats
35 Crouching in the river reeds,
Stalking gentle flesh that feeds
By the river brink; no more
Does the bugle-throated roar
Cry that monarch claws have leapt
40 From the scabbards where they slept.

Silver snakes that once a year
Doff the lovely coats you wear,
Seek no covert in your fear
Lest a mortal eye should see;

45 What's your nakedness to me?
Here no leprous flowers rear
Fierce corollas in the air;
Here no bodies sleek and wet,
Dripping mingled rain and sweat,
50 Tread the savage measures of
Jungle boys and girls in love.
What is last year's snow to me,
Last year's anything? The tree
Budding yearly must forget
55 How its past arose or set—
Bough and blossom, flower, fruit,
Even what shy bird with mute
Wonder at her travail there,
Meekly labored in its hair.
60 *One three centuries removed*
From the scenes his fathers loved,
Spicy grove, cinnamon tree,
What is Africa to me?

So I lie, who find no peace
65 Night or day, no slight release
From the unremittent beat
Made by cruel padded feet
Walking through my body's street.
Up and down they go, and back,
70 Treading out a jungle track.
So I lie, who never quite
Safely sleep from rain at night—
I can never rest at all
When the rain begins to fall;
75 Like a soul gone mad with pain
I must match its weird refrain;
Ever must I twist and squirm,
Writhing like a baited worm,
While its primal measures drip
80 Through my body, crying, "Strip!
Doff this new exuberance.
Come and dance the Lover's Dance!"
In an old remembered way
Rain works on me night and day.

85 Quaint, outlandish heathen gods
Black men fashion out of rods,

Clay, and brittle bits of stone,
In a likeness like their own,
My conversion came high-priced;
90   I belong to Jesus Christ,
Preacher of humility;
Heathen gods are naught to me.

Father, Son, and Holy Ghost,
So I make an idle boast;
95   Jesus of the twice-turned cheek,
Lamb of God, although I speak
With my mouth thus, in my heart
Do I play a double part.
Ever at Thy glowing altar
100   Must my heart grow sick and falter,
Wishing He I served were black,
Thinking then it would not lack
Precedent of pain to guide it,
Let who would or might deride it;
105   Surely then this flesh would know
Yours had borne a kindred woe.
Lord, I fashion dark gods, too,
Daring even to give You
Dark despairing features where,
110   Crowned with dark rebellious hair,
Patience wavers just so much as
Mortal grief compels, while touches
Quick and hot, of anger, rise
To smitten cheek and weary eyes.
115   Lord, forgive me if my need
Sometimes shapes a human creed.
All day long and all night through,
One thing only must I do;
Quench my pride and cool my blood,
120   *Lest I perish in the flood.*
Lest a hidden ember set
Timber that I thought was wet
Burning like the dryest flax,
Melting like the merest wax,
125   *Lest the grave restore its dead.*
Not yet has my heart or head
In the least way realized
They and I are civilized.

1925

Earle Birney

(1904–1995)

Anglosaxon Street

Dawndrizzle ended   dampness steams from
blotching brick and   black plasterwaste
Faded housepatterns   hoary and finicky
unfold stuttering   stick like a phonograph

5 Here is a ghetto   gotten for goyim
O with care denuded   of nigger and kike
No coonsmell rankles   reeks only cellarrot
attar of carexhaust   catcorpse and cookinggrease
Imperial hearts   heave in this haven
10 Cracks across windows   are welded with slogans
There'll Always Be An England   enhances geraniums
and V's for a Victory   vanquish the housefly

Ho! with climbing sun   march the bleached beldames
festooned with shopping bags   farded flatarched
15 bigthewed Saxonwives   stepping over buttrivers
waddling back wienerladen   to suckle smallfry

Hoy! with sunslope   shrieking over hydrants
flood from learningshall   the lean fingerlings
Nordic nobblecheeked   not all clean of nose
20 leaping Commandowise   into leprous lanes

What! after whistleblow!   spewed from wheelboat
after daylong doughtiness   dire handplay
in sewertrench or sandpit   come Saxonthegns
Junebrown Jutekings   jawslack for meat

25 Sit after supper   on smeared doorsteps
not humbly swearing   hatedeeds on Huns
profiteers politicians   pacifists Jews

Then by twobit magic   to muse in movie
unlock picturehoard   or lope to alehall
30 soaking bleakly   in beer skittleless
Home again to hotbox   and humid husbandhood
in slumbertrough adding   sleepily to Anglekin

Alongside in lanenooks   carling and leman
caterwaul and clip   careless of Saxonry
35 with moonglow and haste   and a higher heartbeat

Slumbers now slumtrack   unstinks cooling
waiting brief but milkmaid   mornstar and worldrise

1947

The Bear on the Delhi Road

Unreal   tall as a myth
by the road the Himalayan bear
is beating the brilliant air
with his crooked arms
5 About him two men   bare
spindly as locusts   leap

One pulls on a ring
in the great soft nose   His mate
flicks   flicks with a stick
10 up at the rolling eyes

They have not led him here
down from the fabulous hills
to this bald alien plain
and the clamorous world   to kill
15 but simply to teach him to dance

They are peaceful both   these spare
men of Kashmir   and the bear
alive is their living   too
If   far on the Delhi way
20 around him galvanic they dance
it is merely to wear   wear
from his shaggy body the tranced
wish forever to stay
only an ambling bear
25 four-footed in berries

It is no more joyous for them
in this hot dust to prance
out of reach of the praying claws
sharpened to paw for ants
30 in the shadows of deodars
It is not easy to free
myth from reality
or rear this fellow up
to lurch   lurch with them
35 in the tranced dancing of men

1960

Richard Eberhart

(1904–   )

The Fury of Aerial Bombardment

You would think the fury of aerial bombardment
Would rouse God to relent; the infinite spaces
Are still silent. He looks on shock-pried faces.
History, even, does not know what is meant.

5 You would feel that after so many centuries
God would give man to repent; yet he can kill
As Cain could, but with multitudinous will,
No farther advanced than in his ancient furies.

Was man made stupid to see his own stupidity?
10 Is God by definition indifferent, beyond us all?
Is the eternal truth man's fighting soul
Wherein the Beast ravens in its own avidity?

Of Van Wettering I speak, and Averill,
Names on a list, whose faces I do not recall
15 But they are gone to early death, who late in school
Distinguished the belt feed lever from the belt holding pawl.

1947

On a Squirrel Crossing the Road in Autumn, in New England

It is what he does not know,
Crossing the road under the elm trees,
About the mechanism of my car,
About the Commonwealth of Massachusetts,
5 About Mozart, India, Arcturus,

That wins my praise. I engage
At once in whirling squirrel-praise.

He obeys the orders of nature
Without knowing them.
10 It is what he does not know
That makes him beautiful.
Such a knot of little purposeful nature!

I who can see him as he cannot see himself
Repose in the ignorance that is his blessing.

15 It is what man does not know of God
Composes the visible poem of the world.
. . . Just missed him!

The Groundhog

In June, amid the golden fields,
I saw a groundhog lying dead.
Dead lay he; my senses shook,
And mind outshot our naked frailty.
5   There lowly in the vigorous summer
His form began its senseless change,
And made my senses waver dim
Seeing nature ferocious in him.
Inspecting close his maggots' might
10 And seething cauldron of his being,
Half with loathing, half with a strange love,
I poked him with an angry stick.
The fever arose, became a flame
And Vigour circumscribed the skies,
15 Immense energy in the sun,
And through my frame a sunless trembling.
My stick had done nor good nor harm.
Then stood I silent in the day
Watching the object, as before;
20 And kept my reverence for knowledge
Trying for control, to be still,
To quell the passion of the blood;
Until I had bent down on my knees
Praying for joy in the sight of decay.
25 And so I left; and I returned
In Autumn strict of eye, to see
The sap gone out of the groundhog,
But the bony sodden hulk remained.
But the year had lost its meaning,
30 And in intellectual chains
I lost both love and loathing,
Mured up in the wall of wisdom.
Another summer took the fields again
Massive and burning, full of life,
35 But when I chanced upon the spot
There was only a little hair left,
And bones bleaching in the sunlight
Beautiful as architecture;
I watched them like a geometer,
40 And cut a walking stick from a birch.
It has been three years, now.
There is no sign of the groundhog.

I stood there in the whirling summer,
My hand capped a withered heart,
45 And thought of China and of Greece,
Of Alexander in his tent;
Of Montiagne in his tower,
Of Saint Theresa in her wild lament.

1930

Kenneth Rexroth

(1905–1982)

Vitamins and Roughage

Strong ankled, sun burned, almost naked,
The daughters of California
Educate reluctant humanists;
Drive into their skulls with tennis balls
5 The unhappy realization
That nature is still stronger than man.
The special Hellenic privilege
Of the special intellect seeps out
At last in this irrigated soil.
10 Sweat of athletes and juice of lovers
Are stronger than Socrates' hemlock,
And the games of scrupulous Euclid
Vanish in the gymnopaedia.

1944

Proust's Madeleine

Somebody has given my
Baby daughter a box of
Old poker chips to play with.
Today she hands me one while
5 I am sitting with my tired
Brain at my desk. It is red.
On it is a picture of
An elk's head and the letters
B. P. O. E.—a chip from
10 A small town Elks' Club. I flip
It idly in the air and

Catch it and do a coin trick
To amuse my little girl.
Suddenly everything slips aside.
15 I see my father
Doing the very same thing,
Whistling "Beautiful Dreamer,"
His breath smelling richly
Of whiskey and cigars. I can
20 Hear him coming home drunk
From the Elks' Club in Elkhart
Indiana, bumping the
Chairs in the dark. I can see
Him dying of cirrhosis
25 Of the liver and stomach
Ulcers and pneumonia,
Or, as he said on his deathbed, of
Crooked cards and straight whiskey,
Slow horses and fast women.

                                                    1963

W. H. Auden

(1907–1973)

The Unknown Citizen

(To JS/07/M/378
This Marble Monument
Is Erected by the State)

He was found by the Bureau of Statistics to be
One against whom there was no official complaint,
And all the reports on his conduct agree
That, in the modern sense of an old-fashioned word, he was a saint,
5 For in everything he did he served the Greater Community.
Except for the War till the day he retired
He worked in a factory and never got fired,
But satisfied his employers, Fudge Motors Inc.
Yet he wasn't a scab or odd in his views,
10 For his Union reports that he paid his dues,
(Our report on his Union shows it was sound)
And our Social Psychology workers found
That he was popular with his mates and liked a drink.

The Press are convinced that he bought a paper every day
15 And that his reactions to advertisements were normal in every way.
Policies taken out in his name prove that he was fully insured,
And his Health-card shows he was once in hospital but left it cured.
Both Producers Research and High-Grade Living declare
He was fully sensible to the advantages of the Installment Plan
20 And had everything necessary to the Modern Man,
A phonograph, a radio, a car, and a frigidaire.
Our researchers into Public Opinion are content
That he held the proper opinions for the time of year;
When there was peace, he was for peace; when there was war, he went.
25 He was married and added five children to the population,
Which our Eugenist says was the right number for a parent of his generation,
And our teachers report that he never interfered with their education.
Was he free? Was he happy? The question is absurd:
Had anything been wrong, we should certainly have heard.

1940

Musée des Beaux Arts[1]

About suffering they were never wrong,
The Old Masters: how well they understood
Its human position; how it takes place
While someone else is eating or opening a window or just walking dully along;
5 How, when the aged are reverently, passionately waiting
For the miraculous birth, there always must be
Children who did not specially want it to happen, skating
On a pond at the edge of the wood:
They never forgot
10 That even the dreadful martyrdom must run its course
Anyhow in a corner, some untidy spot
Where the dogs go on with their doggy life and the torturer's horse
Scratches its innocent behind on a tree.

In Brueghel's *Icarus*,[2] for instance: how everything turns away
15 Quite leisurely from the disaster; the plowman may
Have heard the splash, the forsaken cry,
But for him it was not an important failure; the sun shone
As it had to on the white legs disappearing into the green
Water; and the expensive delicate ship that must have seen

---

[1] the Museum of Fine Arts, in Brussels
[2] Icarus, in Greek myth, flew too close to the sun on wings of wax, fell into the sea and drowned. In Brueghel's painting Icarus is a peripheral figure.

20   Something amazing, a boy falling out of the sky,
    Had somewhere to get to and sailed calmly on.

                            1940

In Memory of W. B. Yeats

(d. January, 1939)

1

He disappeared in the dead of winter:
The brooks were frozen, the airports almost deserted,
And snow disfigured the public statues;
The mercury sank in the mouth of the dying day.
5   What instruments we have agree
The day of his death was a dark cold day.

Far from his illness
The wolves ran on through the evergreen forests,
The peasant river was untempted by the fashionable quays;
10   By mourning tongues
The death of the poet was kept from his poems.

But for him it was his last afternoon as himself,
An afternoon of nurses and rumors;
The provinces of his body revolted,
15   The squares of his mind were empty,
Silence invaded the suburbs,
The current of his feeling failed; he became his admirers.

Now he is scattered among a hundred cities
And wholly given over to unfamiliar affections,
20   To find his happiness in another kind of wood
And be punished under a foreign code of conscience.
The words of a dead man
Are modified in the guts of the living.

But in the importance and noise of tomorrow
25   When the brokers are roaring like beasts on the floor of the Bourse,[1]
And the poor have the sufferings to which they are fairly accustomed,
And each in the cell of himself is almost convinced of his freedom,
A few thousand will think of this day
As one thinks of a day when one did something slightly unusual.
30   What instruments we have agree
The day of his death was a dark cold day.

---

[1] the Paris stock exchange

2

You were silly like us; your gift survived it all:
The parish of rich women, physical decay,
Yourself. Mad Ireland hurt you into poetry.
35 Now Ireland has her madness and her weather still,
For poetry makes nothing happen: it survives
In the valley of its making where executives
Would never want to tamper, flows on south
From ranches of isolation and the busy griefs,
40 Raw towns that we believe and die in; it survives,
A way of happening, a mouth.

3

Earth, receive an honored guest:
William Yeats is laid to rest.
Let the Irish vessel lie
45 Emptied of its poetry.

Time that is intolerant
Of the brave and innocent,
And indifferent in a week
To a beautiful physique,

50 Worships language and forgives
Everyone by whom it lives;
Pardons cowardice, conceit,
Lays its honours at their feet.

Time that with this strange excuse
55 Pardoned Kipling and his views,
And will pardon Paul Claudel,
Pardons him for writing well.

In the nightmare of the dark
All the dogs of Europe bark,
60 And the living nations wait,
Each sequestered in its hate;

Intellectual disgrace
Stares from every human face,
And the seas of pity lie
65 Locked and frozen in each eye.

Follow, poet, follow right
To the bottom of the night,
With your unconstraining voice
Still persuade us to rejoice;

70   With the farming of a verse
       Make a vineyard of the curse,
       Sing of human unsuccess
       In a rapture of distress;

       In the deserts of the heart
75   Let the healing fountain start,
       In the prison of his days
       Teach the free man how to praise.

                                                              1940

Epitaph on a Tyrant

Perfection, of a kind, was what he was after,
And the poetry he invented was easy to understand;
He knew human folly like the back of his hand,
And was greatly interested in armies and fleets;
5 When he laughed, respectable senators burst with laughter,
And when he cried the little children died in the streets.

As I Walked Out One Evening

As I walked out one evening,
    Walking down Bristol Street,
The crowds upon the pavement
    Were fields of harvest wheat.

5 And down by the brimming river
    I heard a lover sing
Under an arch of the railway:
    "Love has no ending.

"I'll love you dear, I'll love you
10   Till China and Africa meet,
And the river jumps over the mountain
    And the salmon sing in the street.

"I'll love you till the ocean
    Is folded and hung up to dry,
15 And the seven stars go squawking
    Like geese about the sky.

The years shall run like rabbits,
    For in my arms I hold
The Flower of the Ages,
20   And the first love of the world."

But all the clocks in the city
    Began to whirr and chime:

"O let not Time deceive you,
    You cannot conquer Time.

25 "In the burrows of the Nightmare
    Where Justice naked is,
Time watches from the shadow
    And coughs when you would kiss.

"In headaches and in worry
30   Vaguely life leaks away,
And Time will have his fancy
    Tomorrow or to-day.

"Into many a green valley
    Drifts the appalling snow;
35 Time breaks the threaded dances
    And the diver's brilliant bow.

"O plunge your hands in water,
    Plunge them in up to the wrist;
Stare, stare in the basin
40   And wonder what you've missed.

"The glacier knocks in the cupboard,
    The desert sighs in the bed,
And the crack in the tea-cup opens
    A lane to the land of the dead.

45 "Where the beggars raffle the banknotes
    And the Giant is enchanting to Jack,
And the Lily-white Boy is a Roarer,
    And Jill goes down on her back.

"O look, look in the mirror,
50   O look in your distress;
Life remains a blessing
    Although you cannot bless.

"O stand, stand at the window
    As the tears scald and start;
55 You shall love your crooked neighbor
    With your crooked heart."

It was late, late in the evening,
    The lovers they were gone;
The clocks had ceased their chiming,
60   And the deep river ran on.

                                        1940

"Lay Your Sleeping Head, My Love"

Lay your sleeping head, my love,
Human on my faithless arm;
Time and fevers burn away
Individual beauty from
5   Thoughtful children, and the grave
Proves the child ephemeral:
But in my arms till break of day
Let the living creature lie,
Mortal, guilty, but to me
10 The entirely beautiful.

Soul and body have no bounds:
To lovers as they lie upon
Her tolerant enchanted slope
In their ordinary swoon,
15 Grave the vision Venus sends
Of supernatural sympathy,
Universal love and hope;
While an abstract insight wakes
Among the glaciers and the rocks
20 The hermit's sensual ecstasy.

Certainty, fidelity
On the stroke of midnight pass
Like vibrations of a bell,
And fashionable madmen raise
25 Their pedantic boring cry:
Every farthing of the cost,
All the dreaded cards foretell,
Shall be paid, but from this night
Not a whisper, not a thought,
30 Not a kiss nor look to be lost.

Beauty, midnight, vision dies:
Let the winds of dawn that blow
Softly round your dreaming head
Such a day of sweetness show
35 Eye and knocking heart may bless,
Find the mortal world enough;
Noons of dryness see you fed
By the involuntary powers,
Nights of insult let you pass
40 Watched by every human love.

1945

Stop All the Clocks

Stop all the clocks, cut off the telephone,
Prevent the dog from barking with a juicy bone,
Silence the pianos and with muffled drum
Bring out the coffin, let the mourners come.

5 Let aeroplanes circle moaning overhead
Scribbling on the sky the message He Is Dead,
Put crêpe bows round the white necks of the public doves,
Let the traffic policemen wear black cotton gloves.

He was my North, my South, my East and West,
10 My working week and my Sunday rest,
My noon, my midnight, my talk, my song;
I thought that love would last for ever: I was wrong.

The stars are not wanted now; put out every one:
Pack up the moon and dismantle the sun;
15 Pour away the ocean and sweep up the woods:
For nothing now can ever come to any good.

1940

Theodore Roethke

(1908–1963)

Root Cellar

Nothing would sleep in that cellar, dank as a ditch,
Bulbs broke out of boxes hunting for chinks in the dark,
Shoots dangled and drooped,
Lolling obscenely from mildewed crates,
5 Hung down long yellow evil necks, like tropical snakes.
And what a congress of stinks!—
Roots ripe as old bait,
Pulpy stems, rank, silo-rich,
Leaf-mold, manure, lime, piled against slippery planks.
10 Nothing would give up life:
Even the dirt kept breathing a small breath.

1948

The Waking

I wake to sleep, and take my waking slow.
I feel my fate in what I cannot fear.
I learn by going where I have to go.

We think by feeling. What is there to know?
5 I hear my being dance from ear to ear.
I wake to sleep, and take my waking slow.

Of those so close beside me, which are you?
God bless the Ground! I shall walk softly there,
And learn by going where I have to go.

10 Light takes the Tree; but who can tell us how?
The lowly worm climbs up a winding stair;
I wake to sleep, and take my waking slow.

Great Nature has another thing to do
To you and me; so take the lively air,
15 And, lovely, learn by going where to go.

This shaking keeps me steady. I should know.
What falls away is always. And is near.
I wake to sleep, and take my waking slow.
I learn by going where I have to go.

1953

Dolor

I have known the inexorable sadness of pencils,
Neat in their boxes, dolor of pad and paper-weight,
All the misery of manilla folders and mucilage,
Desolation in immaculate public places,
5 Lonely reception room, lavatory, switchboard,
The unalterable pathos of basin and pitcher,
Ritual of multigraph, paper-clip, comma,
Endless duplication of lives and objects.
And I have seen dust from the walls of institutions,
10 Finer than flour, alive, more dangerous than silica,
Sift, almost invisible, through long afternoons of tedium,
Dropping a fine film on nails and delicate eyebrows,
Glazing the pale hair, the duplicate gray standard faces.

1948

I Knew a Woman

I knew a woman, lovely in her bones,
When small birds sighed, she would sigh back at them;
Ah, when she moved, she moved more ways than one:
The shapes a bright container can contain!
5 Of her choice virtues only gods should speak,
Or English poets who grew up on Greek
(I'd have them sing in chorus, cheek to cheek).

How well her wishes went! She stroked my chin,
She taught me Turn, and Counter-turn, and Stand;
10 She taught me Touch, that undulant white skin;
I nibbled meekly from her proffered hand;
She was the sickle; I, poor I, the rake,
Coming behind her for her pretty sake
(But what prodigious mowing we did make).

15 Love likes a gander, and adores a goose:
Her full lips pursed, the errant note to seize;
She played it quick, she played it light and loose;
My eyes, they dazzled at her flowing knees;
Her several parts could keep a pure repose,
20 Or one hip quiver with a mobile nose
(She moved in circles, and those circles moved).

Let seed be grass, and grass turn into hay:
I'm martyr to a motion not my own;
What's freedom for? To know eternity.
25 I swear she cast a shadow white as stone.
But who would count eternity in days?
These old bones live to learn her wanton ways:
(I measure time by how a body sways).

                                        1958

In a Dark Time

In a dark time, the eye begins to see,
I meet my shadow in the deepening shade;
I hear my echo in the echoing wood—
A lord of nature weeping to a tree.
5 I live between the heron and the wren,
Beasts of the hill and serpents of the den.

What's madness but nobility of soul
At odds with circumstance? The day's on fire!
I know the purity of pure despair,
10 My shadow pinned against a sweating wall.
That place among the rocks—is it a cave,
Or winding path? The edge is what I have.

A steady storm of correspondences!
A night flowing with birds, a ragged moon,
15 And in broad day the midnight come again!
A man goes far to find out what he is—
Death of the self in a long, tearless night,
All natural shapes blazing unnatural light.

Dark, dark my light, and darker my desire.
20 My soul, like some heat-maddened summer fly,
Keeps buzzing at the sill. Which I is *I*?
A fallen man, I climb out of my fear.
The mind enters itself, and God the mind,
And one is One, free in the tearing wind.

1960

My Papa's Waltz

The whiskey on your breath
Could make a small boy dizzy;
But I hung on like death:
Such waltzing was not easy.

5 We romped until the pans
Slid from the kitchen shelf;
My mother's countenance
Could not unfrown itself.

The hand that held my wrist
10 Was battered on one knuckle;
At every step you missed
My right ear scraped a buckle.

You beat time on my head
With a palm caked hard by dirt,
15 Then waltzed me off to bed
Still clinging to your shirt.

1948

The Meadow Mouse

1

In a shoe box stuffed in an old nylon stocking
Sleeps the baby mouse I found in the meadow,
Where he trembled and shook beneath a stick
Till I caught him up by the tail and brought him in,
5 Cradled in my hand,
A little quaker, the whole body of him trembling,
His absurd whiskers sticking out like a cartoon-mouse,
His feet like small leaves,
Little lizard-feet,
10 Whitish and spread wide when he tried to struggle away,
Wriggling like a miniscule puppy.

Now he's eaten his three kinds of cheese and drunk from his bottlecap
    watering-trough—
So much he just lies in one corner,
His tail curled under him, his belly big
15 As his head; his bat-like ears
Twitching, tilting toward the least sound.

Do I imagine he no longer trembles
When I come close to him?
He seems no longer to tremble.

2

20 But this morning the shoe-box house on the back porch is empty.
Where has he gone, my meadow mouse,
My thumb of a child that nuzzled in my palm?—
To run under the hawk's wing,
Under the eye of the great owl watching from the elm-tree,
25 To live by courtesy of the shrike, the snake, the tom-cat.

I think of the nestling fallen into the deep grass,
The turtle gasping in the dusty rubble of the highway,
The paralytic stunned in the tub, and the water rising,—
All things innocent, hapless, forsaken.

A. M. Klein

(1909–1972)

The Rocking Chair

It seconds the crickets of the province. Heard
in the clean lamplit farmhouses of Quebec,—
wooden,—it is no less a national bird;
and rivals, in its cage, the mere stuttering clock.
5 To its time, the evenings are rolled away;
and in its peace the pensive mother knits
contentment to be worn by her family,
grown-up, but still cradled by the chair in which she sits.

It is also the old man's pet, pair to his pipe,
10 the two aids of his arithmetic and plans,
plans rocking and puffing into market-shape;
and it is the toddler's game and dangerous dance.
Moved to the verandah, on summer Sundays, it is,
among the hanging plants, the girls, the boy-friends,

15 sabbatical and clumsy, like the white haloes
dangling above the blue serge suits of the young men.

It has a personality of its own;
is a character (like that old drunk Lacoste,
exhaling amber, and toppling on his pins);
20 it is alive; individual; and no less
an identity than those about it. And
it is tradition. Centuries have been flicked
from its arcs, alternately flicked and pinned.
It rolls with the gait of St. Malo.[1] It is act

25 and symbol, symbol of this static folk
which moves in segments, and returns to base,—
a sunken pendulum: *invoke, revoke;*
loosed yon, leashed hither, motion on no space.
O, like some Anjou[2] ballad, all refrain,
30 which turns about its longing, and seems to move
to make a pleasure out of repeated pain,
its music moves, as if always back to a first love.

1948

Lone Bather

Upon the ecstatic diving board the diver
poised for parabolas, lets go
lets go his manshape to become a bird.
Is bird, and topsy-turvy
5 the pool floats overhead, and the white tiles snow

their crazy hexagons. Is dolphin. Then
is plant with lilies bursting from his heels.
Himself, suddenly mysterious and marine,
bobs up a merman leaning on his hills.

10 Plashes and plays alone the deserted pool;
as those, is free, who think themselves unseen.
He rolls in his heap of fruit,
he slides his belly over
the melonrinds of water, curved and smooth and green.
15 Feels good: and trains, like little acrobats
his echoes dropping from the galleries;
circles himself over a rung of water;
swims fancy and gay; taking a notion, hides

---

[1] a seaport in Brittany
[2] a former province of western France

under the satins of his great big bed,—
20 and then comes up to float until he thinks
the ceiling at his brow, and nowhere any sides.
His thighs are a shoal of fishes: scattered: he
turns with many gloves of greeting
towards the sunnier water and the tiles.

25 Upon the tiles he dangles from his toes
lazily the eight reins of his ponies.

An afternoon, far from the world
a street sound throws like a stone, with paper, through the glass.
Up, he is chipped enamel, grained with hair.
30 The gloss of his footsteps follows him to the showers,
the showers, and the male room, and the towel
which rubs the bird, the plant, the dolphin back again
personable plain.

1948

Stephen Spender

(1909–1995)

I Think Continually of Those Who Were Truly Great

I think continually of those who were truly great.
Who, from the womb, remembered the soul's history
Through corridors of light where the hours are suns
Endless and singing. Whose lovely ambition
5 Was that their lips, still touched with fire,
Should tell of the Spirit clothed from head to foot in song.
And who hoarded from the Spring branches
The desired falling across their bodies like blossoms.

What is precious is never to forget
10 The essential delight of the blood drawn from ageless springs
Breaking through rocks in worlds before our earth.
Never to deny its pleasure in the morning simple light
Nor its grave evening demand for love.
Never to allow gradually the traffic to smother
15 With noise and fog the flowering of the spirit.

Near the snow, near the sun, in the highest fields
See how these names are fêted by the waving grass
And by the streamers of white cloud

And whispers of wind in the listening sky.
20 The names of those who in their lives fought for life
Who wore at their hearts the fire's center.
Born of the sun they traveled a short while towards the sun,
And left the vivid air signed with their honor.

                                                            1932

Charles Olson

(1910–1970)

I, Maximus of Gloucester, to You

Off-shore, by islands hidden in the blood
jewels & miracles, I, Maximus
a metal hot from boiling water, tell you
what is a lance, who obeys the figures of
5   the present dance

                        1

the thing you're after
may lie around the bend
of the nest (second, time slain, the bird! the bird!

And there! (strong) thrust, the mast! flight
10   (of the bird
                                o kylix, o
                                Antony of Padua
                                sweep low, o bless

the roofs, the old ones, the gentle steep ones
15 on whose ridge-poles the gulls sit, from which they depart,

                        And the flake-racks

of my city!

                        2

love is form, and cannot be without
important substance (the weight
20 say, 58 carats each one of us, perforce
our goldsmith's scale

                        feather to feather added
                        (and what is mineral, what
                        is curling hair, the string

25   you carry in your nervous beak, these
make bulk, these, in the end, are
the sum
(o my lady of good voyage
in whose arm, whose left arm rests
30 no boy but a carefully carved wood, a painted face, a schooner!
a delicate mast, as bow-sprit for

forwarding

3

the underpart is, though stemmed, uncertain
is, as sex is, as moneys are, facts!
35 facts, to be dealt with, as the sea is, the demand
that they be played by, that they only can be, that they must
be played by, said he, coldly, the
ear!

By ear, he sd.
40 But that which matters, that which insists, that which will last,
that! o my people, where shall you find it, how, where, where shall you listen
when all is become billboards, when, all, even silence, is spray-gunned?

when even our bird, my roofs,
cannot be heard

45 when even you, when sound itself is neoned in?

when, on the hill, over the water
where she who used to sing,
when the water glowed,
black, gold, the tide
50 outward, at evening

when bells came like boats
over the oil-slicks, milkweed
hulls

And a man slumped,
55 attentionless,
against pink shingles

o sea city)

4

one loves only form,
and form only comes

60 into existence when
the thing is born

> born of yourself, born
> of hay and cotton struts,
> of street-pickings, wharves, weeds
65 you carry in, my bird

> > of a bone of a fish
> > of a straw, or will
> > of a color, of a bell
> > of yourself, torn

5

70 love is not easy
but how shall you know,
New England, now
that pejorocracy is here, how
that street-cars, o Oregon, twitter
75 in the afternoon, offend
a black-gold loin?

> how shall you strike,
> o swordsman, the blue-red back
> when, last night, your aim
80 was mu-sick, mu-sick, mu-sick
> And not the cribbage game?

> > (o Gloucester-man,
> > weave
> > your birds and fingers
85 new, your roof-tops,
> > clean shit upon racks
> > sunned on
> > American
> > braid
90 with others like you, such
> > extricable surface
> > as faun and oral,
> > satyr lesbos vase

> > o kill kill kill kill kill
95 those
> > who advertise you
> > out)

6

in! in! the bow-sprit, bird, the beak
in, the bend is, in, goes in, the form
100 that which you make, what holds, which is
the law of object, strut after strut, what you are, what you must be, what
the force can throw up, can, right now hereinafter erect,
the mast, the mast, the tender
mast!

105   The nest, I say, to you, I Maximus, say
           under the hand, as I see it, over the waters
           from this place where I am, where I hear,
           can still hear

           from where I carry you a feather
110   as though, sharp, I picked up,
           in the afternoon delivered you
           a jewel,
                  it flashing more than a wing,
           than any old romantic thing,
115   than memory, than place,
           then anything other than that which you carry
           than that which is,
           call it a nest, around the head of, call it
           the next second

120   than that which you
           can do!

                                    1953

Elizabeth Bishop

(1911–1979)

The Fish

I caught a tremendous fish
and held him beside the boat
half out of water, with my hook
fast in a corner of his mouth.
5 He didn't fight.
He hadn't fought at all.
He hung a grunting weight,

battered and venerable
and homely. Here and there
10 his brown skin hung in strips
like ancient wall-paper,
and its pattern of darker brown
was like wall-paper:
shapes like full-blown roses
15 stained and lost through age.
He was speckled with barnacles,
fine rosettes of lime,
and infested
with tiny white sea-lice,
20 and underneath two or three
rags of green weed hung down.
While his gills were breathing in
the terrible oxygen
—the frightening gills,
25 fresh and crisp with blood,
that can cut so badly—
I thought of the coarse white flesh
packed in like feathers,
the big bones and the little bones,
30 the dramatic reds and blacks
of his shiny entrails,
and the pink swim-bladder
like a big peony.
I looked into his eyes
35 which were far larger than mine
but shallower, and yellowed,
the irises backed and packed
with tarnished tinfoil
seen through the lenses
40 of old scratched isinglass.
They shifted a little, but not
to return my stare.
—It was more like the tipping
of an object toward the light.
45 I admired his sullen face,
the mechanism of his jaw,
and then I saw
that from his lower lip
—if you could call it a lip—
50 grim, wet, and weapon-like,
hung five old pieces of fish-line,

of four and a wire leader
with the swivel still attached,
with all their five big hooks
55 grown firmly in his mouth.
A green line, frayed at the end
where he broke it, two heavier lines,
and a fine black thread
still crimped from the strain and snap
60 when it broke and he got away.
Like medals with their ribbons
frayed and wavering,
a five-haired beard of wisdom
trailing from his aching jaw.
65 I stared and stared
and victory filled up
the little rented boat,
from the pool of bilge
where oil had spread a rainbow
70 around the rusted engine
to the bailer rusted orange,
the sun-cracked thwarts,
the oarlocks on their strings,
the gunnels—until everything
75 was rainbow, rainbow, rainbow!
And I let the fish go.

1946

Sandpiper

The roaring alongside he takes for granted,
and that every so often the world is bound to shake.
He runs, he runs to the south, finical, awkward,
in a state of controlled panic, a student of Blake.

5 The beach hisses like fat. On his left, a sheet
of interrupting water comes and goes
and glazes over his dark and brittle feet.
He runs, he runs straight through it, watching his toes.

—Watching, rather, the spaces of sand between them,
10 where (no detail too small) the Atlantic drains
rapidly backwards and downwards. As he runs,
he stares at the dragging grains.

The world is a mist. And then the world is
minute and vast and clear. The tide

15 is higher or lower. He couldn't tell you which.
His beak is focused; he is preoccupied,
looking for something, something, something.
Poor bird, he is obsessed!
The millions of grains are black, white, tan, and gray,
20 mixed with quartz grains, rose and amethyst.

1962

In the Waiting Room

In Worcester, Massachusetts,
I went with Aunt Consuelo
to keep her dentist's appointment
and sat and waited for her
5 in the dentist's waiting room.
It was winter. It got dark
early. The waiting room
was full of grown-up people,
arctics and overcoats,
10 lamps and magazines.
My aunt was inside
what seemed like a long time
and while I waited I read
the *National Geographic*
15 (I could read) and carefully
studied the photographs:
The inside of a volcano,
black, and full of ashes;
then it was spilling over
20 in rivulets of fire.
Osa and Martin Johnson
dressed in riding breeches,
laced boots, and pith helmets.
A dead man slung on a pole
25 —"Long Pig," the caption said.
Babies with pointed heads
wound round and round with string;
black, naked women with necks
wound round and round with wire
30 like the necks of light bulbs.
Their breasts were horrifying.
I read it right straight through.
I was too shy to stop.
And then I looked at the cover:
35 the yellow margins, the date.

Suddenly, from inside,
came an *oh!* of pain
—Aunt Consuelo's voice—
not very loud or long.
40 I wasn't at all surprised;
even then I knew she was
a foolish, timid woman.
I might have been embarrassed,
but wasn't. What took me
45 completely by surprise
was that it was *me:*
my voice, in my mouth.
Without thinking at all
I was my foolish aunt,
50 I—we—were falling, falling,
our eyes glued to the cover
of the *National Geographic,*
February, 1918.
I said to myself: three days
55 and you'll be seven years old.
I was saying it to stop
the sensation of falling off
the round, turning world
into cold, blue-black space.
60 But I felt: you are an *I,*
you are an *Elizabeth,*
you are one of *them.*
Why should you be one, too?
I scarcely dared to look
65 to see what it was I was.
I gave a sidelong glance
—I couldn't look any higher—
at shadowy gray knees,
trousers and skirts and boots
70 and different pairs of hands
lying under the lamps.
I knew that nothing stranger
had ever happened, that nothing
stranger could ever happen.

75 Why should I be my aunt,
or me, or anyone?
What similarities—
boots, hands, the family voice
I felt in my throat, or even

80 the *National Geographic*
   and those awful hanging breasts—
   held us all together
   or made us all just one?
   How—I didn't know any
85 word for it—how "unlikely" . . .
   How had I come to be here,
   like them, and overhear
   a cry of pain that could have
   got loud and worse but hadn't?

90 The waiting room was bright
   and too hot. It was sliding
   beneath a big black wave,
   another, and another.

   Then I was back in it.
95 The War was on. Outside,
   in Worcester, Massachusetts,
   were night and slush and cold,
   and it was still the fifth
   of February, 1918.

                                              1976

The Moose

For Grace Bulmer Bowers

From narrow provinces
of fish and bread and tea,
home of the long tides
where the bay leaves the sea
5 twice a day and takes
the herrings long rides,

where if the river
enters or retreats
in a wall of brown foam
10 depends on if it meets
the bay coming in,
the bay not at home;

where, silted red,
sometimes the sun sets
15 facing a red sea,
and others, veins the flats'
lavender, rich mud
in burning rivulets;

on red, gravelly roads,
20 down rows of sugar maples,
    past clapboard farmhouses
    and neat, clapboard churches,
    bleached, ridged as clamshells,
    past twin silver birches,

25 through late afternoon
    a bus journeys west,
    the windshield flashing pink,
    pink glancing off of metal,
    brushing the dented flank
30 of blue, beat-up enamel;

    down hollows, up rises,
    and waits, patient, while
    a lone traveller gives
    kisses and embraces
35 to seven relatives
    and a collie supervises.

    Goodbye to the elms,
    to the farm, to the dog.
    The bus starts. The light
40 grows richer; the fog,
    shifting, salty, thin,
    comes closing in.

    Its cold, round crystals
    form and slide and settle
45 in the white hens' feathers,
    in gray glazed cabbages,
    on the cabbage roses
    and lupins like apostles;

    the sweet peas cling
50 to their wet white string
    on the whitewashed fences;
    bumblebees creep
    inside the foxgloves,
    and evening commences.

55 One stop at Bass River.
    Then the Economies—
    Lower, Middle, Upper;
    Five Islands, Five Houses,
    where a woman shakes a tablecloth
60 out after supper.

A pale flickering. Gone.
The Tantramar marshes
and the smell of salt hay.
An iron bridge trembles
65   and a loose plank rattles
but doesn't give way.

On the left, a red light
swims through the dark:
a ship's port lantern.
70   Two rubber boots show,
illuminated, solemn.
A dog gives one bark.

A woman climbs in
with two market bags,
75   brisk, freckled, elderly.
"A grand night. Yes, sir,
all the way to Boston."
She regards us amicably.

Moonlight as we enter
80   the New Brunswick woods,
hairy, scratchy, splintery;
moonlight and mist
caught in them like lamb's wool
on bushes in a pasture.

85   The passengers lie back.
Snores. Some long sighs.
A dreamy divagation
begins in the night,
a gentle, auditory,
90   slow hallucination. . . .

In the creakings and noises,
an old conversation
—not concerning us,
but recognizable, somewhere,
95   back in the bus:
Grandparents' voices

uninterruptedly
talking, in Eternity:
names being mentioned,
100   things cleared up finally;
what he said, what she said,
who got pensioned;

deaths, deaths and sicknesses;
the year he remarried;
105   the year (something) happened.
She died in childbirth.
That was the son lost
when the schooner foundered.

He took to drink. Yes.
110   She went to the bad.
When Amos began to pray
even in the store and
finally the family had
to put him away.

115   "Yes . . ." that peculiar
affirmative. "Yes . . ."
A sharp, indrawn breath,
half groan, half acceptance,
that means "Life's like that.
120   We know *it* (also death)."

Talking the way they talked
in the old featherbed,
peacefully, on and on,
dim lamplight in the hall,
125   down in the kitchen, the dog
tucked in her shawl.

Now, it's all right now
even to fall asleep
just as on all those nights
130   —Suddenly the bus driver
stops with a jolt,
turns off his lights.

A moose has come out of
the impenetrable wood
135   and stands there, looms, rather,
in the middle of the road.
It approaches; it sniffs at
the bus's hot hood.

Towering, antlerless,
140   high as a church,
homely as a house
(or, safe as houses).
A man's voice assures us
"Perfectly harmless. . . ."

145 Some of the passengers
    exclaim in whispers,
    childishly, softly,
    "Sure are big creatures."
    "It's awful plain."
150 "Look! It's a she!"

    Taking her time,
    she looks the bus over,
    grand, otherworldly.
    Why, why do we feel
155 (we all feel) this sweet
    sensation of joy?

    "Curious creatures,"
    says our quiet driver,
    rolling his *r*'s.
160 "Look at that, would you."
    Then he shifts gears.
    For a moment longer,

    by craning backward,
    the moose can be seen
165 on the moonlit macadam;
    then there's a dim
    smell of moose, an acrid
    smell of gasoline.

One Art

    The art of losing isn't hard to master;
    so many things seem filled with the intent
    to be lost that their loss is no disaster.

    Lose something every day. Accept the fluster
  5 of lost door keys, the hour badly spent.
    The art of losing isn't hard to master.

    Then practice losing farther, losing faster:
    places, and names, and where it was you meant
    to travel. None of these will bring disaster.

 10 I lost my mother's watch. And look! my last, or
    next-to-last, of three loved houses went.
    The art of losing isn't hard to master.

    I lost two cities, lovely ones. And, vaster,
    some realms I owned, two rivers, a continent.
 15 I miss them, but it wasn't a disaster.

—Even losing you (the joking voice, a gesture
I love) I shan't have lied. It's evident
the art of losing's not too hard to master
though it may look like (*Write it!*) like disaster.

Sonnet

Caught—the bubble
in the spirit-level,
a creature divided;
and the compass needle
5 wobbling and wavering,
undecided.
Freed—the broken
thermometer's mercury
running away;
10 and the rainbow-bird
from the narrow bevel
of the empty mirror,
flying wherever
it feels like, gay!

1979

Kenneth Patchen

(1911–1972)

The Character of Love Seen as a Search for the Lost

You, the woman; I, the man; this, the world:
And each is the work of all.

There is the muffled step in the snow; the stranger;
The crippled wren; the nun; the dancer; the Jesus-wing
5 Over the walkers in the village; and there are
Many beautiful arms about us and the things we know.

See how those stars tramp over heaven on their sticks
Of ancient light: with what simplicity that blue
Takes eternity into the quiet cave of God, where Caesar
10 And Socrates, like primitive paintings on a wall,
Look, with idiot eyes, on the world where we two are.

You, the sought for; I, the seeker; this, the search:
And each is the mission of all.

For greatness is only the drayhorse that coaxes
15 The built cart out; and where we go is reason.
But genius is an enormous littleness, a trickling
Of heart that covers alike the hare and the hunter.

How smoothly, like the sleep of a flower, love,
The grassy wind moves over night's tense meadow:
20 See how the great wooden eyes of the forest
Stare upon the architecture of our innocence.

You, the village; I, the stranger; this, the road:
And each is the work of all.

Then, not that man do more, or stop pity; but that he be
25 Wider in living; that all his cities fly a clean flag . . .
We have been alone too long, love; it is terribly late
For the pierced feet on the water and we must not die now.

Have you wondered why all the windows in heaven were broken?
Have you seen the homeless in the open grave of God's hand?
30 Do you want to acquaint the larks with the fatuous music of war?

There is the muffled step in the snow; the stranger;
The crippled wren; the nun; the dancer; the Jesus-wing
Over the walkers in the village; and there are
Many desperate arms about us and the things we know.

Do the Dead Know What Time It Is?

The old guy put down his beer.
Son, he said,
    (and a girl came over to the table where we were:
    asked us by Jack Christ to buy her a drink.)
5 Son, I am going to tell you something
The like of which nobody ever was told.
    (and the girl said, I've got nothing on tonight;
    how about you and me going to your place?)
I am going to tell you the story of my mother's
10 Meeting with God.
    (and I whispered to the girl: I don't have a room,
    but maybe . . .)
She walked up to where the top of the world is
And He came right up to her and said
15 So at last you've come home.
    (but maybe what?
    I thought I'd like to stay here and talk to you.)

My mother started to cry and God
Put His arms around her.
20   (about what?
        Oh, just talk . . . we'll find something.)
She said it was like a fog coming over her face
And light was everywhere and a soft voice saying
You can stop crying now.
25   (what can we talk about that will take all night?
        and I said that I didn't know.)
You can stop crying now.

Irving Layton

(1912–   )

Party at Hydra[1]

For Marianne

The white cormorants shaped like houses stare down at you.
A Greek Chagall[2] perched them there on the crooked terraces.
The steep ascent is through a labyrinth of narrow streets
Cobbled with huge stones that speak only Arvanitika.[3]
5 A surfeit of wisdom has made the stars above you eternally silent.
Many are ambushed by the silence and many never find their way
To the house where the perpetual party is going on.
If you are on the lookout for monsters or demons
You will not find their legs sprawled out in the terraces.
10 They are all assembled at the house threshing one another
With extracts from diaries whose pages fly open releasing beetles
That crawl along the grapevines and disappear into a night of ears.
Though only one head can be seen, several monsters have seven
And some have three and some no more than two. Beware of the one
15 Headed monster with an aspirin in his hand who'll devour you instead.
You know the number of heads each has by the small sucking winds
They make as they dissolve the salads and meats on their plates. So
Listen carefully holding a lighted incense stick for a talisman.
A rutting woman lets her smile float on your glass of punch.

---

[1]an island in the Aegean Sea
[2]Marc Chagall (b. 1887), famous for his dreamlike paintings
[3]an Albanian language

20 You scoop it up to hand back to her on a soaked slice of lemonpeel.
A poet announces to everyone not listening he has begun a new poem.
He hears a spider growling at him from a suntanned cleavage
And at once pierces it with a metaphor using its blood for glue.
A married man discourses tenderly on love and poultices.
25 It is almost dark when a goddess appears beside you.
She guides your hand under her white robe and murmurs
"The sweat of invalids in medicine bottles is not love
And wisdom is love that has lost one of its testicles.
Desire is love's lubricant yet love is no wheel spinning in a groove.
30 Love resides neither in the body nor in the soul
But is a volatile element reconciling spirit to flesh.
Love is the holy seal of their interpenetration and unity
When they come together in the perfect moment of fusion.
If you wish to know more about love listen to the crickets on the moon
35 And emulate the silent shining of the stars but do not become one."
When she vanishes your hand is a river you swim in forever.

Berry Picking

Silently my wife walks on the still wet furze
Now darkgreen the leaves are full of metaphors
Now lit up is each tiny lamp of blueberry.
The white nails of rain have dropped and the sun is free.

5 And whether she bends or straightens to each bush
To find the children's laughter among the leaves
Her quiet hands seem to make the quiet summer hush—
Berries or children, patient she is with these.

I only vex and perplex her; madness, rage
10 Are endearing perhaps put down upon the page;
Even silence daylong and sullen can then
Enamour as restraint or classic discipline.

So I envy the berries she puts in her mouth,
The red and succulent juice that stains her lips;
15 I shall never taste that good to her, nor will they
Displease her with a thousand barbarous jests.

How they lie easily for her hand to take,
Part of the unoffending world that is hers;
Here beyond complexity she stands and stares
20 And leans her marvellous head as if for answers.

No more the easy soul my childish craft deceives
Nor the simpler one for whom yes is always yes;

No, now her voice comes to me from a far way off
Though her lips are redder than the raspberries.

1958

Robert Hayden

(1913–1980)

Those Winter Sundays

Sundays too my father got up early
and put his clothes on in the blueblack cold,
then with cracked hands that ached
from labor in the weekday weather made
5 banked fires blaze. No one ever thanked him.

I'd wake and hear the cold splintering, breaking.
When the rooms were warm, he'd call,
and slowly I would rise and dress,
fearing the chronic angers of that house,

10 Speaking indifferently to him,
who had driven out the cold
and polished my good shoes as well.
What did I know, what did I know
of love's austere and lonely offices?

1962

Frederick Douglass

When it is finally ours, this freedom, this liberty, this beautiful
and terrible thing, needful to man as air,
usable as earth; when it belongs at last to all,
when it is truly instinct, brain matter, diastole, systole,
5 reflex action; when it is finally won; when it is more
than the gaudy mumbo jumbo of politicians;
this man, this Douglass, this former slave, this Negro
beaten to his knees, exiled, visioning a world
where none is lonely, none hunted, alien,
10 this man, superb in love and logic, this man
shall be remembered. Oh, not with statues' rhetoric,
not with legends and poems and wreaths of bronze alone,
but with the lives grown out of his life, the lives
fleshing his dream of the beautiful, needful thing.

John Berryman

(1914–1972)

A Professor's Song

(. . rabid or dog-dull.) Let me tell you how
The Eighteenth Century couplet ended. Now
Tell me. Troll me the sources of that Song—
Assigned last week—by Blake. Come, come along,
5 Gentlemen. (Fidget and huddle, do. Squint soon.)
I want to end these fellows all by noon.

"That deep romantic chasm"—an early use;
The word is from the French, by our abuse
Fished out a bit. (Red all your eyes. O when?)
10 "A poet is a man speaking to men":
But I am then a poet, am I not?—
Ha ha. The radiator, please. Well, what?

Alive now—no—Blake would have written prose,
But movement following movement crisply flows,
15 So much the better, better the much so,
As burbleth Mozart. Twelve. The class can go.
Until I meet you, then, in Upper Hell
Convulsed, foaming immortal blood: farewell.

1948

Dream Song #14

Life, friends, is boring. We must not say so.
After all, the sky flashes, the great sea yearns,
we ourselves flash and yearn,
and moreover my mother told me as a boy
5 (repeatingly) "Ever to confess you're bored
means you have no

Inner Resources." I conclude now I have no
inner resources, because I am heavy bored.
Peoples bore me,
10 literature bores me, especially great literature,
Henry bores me, with his plights & gripes
as bad as achilles,

who loves people and valiant art, which bores me.
And the tranquil hills, & gin, look like a drag
15 and somehow a dog

has taken itself & its tail considerably away
into mountains or sea or sky, leaving
behind: me, wag.

1969

David Ignatow

(1914–   )

Sunday at the State Hospital

I am sitting across the table
eating my visit sandwich.
The one I brought him stays suspended
near his mouth; his eyes focus
5 on the table and seem to think,
his shoulders hunched forward.
I chew methodically,
pretending to take him
as a matter of course.
10 The sandwich tastes mad
and I keep chewing.
My past is sitting in front of me
filled with itself
and trying with almost no success
15 to bring the present to its mouth.

Moonlight Poem

I wish you would get happy again
so I could knock it out of you.
It's a way of entertaining myself
because I can't stand
5 your beatific face
in the moonlight.

No Theory

No theory will stand up to a chicken's guts
being cleaned out, a hand rammed up
to pull out the wriggling entrails,
the green bile and the bloody liver;
5 no theory that does not grow sick
at the odor escaping.

The Bagel

I stopped to pick up the bagel
rolling away in the wind,
annoyed with myself
for having dropped it
5   as it were a portent.
Faster and faster it rolled,
with me running after it
bent low, gritting my teeth,
and I found myself doubled over
10   and rolling down the street
head over heels, one complete somersault
after another like a bagel
and strangely happy with myself.

Randall Jarrell

(1914–1965)

The Death of the Ball Turret Gunner

From my mother's sleep I fell into the State,
And I hunched in its belly till my wet fur froze.
Six miles from earth, loosed from its dream of life,
I woke to black flak and the nightmare fighters.
5   When I died they washed me out of the turret with a hose.

1945

Nestus Gurley

Sometimes waking, sometimes sleeping,
Late in the afternoon, or early
In the morning, I hear on the lawn,
On the walk, on the lawn, the soft quick step,
5   The sound half song, half breath: a note or two
That with a note or two would be a tune.
It is Nestus Gurley.

It is an old
Catch or snatch or tune
10   In the Dorian mode: the mode of the horses
That stand all night in the fields asleep
Or awake, the mode of the cold

Hunter, Orion, wheeling upside-down,
All space and stars, in cater-cornered Heaven.
15 When, somewhere under the east,
The great march begins, with birds and silence;
When, in the day's first triumph, dawn
Rides over the houses, Nestus Gurley
Delivers to me my lot.

20 As the sun sets, I hear my daughter say:
"He has four routes and makes a hundred dollars."
Sometimes he comes with dogs, sometimes with children,
Sometimes with dogs and children.
He collects, today.
25 I hear my daughter say:
"Today Nestus has got on his derby."
And he says, after a little: "It's two-eighty."
"How could it be two-eighty?"
"Because this month there're five Sundays: it's two-eighty."

30 He collects, delivers. Before the first, least star
Is lost in the paling east; at evening
While the soft, side-lit, gold-leafed day
Lingers to see the stars, the boy Nestus
Delivers to me the Morning Star, the Evening Star
35 —Ah no, only the Morning *News*, the Evening *Record*
Of what I have done and what I have not done
Set down and held against me in the Book
Of Death, on paper yellowing
Already, with one morning's sun, one evening's sun.

40 Sometimes I only dream him. He brings then
News of a different morning, a judgment not of men.
The bombers have turned back over the Pole,
Having met a star. . . . I look at that new year
And, waking, think of our Moravian Star
45 Not lit yet, and the pure beeswax candle
With its red flame-proofed paper pompom
Not lit yet, and the sweetened
Bun we brought home from the love-feast, still not eaten,
And the song the children sang: *O Morning Star*—

50 And at this hour, to the dew-hushed drums
Of the morning, Nestus Gurley
Marches to me over the lawn; and the cat Elfie,
Furred like a musk-ox, coon-tailed, gold-leaf-eyed,
Looks at the paper boy without alarm

55 But yawns, and stretches, and walks placidly
   Across the lawn to his ladder, climbs it, and begins to purr.

   I let him in,
   Go out and pick up from the grass the paper hat
   Nestus has folded: this tricorne fit for a Napoleon
60 Of our days and institutions, weaving
   Baskets, being bathed, receiving
   Electric shocks, Rauwolfia. . . . I put it on
   —Ah no, only unfold it.
   There is dawn inside; and I say to no one
65 About—
                    it is a note or two
   That with a note or two would—
                                    say to no one
   About nothing: "He delivers dawn."

70 When I lie coldly
   —Lie, that is, neither with coldness nor with warmth—
   In the darkness that is not lit by anything,
   In the grave that is not lit by anything
   Except our hope: the hope
75 That is not proofed against anything, but pure
   And shining as the first, least star
   That is lost in the east on the morning of Judgment—
   May I say, recognizing the step
   Or tune or breath. . . .
80   recognizing the breath,
   May I say, "It is Nestus Gurley."

                                                                1960

Dudley Randall

(1914–   )

Ballad of Birmingham

(On the bombing of a church in Birmingham, Alabama, 1963)

"Mother dear, may I go downtown
Instead of out to play,
And march the streets of Birmingham
In a Freedom March today?"

5 "No, baby, no, you may not go,
   For the dogs are fierce and wild,
   And clubs and hoses, guns and jails
   Aren't good for a little child."

   "But, mother, I won't be alone.
10 Other children will go with me,
   And march the streets of Birmingham
   To make our country free."

   "No, baby, no, you may not go,
   For I fear those guns will fire.
15 But you may go to church instead
   And sing in the children's choir."

   She has combed and brushed her night-dark hair,
   And bathed rose petal sweet,
   And drawn white gloves on her small brown hands,
20 And white shoes on her feet.

   The mother smiled to know her child
   Was in the sacred place,
   But that smile was the last smile
   To come upon her face.

25 For when she heard the explosion,
   Her eyes grew wet and wild.
   She raced through the streets of Birmingham
   Calling for her child.

   She clawed through bits of glass and brick,
30 Then lifted out a shoe.
   "O, here's the shoe my baby wore,
   But, baby, where are you?"

William Stafford

(1914–1993)

At the Un-National Monument Along the Canadian Border

This is the field where the battle did not happen,
where the unknown soldier did not die.
This is the field where grass joined hands,
Where no monument stands,
5 and the only heroic thing is the sky.

Birds fly here without any sound,
unfolding their wings across the open.
No people killed—or were killed—on this ground
hallowed by neglect and an air so tame
10   that people celebrate it by forgetting its name.

1977

Traveling Through the Dark

Traveling through the dark I found a deer
dead on the edge of the Wilson River road.
It is usually best to roll them into the canyon:
that road is narrow; to swerve might make more dead.

5   By glow of the tail-light I stumbled back of the car
and stood by the heap, a doe, a recent killing;
she had stiffened already, almost cold.
I dragged her off; she was large in the belly.

My fingers touching her side brought me the reason—
10   her side was warm; her fawn lay there waiting,
alive, still, never to be born.
Beside that mountain road I hesitated.

The car aimed ahead its lowered parking lights;
under the hood purred the steady engine.
15   I stood in the glare of the warm exhaust turning red;
around our group I could hear the wilderness listen.

I thought hard for us all—my only swerving—
then pushed her over the edge into the river.

1962

Dylan Thomas

(1914–1953)

A Refusal to Mourn the Death, by Fire, of a Child in London

Never until the mankind making
Bird beast and flower
Fathering and all humbling darkness
Tells with silence the last light breaking
5   And the still hour
Is come out of the sea tumbling in harness

And I must enter again the round
Zion of the water bead
And the synagogue of the ear of corn
10 Shall I let pray the shadow of a sound
Or sow my salt seed
In the least valley of sackcloth to mourn

The majesty and burning of the child's death.
I shall not murder
15 The mankind of her going with a grave truth
Nor blaspheme down the stations of the breath
With any further
Elegy of innocence and youth.

Deep with the first dead lies London's daughter,
20 Robed in the long friends,
The grains beyond age, the dark veins of her mother,
Secret by the unmourning water
Of the riding Thames.
After the first death, there is no other.

1946

In My Craft or Sullen Art

In my craft or sullen art
Exercised in the still night
When only the moon rages
And the lovers lie abed
5 With all their griefs in their arms,
I labor by singing light
Not for ambition or bread
Or the strut and trade of charms
On the ivory stages
10 But for the common wages
Of their most secret heart.

Not for the proud man apart
From the raging moon I write
On these spindrift pages
15 Nor for the towering dead
With their nightingales and psalms
But for the lovers, their arms
Round the griefs of the ages,
Who pay no praise or wages
20 Nor heed my craft or art.

1946

Fern Hill

Now as I was young and easy under the apple boughs
About the lilting house and happy as the grass was green,
    The night above the dingle starry,
      Time let me hail and climb
5   Golden in the heydays of his eyes,
And honored among wagons I was prince of the apple towns
And once below a time I lordly had the trees and leaves
      Trail with daisies and barley
    Down the rivers of the windfall light.

10 And as I was green and carefree, famous among the barns
About the happy yard and singing as the farm was home,
    In the sun that is young once only,
      Time let me play and be
    Golden in the mercy of his means,
15 And green and golden I was huntsman and herdsman, the calves
Sang to my horn, the foxes on the hills barked clear and cold,
      And the sabbath rang slowly
    In the pebbles of the holy streams.

All the sun long it was running, it was lovely, the hay
20 Fields high as the house, the tunes from the chimneys, it was air
    And playing, lovely and watery
      And fire green as grass.
    And nightly under the simple stars
As I rode to sleep the owls were bearing the farm away,
25 All the moon long I heard, blessed among stables, the night-jars
    Flying with the ricks, and the horses
      Flashing into the dark.

And then to awake, and the farm, like a wanderer white
With the dew, come back, the cock on his shoulder: it was all
30   Shining, it was Adam and maiden,
      The sky gathered again
    And the sun grew round that very day.
So it must have been after the birth of the simple light
In the first, spinning place, the spellbound horses walking warm
35   Out of the whinnying green stable
      On to the fields of praise.

And honored among foxes and pheasants by the gay house
Under the new made clouds and happy as the heart was long,
    In the sun born over and over,

40   I ran my heedless ways,
        My wishes raced through the house high hay
    And nothing I cared, at my sky blue trades, that time allows
    In all his tuneful turning so few and such morning songs
        Before the children green and golden
45   Follow him out of grace,

    Nothing I cared, in the lamb white days, that time would take me
    Up to the swallow thronged loft by the shadow of my hand,
        In the moon that is always rising,
            Nor that riding to sleep
50   I should hear him fly with the high fields
    And wake to the farm forever fled from the childless land.
    Oh as I was young and easy in the mercy of his means,
            Time held me green and dying
        Though I sang in my chains like the sea.

                                                            1946

Do Not Go Gentle into That Good Night

Do not go gentle into that good night,
Old age should burn and rave at close of day;
Rage, rage against the dying of the light.

Though wise men at their end know dark is right,
5 Because their words had forked no lightning they
Do not go gentle into that good night.

Good men, the last wave by, crying how bright
Their frail deeds might have danced in a green bay,
Rage, rage against the dying of the light.

10 Wild men who caught and sang the sun in flight,
And learn, too late, they grieved it on its way,
Do not go gentle into that good night.

Grave men, near death, who see with blinding sight
Blind eyes could blaze like meteors and be gay,
15 Rage, rage against the dying of the light.

And you, my father, there on the sad height,
Curse, bless, me now with your fierce tears, I pray.
Do not go gentle into that good night.
Rage, rage against the dying of the light.

                                                            1952

Isabella Gardner

(1915–1981)

Timeo

Dear God (safe ambiguity)
If I address you faithlessly
the fear of heaven devils me.
Could I be sure of purgatory
5 Sure I could praise and not adore thee
I might a tepid faith embrace.
But I am terrified of grace.
Gethsemane is any place.

1955

Summers Ago

For Edith Sitwell

> The Ferryman fairied us out to sea
> Gold gold gold sang the apple tree

Children I told you I tell you our sun was a hail of gold!
I say that sun stoned, that sun stormed our tranquil, our blue bay
bellsweet saltfresh water (bluer than tongue-can-tell, daughter)
and dazed us, darlings, and dazzled us, I say that sun crazed
5 (that sun clove) our serene as ceramic selves and our noon glazed cove,
and children all that grew wild by the wonderful water shot tall
as tomorrow, reeds suddenly shockingly green had sprouted like sorrow
and crimson explosions of roses arose in that flurry of Danaean glory
while at night we did swoon ah we swanned to a silverer moonlight than
      listen or lute,
10 we trysted in gondolas blown from glass and kissed in fluted Venetian bliss.

> Sister and brother I your mother
> Once was a girl in skirling weather
> Though summer and swan must alter, falter,
> I waltzed on the water once, son and daughter.

1961

Knowing

Mon moi, Ils m'arrachent mon moi

—MICHELET

I will be lonely at half past dead
Weep none one or many beside my bed.
At the dead center of all alone

I must unwillingly work at dying
5 I will be crying crying crying
Not I not I this flesh these bones.

1980

P. K. Page

(1916–)

The Stenographers

After the brief bivouac of Sunday,
their eyes, in the forced march of Monday to Saturday,
hoist the white flag, flutter in the snow storm of paper,
haul it down and crack in the midsun of temper.

5 In the pause between the first draft and the carbon
they glimpse the smooth hours when they were children—
the ride in the ice-cart, the ice-man's name,
the end of the route and the long walk home;

remember the sea where floats at high tide
10 were sea marrows growing on the scatter-green vine
or spools of gray toffee, or wasps' nests on water;
remember the sand and the leaves of the country.

Bell rings and they go and the voice draws their pencil
like a sled across snow; when its runners are frozen
15 rope snaps and the voice then is pulling no burden
but runs like a dog on the winter of paper.

Their climates are winter and summer—no wind
for the kites of their hearts—no wind for a flight;
a breeze at the most, to tumble them over
20 and leave them like rubbish—the boy-friends of blood.

In the inch of the noon as they move they are stagnant.
The terrible calm of the noon is their anguish;
the lip of the counter, the shapes of the straws
like icicles breaking their tongues are invaders.

25 Their beds are their oceans—salt water of weeping
the waves that they know—the tide before sleep;
and fighting to drown they assemble their sheep
in columns and watch them leap desks for their fences
and stare at them with their own mirror-worn faces.

30 In the felt of the morning the calico minded,
   sufficiently starched, insert papers, hit keys,
   efficient and sure as their adding machines;
   yet they weep in the vault, they are taut as net curtains
   stretched upon frames. In their eyes I have seen
35 the pin men of madness in marathon trim
   race round the track of the stadium pupil.

                                                    1946

Schizophrenic

Nobody knew when it would start again—
the extraordinary beast go violent in her blood;
nobody knew the virtue of her need
to shape her face to the giant in her brain.

5 Certainly friends were sympathetic, kind,
gave her small handkerchiefs and showed her tricks,
built her life to a sort of 'pick-up sticks'
simplification—as if she were a child.

Malleable she wore her lustre nails
10 daily like a debutante and smoked,
watching the fur her breath made as they joked,
caught like a wind in the freedom of their sails.

While always behind her face, the giant's face
struggled to break the matte mask of her skin—
15 and, turned about at last, be looking in—
tranquilly *in* to that imprisoned place.

Strong for the dive he dived one day at tea—
the cakes like flowers, the cups dreamy with cream—
he saw the window a lake and with a scream
20 nobody heard, shot by immediacy

he forced the contours of her features out.
Her tea-time friends were statues as she passed,
pushed, but seemingly drawn towards the glass;

her tea-time friends were blind, they did not see
25 the violence of his struggle to get free,
and deaf, and deaf, they did not hear his shout.

The waters of his lake were sharp and cold—
splashed and broke, triangular on the floor
after the dive from his imagined shore
30 in a land where all the inhabitants are old.

Gwendolyn Brooks

(1917–   )

The Bean Eaters

They eat beans mostly, this old yellow pair.
Dinner is a casual affair.
Plain chipware on a plain and creaking wood,
Tin flatware.

5 Two who are Mostly Good.
Two who have lived their day,
But keep on putting on their clothes
And putting things away.

And remembering . . .
10 Remembering, with twinklings and twinges,
As they lean over the beans in their rented back room that is full of beads and
    receipts and dolls and clothes, tobacco crumbs, vases and fringes.

1960

We Real Cool

The Pool Players.
Seven at the Golden Shovel.

We real cool. We
Left school. We

Lurk late. We
Strike straight. We

5 Sing sin. We
Thin gin. We

Jazz June. We
Die soon.

1960

Robert Lowell

(1917–1977)

Mr. Edwards and the Spider

I saw the spiders marching through the air,
Swimming from tree to tree that mildewed day
    In latter August when the hay

Came creaking to the barn. But where
5   The wind is westerly,
Where gnarled November makes the spiders fly
Into the apparitions of the sky,
They purpose nothing but their ease and die
Urgently beating east to sunrise and the sea;

10   What are we in the hands of the great God?
It was in vain you set up thorn and briar
       In battle array against the fire
       And treason crackling in your blood;
          For the wild thorns grow tame
15   And will do nothing to oppose the flame;
Your lacerations tell the losing game
You play against a sickness past your cure
How will the hands be strong? How will the heart endure?

A very little thing, a little worm,
20   Or hourglass-blazoned spider, it is said,
          Can kill a tiger. Will the dead
          Hold up his mirror and affirm
             To the four winds the smell
And flash of his authority? It's well
25   If God who holds you to the pit of hell,
Much as one holds a spider, will destroy,
Baffle and dissipate your soul. As a small boy

On Windsor Marsh, I saw the spider die
When thrown into the bowels of fierce fire:
30   There's no long struggle, no desire
          To get up on its feet and fly—
             It stretches out its feet
And dies. This is the sinner's last retreat;
Yes, and no strength exerted on the heat
35   Then sinews the abolished will, when sick
And full of burning, it will whistle on a brick.

But who can plumb the sinking of that soul?
Josiah Hawley, picture yourself cast
          Into a brick-kiln where the blast
40   Fans your quick vitals to a coal—
             If measured by a glass,
How long would it seem burning! Let there pass
A minute, ten, ten trillion; but the blaze
Is infinite, eternal: this is death,
45 To die and know it. This is the Black Widow, death.

1946

Skunk Hour

For Elizabeth Bishop

Nautilus Island's hermit
heiress still lives through winter in her Spartan cottage;
her sheep still graze above the sea.
Her son's a bishop. Her farmer
5 is first selectman in our village;
she's in her dotage.

Thirsting for
the hierarchic privacy
of Queen Victoria's century,
10 she buys up all
the eyesores facing her shore,
and lets them fall.

The season's ill—
we've lost our summer millionaire,
15 who seemed to leap from an L. L. Bean
catalogue. His nine-knot yawl
was auctioned off to lobstermen.
A red fox stain covers Blue Hill.

And now our fairy
20 decorator brightens his shop for fall;
his fishnet's filled with orange cork,
orange, his cobbler's bench and awl;
there is no money in his work,
he'd rather marry.

25 One dark night,
my Tudor Ford climbed the hill's skull;
I watched for love-cars. Lights turned down,
they lay together, hull to hull,
where the graveyard shelves on the town. . . .
30 My mind's not right.

A car radio bleats,
"Love, O careless Love. . . ." I hear
my ill-spirit sob in each blood cell,
as if my hand were at its throat. . . .
35 I myself am hell;
nobody's here—

only skunks, that search
in the moonlight for a bite to eat.
They march on their soles up Main Street:

40 white stripes, moonstruck eyes' red fire
    under the chalk-dry and spar spire
    of the Trinitarian Church.

    I stand on top
    of our back steps and breathe the rich air–
45 a mother skunk with her column of kittens swills the garbage pail.
    She jabs her wedge-head in a cup
    of sour cream, drops her ostrich tail,
    and will not scare.

                                                                1957

Water

    It was a Maine lobster town—
    each morning boatloads of hands
    pushed off for granite
    quarries on the islands,

5   and left dozens of bleak
    white frame houses stuck
    like oyster shells
    on a hill of rock,

    and below us, the sea lapped
10 the raw little match-stick
    mazes of a weir,
    where the fish for bait were trapped.

    Remember? We sat on a slab of rock.
    From this distance in time,
15 it seems the color
    of iris, rotting and turning purpler,

    but it was only
    the usual gray rock
    turning the usual green
20 when drenched by the sea.

    The sea drenched the rock
    at our feet all day,
    and kept tearing away
    flake after flake.

25 One night you dreamed
    you were a mermaid clinging to a wharf-pile,
    and trying to pull
    off the barnacles with your hands.

We wished our two souls
30 might return like gulls
to the rock. In the end,
the water was too cold for us.

1964

For the Union Dead

"Relinquunt Omnia Servare Rem Publican."[1]

The old South Boston Aquarium stands
in a Sahara of snow now. Its broken windows are boarded.
The bronze weathervane cod has lost half its scales.
The airy tanks are dry.

5 Once my nose crawled like a snail on the glass;
my hand tingled
to burst the bubbles
drifting from the noses of the cowed, compliant fish.

My hand draws back. I often sigh still
10 for the dark downward and vegetating kingdom
of the fish and reptile. One morning last March,
I pressed against the new barbed and galvanized

fence on the Boston Common. Behind their cage,
yellow dinosaur steamshovels were grunting
15 as they cropped up tons of mush and grass
to gouge their underworld garage.

Parking spaces luxuriate like civic
sandpiles in the heart of Boston.
A girdle of orange, Puritan-pumpkin colored girders
20 braces the tingling Statehouse,

shaking over the excavations, as it faces Colonel Shaw
and his bell-cheeked Negro infantry
on St. Gaudens' shaking Civil War relief,
propped by a plank splint against the garage's earthquake.

25 Two months after marching through Boston,
half the regiment was dead;
at the dedication,
William James could almost hear the bronze Negroes breathe.

Their monument sticks like a fishbone
30 in the city's throat.

---

[1]"They gave up all to serve the republic."

Its Colonel is as lean
as a compass-needle.

He has an angry wrenlike vigilance,
a greyhound's gentle tautness;
35 he seems to wince at pleasure,
and suffocate for privacy.

He is out of bounds now. He rejoices in man's lovely,
peculiar power to choose life and die—
when he leads his black soldiers to death,
40 he cannot bend his back.

On a thousand small town New England greens,
the old white churches hold their air
of sparse, sincere rebellion; frayed flags
quilt the graveyards of the Grand Army of the Republic.

45 The stone statues of the abstract Union Soldier
grow slimmer and younger each year—
wasp-waisted, they doze over muskets
and muse through their sideburns . . .

Shaw's father wanted no monument
50 except the ditch,
where his son's body was thrown
and lost with his "niggers."

The ditch is nearer.
There are no statues for the last war here;
55 on Boylston Street, a commercial photograph
shows Hiroshima boiling

over a Mosler Safe, the "Rock of Ages"
that survived the blast. Space is nearer.
When I crouch to my television set,
60 the drained faces of Negro school-children rise like balloons.

Colonel Shaw
is riding on his bubble,
he waits
for the blessèd break.

65 The Aquarium is gone. Everywhere,
giant finned cars nose forward like fish;
a savage servility
slides by on grease.

1964

Margaret Avison

(1918–   )

A Nameless One

Hot in June a narrow winged
long-elbowed-thread-legged
living insect lived
and died within
5 the lodgers' second-floor bathroom here.

At six a.m.
wafting ceilingward,
no breeze but what it living made there;

at noon standing
10 still as a constellation of spruce needles
before the moment of
making it, whirling;

at four a
wilted flotsam, cornsilk, on the linoleum:
15 now that it is
over, I
look with new eyes
upon this room
adequate for one to
20 be, in.

It's insect-day
has threaded a needle
for me for my eyes dimming
over rips and tears and
25 thin places.

1991

Alfred Purdy

(1918–   )

The Cariboo Horses

At 100 Mile House the cowboys ride in rolling
stagey cigarettes with one hand reining
restive equine rebels on a morning grey as stone
—so much like riding dangerous women
5   with whiskey coloured eyes—

such women as once fell dead with their lovers
with fire in their heads and slippery froth on thighs
—Beaver and Carrier women maybe or
                    Blackfoot squaws far past the edge of this valley
10 on the other side of those two toy mountain ranges
                    from the sunfierce plains beyond—

But only horses
                    waiting in stables
hitched at taverns
15   standing at dawn
pastured outside the town with
jeeps and fords and chevvys and
busy muttering stake trucks rushing
importantly over roads of man's devising
20 over the safe known roads of the ranchers
families and merchants of the town—
                    On the high prairie
are only horse and rider
                    wind in dry grass
25 clopping in silence under the toy mountains
dropping sometimes and
                    lost in the dry grass
                    golden oranges of dung—

Only horses
30   no stopwatch memories or palace ancestors
not Kiangs hauling undressed stone in the Nile Valley
and having stubborn Egyptian tantrums or
Onagers racing thru Hither Asia and
the last Quagga screaming in African highlands
35   lost relatives of these
                    whose hooves were thunder
the ghosts of horses battering thru the wind
whose names were the wind's common usage
whose life was the sun's
40   arriving here at chilly noon
                    in the gasoline smell of the
                    dust and waiting 15 minutes
                    at the grocer's—

Wilderness Gothic
Across Roblin Lake, two shores away,
they are sheathing the church spire
with new metal. Someone hangs in the sky
over there from a piece of rope,

5 hammering and fitting God's belly-scratcher,
working his way up along the spire
until there's nothing left to nail on—
Perhaps the workman's faith reaches beyond:
touches intangibles, wrestles with Jacob,
10 replacing rotten timber with pine thews,
pounds hard in the blue cave of the sky,
contends heroically with difficult problems of
gravity, sky navigation and mythopeia,
his volunteer time and labor denoted to God,
15 minus sick benefits of course on a non-union job—
Fields around are yellowing into harvest,
nestling and fingering are sky and water borne,
death is yodeling quiet in green woodlots,
and bodies of three young birds have disappeared
20 in the sub-surface of the new county highway—
That picture is incomplete, part left out
that might alter the whole Dürer landscape:
gothic ancestors peer from medieval sky,
dour faces trapped in photograph albums escaping
25 to clop down iron roads with matched grays:
work-sodden wives groping inside their flesh
for what keeps moving and changing and flashing
beyond and past the long frozen Victorian day.
A sign of fire and brimstone? A two-headed calf
30 born in the barn last night? A sharp female agony?
An age and a faith moving into transition,
the dinner cold and new-baked bread a failure,
deep woods shiver and water drops hang pendant,
double yolked eggs and the house creaks a little—
35 Something is about to happen. Leaves are still.
Two shores away, a man hammering in the sky.
Perhaps he will fall.

1968

Lawrence Ferlinghetti

(1919–   )

In Goya's greatest scenes we seem to see

In Goya's greatest scenes we seem to see

                               the people of the world

     exactly at the moment when

they first attained the title of
"suffering humanity"

5
They writhe upon the page
in a veritable rage
of adversity

Heaped up
10
groaning with babies and bayonets
under cement skies
in an abstract landscape of blasted trees
bent statues bats wings and beaks
slippery gibbets
15
cadavers and carnivorous cocks
and all the final hollering monsters
of the
"imagination of disaster"
they are so bloody real
20
it is as if they really still existed
And they do

Only the landscape is changed

They still are ranged along the roads
plagued by legionnaires
25
false windmills and demented roosters

They are the same people
only further from home
on freeways fifty lanes wide
on a concrete continent
30
spaced with bland billboards
illustrating imbecile illusions of happiness
The scene shows fewer tumbrils
but more maimed citizens
in painted cars
35
and they have strange license plates
and engines
that devour America

1958

The pennycandystore beyond the El

The pennycandystore beyond the El
is where I first
fell in love
with unreality

5 Jellybeans glowed in the semi-gloom
of that september afternoon
A cat upon the counter moved among
                              the licorice sticks
                  and tootsie rolls
10   and Oh Boy Gum

Outside the leaves were falling as they died

A wind had blown away the sun

A girl ran in
Her hair was rainy
15 Her breasts were breathless in the little room

Outside the leaves were falling
                  and they cried
                              Too soon! too soon!

1958

Howard Nemerov

(1920–1991)

The Goose Fish

On the long shore, lit by the moon
To show them properly alone,
Two lovers suddenly embraced
So that their shadows were as one.
5 The ordinary night was graced
For them by the swift tide of blood
That silently they took at flood,
And for a little time they prized
    Themselves emparadised.

10 Then, as if shaken by stage-fright
Beneath the hard moon's bony light,
They stood together on the sand
Embarrassed in each other's sight
But still conspiring hand in hand,
15 Until they saw, there underfoot,
As though the world had found them out,
The goose fish turning up, though dead,
    His hugely grinning head.

There in the china light he lay,
20 Most ancient and corrupt and gray
They hesitated at his smile,
Wondering what it seemed to say
To lovers who a little while
Before had thought to understand,
25 By violence upon the sand,
The only way that could be known
    To make a world their own.

It was a wide and moony grin
Together peaceful and obscene;
30 They knew not what he would express,
So finished a comedian
He might mean failure or success,
But took it for an emblem of
Their sudden, new and guilty love
35 To be observed by, when they kissed,
    That rigid optimist.

So he became their patriarch,
Dreadfully mild in the half-dark.
His throat that the sand seemed to choke,
40 His picket teeth, these left their mark
But never did explain the joke
That so amused him, lying there
While the moon went down to disappear
Along the still and tilted track
45   That bears the zodiac.

                                                1960

I Only Am Escaped Alone To Tell Thee

I tell you that I see her still
At the dark entrance of the hall.
One gas lamp burning near her shoulder
Shone also from her other side
5 Where hung the long inaccurate glass
Whose pictures were as troubled water.
An immense shadow had its hand
Between us on the floor, and seemed
To hump the knuckles nervously,
10 A giant crab readying to walk,
Or a blanket moving in its sleep.

You will remember, with a smile
Instructed by movies to reminisce,
How strict her corsets must have been,
15 How the huge arrangements of her hair
Would certainly betray the least
Impassionate displacement there.
It was no rig for dallying,
And maybe only marriage could
20 Derange that queenly scaffolding—
As when a great ship, coming home,
Coasts in the harbor, dropping sail
And loosing all the tackle that had laced
Her in the long lanes . . .
25   I know
We need not draw this figure out
But all that whalebone came from whales
And all the whales lived in the sea,
In calm beneath the troubled glass,
30 Until the needle drew their blood.
I see her standing in the hall,
Where the mirror's lashed to blood and foam,
And the black flukes of agony
Beat at the air till the light blows out.

                                                   1955

Richard Wilbur

(1921–   )

In a Churchyard

That flower unseen, that gem of purest ray,
Bright thoughts uncut by men:
Strange that you need but speak them, Thomas Gray,
And the mind skips and dives beyond its ken,

5 Finding at once the wild supposèd bloom
Or in the imagined cave
Some pulse of crystal staving off the gloom
As covertly as phosphorus in a grave.

Void notions proper to a buried head!
10 Beneath these tombstones here
Unseenness fills the sockets of the dead,
Whatever to their souls may now appear;

And who but those unfathomably deaf
Who quiet all this ground
15 Could catch, within the ear's diminished clef,
A music innocent of time and sound?

What do the living hear, then, when the bell
Hangs plumb within the tower
Of the still church, and still their thoughts compel
20 Pure tollings that intend no mortal hour?

As when a ferry for the shore of death
Glides looming toward the dock,
Her engines cut, her spirits bating breath
As the ranked pilings narrow toward the shock,

25 So memory and expectation set
Some pulseless clangor free
Of circumstance, and charm us to forget
This twilight crumbling in the churchyard tree,

Those swifts or swallows which do not pertain,
30 Scuffed voices in the drive,
That light flicked on behind the vestry pane,
Till, unperplexed from all that is alive,

It shadows all our thought, balked imminence
Of uncommitted sound,
35 And still would tower at the sill of sense
Were not, as now, its honeyed abeyance crowned

With a mauled boom of summons far more strange
Than any stroke unheard,
Which breaks again with unimagined range
40 Through all reverberations of the word,

Pooling the mystery of things that are,
The buzz of prayer said,
The scent of grass, the earliest-blooming star,
These unseen gravestones, and the darker dead.

1969

Exeunt

Piecemeal the summer dies;
At the field's edge a daisy lives alone;
A last shawl of burning lies
On the gray field-stone.

5   All cries are thin and terse;
The field has droned the summer's final mass;
    A cricket like a dwindled hearse
      Crawls from the dry grass.

1956

Place Pigalle

Now homing tradesmen scatter through the streets
Toward suppers, thinking on improved conditions,
While evening, with a million simple fissions,
Takes up its warehouse watches, storefront beats,
5 By nursery windows its assigned positions.

Now at the corners of the Place Pigalle
Bright bars explode against the dark's embraces;
The soldiers come, the boys with ancient faces,
Seeking their ancient friends, who stroll and loll
10 Amid the glares and glass: electric graces.

The puppies are asleep, and snore the hounds;
But here wry hares, the soldier and the whore,
Mark off their refuge with a gaudy door,
Brazen at bay, and boldly out of bounds:
15 The puppies dream, the hounds superbly snore.

Ionized innocence: this pair reclines,
She on the table, he in a tilting chair,
With Arden ease; her eyes as pale as air
Travel his priestgoat face; his hand's thick tines
20 Touch the gold whorls of her Corinthian hair.

"Girl, if I love thee not, then let me die;
Do I not scorn to change my state with kings?
Your muchtouched flesh, incalculable, which wrings
Me so, now shall I gently seize in my
25 Desperate soldier's hands which kill all things."

1947

Love Calls Us to the Things of This World

    The eyes open to a cry of pulleys,
And spirited from sleep, the astounded soul
Hangs for a moment bodiless and simple
As false dawn.
5   Outside the open window
The morning air is all awash with angels.

Some are in bed-sheets, some are in blouses,
Some are in smocks: but truly there they are.
Now they are rising together in calm swells
10 Of halcyon feeling, filling whatever they wear
With the deep joy of their impersonal breathing;

Now they are flying in place, conveying
The terrible speed of their omnipresence, moving
And staying like white water; and now of a sudden
15 They swoon down into so rapt a quiet
That nobody seems to be there.
                          The soul shrinks

From all that it is about to remember,
From the punctual rape of every blessèd day,
20 And cries,
            "Oh, let there be nothing on earth but laundry,
Nothing but rosy hands in the rising steam
And clear dances done in the sight of heaven."

Yet, as the sun acknowledges
25 With a warm look the world's hunks and colors,
The soul descends once more in bitter love
To accept the waking body, saying now
In a changed voice as the man yawns and rises,

"Bring them down from their ruddy gallows;
30 Let there be clean linen for the backs of thieves;
Let lovers go fresh and sweet to be undone,
And the heaviest nuns walk in a pure floating
Of dark habits,
              keeping their difficult balance."

1956

Year's-End

Now winter downs the dying of the year,
And night is all a settlement of snow;
From the soft street the rooms of houses show
A gathered light, a shapen atmosphere,
5 Like frozen-over lakes whose ice is thin
And still allows some stirring down within.

I've known the wind by water banks to shake
The late leaves down, which frozen where they fell
And held in ice as dancers in a spell
10 Fluttered all winter long into a lake;

Graved on the dark in gestures of descent,
They seemed their own most perfect monument.

There was perfection in the death of ferns
Which laid their fragile cheeks against the stone
15 A million years. Great mammoths overthrown
Composedly have made their long sojourns,
Like palaces of patience, in the gray
And changeless lands of ice. And at Pompeii

The little dog lay curled and did not rise
20 But slept the deeper as the ashes rose
And found the people incomplete, and froze
The random hands, the loose unready eyes
Of men expecting yet another sun
To do the shapely thing they had not done.

25 These sudden ends of time must give us pause.
We fray into the future, rarely wrought
Save in the tapestries of afterthought.
More time, more time. Barrages of applause
Come muffled from a buried radio.
30 The New-year bells are wrangling with the snow.

1950

Philip Larkin

(1922–1985)

Church Going

Once I am sure there's nothing going on
I step inside, letting the door thud shut.
Another church: matting, seats, and stone,
And little books; sprawlings of flowers, cut
5 For Sunday, brownish now; some brass and stuff
Up at the holy end; the small neat organ;
And a tense, musty, unignorable silence,
Brewed God knows how long. Hatless, I take off
My cycle-clips in awkward reverence,

10 Move forward, run my hand around the font.
From where I stand, the roof looks almost new—
Cleaned, or restored? Someone would know: I don't.
Mounting the lectern, I peruse a few

Hectoring large-scale verses, and pronounce
15 "Here endeth" much more loudly than I'd meant.
The echoes snigger briefly. Back at the door
I sign the book, donate an Irish sixpence,
Reflect the place was not worth stopping for.

Yet stop I did: in fact I often do,
20 And always end much at a loss like this,
Wondering what to look for; wondering, too,
When churches fall completely out of use
What we shall turn them into, if we shall keep
A few cathedrals chronically on show,
25 Their parchment, plate and pyx in locked cases,
And let the rest rent-free to rain and sheep.
Shall we avoid them as unlucky places?

Or, after dark, will dubious women come
To make their children touch a particular stone;
30 Pick simples for a cancer; or on some
Advised night see walking a dead one?
Power of some sort or other will go on
In games, in riddles, seemingly at random;
But superstition, like belief, must die,
35 And what remains when disbelief has gone?
Grass, weedy pavement, brambles, buttress, sky,

A shape less recognizable each week,
A purpose more obscure. I wonder who
Will be the last, the very last, to seek
40 This place for what it was; one of the crew
That tap and jot and know what rood-lofts were?
Some ruin-bibber, randy for antique,
Or Christmas-addict, counting on a whiff
Of gown-and-bands and organ-pipes and myrrh?
45 Or will he be my representative,

Bored, uninformed, knowing the ghostly silt
Dispersed, yet tending to this cross of ground
Through suburb scrub because it held unspilt
So long and equably what since is found
50 Only in separation—marriage, and birth,
And death, and thoughts of these—for whom was built
This special shell? For, though I've no idea
What this accoutred frowsty barn is worth,
It pleases me to stand in silence here;

55 A serious house on serious earth it is,
   In whose blent air all our compulsions meet,
   Are recognised, and robed as destinies,
   And that much never can be obsolete,
   Since someone will forever be surprising
60 A hunger in himself to be more serious,
   And gravitating with it to this ground,
   Which, he once heard, was proper to grow wise in,
   If only that so many dead lie round.

                                                        1955

The Whitsun Weddings[1]

That Whitsun, I was late getting away:
     Not till about
One-twenty on the sunlit Saturday
Did my three-quarters-empty train pull out,
5 All windows down, all cushions hot, all sense
Of being in a hurry gone. We ran
Behind the backs of houses, crossed a street
Of blinding windscreens, smelt the fish-dock; thence
The river's level drifting breadth began,
10 Where sky and Lincolnshire and water meet.

All afternoon, through the tall heat that slept
     For miles inland,
A slow and stopping curve southwards we kept.
Wide farms went by, short-shadowed cattle, and
15 Canals with floatings of industrial froth;
A hothouse flashed uniquely: hedges dipped
And rose: and now and then a smell of grass
Displaced the reek of buttoned carriage-cloth
Until the next town, new and nondescript,
20 Approached with acres of dismantled cars.

At first, I didn't notice what a noise
     The weddings made
Each station that we stopped at: sun destroys
The interest of what's happening in the shade,
25 And down the long cool platforms whoops and skirls
I took for porters larking with the mails,
And went on reading. Once we started, though,
We passed them, grinning and pomaded, girls

---
[1]Whitsunday is the seventh Sunday after Easter.

In parodies of fashion, heels and veils,
30 All posed irresolutely, watching us go,

As if out on the end of an event
     Waving goodbye
To something that survived it. Struck, I leant
More promptly out next time, more curiously,
35 And saw it all again in different terms:
The fathers with broad belts under their suits
And seamy foreheads; mothers loud and fat;
An uncle shouting smut; and then the perms,
The nylon gloves and jewelry-substitutes,
40 The lemons, mauves and olive-ochers that

Marked off the girls unreally from the rest.
     Yes, from cafés
And banquet-halls up yards, and bunting-dressed
Coach-party annexes, the wedding-days
45 Were coming to an end. All down the line
Fresh couples climbed aboard: the rest stood round;
The last confetti and advice were thrown,
And, as we moved, each face seemed to define
Just what it saw departing; children frowned
50 At something dull; fathers had never known

Success so huge and wholly farcical;
     The women shared
The secret like a happy funeral;
While girls, gripping their handbags tighter, stared
55 At a religious wounding. Free at last,
And loaded with the sum of all they saw,
We hurried towards London, shuffling gouts of steam.
Now fields were building-plots, and poplars cast
Long shadows over major roads, and for
60 Some fifty minutes, that in time would seem

Just long enough to settle hats and say
     I nearly died,
A dozen marriages got under way.
They watched the landscape, sitting side by side
65 —An Odeon went past, a cooling tower,
And someone running up to bowl—and none
Thought of the others they would never meet
Or how their lives would all contain this hour.
I thought of London spread out in the sun,
70 Its postal districts packed like squares of wheat:

There we were aimed. And as we raced across
   Bright knots of rail
Past standing Pullmans, walls of blackened moss
Came close, and it was nearly done, this frail
75 Traveling coincidence; and what it held
Stood ready to be loosed with all the power
That being changed can give. We slowed again,
And as the tightened brakes took hold, there swelled
A sense of falling, like an arrow-shower
80 Sent out of sight, somewhere becoming rain.

1964

James Dickey

(1923–   )

The Heaven of Animals

Here they are. The soft eyes open.
If they have lived in a wood
It is a wood.
If they have lived on plains
5 It is grass rolling
Under their feet forever.

Having no souls, they have come,
Anyway, beyond their knowing.
Their instincts wholly bloom
10 And they rise.
The soft eyes open.

To match them, the landscape flowers,
Outdoing, desperately
Outdoing what is required:
15 The richest wood,
The deepest field.

For some of these,
It could not be the place
It is, without blood.
20 These hunt, as they have done
But with claws and teeth grown perfect,

More deadly than they can believe.
They stalk more silently,

And crouch on the limbs of trees,
25 And their descent
Upon the bright backs of their prey

May take years
In a sovereign floating of joy.
And those that are hunted
30 Know this as their life,
Their reward: to walk

Under such trees in full knowledge
Of what is in glory above them,
And to feel no fear,
35 But acceptance, compliance.
Fulfilling themselves without pain

At the cycle's center,
They tremble, they walk
Under the tree,
40 They fall, they are torn,
They rise, they walk again.

1962

Buckdancer's Choice

So I would hear out those lungs,
The air split into nine levels,
Some gift of tongues of the whistler

In the invalid's bed: my mother,
5 Warbling all day to herself
The thousand variations of one song;

It is called Buckdancer's Choice.
For years, they have all been dying
Out, the classic buck-and-wing men

10 Of traveling minstrel shows;
With them also an old woman
Was dying of breathless angina,

Yet still found breath enough
To whistle up in my head
15 A sight like a one-man band,

Freed black, with cymbals at heel,
An ex-slave who thrivingly danced
To the ring of his own clashing light

Through the thousand variations of one song
20 All day to my mother's prone music,
The invalid's warbler's note,

While I crept close to the wall
Sock-footed, to hear the sounds alter,
Her tongue like a mockingbird's break

25 Through stratum after stratum of a tone
Proclaiming what choices there are
For the last dancers of their kind,

For ill women and for all slaves
Of death, and children enchanted at walls
30 With a brass-beating glow underfoot,

Not dancing but nearly risen
Through barnlike, theatrelike houses
On the wings of the buck and wing.

1965

Denise Levertov

(1923–1997)

Six Variations (part iii)

Shlup, shlup, the dog
as it laps up
water
makes intelligent
5 music, resting
now and then to take breath in irregular
measure.

1958

Come into Animal Presence

Come into animal presence.
No man is so guileless as
the serpent. The lonely white
rabbit on the roof is a star
5 twitching its ears at the rain.
The llama intricately
folding its hind legs to be seated
not disdains but mildly

disregards human approval.
10 What joy when the insouciant
armadillo glances at us and doesn't
· quicken its trotting
across the track into the palm brush.

What is this joy? That no animal
15 falters, but knows what it must do?
That the snake has no blemish,
that the rabbit inspects his strange surroundings
in white star-silence? The llama
rests in dignity, the armadillo
20 has some intention to pursue in the palm-forest.
Those who were sacred have remained so,
holiness does not dissolve, it is a presence
of bronze, only the sight that saw it
faltered and turned from it.
25 An old joy returns in holy presence.

1961

What Were They Like?

1) Did the people of Viet Nam
   use lanterns of stone?
2) Did they hold ceremonies
   to reverence the opening of buds?
5 3) Were they inclined to rippling laughter?
4) Did they use bone and ivory,
   jade and silver, for ornament?
5) Had they an epic poem?
6) Did they distinguish between speech and singing?

10 1) Sir, their light hearts turned to stone.
   It is not remembered whether in gardens
   stone lanterns illumined pleasant ways.
2) Perhaps they gathered once to delight in blossom,
   but after the children were killed
15 there were no more buds.
3) Sir, laughter is bitter to the burned mouth.
4) A dream ago, perhaps. Ornament is for joy.
   All the bones were charred.
5) It is not remembered. Remember,
20 most were peasants; their life
   was in rice and bamboo.
   When peaceful clouds were reflected in the paddies
   and the water buffalo stepped surely along terraces,

maybe fathers told their sons old tales.
25   When bombs smashed the mirrors
there was time only to scream.
There is an echo yet, it is said,
of their speech which was like a song.
It is reported their singing resembled
30   the flight of moths in moonlight.
Who can say? It is silent now.

1971

Losing Track

Long after you have swung back
away from me
I think you are still with me:

you come in close to the shore
5   on the tide
and nudge me awake the way

a boat adrift nudges the pier:
am I a pier
half-in half-out of the water?

10   and in the pleasure of that communion
I lose track,
the moon I watch goes down, the

tide swings you away before
I know I'm
15   alone again long since,

mud sucking at gray and black
timbers of me,
a light growth of green dreams drying.

1962

Maxine Kumin

(1925–   )

Morning Swim

Into my empty head there come
a cotton beach, a dock wherefrom

I set out, oily and nude
through mist, in chilly solitude.

5 There was no line, no roof or floor
to tell the water from the air.

Night fog thick as terry cloth
closed me in its fuzzy growth.

I hung my bathrobe on two pegs.
10 I took the lake between my legs.

Invaded and invader, I
went overhand on that flat sky.

Fish twitched beneath me, quick and tame.
In their green zone they sang my name

15 and in the rhythm of the swim
I hummed a two-four-time slow hymn.

I hummed *Abide with Me.* The beat
rose in the fine thrash of my feet,

rose in the bubbles I put out
20 slantwise, trailing through my mouth.

My bones drank water; water fell
through all my doors. I was the well

that fed the lake that met my sea
in which I sang *Abide with Me.*

1965

Woodchucks

Gassing the woodchucks didn't turn out right.
The knockout bomb from the Feed and Grain Exchange
was featured as merciful, quick at the bone
and the case we had against them was airtight,
5 both exits shoehorned shut with puddingstone,
but they had a sub-sub-basement out of range.

Next morning they turned up again, no worse
for the cyanide than we for our cigarettes
and state-store Scotch, all of us up to scratch.
10 They brought down the marigolds as a matter of course
and then took over the vegetable patch
nipping the broccoli shoots, beheading the carrots.

The food from our mouths, I said, righteously thrilling
to the feel of the .22, the bullets' neat noses.
15 I, a lapsed pacifist fallen from grace
puffed with Darwinian pieties for killing,

now drew a bead on the littlest woodchuck's face.
He died down in the everbearing roses.

Ten minutes later I dropped the mother. She
20 flipflopped in the air and fell, her needle teeth
still hooked in a leaf of early Swiss chard.
Another baby next. O one-two-three
the murderer inside me rose up hard,
the hawkeye killer came on stage forthwith.

25 There's one chuck left. Old wily fellow, he keeps
me cocked and ready day after day after day
All night I hunt his humped-up form. I dream
I sight along the barrel in my sleep.
If only they'd all consented to die unseen
30 gassed underground the quiet Nazi way.

1972

Edward Field

(1924–   )

The Bride of Frankenstein

The Baron has decided to mate the monster,
to breed him perhaps,
in the interests of pure science, his only god.
So he goes up into his laboratory
5 which he has built in the tower of the castle
to be as near the interplanetary forces as possible,
and puts together the prettiest monster-woman you ever saw
with a body like a pin-up girl
and hardly any stitching at all
10 where he sewed on the head of a raped and murdered beauty queen.

He sets his liquids burping, and coils blinking and buzzing,
and waits for an electric storm to send through the equipment
the spark vital for life.
The storm breaks over the castle
15 and the equipment really goes crazy
like a kitchen full of modern appliances
as the lightning juice starts oozing right into that pretty corpse.

He goes to get the monster
so he will be right there when she opens her eyes,
20 for she might fall in love with the first thing she sees

as ducklings do.
That monster is already straining at his chains and slurping
ready to go right to it:
He has been well prepared for coupling
25 by his pinching leering keeper who's been saying for weeks,
"You gonna get a little nookie, kid,"
or "How do you go for some poontag, baby."
All the evil in him is focused on this one thing now
as he is led into her very presence.

30 She awakens slowly,
she bats her eyes,
she gets up out of the equipment,
and finally she stands in all her seamed glory,
a monster princess with a hairdo like a fright-wig,
35 lightning flashing in the background
like a halo and a wedding veil,
like a photographer snapping pictures of great moments.

She stands and stares with her electric eyes,
beginning to understand that in this life too
40 she was just another body to be raped.

The monster is ready to go:
He roars with joy at the sight of her,
so they let him loose and he goes right for those knockers.
And she starts screaming to break your heart
45 and you realize that she was just born:
In spite of her big tits she was just a baby.

But her instincts are right—
rather death than that green slobber:
She jumps off the parapet.

50 And then the monster's sex drive goes wild.
Thwarted, it turns to violence, demonstrating sublimation crudely,
and he wrecks the lab, those burping acids and buzzing coils,
overturning the control panel so the equipment goes off like a bomb,
the stone castle crumbling and crashing in the storm
55 destroying them all . . . perhaps.

Perhaps somehow the Baron got out of that wreckage of his dreams
with his evil intact if not his good looks
and more wicked than ever went on with his thrilling career.

And perhaps even the monster lived
60 to roam the earth, his desire still ungratified,

and lovers out walking in shadowy and deserted places
will see his shape loom up over them, their doom—
and children sleeping in their beds
will wake up in the dark night screaming
65 as his hideous body grabs them.

Catherine Davis

(1924–   )

After a Time

After a time, all losses are the same.
One more thing lost is one thing less to lose;
And we go stripped at last the way we came.

Though we shall probe, time and again, our shame,
5 Who lack the wit to keep or to refuse,
After a time, all losses are the same.

No wit, no luck can beat a losing game;
Good fortune is a reassuring ruse:
And we go stripped at last the way we came.

10 Rage as we will for what we think to claim,
Nothing so much as this bare thought subdues:
After a time, all losses are the same.

The sense of treachery—the want, the blame—
Goes in the end, whether or not we choose,
15 And we go stripped at last the way we came.

So we, who would go raging, will go tame
When what we have we can no longer use:
After a time, all losses are the same;
And we go stripped at last the way we came.

1957

What Does It Mean?

after Thomas Wyatt

What does it mean? I lie awake;
My mind needs rest, my bones all ache:
So needy and so loath to take?
        What does it mean?

5   When I should most be comforted,
Covers and pillow, limbs and head,
Are every which way in the bed.
    What does it mean?

I toss, I turn, I cough, I curse;
10 I must, it seems, all night rehearse,
Revile my days and make them worse:
    What does it mean?

I doze a little, dream, and start:
The random terrors of the heart
15 Wake me—they take my dæmon's part:
    What does it mean?

My dæmon says, they cheat, they lie,
Run from themselves, themselves awry,
Who say it's love that makes them cry
20   What does it mean?

How little they must need to know!
Nothing but love can rouse them so,
When a whole life is touch and go!
    What does it mean?

25 Thus it is I spend the night,
Conscious that in my dæmon's sight
The waking heart must see things right:
    What does it mean?

What does it matter that the past
30 And my own dæmon hold me fast?
I shall get sleep enough at last:
    What does it mean?

        1962

Donald Justice

(1925–   )

Here in Katmandu[1]

We have climbed the mountain,
There's nothing more to do.
It is terrible to come down
To the valley

---

[1]capital of Nepal, west of Mt. Everest

5 Where, amidst many flowers,
   One thinks of snow,

   As, formerly, amidst snow,
   Climbing the mountain,
   One thought of flowers,
10 Tremulous, ruddy with dew,
   In the valley.
   One caught their scent coming down.

   It is difficult to adjust, once down,
   To the absence of snow.
15 Clear days, from the valley,
   One looks up at the mountain.
   What else is there to do?
   Prayerwheels, flowers!

   Let the flowers
20 Fade, the prayerwheels run down.
   What have these to do
   With us who have stood atop the snow
   Atop the mountain,
   Flags seen from the valley?

25 It might be possible to live in the valley,
   To bury oneself among flowers,
   If one could forget the mountain,
   How, setting out before dawn,
   Blinded with snow,
30 One knew what to do.

   Meanwhile it is not easy here in Katmandu,
   Especially when to the valley
   That wind which means snow
   Elsewhere, but here means flowers,
35 Comes down,
   As soon it must, from the mountain.

                               1960

Luxury

   You are like a sun of the tropics
   Peering through blinds

   Drawn for siesta.
   Already you teach me

5 The Spanish for sunflower.
   You, alone on the clean sheet.

You, like the spilt moon.
You, like a star

Hidden by sun-goggles.
10 You shall have a thousand lovers.

You, spread here like butter,
Like doubloons, like flowers.

1973

Anonymous Drawing

A delicate young Negro stands
With the reins of a horse clutched loosely in his hands;
So delicate, indeed, that we wonder if he can hold the spirited creature
    beside him
Until the master shall arrive to ride him.
5   Already the animal's nostrils widen with rage or fear.
But if we imagine him snorting, about to rear,
This boy, who should know about such things better than we,
Only stands smiling, passive and ornamental, in a fantastic livery
Of ruffles and puffed breeches,
10 Watching the artist, apparently, as he sketches.
Meanwhile the petty lord who must have paid
For the artist's trip up from Perugia, for the horse, for the boy, for everything
    here, in fact, has been delayed,
Kept too long by his steward, perhaps, discussing
Some business concerning the estate, or fussing
15 Over the details of his impeccable toilet
With a manservant whose opinion is that any alteration at all would spoil it.
However fast he should come hurrying now
Over this vast greensward, mopping his brow
Clear of the sweat of the fine Renaissance morning, it would be too late:
20 The artist will have had his revenge for being made to wait,
A revenge not only necessary but right and clever—
Simply to leave him out of the scene forever.

1967

Landscape with Little Figures

There once were some pines, a canal, a piece of sky.
The pines are the houses now of the very poor,
Huddled together, in a blue, ragged wind.
Children go whistling their dogs, down by the mud flats,
5   Once the canal. There's a red ball lost in the weeds.

It's winter, it's after supper, it's goodbye.
O goodbye to the houses, the children, the little red ball.
And the pieces of sky that will go on now falling for days.

1960

Robert Bly

(1926–)

Driving to Town Late to Mail a Letter

It is a cold and snowy night. The main street is deserted.
The only things moving are swirls of snow.
As I lift the mailbox door, I feel its cold iron.
There is a privacy I love in this snowy night.
5 Driving around, I will waste more time.

1962

Robert Creeley

(1926–)

Oh No

If you wander far enough
you will come to it
and when you get there
they will give you a place to sit
5 for yourself only, in a nice chair,
and all your friends will be there
with smiles on their faces
and they will likewise all have places.

1955

Naughty Boy

When he brings home a whale,
she laughs and says, that's not for real.

And if he won the Irish sweepstakes,
she would say, where were you last night?

5 Where are you now, for that matter? Am
   I always (she says) to be looking

   at you? She says,
   if I thought it would get any better I

   would shoot you, you
10 nut, you. Then pats her hair

   into place, and waits
   for Uncle Jim's deep-fired, all-fat, real gone

   whale steaks.

                                                           1955

Allen Ginsberg

(1926–1997)

From **Howl**

For Carl Solomon[1]

                              I

I saw the best minds of my generation destroyed by madness, starving hysterical
     naked,
dragging themselves through the negro streets at dawn looking for an angry fix,
angelheaded hipsters burning for the ancient heavenly connection to the starry
     dynamo in the machinery of night,
who poverty and tatters and hollow-eyed and high sat up smoking in the
     supernatural darkness of cold-water flats floating across the tops of cities
     contemplating jazz,
5 who bared their brains to Heaven under the El[2] and saw Mohammedan angels
     staggering on tenement roofs illuminated,
who passed through universities with radiant cool eyes hallucinating Arkansas
     and Blake-light[3] tragedy among the scholars of war,
who were expelled from the academies for crazy & publishing obscene odes on
     the windows of the skull,[4]

---

[1]friend of Ginsberg and fellow psychiatric patient in 1949
[2]the elevated railway
[3]refers to English poet William Blake (1757–1827)
[4]Ginsberg was expelled from Columbia for writing an obscenity on his windowpane.

who cowered in unshaven rooms in underwear, burning their money in
wastebaskets and listening to the Terror through the wall,

who got busted in their pubic beards returning through Laredo with a belt of
marijuana for New York,

10 who ate fire in paint hotels or drank turpentine in Paradise Alley,[5] death, or
purgatoried their torsos night after night

with dreams, with drugs, with waking nightmares, alcohol and cock and endless
balls,

incomparable blind streets of shuddering cloud and lightning in the mind
leaping toward poles of Canada & Paterson, illuminating all the motionless
world of Time between,

Peyote solidities of halls, backyard green tree cemetery dawns, wine
drunkenness over the rooftops, storefront boroughs of teahead joyride neon
blinking traffic light, sun and moon and tree vibrations in the roaring winter
dusks of Brooklyn, ashcan rantings and kind king light of mind,

who chained themselves to subways for the endless ride from Battery to holy
Bronx on benzedrine until the noise of wheels and children brought them
down shuddering mouth-wracked and battered bleak of brain all drained of
brilliance in the drear light of Zoo,

15 who sank all night in submarine light of Bickford's[6] floated out and sat through
the stale beer afternoon in desolate Fugazzi's,[7] listening to the crack of doom
on the hydrogen jukebox,

who talked continuously seventy hours from park to pad to bar to Bellevue[8] to
museum to the Brooklyn Bridge,

a lost battalion of platonic conversationalists jumping down the stoops off fire
escapes off windowsills off Empire State out of the moon,

yacketayakking screaming vomiting whispering facts and memories and
anecdotes and eyeball kicks and shocks of hospitals and jails and wars,

whole intellects disgorged in total recall for seven days and nights with brilliant
eyes, meat for the Synagogue cast on the pavement,

20 who vanished into nowhere Zen New Jersey leaving a trail of ambiguous picture
postcards of Atlantic City Hall,

suffering Eastern sweats and Tangerian bone-grindings and migraines of China
under junk-withdrawal in Newark's bleak furnished room,

who wandered around and around at midnight in the railroad yard wondering
where to go, and went, leaving no broken hearts,

who lit cigarettes in boxcars boxcars boxcars racketing through snow toward
lonesome farms in grandfather night,

---

[5] a slum courtyard on the East Side
[6] cafeteria
[7] bar in Greenwich Village
[8] N.Y. City public hospital

who studied Plotinus Poe St. John of the Cross[9] telepathy and bop kaballa[10]
    because the cosmos instinctively vibrated at their feet in Kansas,

25 who loned it through the streets of Idaho seeking visionary indian angels who
    were visionary indian angels,

who thought they were only mad when Baltimore gleamed in supernatural
    ecstasy,

who jumped in limousines with the Chinaman of Oklahoma on the impulse of
    winter midnight streetlight smalltown rain,

who lounged hungry and lonesome through Houston seeking jazz or sex or
    soup, and followed the brilliant Spaniard to converse about America and
    Eternity, a hopeless task, and so took ship to Africa,

who disappeared into the volcanoes of Mexico leaving behind nothing but the
    shadow of dungarees and the lava and ash of poetry scattered in fireplace
    Chicago,

30 who reappeared on the West Coast investigating the F.B.I. in beards and shorts
    with big pacifist eyes sexy in their dark skin passing out incomprehensible
    leaflets,

who burned cigarette holes in their arms protesting the narcotic tobacco haze of
    Capitalism,

who distributed Supercommunist pamphlets in Union Square weeping and
    undressing while the sirens of Los Alamos wailed them down, and wailed
    down Wall, and the Staten Island ferry also wailed,

who broke down crying in white gymnasiums naked and trembling before the
    machinery of other skeletons,

who bit detectives in the neck and shrieked with delight in policecars for
    committing no crime but their own wild cooking pederasty and intoxication,

35 who howled on their knees in the subway and were dragged off the roof waving
    genitals and manuscripts,

who let themselves be fucked in the ass by saintly motorcyclists, and screamed
    with joy,

who blew and were blown by those human seraphim, the sailors, caresses of
    Atlantic and Caribbean love,

who balled in the morning in the evenings in rosegardens and the grass of
    public parks and cemeteries scattering their semen freely to whomever come
    who may,

who hiccupped endlessly trying to giggle but wound up with a sob behind a
    partition in a Turkish Bath when the blonde & naked angel came to pierce
    them with a sword,

---

[9]Plotinus (205–270), Roman philosopher; Edgar Allan Poe (1809–1849); St. John of the Cross
(1542–1591), Spanish poet
[10]cf. *cabala:* esoteric interpretation of Hebrew scriptures

40 who lost their loveboys to the three old shrews of fate the one eyed shrew of the
heterosexual dollar the one eyed shrew that winks out of the womb and the
one eyed shrew that does nothing but sit on her ass and snip the intellectual
golden threads of the craftsman's loom,

who copulated ecstatic and insatiate with a bottle of beer a sweetheart a
package of cigarettes a candle and fell off the bed, and continued along the
floor and down the hall and ended fainting on the wall with a vision of
ultimate cunt and come eluding the last gyzym of consciousness,

who sweetened the snatches of a million girls trembling in the sunset, and were
red eyed in the morning but prepared to sweeten the snatch of the sunrise,
flashing buttocks under barns and naked in the lake,

who went out whoring through Colorado in myriad stolen night-cars, N.C.,[11]
secret hero of these poems, cocksman and Adonis of Denver—joy to the
memory of his innumerable lays of girls in empty lots & diner backyards,
moviehouses' rickety rows, on mountaintops in caves or with gaunt
waitresses in familiar roadside lonely petticoat upliftings & especially secret
gas-station solipsisms of johns, & hometown alleys too,

who faded out in vast sordid movies, were shifted in dreams, woke on a sudden
Manhattan, and picked themselves up out of basements hungover with
heartless Tokay and horrors of Third Avenue iron dreams & stumbled to
unemployment offices,

45 who walked all night with their shoes full of blood on the snowbank docks
waiting for a door in the East River to open to a room full of steamheat and
opium,

who created great suicidal dramas on the apartment cliff-banks of the Hudson
under the wartime blue floodlight of the moon & their heads shall be
crowned with laurel in oblivion,

who ate the lamb stew of the imagination or digested the crab at the muddy
bottom of the rivers of Bowery,

who wept at the romance of the streets with their pushcarts full of onions and
bad music,

who sat in boxes breathing in the darkness under the bridge, and rose up to
build harpsichords in their lofts,

50 who coughed on the sixth floor of Harlem crowned with flame under the
tubercular sky surrounded by orange crates of theology,

who scribbled all night rocking and rolling over lofty incantations which in the
yellow morning were stanzas of gibberish,

who cooked rotten animals lung heart feet tail borscht & tortillas dreaming of
the pure vegetable kingdom,

who plunged themselves under meat trucks looking for an egg,

---

[11]Neal Cassady, friend of Ginsberg and Jack Kerouac

who threw their watches off the roof to cast their ballot for Eternity outside of
Time, & alarm clocks fell on their heads every day for the next decade,

55 who cut their wrists three times successively unsuccessfully, gave up and were
forced to open antique stores where they thought they were growing old and
cried,

who were burned alive in their innocent flannel suits on Madison Avenue amid
blasts of leaden verse & the tanked-up clatter of the iron regiments of fashion
& the nitroglycerine shrieks of the fairies of advertising & the mustard gas of
sinister intelligent editors, or were run down by the drunken taxicabs of
Absolute Reality,

who jumped off the Brooklyn Bridge this actually happened and walked away
unknown and forgotten into the ghostly daze of Chinatown soup alleyways &
firetrucks, not even one free beer,

who sang out of their windows in despair, fell out of the subway window,
jumped in the filthy Passaic, leaped on negroes, cried all over the street,
danced on broken wineglasses barefoot smashed phonograph records of
nostalgic European 1930's German jazz finished the whiskey and threw up
groaning into the bloody toilet, moans in their ears and the blast of colossal
steamwhistles,

who barreled down the highways of the past journeying to each other's
hotrod-Golgotha[12] jail-solitude watch or Birmingham jazz incarnation,

60 who drove crosscountry seventytwo hours to find out if I had a vision or you
had a vision or he had a vision to find out Eternity,

who journeyed to Denver, who died in Denver, who came back to Denver &
waited in vain, who watched over Denver & brooded & loned in Denver and
finally went away to find out the Time, & now Denver is lonesome for her
heroes,

who fell on their knees in hopeless cathedrals praying for each other's salvation
and light and breasts, until the soul illuminated its hair for a second,

who crashed through their minds in jail waiting for impossible criminals with
golden heads and the charm of reality in their hearts who sang sweet blues to
Alcatraz,

who retired to Mexico to cultivate a habit, or Rocky Mount to tender Buddha or
Tangiers to boys or Southern Pacific to the black locomotive or Harvard to
Narcissus to Woodlawn[13] to the daisychain or grave,

65 who demanded sanity trials accusing the radio of hypnotism & were left with
their insanity & their hands & a hung jury,

who threw potato salad at CCNY lecturers on Dadaism and subsequently
presented themselves on the granite steps of the madhouse with shaven heads
and harlequin speech of suicide, demanding instantaneous lobotomy,

---

[12]scene of Jesus' crucifixion
[13]Bronx cemetery

and who were given instead the concrete void of insulin metrasol electricity
hydrotherapy psychotherapy occupational therapy pingpong & amnesia,

who in humorless protest overturned only one symbolic pingpong table, resting
briefly in catatonia,

returning years later truly bald except for a wig of blood, and tears and fingers,
to the visible madman doom of the wards of the madtowns of the East,

70 Pilgrim State's Rockland's and Greystone's[14] foetid halls, bickering with the
echoes of the soul, rocking and rolling in the midnight-solitude-bench
dolmen-realms of love, dream of life a nightmare, bodies turned to stone as
heavy as the moon,

with mother finally ******, and the last fantastic book flung out of the
tenement window, and the last door closed at 4 AM and the last telephone
slammed at the wall in reply and the last furnished room emptied down to
the last piece of mental furniture, a yellow paper rose twisted on a wire
hanger in the closet, and even that imaginary, nothing but a hopeful little bit
of hallucination—

ah, Carl, while you are not safe I am not safe, and now you're really in the total
animal soup of time—

and who therefore ran through the icy streets obsessed with a sudden flash of
the alchemy of the use of the ellipse the catalog the meter & the vibrating
plane,

who dreamt and made incarnate gaps in Time & Space through images
juxtaposed, and trapped the archangel of the soul between 2 visual images
and joined the elemental verbs and set the noun and dash of consciousness
together jumping with sensation of Pater Omnipotens Aeterna Deus[15]

75 to recreate the syntax and measure of poor human prose and stand before you
speechless and intelligent and shaking with shame, rejected yet confessing
out the soul to conform to the rhythm of thought in his naked and endless
head,

the madman bum and angel beat in Time, unknown, yet putting down here
what might be left to say in time come after death,

and rose incarnate in the ghostly clothes of jazz in the goldhorn shadow of the
band and blew the suffering of America's naked mind for love into an eli eli
lamma lamma sabacthani[16] saxophone cry that shivered the cities down to the
last radio

with the absolute heart of the poem of life butchered out of their own bodies
good to eat a thousand years.

1956

---

[14]mental hospitals in New York and New Jersey

[15]Latin: "Omnipotent Father Eternal God," from a letter of French painter Paul Cézanne (1839–1906)

[16]Hebrew: "My God, my God, why hast thou forsaken me?"; Christ's words on the cross (Matthew 27:46)

A Supermarket in California

What thoughts I have of you tonight, Walt Whitman, for I walked down the sidestreets under the trees with a headache self-conscious looking at the full moon.

In my hungry fatigue, and shopping for images, I went into the neon fruit supermarket, dreaming of your enumerations!

What peaches and what penumbras! Whole families shopping at night! Aisles full of husbands! Wives in the avocados, babies in the tomatoes!—and you, García Lorca,[1] what were you doing down by the watermelons?

I saw you, Walt Whitman, childless, lonely old grubber, poking among the meats in the refrigerator and eyeing the grocery boys.

5   I heard you asking questions of each: Who killed the pork chops? What price bananas? Are you my Angel?

I wandered in and out of the brilliant stacks of cans following you, and followed in my imagination by the store detective.

We strode down the open corridors together in our solitary fancy tasting artichokes, possessing every frozen delicacy, and never passing the cashier.

Where are we going, Walt Whitman? The doors close in an hour. Which way does your beard point tonight?

(I touch your book and dream of our odyssey in the supermarket and feel absurd.)

10   Will we walk all night through solitary streets? The trees add shade to shade, lights out in the houses, we'll both be lonely.

Will we stroll dreaming of the lost America of love past blue automobiles in driveways, home to our silent cottage?

Ah, dear father, graybeard, lonely old courage-teacher, what America did you have when Charon quit poling his ferry and you got out on a smoking bank and stood watching the boat disappear on the black waters of Lethe?[2]

1955

Ode to Failure

Many prophets have failed, their voices silent
ghost-shouts in basements nobody heard dusty laughter in family attics
nor glanced them on park benches weeping with relief under empty sky
Walt Whitman viva'd local losers — courage to Fat Ladies in the Freak
    Show! nervous prisoners whose mustached lips dripped sweat on chow
    lines —
5 Mayakovsky cried, Then die! my verse, die like the workers' rank & file
    fusilladed in Petersburg!

---

[1]Federico García Lorca (1899–1936), Spanish poet and playwright; he was murdered at the start of the Spanish Civil War, and his works were suppressed by the Franco government.
[2]Charon, in Greek myth, ferried the shades of the dead to Hades across Lethe, River of Forgetfulness.

Prospero burned his Power books & plummeted his magic wand to the
   bottom of dragon seas
Alexander the Great failed to find more worlds to conquer!
O Failure I chant your terrifying name, accept me your 54 year old
   Prophet
epicking Eternal Flop! I join your Pantheon of mortal bards, & hasten
   this ode with high blood pressure
10 rushing to the top of my skull as if I wouldn't last another minute, like
   the Dying Gaul! to
You, Lord of blind Monet, deaf Beethoven, armless Venus de Milo,
   headless Winged Victory!
I failed to sleep with every bearded rosy-cheeked boy I jacked off over
My tirades destroyed no Intellectual Unions of KGB & CIA in turtlenecks
   & underpants, their woolen suits and tweeds
I never dissolved Plutonium or dismantled the nuclear Bomb before my
   skull lost hair
15 I have not yet stopped the Armies of entire Mankind in their march toward
   World War III
I never got to Heaven, Nirvana, X, Whatchamacallit, I never left Earth,
I never learned to die.

1980

James Merrill

(1926–1995)

Charles on Fire

Another evening we sprawled about discussing
Appearances. And it was the consensus
That while uncommon physical good looks
Continued to launch one, as before, in life
5 (Among its vaporous eddies and false calms),
Still, as one of us said into his beard,
"Without your intellectual and spiritual
Values, man, you are sunk." No one but squared
The shoulders of his own unloveliness.
10 Long-suffering Charles, having cooked and served the meal,
Now brought out little tumblers finely etched
He filled with amber liquor and then passed.
"Say," said the same young man, "in Paris, France,
They do it this way"—bounding to his feet
15 And touching a lit match to our host's full glass.

A blue flame, gentle, beautiful, came, went
Above the surface. In a hush that fell
We heard the vessel crack. The contents drained
As who should step down from a crystal coach.
20   Steward of spirits, Charles's glistening hand
All at once gloved itself in eeriness.
The moment passed. He made two quick sweeps and
Was flesh again. "It couldn't matter less,"
He said, but with a shocked, unconscious glance
25   Into the mirror. Finding nothing changed,
He filled a fresh glass and sank down among us.

1966

Maisie

1

One morning I shall find
I have slept with your full weight upon my heart,
Your motors and my breathing reconciled.
The edges of the blind,

5   The crack beneath the door will have blanched with day,
The walls will be about to jar apart
And sun to dust my lids deep in the opened flower.
And still I shall not have sent you away.

2

When you came home without your sex
10   You hid in the cupboard under the sink.
Its gasps and gurglings must have helped somehow.

The second noon you ventured forth,
A silent star, furred up to tragic eyes.
Hazarding recognition in a restaurant.

15   It was horrible to see how much
You honestly cared about food and comfort.
The dishes refused! The chairs tried one by one!

Eunuch and favorite both,
You loll about, exuding that old magic
20   There is mercifully no longer a market for.

3

For the good of the guest who has not yet looked over
The roof garden's brink to the eaves just below,
You shudder there long enough only to shriek

(If eyes could shriek, and if they were ever
25 Eyes, those chalcedony bonfires): *O*
Scarpia! Avanti a Dio!—then plummet from view,
Leaving the newcomer aghast and weak.

1966

Frank O'Hara

(1926–1966)

The Day Lady Died

It is 12:20 in New York a Friday
three days after Bastille day, yes
it is 1959 and I go get a shoeshine
because I will get off the 4:19 in Easthampton
5 at 7:15 and then go straight to dinner
and I don't know the people who will feed me

I walk up the muggy street beginning to sun
and have a hamburger and a malted and buy
an ugly NEW WORLD WRITING to see what the poets
10 in Ghana are doing these days
         I go on to the bank
and Miss Stillwagon (first name Linda I once heard)
doesn't even look up my balance for once in her life
and in the GOLDEN GRIFFIN I get a little Verlaine
15 for Patsy with drawings by Bonnard although I do
think of Hesiod, trans. Richmond Lattimore or
Brendan Behan's new play or *Le Balcon or Les Nègres*
of Genet, but I don't, I stick with Verlaine
after practically going to sleep with quandariness
20 and for Mike I just stroll into the PARK LANE
Liquor Store and ask for a bottle of Strega and
then I go back where I came from to 6th Avenue
and the tobacconist in the Ziegfeld Theatre and
casually ask for a carton of Gauloises and a carton
25 of Picayunes, and a NEW YORK POST with her face on it

and I am sweating a lot by now and thinking of
leaning on the john door in the 5 SPOT
while she whispered a song along the keyboard
to Mal Wandron and everyone and I stopped breathing

1964

Autobiographia Literaria

When I was a child
I played by myself in a
corner of the schoolyard
all alone.

5 I hated dolls and I
hated games, animals were
not friendly and birds
flew away.

If anyone was looking
10 for me I hid behind a
tree and cried out "I am
an orphan."

And here I am, the
center of all beauty!
15 writing these poems!
Imagine!

1967

A True Account of Talking
to the Sun at Fire Island

The Sun woke me this morning loud
and clear, saying "Hey! I've been
trying to wake you up for fifteen
minutes. Don't be so rude, you are
5 only the second poet I've ever chosen
to speak to personally
                        so why
aren't you more attentive? If I could
burn you through the window I would
10 to wake you up. I can't hang around
here all day."
                "Sorry, Sun, I stayed
up late last night talking to Hal."

"When I woke up Mayakovsky he was
15 a lot more prompt," the Sun said
petulantly. "Most people are up
already waiting to see if I'm going
to put in an appearance."
                        I tried
20 to apologize "I missed you yesterday."
"That's better" he said. "I didn't

know you'd come out." "You may be
wondering why I've come so close?"
"Yes" I said beginning to feel hot
25 wondering if maybe he wasn't burning me
anyway.

      "Frankly I wanted to tell you
I like your poetry. I see a lot
on my rounds and you're okay. You may
30 not be the greatest thing on earth, but
you're different. Now, I've heard some
say you're crazy, they being excessively
calm themselves to my mind, and other
crazy poets think that you're a boring
35 reactionary. Not me.

      Just keep on
like I do and pay no attention. You'll
find that people always will complain
about the atmosphere, either too hot
40 or too cold too bright or too dark, days
too short or too long.

      If you don't appear
at all one day they think you're lazy
or dead. Just keep right on, I like it.

45 And don't worry about your lineage
poetic or natural. The Sun shines on
the jungle, you know, on the tundra
the sea, the ghetto. Wherever you were
I knew it and saw you moving. I was waiting
50 for you to get to work.

      And now that you
are making your own days, so to speak,
even if no one reads you but me
you won't be depressed. Not
55 everyone can look up, even at me. It
hurts their eyes."

      "Oh Sun, I'm so grateful to you!"

"Thanks and remember I'm watching. It's
easier for me to speak to you out
60 here. I don't have to slide down
between buildings to get your ear.
I know you love Manhattan, but
you ought to look up more often.

      And
65 always embrace things, people earth

sky stars, as I do, freely and with
the appropriate sense of space. That
is your inclination, known in the heavens
and you should follow it to hell, if
70 necessary, which I doubt.
                        Maybe we'll
speak again in Africa, of which I too
am specially fond. Go back to sleep now
Frank, and I may leave a tiny poem
75 in that brain of yours as a farewell."

"Sun, don't go!" I was awake
at last. "No, go I must, they're calling
me."
       "Who are they?"
80   Rising he said "Some
day you'll know. They're calling to you
too." Darkly he rose, and then I slept.

                                                1966

John Ashbery

(1927–   )

City Afternoon

A veil of haze protects this
Long-ago afternoon forgotten by everybody
In this photograph, most of them now
Sucked screaming through old age and death.

5 If one could seize America
Or at least a fine forgetfulness
That seeps into our outline
Defining our volumes with a stain
That is fleeting too

10 But commemorates
Because it does define, after all:
Gray garlands, that threesome
Waiting for the light to change,
Air lifting the hair of one
15 Upside down in the reflecting pool.

Paradoxes and Oxymorons

This poem is concerned with language on a very plain level.
Look at it talking to you. You look out a window
Or pretend to fidget. You have it but you don't have it.
You miss it, it misses you. You miss each other.

5 The poem is sad because it wants to be yours, and cannot.
What's a plain level? It is that and other things,
Bringing a system of them into play. Play?
Well, actually, yes, but I consider play to be

A deeper outside thing, a dreamed role-pattern,
10 As in the division of grace these long August days
Without proof. Open-ended. And before you know
It gets lost in the steam and chatter of typewriters.

It has been played once more. I think you exist only
To tease me into doing it, on your level, and then you aren't there
15 Or have adopted a different attitude. And the poem
Has set me softly down beside you. The poem is you.

1980

Galway Kinnell

(1927–)

Flower Herding on Mount Monadnock

1

I can support it no longer.
Laughing ruefully at myself
For all I claim to have suffered
I get up. Damned nightmarer!

5 It is New Hampshire out here,
It is nearly the dawn.
The song of the whippoorwill stops
And the dimension of depth seizes everything.

2

The song of a peabody bird goes overhead
10 Like a needle pushed five times through the air,
It enters the leaves, and comes out little changed.

The air is so still
That as they go off through the trees
The love songs of birds do not get any fainter.

3

15 The last memory I have
Is of a flower which cannot be touched,

Through the bloom of which, all day,
Fly crazed, missing bees.

4

As I climb sweat gets up my nostrils,
20 For an instant I think I am at the sea,

One summer off Cap Ferrat we watched a black seagull
Straining for the dawn, we stood in the surf,

Grasshoppers splash up where I step,
The mountain laurel crashes at my thighs.

5

25 There is something joyous in the elegies
Of birds. They seem
Caught up in a formal delight,
Though the mourning dove whistles of despair.

But at last in the thousand elegies
30 The dead rise in our hearts,
On the brink of our happiness we stop
Like someone on a drunk starting to weep.

6

I kneel at a pool,
I look through my face
35 At the bacteria I think
I see crawling through the moss.

My face sees me,
The water stirs, the face,
Looking preoccupied,
40 Gets knocked from its bones.

7

I weighed eleven pounds
At birth, having stayed on
Two extra weeks in the womb.

Tempted by room and fresh air
45   I came out big as a policeman
Blue-faced, with narrow red eyes.
It was eight days before the doctor
Would scare my mother with me.

Turning and craning in the vines
50   I can make out through the leaves
The old, shimmering nothingness, the sky.

8

Green, scaly moosewoods ascend,
Tenants of the shaken paradise,

At every wind last night's rain
55   Comes splattering from the leaves,

It drops in flurries and lies there,
The footsteps of some running start.

9

From a rock
A waterfall,
60   A single trickle like a strand of wire,
Breaks into beads halfway down.

I know
The birds fly off
But the hug of the earth wraps
65   With moss their graves and the giant boulders.

10

In the forest I discover a flower.
The invisible life of the thing
Goes up in flames that are invisible
Like cellophane burning in the sunlight.

70   It burns up. Its drift is to be nothing.
In its covertness it has a way
Of uttering itself in place of itself,
Its blossoms claim to float in the Empyrean,

A wrathful presence on the blur of the ground.

75   The appeal to heaven breaks off.
The petals begin to fall, in self-forgiveness.
It is a flower. On this mountainside it is dying.

To Christ Our Lord

The legs of the elk punctured the snow's crust
And wolves floated lightfooted on the land
Hunting Christmas elk living and frozen;
Inside snow melted in a basin, and a woman basted
5   A bird spread over coals by its wings and head.

Snow had scaled the windows; candles lit
The Christmas meal. The Christmas grace chilled
The cooked bird, being long-winded and the room cold
During the words a boy thought, is it fitting
10   To eat this creature killed on the wing?

He had killed it himself, climbing out
Alone on snowshoes in the Christmas dawn,
The fallen snow swirling and the snowfall gone,
Heard its throat scream as the gunshot scattered,
15   Watched it drop, and fished from the snow the dead.

He had not wanted to shoot. The sound
Of wings beating into the hushed air
Had stirred his love, and his fingers
Froze in his gloves, and he wondered,
20   Famishing, could he fire? Then he fired.

Now the grace praised his wicked act. At its end
The bird on the plate
Stared at his stricken appetite.
There had been nothing to do but surrender,
25   To kill and to eat; he ate as he had killed, with wonder.

At night on snowshoes on the drifting field
He wondered again, for whom had love stirred?
The stars glittered on the snow and nothing answered.
Then the Swan spread her wings, cross of the cold north,
30   The pattern and mirror of the acts of earth.

1960

W. S. Merwin

(1927–   )

The River of Bees

In a dream I returned to the river of bees
Five orange trees by the bridge and
Beside two mills my house

Into whose courtyard a blind man followed
5 The goats and stood singing
Of what was older

Soon it will be fifteen years

He was old he will have fallen into his eyes

I took my eyes
10 A long way to the calendars
Room after room asking how shall I live

One of the ends is made of streets
One man processions carry through it
Empty bottles their
15 Image of hope
It was offered to me by name

Once once and once
In the same city I was born
Asking what shall I say

20 He will have fallen into his mouth
Men think they are better than grass

I return to his voice rising like a forkful of hay

He was old he is not real nothing is real
Nor the noise of death drawing water

25 We are the echo of the future

On the door it says what to do to survive
But we were not born to survive
Only to live

1967

The Moths

It is cold here
In the steel grass
At the foot of the invisible statue
Made by the incurables and called
5 Justice

At a great distance
An audience of rubber tombstones is watching
The skulls of
The leaders
10 Strung on the same worm

Darkness moves up the nail

And I am returning to a night long since past
In which the rain is falling and
A crying comes from the stations
15 And near at hand a voice a woman's
In a jug under the wind
Is trying to sing

No one has shown her
Any statue and
20 The music keeps rising through her
Almost beginning and
The moths
Lie in the black grass waiting

1967

James Wright

(1927–1980)

Autumn Begins in Martins Ferry, Ohio

In the Shreve High football stadium,
I think of Polacks nursing long beers in Tiltonsville,
And gray faces of Negroes in the blast furnace at Benwood,
And the ruptured night watchman of Wheeling Steel,
5 Dreaming of heroes.

All the proud fathers are ashamed to go home.
Their women cluck like starved pullets,
Dying for love.

Therefore,
10 Their sons grow suicidally beautiful
At the beginning of October,
And gallop terribly against each other's bodies.

1966

Two Postures Beside a Fire

1

Tonight I watch my father's hair,
As he sits dreaming near his stove.
Knowing my feather of despair,
He sent me an owl's plume for love,

5 Lest I not know, so I've come home.
Tonight Ohio, where I once
Hounded and cursed my loneliness,
Shows me my father, who broke stones,
Wrestled and mastered great machines,
10 And rests, shadowing his lovely face.

2

Nobly his hands fold together in his repose.
He is proud of me, believing
I have done strong things among men and become a man
Of place among men of place in the large cities.
15 I will not waken him.
I have come home alone, without wife or child
To delight him. Awake, solitary and welcome,
I too sit near his stove, the lines
Of an ugly age scarring my face, and my hands
20 Twitch nervously about.

1968

Philip Levine

(1928–   )

To a Child Trapped in a Barber Shop

You've gotten in through the transom
    and you can't get out
till Monday morning or, worse,
    till the cops come.

5 That six-year-old red face
    calling for mama
is yours; it won't help you
    because your case

is closed forever, hopeless.
10   So don't drink
the Lucky Tiger, don't
    fill up on grease

because that makes it a lot worse,
    that makes it a crime
15 against property and the state
    and that costs time.

We've all been here before,
    we took our turn
under the electric storm
20   of the vibrator

and stiffened our wills to meet
    the close clippers
and heard the true blade mowing
    back and forth

25 on a strip of dead skin,
    and we stopped crying.
You think your life is over?
    It's just begun.

1968

You Can Have It

My brother comes home from work
and climbs the stairs to our room.
I can hear the bed groan and his shoes drop
one by one. You can have it, he says.

5 The moonlight streams in the window
and his unshaven face is whitened
like the face of the moon. He will sleep
long after noon and waken to find me gone.

Thirty years will pass before I remember
10 that moment when suddenly I knew each man
has one brother who dies when he sleeps
and sleeps when he rises to face this life,

and that together they are only one man
sharing a heart that always labors, hands
15 yellowed and cracked, a mouth that gasps
for breath and asks, Am I gonna make it?

All night at the ice plant he had fed
the chute its silvery blocks, and then I
stacked cases of orange soda for the children
20 of Kentucky, one gray boxcar at a time

with always two more waiting. We were twenty
for such a short time and always in
the wrong clothes, crusted with dirt
and sweat. I think now we were never twenty.

25 In 1948 in the city of Detroit, founded
by de la Mothe Cadillac for the distant purposes
of Henry Ford, no one wakened or died,
no one walked the streets or stoked a furnace,

for there was no such year, and now
30 that year has fallen off all the old newspapers,
calendars, doctors' appointments, bonds,
wedding certificates, drivers licenses.

The city slept. The snow turned to ice.
The ice to standing pools or rivers
35 racing in the gutters. Then bright grass rose
between the thousands of cracked squares,

and that grass died. I give you back 1948.
I give you all the years from then
to the coming one. Give me back the moon
40 with its frail light falling across a face.

Give me back my young brother, hard
and furious, with wide shoulders and a curse
for God and burning eyes that look upon
all creation and say, You can have it.

1968

Donald Petersen

(1928–   )

The Ballad of Dead Yankees

Where's Babe Ruth, the King of Swat,
Who rocked the heavens with his blows?
Grabowski, Pennock, and Malone—
Mother of mercy, where are those?

5 Where's Tony (Poosh 'em up) Lazzeri,
The quickest man that ever played?
Where's the gang that raised the roof
In the house that Colonel Ruppert made?

Where's Lou Gehrig, strong and shy,
10 Who never missed a single game?
Where's Tiny Bonham, where's Jake Powell
And many another peerless name?

Where's Steve Sundra, good but late,
Who for a season had his fling?
15   Where are the traded, faded ones?
Lord, can they tell us anything?

Where's the withered nameless dwarf
Who sold us pencils at the gate?
Hurled past the clamor of our cheers?
20   Gone to rest with the good and great?

Where's the swagger, where's the strut,
Where's the style that was the hitter?
Where's the pitcher's swanlike motion?
What in God's name turned life bitter?

25   For strong-armed Steve, who lost control
And weighed no more than eighty pounds,
No sooner benched than in his grave,
Where's the cleverness that confounds?

For Lou the man, erect and clean,
30   Wracked with a cruel paralysis,
Gone in his thirty-seventh year,
Where's the virtue that was his?

For nimble Tony, cramped in death,
God knows why and God knows how,
35   Shut in a dark and silent house,
Where's the squirrel quickness now?

For big brash Babe in an outsize suit,
Himself grown thin and hoarse with cancer,
Still autographing balls for boys,
40   Mother of mercy, what's the answer?

Is there a heaven with rainbow flags,
Silver trophies hung on walls,
A horseshoe grandstand, mobs of fans,
Webbed gloves and official balls?

45   Is there a power in judgment there
To stand behind the body's laws,
A stern-faced czar whose slightest word
Is righteous as Judge Kenesaw's?

And if there be no turnstile gate
50   At that green park, can we get in?
Is the game suspended or postponed,
And do the players play to win?

Mother of mercy, if you're there,
Pray to the high celestial czar
55 For all of these, the early dead,
Who've gone where no ovations are.

1964

Anne Sexton

(1928–1974)

Her Kind

I have gone out, a possessed witch,
haunting the black air, braver at night;
dreaming evil, I have done my hitch
over the plain houses, light by light:
5 lonely thing, twelve-fingered, out of mind.
A woman like that is not a woman, quite.
I have been her kind.

I have found the warm caves in the woods,
filled them with skillets, carvings, shelves,
10 closets, silks, innumerable goods;
fixed the suppers for the worms and the elves:
whining, rearranging the disaligned.
A woman like that is misunderstood.
I have been her kind.

15 I have ridden in your cart, driver,
waved my nude arms at villages going by,
learning the last bright routes, survivor
where your flames still bite my thigh
and my ribs crack where your wheels wind.
20 A woman like that is not ashamed to die.
I have been her kind.

1960

Cinderella

You always read about it:
the plumber with twelve children
who wins the Irish Sweepstakes.
From toilets to riches.
5 That story.

Or the nursemaid,
some luscious sweet from Denmark
who captures the oldest son's heart.
From diapers to Dior.
10 That story.

Or a milkman who serves the wealthy,
eggs, cream, butter, yogurt, milk,
the white truck like an ambulance
who goes into real estate
15 and makes a pile.
From homogenized to martinis at lunch.

Or the charwoman
who is on the bus when it cracks up
and collects enough from the insurance.
20 From mops to Bonwit Teller.
That story.

Once
the wife of a rich man was on her deathbed
and she said to her daughter Cinderella:
25 Be devout. Be good. Then I will smile
down from heaven in the seam of a cloud.
The man took another wife who had
two daughters, pretty enough
but with hearts like blackjacks.
30 Cinderella was their maid.
She slept on the sooty hearth each night
and walked around looking like Al Jolson.
Her father brought presents home from town,
jewels and gowns for the other women
35 but the twig of a tree for Cinderella.
She planted that twig on her mother's grave
and it grew to a tree where a white dove sat.
Whenever she wished for anything the dove
would drop it like an egg upon the ground.
40 The bird is important, my dears, so heed him.

Next came the ball, as you all know.
It was a marriage market.
The prince was looking for a wife.
All but Cinderella were preparing
45 and gussying up for the big event.
Cinderella begged to go too.
Her stepmother threw a dish of lentils

into the cinders and said: Pick them
up in an hour and you shall go.
50   The white dove brought all his friends;
all the warm wings of the fatherland came,
and picked up the lentils in a jiffy.
No, Cinderella, said the stepmother,
you have no clothes and cannot dance.
55   That's the way with stepmothers.

Cinderella went to the tree at the grave
and cried forth like a gospel singer:
Mama! Mama! My turtledove,
send me to the prince's ball!
60   The bird dropped down a golden dress
and delicate little gold slippers.
Rather a large package for a simple bird.
So she went. Which is no surprise.
Her stepmother and sisters didn't
65   recognize her without her cinder face
and the prince took her hand on the spot
and danced with no other the whole day.

As nightfall came she thought she'd better
get home. The prince walked her home
70   and she disappeared into the pigeon house
and although the prince took an axe and broke
it open she was gone. Back to her cinders.
These events repeated themselves for three days.
However on the third day the prince
75   covered the palace steps with cobbler's wax
and Cinderella's gold shoe stuck upon it.

Now he would find whom the shoe fit
and find his strange dancing girl for keeps.
He went to their house and the two sisters
80   were delighted because they had lovely feet.
The eldest went into a room to try the slipper on
but her big toe got in the way so she simply
sliced it off and put on the slipper.
The prince rode away with her until the white dove
85   told him to look at the blood pouring forth.
That is the way with amputations.
They don't just heal up like a wish.
The other sister cut off her heel
but the blood told as blood will.

90 The prince was getting tired.
He began to feel like a shoe salesman.
But he gave it one last try.
This time Cinderella fit into the shoe
like a love letter into its envelope.
95 At the wedding ceremony
the two sisters came to curry favor
and the white dove pecked their eyes out.
Two hollow spots were left
like soup spoons.

100 Cinderella and the prince
lived, they say, happily ever after,
like two dolls in a museum case
never bothered by diapers or dust,
never arguing over the timing of an egg,
105 never telling the same story twice,
never getting a middle-aged spread,
their darling smiles pasted on for eternity.
Regular Bobbsey Twins.
That story.

1971

In Celebration of My Uterus

Everyone in me is a bird.
I am beating all my wings.
They wanted to cut you out
but they will not.
5 They said you were immeasurably empty
but you are not.
They said you were sick unto dying
but they were wrong.
You are singing like a school girl.
10 You are not torn.

Sweet weight,
in celebration of the woman I am
and of the soul of the woman I am
and of the central creature and its delight
15 I sing for you. I dare to live.
Hello, spirit. Hello, cup.
Fasten, cover. Cover that does contain.
Hello to the soil of the fields.
Welcome, roots.

20 Each cell has a life.
There is enough here to please a nation.
It is enough that the populace own these goods.
Any person, any commonwealth would say of it,
"It is good this year that we may plant again
25 and think forward to a harvest.
A blight had been forecast and has been cast out."
Many women are singing together of this:
one is in a shoe factory cursing the machine,
one is at the aquarium tending a seal,
30 one is dull at the wheel of her Ford,
one is at the toll gate collecting,
one is tying the cord of a calf in Arizona,
one is straddling a cello in Russia,
one is shifting pots on the stove in Egypt,
35 one is painting her bedroom walls moon color,
one is dying but remembering a breakfast,
one is stretching on her mat in Thailand,
one is wiping the ass of her child,
one is staring out the window of a train
40 in the middle of Wyoming and one is
anywhere and some are everywhere and all
seem to be singing, although some can not
sing a note.

Sweet weight,
45 in celebration of the woman I am
let me carry a ten-foot scarf,
let me drum for the nineteen-year-olds,
let me carry bowls for the offering
(if that is my part).
50 Let me study the cardiovascular tissue,
let me examine the angular distance of meteors,
let me suck on the stems of flowers
(if that is my part).
Let me make certain tribal figures
55 (if that is my part).
For this thing the body needs
let me sing
for the supper,
for the kissing,
60 for the correct
yes.

1967

Thom Gunn

(1929–   )

Street Song

I am too young to grow a beard
But yes man it was me you heard
In dirty denim and dark glasses.
I look through everyone who passes
5   But ask him clear, I do not plead,
Keys lids acid and speed.

My grass is not oregano.
Some of it grew in Mexico.
You cannot guess the weed I hold,
10   Clara Green, Acapulco Gold,
Panama Red, you name it man,
Best on the street since I began.

My methedrine, my double-sun,
Will give you two lives in your one,
15   Five days of power before you crash.
At which time use these lumps of hash
—They burn so sweet, they smoke so smooth,
They make you sharper while they soothe.

Now here, the best I've got to show,
20   Made by a righteous cat I know.
Pure acid—it will scrape your brain,
And make it something else again.
Call it heaven, call it hell,
Join me and see the world I sell.

25   Join me, and I will take you there,
Your head will cut out from your hair
Into whichever self you choose.
With Midday Mick man you can't lose,
I'll get you anything you need.
30   *Keys lids acid and speed.*

1971

The Discovery of the Pacific

They lean against the cooling car, backs pressed
Upon the dusts of a brown continent,

And watch the sun, now Westward of their West,
Fall to the ocean. Where it led they went.

5 Kansas to California. Day by day
They travelled emptier of the things they knew.
They improvised new habits on the way,
But lost the occasions, and then lost them too.

One night, no-one and nowhere, she had woken
10 To resin-smell and to the firs' slight sound,
And through their sleeping-bag had felt the broken
Tight-knotted surfaces of the naked ground.

Only his lean quiet body cupping hers
Kept her from it, the extreme chill. By degrees
15 She fell asleep. Around them in the firs
The wind probed, tiding through forked estuaries.

And now their skin is caked with road, the grime
Merely reflecting sunlight as it fails.
They leave their clothes among the rocks they climb,
20 Blunt leaves of iceplant nuzzle at their soles.

Now they stand chin-deep in the sway of ocean,
Firm West, two stringy bodies face to face,
And come, together, in the water's motion,
The full caught pause of their embrace.

1961

Black Jackets

In the silence that prolongs the span
Rawly of music when the record ends,
    The red-haired boy who drove a van
In weekday overalls but, like his friends,

5   Wore cycle boots and jacket here
To suit the Sunday hangout he was in,
    Heard, as he stretched back from his beer,
Leather creak softly round his neck and chin.

Before him, on a coal-black sleeve
10 Remote exertion had lined, scratched, and burned
    Insignia that could not revive
The heroic fall or climb where they were earned.

On the other drinkers bent together,
Concocting selves for their impervious kit,

15   He saw it as no more than leather
       Which, taut across the shoulders grown to it,

           Sent through the dimness of a bar
       As sudden and anonymous hints of light
           As those that shipping give, that are
20   Now flickers in the Bay, now lost in night.

           He stretched out like a cat, and rolled
       The bitterish taste of beer upon his tongue,
           And listened to a joke being told:
       The present was the things he stayed among.

25   If it was only loss he wore,
       He wore it to assert, with fierce devotion,
           Complicity and nothing more.
       He recollected his initiation,

           And one especially of the rites.
30   For on his shoulders they had put tattoos:
           The group's name on the left, The Knights,
       And on the right the slogan Born To Lose.

                                                              1961

X. J. Kennedy

(1929–   )

In a Prominent Bar in Secaucus One Day

*To the Tune of "The Old Orange Flute" or
the Tune of "Sweet Betsy from Pike"*

In a prominent bar in Secaucus one day
Rose a lady in skunk with a topheavy sway,
Raised a knobby red finger—all turned from their beer—
While with eyes bright as snowcrust she sang high and clear:

5   "Now who of you'd think from an eyeload of me
    That I once was a lady as proud as could be?
    Oh I'd never sit down by a tumbledown drunk
    If it wasn't, my dears, for the high cost of junk.

    "All the gents used to swear that the white of my calf
10 Beat the down of the swan by a length and a half.
    In the kerchief of linen I caught to my nose
    Ah, there never fell snot, but a little gold rose.

"I had seven gold teeth and a toothpick of gold,
My Virginia cheroot was a leaf of it rolled
15 And I'd light it each time with a thousand in cash—
Why the bums used to fight if I flicked them an ash.

"Once the toast of the Biltmore, the belle of the Taft,
I would drink bottle beer at the Drake, never draft,
And dine at the Astor on Salisbury steak
20 With a clean tablecloth for each bite I did take.

"In a car like the Roxy I'd roll to the track,
A steel-guitar trio, a bar in the back,
And the wheels made no noise, they turned over so fast,
Still it took you ten minutes to see me go past.

25 "When the horses bowed down to me that I might choose,
I bet on them all, for I hated to lose.
Now I'm saddled each night for my butter and eggs
And the broken threads race down the backs of my legs.

"Let you hold in mind, girls, that your beauty must pass
30 Like a lovely white clover that rusts with its grass.
Keep your bottoms off barstools and marry you young
Or be left—an old barrel with many a bung.

"For when time takes you out for a spin in his car
You'll be hard-pressed to stop him from going too far
35 And be left by the roadside, for all your good deeds,
Two toadstools for tits and a face full of weeds."

All the house raised a cheer, but the man at the bar
Made a phonecall and up pulled a red patrol car
And she blew us a kiss as they copped her away
40 From that prominent bar in Secaucus, N.J.

1985

Nude Descending a Staircase

Toe after toe, a snowing flesh,
a gold of lemon, root and rind,
she sifts in sunlight down the stairs
with nothing on. Nor on her mind.

5 We spy beneath the banister
a constant thresh of thigh on thigh;
her lips imprint the swinging air
that parts to let her parts go by.

One-woman waterfall, she wears
10 her slow descent like any drape
and pausing on the final stair,
collects her motions into shape.

1985

Maurice Kenny

(1929–   )

Listening for the Elders

is summer this bear
    home this tamarack
are these wild berries song
is this hill
5   where my grandmother sleeps
    this river where
    my father fishes
does this winter-house
    light its window for me
10   burn oak for my chill
does this woman sing my pain
does this drum beat
    sounding waters
or does this crow caw
15 does this hickory nut fall
    this corn ripen
    this field yellow
    this prayer-feather hang
    this mother worry
20   this ghost walk
does this fire glow
    this bat swoop
    this night fall
does this star shine
25   over mountains
    for this cousin who has
    no aunt picking sweetgrass
    for a pillow

is summer this wolf
30   this elm leaf
    this pipe smoke
is summer this turtle

home this sumac
home this black-ash
35 is summer this story
is summer home
is twilight home
is summer this tongue
home this cedar
40 these snakes in my hair

reflections on this sky
this summer day
this bear

Legacy

my face is grass
color of April rain;
arms, legs are the limbs
of birch, cedar;
5 my thoughts are winds
which blow;
pictures in my mind
are the climb uphill
to dream in the sun;
10 hawk feathers, and quills
of porcupine running
the edge of the stream
which reflects stories
of my many mornings
15 and the dark faces of night
mingled with victories
of dawn and tomorrow;
corn of the fields and squash . . .
the daughters of my mother
20 who collect honey
and all the fruits;
meadow and sky are the end of my day
the stretch of my night
yet the birth of my dust;
25 my wind is the breath of a fawn
the cry of the cub
the trot of the wolf
whose print covers
the tracks of my feet;
30 my word, my word,
loaned

legacy, the obligation I hand
    to the blood of my flesh
    the sinew of the loins
35 to hold to the sun
and the moon
which direct the river
    that carries my song
    and the beat of the drum
40 to the fires of the village
    which endures.

Adrienne Rich

(1929–   )

A Clock in the Square

This handless clock stares blindly from its tower,
Refusing to acknowledge any hour.
But what can one clock do to stop the game
When others go on striking just the same?
5 Whatever mite of truth the gesture held,

Time may be silenced but will not be stilled,
Nor we absolved by any one's withdrawing
From all the restless ways we must be going
And all the rings in which we're spun and swirled,
10 Whether around a clockface or a world.

                                                      1951

Aunt Jennifer's Tigers

Aunt Jennifer's tigers prance across a screen,
Bright topaz denizens of a world of green.
They do not fear the men beneath the tree;
They pace in sleek chivalric certainty.

5 Aunt Jennifer's fingers fluttering through her wool
Find even the ivory needle hard to pull.
The massive weight of Uncle's wedding band
Sits heavily upon Aunt Jennifer's hand.

When Aunt is dead, her terrified hands will lie
10 Still ringed with ordeals she was mastered by.

The tigers in the panel that she made
Will go on prancing, proud and unafraid.

1951

The Insusceptibles

Then the long sunlight lying on the sea
Fell, folded gold on gold; and slowly we
Took up our decks of cards, our parasols,
The picnic hamper and the sandblown shawls
5 And climbed the dunes in silence. There were two
Who lagged behind as lovers sometimes do,
And took a different road. For us the night
Was final, and by artificial light
We came indoors to sleep. No envy there
10 Of those who might be watching anywhere
The lustres of the summer dark, to trace
Some vagrant splinter blazing out of space.
No thought of them, save in a lower room
To leave a light for them when they should come.

1955

Diving into the Wreck

First having read the book of myths,
and loaded the camera,
and checked the edge of the knife-blade,
I put on
5 the body-armor of black rubber
the absurd flippers
the grave and awkward mask.
I am having to do this
not like Cousteau with his
10 assiduous team
aboard the sun-flooded schooner
but here alone.

There is a ladder.
The ladder is always there
15 hanging innocently
close to the side of the schooner.
We know what it is for,
we who have used it.
otherwise
20 it is a piece of maritime floss
some sundry equipment.

I go down.
Rung after rung and still
the oxygen immerses me
25 the blue light
the clear atoms
of our human air.
I go down.
My flippers cripple me,
30 I crawl like an insect down the ladder
and there is no one
to tell me when the ocean
will begin.

First the air is blue and then
35 it is bluer and then green and then
black I am blacking out and yet
my mask is powerful
it pumps my blood with power
the sea is another story
40 the sea is not a question of power
I have to learn alone
to turn my body without force
in the deep element.

And now; it is easy to forget
45 what I came for
among so many who have always
lived here
swaying their crenellated fans
between the reefs
50 and besides
you breathe differently down here.

I came to explore the wreck.
The words are purposes.
The words are maps.
55 I came to see the damage that was done
and the treasures that prevail.
I stroke the beam of my lamp
slowly along the flank
of something more permanent
60 than fish or weed

the thing I came for:
the wreck and not the story of the wreck
the thing itself and not the myth
the drowned face always staring

65 toward the sun
the evidence of damage
worn by salt and sway into this threadbare beauty
the ribs of the disaster
curving their assertion
70 among the tentative haunters.

This is the place.
And I am here, the mermaid whose dark hair
streams black, the merman in his armored body.
We circle silently
75 about the wreck
we dive into the hold.
I am she: I am he

whose drowned face sleeps with open eyes
whose breasts still bear the stress
80 whose silver, copper, vermeil cargo lies
obscurely inside barrels
half-wedged and left to rot
we are the half-destroyed instruments
that once held to a course
85 the water-eaten log
the fouled compass

We are, I am, you are
by cowardice or courage
the one who find our way
90 back to this scene
carrying a knife, a camera
a book of myths
in which
our names do not appear.

1973

Ted Hughes

(1930–   )

Hawk Roosting

I sit in the top of the wood, my eyes closed.
Inaction, no falsifying dream
Between my hooked head and hooked feet:
Or in sleep rehearse perfect kills and eat.

5 The convenience of the high trees!
   The air's buoyancy and the sun's ray
   Are of advantage to me;
   And the earth's face upward for my inspection.

   My feet are locked upon the rough bark.
10 It took the whole of Creation
   To produce my foot, my each feather:
   Now I hold Creation in my foot

   Or fly up, and revolve it all slowly—
   I kill where I please because it is all mine.
15 There is no sophistry in my body:
   My manners are tearing off heads—

   The allotment of death.
   For the one path of my flight is direct
   Through the bones of the living.
20 No arguments assert my right:

   The sun is behind me.
   Nothing has changed since I began.
   My eye has permitted no change.
   I am going to keep things like this.

                                          1960

Pike

   Pike, three inches long, perfect
   Pike in all parts, green tigering the gold.
   Killers from the egg: the malevolent aged grin.
   They dance on the surface among the flies.

5 Or move, stunned by their own grandeur,
   Over a bed of emerald, silhouette
   Of submarine delicacy and horror.
   A hundred feet long in their world.

   In ponds, under the heat-struck lily pads—
10 Gloom of their stillness:
   Logged on last year's black leaves, watching upwards.
   Or hung in an amber cavern of weeds

   The jaw's hooked clamp and fangs
   Not to be changed at this date;
15 A life subdued to its instrument;
   The gills kneading quietly, and the pectorals.

Three we kept behind glass,
Jungled in weed: three inches, four,
And four and a half: fed fry to them—
20 Suddenly there were two. Finally one

With a sag belly and the grin it was born with.
And indeed they spare nobody.
Two, six pounds each, over two feet long,
High and dry and dead in the willow-herb—

25 One jammed past its gills down the other's gullet:
The outside eye stared: as a vice locks—
The same iron in this eye
Though its film shrank in death.

A pond I fished, fifty yards across,
30 Whose lilies and muscular tench
Had outlasted every visible stone
Of the monastery that planted them—

Stilled legendary depth:
It was as deep as England. It held
35 Pike too immense to stir, so immense and old
That past nightfall I dared not cast

But silently cast and fished
With the hair frozen on my head
For what might move, for what eye might move.
40 The still splashes on the dark pond,

Owls hushing the floating woods
Frail on my ear against the dream
Darkness beneath night's darkness had freed,
That rose slowly towards me, watching.

1960

The Thought-Fox

I imagine this midnight moment's forest:
Something else is alive
Beside the clock's loneliness
And this blank page where my fingers move.

5 Through the window I see no star:
Something more near
Though deeper within darkness
Is entering the loneliness:

Cold, delicately as the dark snow,
10 A fox's nose touches twig, leaf;
Two eyes serve a movement, that now
And again now, and now, and now

Sets neat prints into the snow
Between trees, and warily a lame
15 Shadow lags by stump and in hollow
Of a body that is bold to come

Across clearings, an eye,
A widening deepening greenness,
Brilliantly, concentratedly,
20 Coming about its own business

Till, with a sudden sharp hot stink of fox
It enters the dark hole of the head.
The window is starless still; the clock ticks,
The page is printed.

1957

Gary Snyder

(1930–   )

Before the Stuff Comes Down

Walking out of the "big E"
Dope store of the suburb,
              canned music plugging up your ears
              the wide aisles,
5   miles of wares
              from nowheres,

Suddenly it's California:
Live oak, brown grasses

Butterflies over the parking lot and the freeway
10 A Turkey Buzzard power in the blue air.

A while longer,
Still here.

1967

Derek Walcott

(1930–   )

Sea Canes

Half my friends are dead.
I will make you new ones, said earth.
No, give me them back, as they were, instead,
with faults and all, I cried.

5 Tonight I can snatch their talk
from the faint surf's drone
through the canes, but I cannot walk

on the moonlit leaves of ocean
down that white road alone,
10 or float with the dreaming motion

of owls leaving earth's load.
O earth, the number of friends you keep
exceeds those left to be loved.

The sea-canes by the cliff flash green and silver;
15 they were the seraph lances of my faith,
but out of what is lost grows something stronger

that has the rational radiance of stone,
enduring moonlight, further than despair,
strong as the wind, that through dividing canes

20 brings those we love before us, as they were,
with faults and all, not nobler, just there.

1976

A Far Cry from Africa

A wind is ruffling the tawny pelt
Of Africa. Kikuyu,[1] quick as flies,
Batten down the bloodstreams of the veldt.
Corpses are scattered through a paradise.
5 Only the worm, colonel of carrion, cries:
'Waste no compassion on these separate dead!'
Statistics justify and scholars seize
The salients of colonial policy.
What is that to the white child hacked in bed?
10 To savages, expendable as Jews?

---

[1] a tribe in Kenya who rose against the European colonialists during the 1950s in what Europeans called the Mau Mau Rebellion

Threshed out by beaters, the long rushes break
In a white dust of ibises whose cries
Have wheeled since civilization's dawn
From the parched river or beast-teeming plain.
15 The violence of beast on beast is read
As natural law, but upright man
Seeks his divinity by inflicting pain.

Delirious as these worried beasts, his wars
Dance to the tightened carcass of a drum,
20 While he calls courage still that native dread
Of the white peace contracted by the dead.

Again brutish necessity wipes its hands
Upon the napkin of a dirty cause, again
A waste of our compassion, as with Spain[2]
25 The gorilla wrestles with the superman.

I who am poisoned with the blood of both,
Where shall I turn, divided to the vein?
I who have cursed
The drunken officer of British rule, how choose
30 Between this Africa and the English tongue I love?
Betray them both, or give back what they give?
How can I face such slaughter and be cool?
How can I turn from Africa and live?

1976

Don Summerhayes

(1931–   )

from the corner of one eye

The giraffes wave like long stems
they rub their velvet horns on the walls
do what they do

they are not merely unaware of us
5 they have no sense of living in a world at all

they dance toward their high barrier
making love in their high heads
with the air, the sky, with unimagined verbs

1992

---

[2]a reference to the Spanish Civil War of 1936–1939

her swans in high park

tilt their dizzy eyes skyward
        ludicrous throats unflexed
and flood the highest light
through wide spread wings
5   ribs glowing blue within
white upon white rising

lucy lost her breasts and died

you were the ex-fat girl from the bronx
veteran of commie picnics and summer camps
ex-jew reclaimed at the last by jolly friends

so how did you like the all-faiths chapel
5 did the rabbi the smooth stranger earn his fee
did the sobs of your maudlin aunt get through to you

after the event we went back to your little house
and your daughter explained that she loved california
and making jewellery and balling all the time

10 the food was so-so but auntie couldn't be stopped
she wanted us all to take something to remember you

thank god your uncle louie had had the foresight
to bring a bottle of rye and the charity
to invite a few of us into the back for a snort
15 and a grimace and a sensible clearing of throats

here's looking at you kid and
your ex-pals litotes and hyperbole

you had an etiquette with yourself

1992

Robert Clayton Casto

(1932–1998)

The Salt Pork

This is about the summer and the wheels of sleep
and the man shot through with Adam and dying from the heart

who moves through the night upstairs along a flowered wall
and longs for kitchens in the immense and preoccupied night.

5 He is about to die tomorrow or next week
   and longs for the thing they say he must not have—salt, salt.

A woman stands at the base of the stairs and she looks up:
he has nothing for salt but tears and his tears are like his flesh

big and white in the night and slow to hover and drop,
10 so she brings him in pity salt pork, gray woman as biting as salt.

Picture the two of them poised on that landing, bitter and old,
measuring each other like gods, after the humbug of years;

and though she has long since spun and spun from her discontent
and shifts like a larva now inside her webbed regret,

15 it is the gift that makes her a woman again and she wings

the silence out from her thighs by the movement of offering
to the floods and coagulation of his flesh the pork,

that he may taste salt things again with a wet white tongue
an inch before dying in summer, when sleep is our green cargo.

20 She knows after all and all the biting years, at last
   she will please the both of them and he will be glad on the stairs

to receive at his lips the forbidden and quite lively flavor
of the sharp wife and the offering beyond old duty—it is

the ransom (lord) of Eden. He is glad like a child from his heart
25 and she knows at last from her own: because we are less than gods

we are holy, holy, holy.

1980

Sketch

for Jacques André Emond
1939–1989

The dying decide for them
selves in that room the
soursweet smell of
death the
5 solved and the dis
solved their
township their
jurisdiction they
bubble into space a
10 parliament fierce as
God

      when you were
    there it was so
    important that
15 art of sketching
    atmosphere the
    page already
    filled with words Bo
    bo Bo
20 bo quelle
    heure quelle
    heure de
    cide for themselves the
    brain de
25 bauched and
    grand not what
    has to happen but what
    happens going
    now going thank
30 you for coming good
    bye good
    bye I under
    stand thankyew
    thankyew merci
35 thankyew thank
    you

                                            1989

The Tin-Flute Player

Misters and missues, goddam your picky christian
little rich boys and girls who have hidden my little tin flute,
thinking me evil and sensitive. Lord! give 'em chicken pox,
the croup and the pimples, let 'em grow up to a mortgage and be
5 unpopular. When they played with me once in vacant fields
(now bumby with houses), their laughter was better than innocence.
Now they have mockingly taken my little tin flute and its little tin
                    sweet sweet song.

Jesus! here they make love with the lights on, that is not art nor
manners, but it is their way who watch each other brightly
10 and they watch me too. I have seen from the street blue solid hands
pull skinny curtains back and the doorways filled with misters
silent and butch and the front lawns empty when I pass.
Am I evil and sensitive simply because I have given them something
that whistles alive, more viable even than life-insurance, my
                    sweet sweet song?

15 I saw two solemn seekers, persons of the night,
   paddle intelligent streams, two swans as white as blood,
   and I ask you, were they not birds of indolence and despair?
   were they, among the green tusks of fern and soft green mosses,
   not the two similar parts of a single eminent soul?
20 Living they had no voice, but when they began to die
   I heard them raise up a symphonious honking, as pretty as my own
                              sweet sweet song!

   Goodbye to the fields and the offspring. Well, I can sing all alone
   incredible little tin tunes! They want to see me cry,
   the smart suburban boys and girls, but as long as I live
25 I will sing to spite them, my song shall be full of abuse and despair
   and rich hatred with all the green hunger of living things and my song
   shall be networks of fear, twirling and cruel as the progress of men,
   and my song shall open the fields to great cities ugly as life, my
                              sweet sweet song.

                                                          1980

Rhina P. Espaillat

(1932–   )

Calculus

   "Look," said my son, "think of it as a line
   looped back and forth to bridge an open space
   unbridgeable at last, but narrowed fine
   and finer with each passing of the lace
5 almost to zero, which can never be."
   "Why not?" said I. "That would be certainty,
   absence of error. It would be too much
   to hope for." "Then you orbit round your aim,
   seeking, like Moses, what you'll never touch;
10 or like a poet, hunting for the word
   to reproduce a song he thinks he heard
   and send it hunting in the hearer's mind."
   "Right," laughed my son, "we play the self-same game.
   Sometimes I think the hunt is all we find,
15 whether we search for song, or sign, or zero."

   In the still house we talked into the night
   before I left him, stalking, unafraid,
   some stubborn truth flicking its dragon tails

across the page before him ... my young hero
20 so thinly armored in the flesh I made,
my small moon gone so far and grown so bright
above my gaze, lighting his awesome skies
where I can wield no sort of telescope.
Pondering now what love could be, that fails,
25 as fail it must, to seize the flying prize
and yet endures, cradling the heart like hope,
I tell my son, "Think of it as a line
weaving between your orbiting and mine."

1992

Group Portrait

People who don't applaud
sit like rows of bricks.
Their hands in their laps are crueler
than stones and sticks.

5 People who don't applaud
have eyes of glass;
they give back nothing living
to those who pass.

They nod when meteors crumble
10 in some back road;
they like it when the prince
shrivels to toad.

People who don't applaud
have mouths like wire.
15 Their silence is cocked and aimed
and they fire and fire.

1992

Sylvia Plath

(1932–1963)

Ariel

Stasis in darkness.
Then the substanceless blue
Pour of tor and distances.

God's lioness,
5   How one we grow,
Pivot of heels and knees!—The furrow

Splits and passes, sister to
The brown arc
Of the neck I cannot catch,

10   Nigger-eye
Berries cast dark
Hooks——

Black sweet blood mouthfuls,
Shadows.
15   Something else

Hauls me through air——
Thighs, hair;
Flakes from my heels.

White
20   Godiva, I unpeel——
Dead hands, dead stringencies.

And now I
Foam to wheat, a glitter of seas.
The child's cry

25   Melts in the wall.
And I
Am the arrow,

The dew that flies
Suicidal, at one with the drive
30   Into the red

Eye, the cauldron of morning.

1965

Morning Song

Love set you going like a fat gold watch.
The midwife slapped your footsoles, and your bald cry
Took its place among the elements.

Our voices echo, magnifying your arrival. New statue.
5   In a drafty museum, your nakedness
Shadows our safety. We stand round blankly as walls.

I'm no more your mother
Than the cloud that distils a mirror to reflect its own slow
Effacement at the wind's hand.

10 All night your moth-breath
   Flickers among the flat pink roses. I wake to listen:
   A far sea moves in my ear.

One cry, and I stumble from bed, cow-heavy and floral
In my Victorian nightgown.
15 Your mouth opens clean as a cat's. The window square

Whitens and swallows its dull stars. And now you try
Your handful of notes;
The clear vowels rise like balloons.

                       1961

Medallion

By the gate with star and moon
Worked into the peeled orange wood
The bronze snake lay in the sun

Inert as a shoelace; dead
5 But pliable still, his jaw
Unhinged and his grin crooked,

Tongue a rose-colored arrow.
Over my hand I hung him.
His little vermilion eye

10 Ignited with a glassed flame
As I turned him in the light;
When I split a rock one time

The garnet bits burned like that.
Dust dulled his back to ochre
15 The way sun ruins a trout.

Yet his belly kept its fire
Going under the chainmail,
The old jewels smoldering there

In each opaque belly-scale:
20 Sunset looked at through milk glass.
And I saw white maggots coil

Thin as pins in the dark bruise
Where his innards bulged as if
He were digesting a mouse.

25 Knifelike, he was chaste enough,
Pure death's-metal. The yardman's
Flung brick perfected his laugh.

                       1960

Metaphors

I'm a riddle in nine syllables,
An elephant, a ponderous house,
A melon strolling on two tendrils.
O red fruit, ivory, fine timbers!
5 This loaf's big with its yeasty rising.
Money's new-minted in this fat purse.
I'm a means, a stage, a cow in calf.
I've eaten a bag of green apples,
Boarded the train there's no getting off.

                                                                1960

Daddy

You do not do, you do not do
Any more, black shoe
In which I have lived like a foot
For thirty years, poor and white,
5 Barely daring to breath or Achoo.

Daddy, I have had to kill you.
You died before I had time—
Marble-heavy, a bag full of God,
Ghastly statue with one gray toe
10 Big as a Frisco seal

And a head in the freakish Atlantic
Where it pours bean green over blue
In the waters off beautiful Nauset.
I used to pray to recover you.
15 Ach, du.

In the German tongue, in the Polish town
Scraped flat by the roller
Of wars, wars, wars.
But the name of the town is common.
20 My Polack friend

Says there are a dozen or two.
So I never could tell where you
Put your foot, your root,
I never could talk to you.
25 The tongue stuck in my jaw.

It stuck in a barb wire snare.
Ich, ich, ich, ich,
I could hardly speak.

I thought every German was you.
30 And the language obscene

An engine, an engine
Chuffing me off like a Jew.
A Jew to Dachau, Auschwitz, Belsen.
I began to talk like a Jew.
35 I think I may well be a Jew.

The snows of the Tyrol, the clear beer of Vienna
Are not very pure or true.
With my gypsy ancestress and my weird luck
And my Taroc pack and my Taroc pack
40 I may be a bit of a Jew.

I have always been scared of *you,*
With your Luftwaffe, your gobbledygoo.
And your neat moustache
And your Aryan eye, bright blue.
45 Panzer-man, panzer-man, O You—

Not God but a swastika
So black no sky could squeak through.
Every woman adores a Fascist,
The boot in the face, the brute
50 Brute heart of a brute like you.

You stand at the blackboard, daddy,
In the picture I have of you.
A cleft in your chin instead of your foot
But no less a devil for that, no not
55 Any less the black man who

Bit my pretty red heart in two.
I was ten when they buried you.
At twenty I tried to die
And get back, back, back to you.
60 I thought even the bones would do.

But they pulled me out of the sack,
And they stuck me together with glue,
And then I knew what to do.
I made a model of you,
65 A man in black with a Meinkampf look

And a love of the rack and the screw.
And I said I do, I do.
So daddy, I'm finally through.

The black telephone's off at the root,
70 The voices just can't worm through.

If I've killed one man, I've killed two—
The vampire who said he was you
And drank my blood for a year,
Seven years, if you want to know.
75 Daddy, you can lie back now.

There's a stake in your fat black heart
And the villagers never liked you.
They are dancing and stamping on you.
They always *knew* it was you.
80 Daddy, daddy, you bastard, I'm through.

1962

Lady Lazarus

I have done it again.
One year in every ten
I manage it—

A sort of walking miracle, my skin
5 Bright as a Nazi lampshade,
My right foot

A paperweight,
My face a featureless, fine
Jew linen.

10 Peel off the napkin
O my enemy.
Do I terrify?—

The nose, the eye pits, the full set of teeth?
The sour breath
15 Will vanish in a day.

Soon, soon the flesh
The grave cave ate will be
At home on me

And I a smiling woman.
20 I am only thirty.
And like the cat I have nine times to die.

This is Number Three.
What a trash
To annihilate each decade.

25 What a million filaments.
The peanut-crunching crowd
Shoves in to see

Them unwrap me hand and foot—
The big strip tease.
30 Gentleman, ladies,

These are my hands,
My knees.
I may be skin and bone,

Nevertheless, I am the same, identical woman.
35 The first time it happened I was ten.
It was an accident.

The second time I meant
To last it out and not come back at all.
I rocked shut

40 As a seashell.
They had to call and call
And pick the worms off me like sticky pearls.

Dying
Is an art, like everything else.
45 I do it exceptionally well.

I do it so it feels like hell.
I do it so it feels real.
I guess you could say I've a call.

It's easy enough to do it in a cell.
50 It's easy enough to do it and stay put.
It's the theatrical

Comeback in broad day
To the same place, the same face, the same brute
Amused shout:

55 "A miracle!"
That knocks me out.
There is a charge

For the eyeing of my scars, there is a charge
For the hearing of my heart—
60 It really goes.

And there is a charge, a very large charge,
For a word or a touch
Or a bit of blood

Or a piece of my hair or my clothes.
65 So, so, Herr Doktor.
So, Herr Enemy.

I am your opus,
I am your valuable,
The pure gold baby

70 That melts to a shriek.
I turn and burn.
Do not think I underestimate your great concern.

Ash, ash—
You poke and stir.
75 Flesh, bone, there is nothing there—

A cake of soap,
A wedding ring,
A gold filling.

Herr God, Herr Lucifer,
80 Beware
Beware.

Out of the ash
I rise with my red hair
And I eat men like air.

1966

Fever 103°

Pure? What does it mean?
The tongues of hell
Are dull, dull as the triple

Tongues of dull, fat Cerberus
5 Who wheezes at the gate. Incapable
Of licking clean

The aguey tendon, the sin, the sin.
The tinder cries.
The indelible smell

10 Of a snuffed candle!
Love, love, the low smokes roll
From me like Isadora's scarves, I'm in a fright

One scarf will catch and anchor in the wheel.
Such yellow sullen smokes
15 Make their own element. They will not rise,

But trundle round the globe
Choking the aged and the meek,
The weak

Hothouse baby in its crib,
20   The ghastly orchid
Hanging its hanging garden in the air,

Devilish leopard!
Radiation turned it white
And killed it in an hour.

25   Greasing the bodies of adulterers
Like Hiroshima ash and eating in.
The sin. The sin.

Darling, all night
I have been flickering, off, on, off, on.
30   The sheets grow heavy as a lecher's kiss.

Three days. Three nights.
Lemon water, chicken
Water, water make me retch.

I am too pure for you or anyone.
35   Your body
Hurts me as the world hurts God. I am a lantern—

My head a moon
Of Japanese paper, my gold beaten skin
Infinitely delicate and infinitely expensive.

40   Does not my heat astound you. And my light.
All by myself I am a huge camellia
Glowing and coming and going, flush on flush.

I think I am going up,
I think I may rise—
45   The beads of hot metal fly, and I, love, I

Am a pure acetylene
Virgin
Attended by roses,

By kisses, by cherubim,
50   By whatever these pink things mean.
Not you, nor him

Not him, nor him
(My selves dissolving, old whore petticoats)—
To Paradise.

                                                                1966

Etheridge Knight

(1933–1991)

For Black Poets Who Think of Suicide

Black Poets should live—not leap
From steel bridges (like the white boys do).

Black Poets should *live*—not lay
Their necks on railroad tracks (like the white boys do).
5 Black Poets should seek, but not search
Too much in sweet dark caves
Or hunt for snipes down psychic trails—
(Like the white boys do).
For Black Poets belong to Black People.
10 Are the flutes of Black Lovers—Are
The organs of Black Sorrows—Are
The trumpets of Black Warriors.
Let all Black Poets die as trumpets,
And be buried in the dust of marching feet.

Amiri Baraka (LeRoi Jones)

(1934–   )

W. W.

Back home the black women are all beautiful,
and the white ones fall back, cutoff from 1000
years stacked booty, and Charles of the Ritz
where jooshladies turn into billy burke in blueglass
5 kicks. With wings, and jingly bew-teeful things.
The black women in Newark are fine. Even with all that grease
in their heads. I mean even the ones where the wigs
slide around, and they coming at you 75 degrees off course.
I could talk to them. Bring them around. To something.
10 Some kind of quick course, on the sidewalk, like Hey baby

why don't you take that thing off yo' haid. You look like
Miss Muffet in a runaway ugly machine. I mean. Like that.

1966

Leonard Cohen

(1934–   )

Elegy

Do not look for him
In brittle mountain streams:
They are too cold for any god;
And do not examine the angry rivers
5 For shreds of his soft body
Or turn the shore stones for his blood;
But in the warm salt ocean
He is descending through cliffs
Of slow green water
10 And the hovering colored fish
Kiss his snow-bruised body
And build their secret nests
In his fluttering winding-sheet.

1964

The Bus

I was the last passenger of the day,
I was alone on the bus,
I was glad they were spending all that money
just getting me up Eighth Avenue.
5 Driver! I shouted, it's you and me tonight,
let's run away from this big city
to a smaller city more suitable to the heart,
let's drive past the swimming pools of Miami Beach,
you in the driver's seat, me several seats back,
10 but in the racial cities we'll change places
so as to show how well you've done up North,
and let us find ourselves some tiny American fishing village
in unknown Florida
and park right at the edge of the sand,
15 a huge bus pointing out,
metallic, painted, solitary,
with New York plates.

1964

Audre Lorde

(1934–1992)

Coal

I
is the total black, being spoken
from the earth's inside.
There are many kinds of open
5 how a diamond comes into a knot of flame
how sound comes into a word, colored
by who pays what for speaking.
Some words are open like a diamond
on glass windows
10 singing out within the passing crash of sun
Then there are words like stapled wagers
in a perforated book—buy and sign and tear apart—
and come whatever wills all chances
the stub remains
15 and ill-pulled tooth with a ragged edge.
Some words live in my throat
breeding like adders. Others know sun
seeking like gypsies over my tongue
to explode through my lips
20 like young sparrows bursting from shell.
Some words
bedevil me.

Love is a word, another kind of open.
As the diamond comes into a knot of flame
25 I am Black because I come from the earth's inside
now take my word for jewel in the open light.

                                                   1976

Love Poem

Speak earth and bless me with what is richest
make sky flow honey out of my hips
rigid as mountains
spread over a valley
5 carved out by the mouth of rain.

And I knew when I entered her I was
high wind in her forests hollow
fingers whispering sound

honey flowed
10 from the split cup
impaled on a lance of tongues
on the tips of her breasts on her navel
and my breath
howling into her entrances
15 through lungs of pain.

Greedy as herring-gulls
or a child
I swing out over the earth
over and over
20 again.

1974

Power

The difference between poetry and rhetoric
is being
ready to kill
yourself
5 instead of your children.

I am trapped on a desert of raw gunshot wounds
and a dead child dragging his shattered black
face off the edge of my sleep
blood from his punctured cheeks and shoulders
10 is the only liquid for miles and my stomach
churns at the imagined taste while
my mouth splits into dry lips
without loyalty or reason
thirsting for the wetness of his blood
15 as it sinks into the whiteness
of the desert where I am lost
without imagery or magic
trying to make power out of hatred and destruction
trying to heal my dying son with kisses
20 only the sun will bleach his bones quicker.

The policeman who shot down a 10-year-old in Queens
stood over the boy with his cop shoes in childish blood
and a voice said "Die you little motherfucker" and
there are tapes to prove that. At his trial
25 this policeman said in his own defense
"I didn't notice the size or nothing else

only the color." and
there are tapes to prove that, too.

Today that 37-year-old white man with 13 years of police forcing
30   has been set free
by 11 white men who said they were satisfied
justice had been done
and one black woman who said
"They convinced me" meaning
35   they had dragged her 4'10" black woman's frame
over the hot coals of four centuries of white male approval
until she let go the first real power she ever had
and lined her own womb with cement
to make a graveyard for our children.

40   I have not been able to touch the destruction within me.
But unless I learn to use
the difference between poetry and rhetoric
my power too will run corrupt as poisonous mold
or lie limp and useless as an unconnected wire
45   and one day I will take my teenaged plug
and connect it to the nearest socket
raping an 85-year-old white woman
who is somebody's mother
and as I beat her senseless and set a torch to her bed
50   a greek chorus will be singing in ¾ time
"Poor thing. She never hurt a soul. What beasts they are."

                                                                    1978

A Question of Climate

I learned to be honest
the way I learned to swim
dropped into the inevitable
my father's thumbs in my hairless armpits
5   about to give way
I am trying
to surface   carefully
remembering
the water's shadow-legged musk
10   cannons of salt   exploding
my nostrils' rage
and for years
my powerful breast stroke
was a declaration of war.

                                                                    1986

Mark Strand

(1934–)

The Dead

The graves grow deeper.
The dead are more dead each night.

Under the elms and the rain of leaves,
The graves grow deeper.

5 The dark folds of the wind
Cover the ground. The night is cold.

The leaves are swept against the stones.
The dead are more dead each night.

A starless dark embraces them.
10 Their faces dim.

We cannot remember them
Clearly enough. We never will.

1963

The Tunnel

A man has been standing
in front of my house
for days. I peek at him
from the living room
5 window and at night,
unable to sleep,
I shine my flashlight
down on the lawn.
He is always there.

10 After a while
I open the front door
just a crack and order
him out of my yard.
He narrows his eyes
15 and moans. I slam
the door and dash back
to the kitchen, then up
to the bedroom, then down.

I weep like a schoolgirl
20 and make obscene gestures
through the window. I

write large suicide notes
and place them so he
can read them easily.
25 I destroy the living
room furniture to prove
I own nothing of value.

When he seems unmoved
I decide to dig a tunnel
30 to a neighboring yard.
I seal the basement off
from the upstairs with
a brickwall. I dig hard
and in no time the tunnel
35 is done. Leaving my pick
and shovel below,

I come out in front of a house
and stand there too tired to
move or even speak, hoping
40 someone will help me.
I feel I'm being watched
and sometimes I hear
a man's voice,
but nothing is done
45 and I have been waiting for days.

1963

Keeping Things Whole

In a field
I am the absence
of field.

This is
5 always the case.
Wherever I am
I am what is missing.

When I walk
I part the air
10 and always
the air moves in
to fill the spaces
where my body's been.

We all have reasons
15 for moving.

I move
to keep things whole.

1968

Eating Poetry

Ink runs from the corners of my mouth.
There is no happiness like mine.
I have been eating poetry.

The librarian does not believe what she sees.
5   Her eyes are sad
and she walks with her hands in her dress.

The poems are gone.
The light is dim.
The dogs are on the basement stairs and coming up.

10 Their eyeballs roll,
their blond legs burn like brush.
The poor librarian begins to stamp her feet and weep.
She does not understand.
When I get on my knees and lick her hand,
15 she screams.

I am a new man.
I snarl at her and bark.
I romp with joy in the bookish dark.

1968

Some Last Words

1

It is easier for a needle to pass through a camel
Than for a poor man to enter a woman of means.
Just go to the graveyard and ask around.

2

Eventually, you slip outside, letting the door
5   Bang shut on your latest thought. What was it anyway?
Just go to the graveyard and ask around.

3

"Negligence" is the perfume I love.
O Fedora. Fedora. If you want any,
Just go to the graveyard and ask around.

4

10 The bones of the buffalo, the rabbit at sunset,
     The wind and its double, the tree, the town . . .
     Just go to the graveyard and ask around.

5

     If you think good things are on their way
     And the world will improve, don't hold your breath.
15 Just go to the graveyard and ask around.

6

     You over there, why do you ask if this is the valley
     Of limitless blue, and if we are its prisoners?
     Just go to the graveyard and ask around.

7

     Life is a dream that is never recalled when the sleeper awakes.
20 If this is beyond you, Magnificent One,
     Just go to the graveyard and ask around.

                                                              1997

Jean Valentine

(1934–   )

The River at Wolf

     Coming east we left the animals
     pelican beaver osprey muskrat and snake
     their hair and skin and feathers
     their eyes in the dark: red and green.
5   Your finger drawing my mouth.

     Blessed are they who remember
     that what they now have they once longed for.

     A day a year ago last summer
     God filled me with himself, like gold, inside,
10 deeper inside than marrow.
     This close to God this close to you:
     walking into the river at Wolf with
     the animals. The snake's
     green skin, lit from inside. Our second life.

X

I have decorated this banner to honor my brother. Our parents did not want his name used publicly.

—FROM AN UNNAMED CHILD'S BANNER IN THE
AIDS MEMORIAL QUILT

The boatpond, broken off, looks back at the sky.
I remember looking at you, X, this way,
taking in your red hair, your eyes' light, and I miss you
so. I know,
5 you are you, and real, standing there in the doorway,
whether dead or whether living, real. —Then Y
said, "Who will remember me three years after I die?
What is there for my eye
to read then?"
10 The lamb should not have given
his wool.
He was so small. At the end, X, you were so small.
Playing with a stone
on your bedspread at the edge of the ocean.

Mary Oliver

(1935–   )

Landscape

Isn't it plain the sheets of moss, except that
they have no tongues, could lecture
all day if they wanted about

spiritual patience? Isn't it clear
5 the black oaks along the path are standing
as though they were the most fragile of flowers?

Every morning I walk like this around
the pond, thinking: if the doors of my heart
ever close, I am as good as dead.

10 Every morning, so far, I'm alive. And now
the crows break off from the rest of the darkness
and burst up into the sky—as though

all night they had thought of what they would like
their lives to be, and imagined
15 their strong, thick wings.

1986

Bats

In the blue air
the bats float
touching no leaf.

Science
5 has shown how they capture
their prey—

moths, mosquitoes—in
the middle of flight
in the fold of a wing,

10 and how they hang
by the millions,
socially, in caves.

But in the night
still comes
15 the unexplained figure

slipping in and out
of bedrooms, in and out
the soft throats of women.

For science is only
20 the golden boat
on the dark river

of blood, where women dream
such fur on the cheeks, such teeth
behind the kiss.

1986

Beyond the Snow Belt

Over the local stations, one by one,
Announcers list disasters like dark poems
That always happen in the skull of winter.
But once again the storm has passed us by:
5 Lovely and moderate, the snow lies down
While shouting children hurry back to play,

And scarved and smiling citizens once more
Sweep down their easy paths of pride and welcome.

And what else might we do? Let us be truthful.
10 Two counties north the storm has taken lives.
Two counties north, to us, is far away, —
A land of trees, a wing upon a map,
A wild place never visited, — so we
Forget with ease each far mortality.

15 Peacefully from our frozen yards we watch
Our children running on the mild white hills.
This is the landscape that we understand, —
And till the principle of things takes root,
How shall examples move us from our calm?
20 I do not say that it is not a fault.
I only say, except as we have loved,
All news arrives as from a distant land.

1965

Lucille Clifton

(1936–   )

in the inner city

in the inner city
or
like we call it
home
5 we think a lot about uptown
and the silent nights
and the houses straight as
dead men
and the pastel lights
10 and we hang on to our no place
happy to be alive
and in the inner city
or
like we call it
15 home

1969

Marge Piercy

(1936–   )

A Battle of Wills Disguised

You and I, are we in the same story?
Sometimes, never, on Tuesdays and Fridays?
I never ordered this Mama costume.
I don't want to be Joan Crawford: she dies
5   in the last reel, relinquishing all.
This is my movie too, you know. Why
is there a woman in it trying to kill me?
I thought this was a love story, but
of how much you and I both love you?

10   You and I, are we fighting the same war?
Then why do you lie on the telephone,
your voice fuzzy with the lint of guilt?
If the enemy is north, why do the guns
point at my house? Why do you study karate
15   instead of artillery and guerilla warfare?
Two generals command the armies of their bodies,
feinting, withdrawing, attacking. If it's the same
war, are you sure we're fighting on the same side?

You and I, are we in the same relationship?
20   Then when you say what a good night we had why
do I writhe awake? Why do you explain how much
better things are getting as you race
out the door, leap the hedge and catch the last
train to the city? After a week you call
25   from the Coast to say how close you're feeling.
If this is a detective story I know who did it,
but who are the cops I can call? Just you. Just me.

1977

When a Friend Dies

When a friend dies
the salmon run no fatter.
The wheat harvest will feed no more bellies.
Nothing is won by endurance
5   but endurance.
A hunger sucks at the mind
for gone color after the last bronze
chrysanthemum is withered by frost.

A hunger drains the day,
10 a homely sore gap
after a tooth is pulled,
a red giant gone nova,
an empty place in the sky
sliding down the arch
15 after Orion in night as wide
as a sleepless staring eye.
When pain and fatigue wrestle
fatigue wins. The eye shuts.
Then the pain rises again at dawn.
20 At first you can stare at it.
Then it blinds you.

1977

Diane Wakoski

(1937–   )

The Canoer

the hush of
the river
at 4 a.m.,
fish flipper their bellies across moss,
5 trees walk down to the very shoreline
thinking nobody is watching them,
his paddle darts in and out of
the water, getting better acquainted
each time with its own slippery
10 texture,
hands boggle out of the river
offering foam money in the corner of his eye.

In my own mind
I change the texture of the river,
15 super-imposing on it
a buffalo, bleeding in the hindquarters,
not raging but calm and taking
the waters. The river dries up
around him, and the skeleton of the buffalo
20 walks down the dried-out bed of an old river.

1977

The Singer

All songs
are tattoos
on his fingers and toes

As he moves
5 from year to year
walking on telegrams.

His throat a pipe
is carved with ancient animals;
and telephone wires imitate his hello.

10 Under his arm
the dream-tortoise struggles
trying to evaporate into the air.

This organ
the red slippery heart
15 beating in the cushion of each finger
is singu-
lar

a rhythm,
the snow slowly shifting
20 to cause an avalanche

the dust accumulating
on a window
sill.

1977

Joseph DeRoche

(1938–   )

Bagging Autumn Leaves

Some things that come with autumn do not change.
Once you've felt fall once, you smell the chill,
not feel it. Half-remembered cold seems strange.
But green goes gold. Or red. And leavings spill

5 a paper rustle cross the driveway and the lawn.
As ever, we rake leaves up the same, and feel

the weight each gathers as we pull upon
the pile we lumber when we haul the real.

Years past, my father and I made a mound.
10 We took a match and turned the leaves to flame.
A smoke and incense fumed the neighborhood around.
Like sacrifice, we immolated every year the same.

I smell those years, burnt spice. My father's dead.
I did not wrap him greenly up when I let go,
15 but like the leaves the trees obscenely shed,
I carried him in smoke and ash to snow.

1985

Blond

I am not going to invite you,
For once, into my life.

Others may call you beautiful
Or handsome, but not from my lips

5 Any praises. This is the way
It should be with strangers,

Always. What if your hair be
The hair that shines bright in

Dark places? So does the sun
10 In the eye of the storm and,

O, we are just winds flying
About you. But not from my

Lips will you hear a sharp
Cry in the street—some summons

15 To follow. What if I dodge you
All night? Loiter behind you?

What matter? Off you go!
Home to your cloister of ciphers!

I will not praise you. I sprawl,
20 Instead, on a splendor of pillows.

In the late guttering light,
Tilted to sleep, I am biting my lips.

1970

Michael S. Harper

(1938–   )

Dear John, Dear Coltrane

a love supreme, a love supreme
a love supreme, a love supreme

Sex fingers toes
in the marketplace
near your father's church
in Hamlet, North Carolina—
5   witness to this love
in this calm fallow
of these minds,
there is no substitute for pain:
genitals gone or going,
10   seed burned out,
you tuck the roots in the earth,
turn back, and move
by river through the swamps,
singing: *a love supreme, a love supreme;*
15   what does it all mean?
Loss, so great each black
woman expects your failure
in mute change, the seed gone.
You plod up into the electric city—
20   your song now crystal and
the blues. You pick up the horn
with some will and blow
into the freezing night:
a love supreme, a love supreme—

25   Dawn comes and you cook
up the thick sin 'tween
impotence and death, fuel
the tenor sax cannibal
heart, genitals and sweat
30   that makes you clean—
a love supreme, a love supreme—
Why you so black?
cause I am
why you so funky?
35   *cause I am*
why you so black?

> *cause I am*
> *why you so sweet?*
> *cause I am*
> 40 *why you so black?*
> *cause I am*
> *a love supreme, a love supreme:*

So sick
you couldn't play *Naima,*
45 so flat we ached
for song you'd concealed
with your own blood,
your diseased liver gave
out its purity,
50 the inflated heart
pumps out, the tenor kiss,
tenor love:
a love supreme, a love supreme—
a love supreme, a love supreme—

1977

Charles Simic

(1938–   )

The Partial Explanation

Seems like a long time
Since the waiter took my order.
Grimy little luncheonette,
The snow falling outside.

5 Seems like it has grown darker
Since I last heard the kitchen door
Behind my back
Since I last noticed
Anyone pass on the street.

10 A glass of ice water
Keeps me company
At this table I chose myself
Upon entering.

And a longing,
15 Incredible longing

To eavesdrop
On the conversation
Of cooks.

1977

Watermelons

Green Buddhas
On the fruit stand.
We eat the smile
And spit out the teeth.

1983

Fork

This strange thing must have crept
Right out of hell.
It resembles a bird's foot
Worn around the cannibal's neck.

5   As you hold it in your hand,
As you stab with it into a piece of meat,
It is possible to imagine the rest of the bird:
Its head which like your fist
Is large, bald, beakless and blind.

1983

Margaret Atwood

(1939–   )

It Is Dangerous to Read Newspapers

While I was building neat
castles in the sandbox,
the hasty pits were
filling with bulldozed corpses

5   and as I walked to the school
washed and combed, my feet
stepping on the cracks in the cement
detonated red bombs.

Now I am grownup
10 and literate, and I sit in my chair
as quietly as a fuse

and the jungles are flaming, the underbrush is charged with soldiers,
the names on the difficult
15　maps go up in smoke.

I am the cause, I am a stockpile of chemical
toys, my body
is a deadly gadget,
I reach out in love, my hands are guns,
20　my good intentions are completely lethal.

Even my
passive eyes transmute
everything I look at to the pocked
black and white of a war photo,
25　how
can I stop myself

It is dangerous to read newspapers.

Each time I hit a key
on my electric typewriter,
30　speaking of peaceful trees

another village explodes.

1968

Seamus Heaney

(1939–　)

Bogland

for T. P. Flanagan

We have no prairies
To slice a big sun at evening—
Everywhere the eye concedes to
Encroaching horizon,

5　Is wooed into the cyclops' eye[1]
Of a tarn. Our unfenced country
Is bog that keeps crusting
Between the sights of the sun.

They've taken the skeleton
10　Of the Great Irish Elk

---

[1]In Homer's *Odyssey,* the Cyclopes are one-eyed giants.

Out of the peat, set it up
An astounding crate full of air.

Butter sunk under
More than a hundred years
15 Was recovered salty and white.
The ground itself is kind, black butter

Melting and opening underfoot,
Missing its last definition
By millions of years.
20 They'll never dig coal here,

Only the waterlogged trunks
Of great firs, soft as pulp.
Our pioneers keep striking
Inwards and downwards.

25 Every layer they strip
Seems camped on before.
The bogholes might be Atlantic seepage.
The wet centre is bottomless.

1969

Waterfall

The burn drowns steadily in its own downpour,
A helter-skelter of muslin and glass
That skids to a halt, crashing up suds.

Simultaneous acceleration
5 And sudden braking; water goes over
Like villains dropped screaming to justice.

It appears an athletic glacier
Has reared into reverse: is swallowed up
And regurgitated through this long throat.

10 My eye rides over and downwards, falls with
Hurtling tons that slabber and spill,
Falls, yet records the tumult thus standing still.

1966

Docker

There, in the corner, staring at his drink.
The cap juts like a gantry's crossbeam,
Cowling plated forehead and sledgehead jaw.
Speech is clamped in the lips' vice.

5 That fist would drop a hammer on a Catholic—
Oh yes, that kind of thing could start again;
The only Roman collar he tolerates
Smiles all round his sleek pint of porter.

Mosaic imperatives bang home like rivets;
10 God is a foreman with certain definite views
Who orders life in shifts of work and leisure.
A factory horn will blare the Resurrection.

He sits strong and blunt as a Celtic cross,
Clearly used to silence and an armchair:
15 Tonight the wife and children will be quiet
At slammed door and smoker's cough in the hall.

1966

Lola Lemire Tostevin

(1939–   )

for Peter

your eyes are a million tiny organisms darting
in different directions   each one carrying
its own aquarium a map I'll return to all my life

as a boy you loved sagas about Polynesians crossing
5 the Pacific without as much as a compass and Chinese
sailors building the first one to help them navigate
their seas

some claim a giant lodestone mountain
in the far north towards which they strain
10 while others feeling more maternal give magnets
a face   a grin that fastens so they can never
get anywhere from here

1992

From **The Song of Songs**

8

the muse has learned to write

words fall gently in this weed and rain filled garden
their intimate touch awaken the measure of an extended
hand from which is offered another apple *un appel une pomme*

5 a poem the gold red rind of a rhyme *a rimmon* a garnet
the bony pulp of a pomegranate the acid taste of crimson the
sensuous pleasure of seeds that speak to the tip of the tongue
the curving stem of knotted rootstock the nodding flowers of
Solomon's seal it is all here in song in this weed and rain
10 filled garden (where voice is the site) its body distinct
from the metaphor so I can love you now that I am no longer
spoken for

1992

Martha Collins

(1940–   )

A History of Small Life on a Windy Planet

First they came in ones
but that was not enough:
they blew away.

Then in twos, hooked together
5 like scissors, pants, they held
each other down.

But one kept kicking up
its heels, muttering *three*,
unhitching itself,

10 drifting
into some pair's
pitiful garden.

This went on, you
can imagine: one goes in
15 to two plus one and three

became the rage but so what?
Say *history* these days
and people sneer:

better the box lunch—
20 if we eat enough
we'll stay fixed:

nothing, not even love,
can sweep us away.
It's only a matter

25 of time, after all, dust
　　is the into and out of
　　stuff, the girl the wind's loved

　　since they were kids.
　　Here's a note, over
30 the shoulder, under

　　the desk: It won't
　　be long. Relax, enjoy.
　　One's enough. Love—

1993

Owl

　　Owl leans into the tree and disappears.
　　A friend disappears down the long concourse,
　　Palestinian scarf over his thin
　　shoulders, thin legs, thinned blood,
5 and we wonder, his former lover and I, how long.

　　The eyes of owl see better because they cannot
　　shift, the ears of owl hear better because
　　they are wide, owl seems wise because of these features,
　　I learn the day my friend leaves, but we
10 fear owl: the bird of night by day means death.

　　The next week, while I'm writing this poem, a notice
　　arrives that says I'm not to *promote* or *produce*,
　　and then some words and *homoerotic* and more
　　words, and I wonder if this could be homoerotic,
15 a friend embracing a former lover, and could

　　the disease be homoerotic, could this woman's pen
　　on this woman's page, snow falling on snow,
　　hand over hand? Eye to eye, death
　　on death, could feather on feather on owl's gray back,
20 check on check on the silky black-and-white scarf?

　　Like to like, except in sex: to attract
　　an owl we hooted like owls; to attract a woman
　　a man may hoot and howl, while the woman coos.
　　Before he left, my friend let me choose a drawing
25 from his sketchbook. The woman I chose, nude,

　　hangs on my wall, while my friend waits and we wait,
　　everyone waits, day after day, for news—
　　words travel, in written or silent lines.

Owl makes no sound when he moves at night,
30 but just before dawn he may answer if you call.

1993

Robert Pinsky

(1940–   )

Exile

Every few years you move
From one city to another
As if to perform this ritual.
Pictures to arrange, and furniture,

5 Cartons of books to shelve—
And here, bundled in newspaper,
Memory's mortal tokens, treasure
Of a life unearthed:

Clouded honey, seizures
10 Of hopelessness and passion,
Good nights or bad ones,
Days of minor victories and scars

Tasting of silver or iron.
Touch, loss, shouts, arts,
15 Gestures, whispers,
Helpless violence of sensation

Like rain flailing a window—
Then a clap of light, the body blinded
You could not say whether by
20 Restitution or disaster,

Clarified by tears and thunder.
Now you begin. For an instant
Everything reassures you
The long exile is over.

1990

Sonnet

Afternoon sun on her back,
calm irregular slap
of water against a dock.

Thin pines clamber
5 over the hill's top—
nothing to remember,

only the same lake
that keeps making the same
sounds under her cheek

10 and flashing the same color.
No one to say her name,
no need, no one to praise her,

only the lake's voice—over
and over, to keep it before her.

1990

Sharon Olds

(1942–   )

The Death of Marilyn Monroe

The ambulance men touched her cold
body, lifted it, heavy as iron,
onto the stretcher, tried to close the
mouth, closed the eyes, tied the
5 arms to the sides, moved a caught
strand of hair, as if it mattered,
saw the shape of her breasts, flattened by
gravity, under the sheet,
carried her, as if it were she,
10 down the steps.

These men were never the same. They went out
afterwards, as they always did,
for a drink or two, but they could not meet
each other's eyes.
15   Their lives took
a turn—one had nightmares, strange
pains, impotence, depression. One did not
like his work, his wife looked
different, his kids. Even death
20 seemed different to him—a place where she
would be waiting,

and one found himself standing at night
in the doorway to a room of sleep, listening to a

woman breathing, just an ordinary
25 woman
breathing.

1983

Sex Without Love

How do they do it, the ones who make love
without love? Beautiful as dancers,
gliding over each other like ice-skaters
over the ice, fingers hooked
5 inside each other's bodies, faces
red as steak, wine, wet as the
children at birth whose mothers are going to
give them away. How do they come to the
come to the   come to the   God   come to the
10 still waters, and not love
the one who came there with them, light
rising slowly as steam off their joined
skin? These are the true religious,
the purists, the pros, the ones who will not
15 accept a false Messiah, love the
priest instead of the God. They do not
mistake the lover for their own pleasure,
they are like great runners: they know they are alone
with the road surface, the cold, the wind,
20 the fit of their shoes, their over-all cardiovascular health—just factors, like the partner
in the bed, and not the truth, which is the
single body alone in the universe
against its own best time.

1983

Nikki Giovanni

(1943–   )

Nikki-Rosa

childhood remembrances are always a drag
if you're Black
you always remember things like living in Woodlawn[1]

---

[1] a working-class suburb of Cincinnati

with no inside toilet
5   and if you become famous or something
they never talk about how happy you were to have your mother
all to your self and
how good the water felt when you got your bath from one of those
big tubs that folk in chicago barbecue in
10 and somehow when you talk about home
it never gets across how much you
understood their feelings
as the whole family attended meetings about Hollydale[2]
and even though you remember
15 your biographers never understand
your father's pain as he sells his stock
and another dream goes
and though you're poor it isn't poverty that
concerns you
20 and though they fought a lot
it isn't your father's drinking that makes any difference
but only that everybody is together and you
and your sister have happy birthdays and very good christmasses
and I really hope no white person ever has cause to write about me
25 because they never understand Black love is Black wealth and they'll
probably talk about my hard childhood and never understand that
all the while I was quite happy.

1968

Louise Glück

(1943–   )

Mock Orange

It is not the moon, I tell you.
It is these flowers
lighting the yard.

I hate them.
5   I hate them as I hate sex,
the man's mouth
sealing my mouth, the man's
paralyzing body—

---
[2]a subdivision of single-family homes, launched in the 1950s

and the cry that always escapes,
10 the low, humiliating
premise of union—

In my mind tonight
I hear the question and pursuing answer
fused in one sound
15 that mounts and mounts and then
is split into the old selves,
the tired antagonisms. Do you see?
We were made fools of.
And the scent of mock orange
20 drifts through the window.

How can I rest?
How can I be content
when there is still
that odor in the world?

1985

The Mountain

My students look at me expectantly.
I explain to them that the life of art is a life
of endless labor. Their expressions
hardly change; they need to know
5 a little more about endless labor.
So I tell them the story of Sisyphus,
how he was doomed to push
a rock up a mountain, knowing nothing
would come of this effort
10 but that he would repeat it
indefinitely. I tell them
there is joy in this, in the artist's life,
that one eludes
judgment, and as I speak
15 I am secretly pushing a rock myself,
slyly pushing it up the steep
face of a mountain. Why do I lie
to these children? They aren't listening,
they aren't deceived, their fingers
20 tapping at the wooden desks—
So I retract
the myth; I tell them it occurs
in hell, and that the artist lies

because he is obsessed with attainment,
25   that he perceives the summit
as that place where he will live forever,
a place about to be
transformed by his burden: with every breath,
I am standing at the top of the mountain.
30   Both my hands are free. And the rock has added
height to the mountain.

1985

Michael Ondaatje

(1943–)

(Inner Tube)

On the warm July river
head back

upside down river
for a roof

5 slowly paddling
towards an estuary between trees

there's a dog
learning to swim near me
friends on shore

10 my head
dips
back to the eyebrow
I'm the prow
on an ancient vessel,
15 this afternoon
I'm going down to Peru
soul between my teeth

a blue heron
with its awkward
20 broken backed flap
upside down

one of us is wrong

he
his blue grey thud

25 thinking he knows
the blue way
out of here

or me

1984

James Tate

(1943–   )

The Lost Pilot

for my father, 1922–1944

Your face did not rot
like the others—the co-pilot,
for example, I saw him

yesterday. His face is corn-
5 mush: his wife and daughter,
the poor ignorant people, stare

as if he will compose soon.
He was more wronged than Job.
But your face did not rot

10 like the others—it grew dark,
and hard like ebony;
the features progressed in their

distinction. If I could cajole
you to come back for an evening,
15 down from your compulsive

orbiting, I would touch you,
read your face as Dallas,
your hoodlum gunner, now,

with the blistered eyes, reads
20 his braille editions. I would
touch your face as a disinterested

scholar touches an original page.
However frightening, I would
discover you, and I would not

25 turn you in; I would not make
you face your wife, or Dallas,
or the co-pilot, Jim. You

could return to your crazy
orbiting, and I would not try
30 to fully understand what

it means to you. All I know
is this: when I see you,
as I have seen you at least

once every year of my life,
35 spin across the wilds of the sky
like a tiny, African god,

I feel dead. I feel as if I were
the residue of a stranger's life,
that I should pursue you.

40 My head cocked toward the sky,
I cannot get off the ground,
and, you, passing over again,

fast, perfect, and unwilling
to tell me that you are doing
45 well, or that it was mistake

that placed you in that world,
and me in this; or that misfortune
placed these worlds in us.

1978

The Blue Booby

The blue booby lives
on the bare rocks
of Galápagos
and fears nothing.
5 It is a simple life:
they live on fish,
and there are few predators.
Also, the males do not
make fools of themselves
10 chasing after the young
ladies. Rather,
they gather the blue
objects of the world
and construct from them

15 a nest—an occasional
Gaulois package,
a string of beads,

a piece of cloth from
a sailor's suit. This
20 replaces the need for
dazzling plumage;
in fact, in the past
fifty million years
the male has grown
25 considerably duller,
nor can he sing well.
The female, though,

asks little of him—
the blue satisfies her
30 completely, has
a magical effect
on her. When she returns
from her day of
gossip and shopping,
35 she sees he has found her
a new shred of blue foil:
for this she rewards him
with her dark body,
the stars turn slowly
40 in the blue foil beside them
like the eyes of a mild savior.

1969

Consumed

Why should you believe in magic,
pretend an interest in astrology
or the tarot? Truth is, you are

free, and what might happen to you
5 today, nobody knows. And your
personality may undergo a radical

transformation in the next half
hour. So it goes. You are consumed
by your faith in justice, your

10 hope for a better day, the rightness
of fate, the dreams, the lies
the taunts—Nobody gets what he

wants. A dark star passes through
you on your way home from
15 the grocery: never again are you

the same—an experience which is
impossible to forget, impossible
to share. The longing to be pure

is over. You are the stranger
20 who gets stranger by the hour.

1969

Amber Coverdale Sumrall

(1945–   )

Upon entering this world the
Hopi were offered corn of various
colors by the Great Spirit, a
choice that would determine their
destiny. They chose blue, signifying
that although their life would be
difficult they would survive
all other tribes.

Keams Canyon, Black Mesa

It is unwise to enter this place
without a spirit guide
a sense of what is sacred

Stretched between two worlds
5 I lie on red earth
reaching for sleep
the shaman's voice   insistent
rattles in my ear
hisses a strange language of warning

10 No rain falls here
radioactive tailings gouge
huge welts upon this land
already a graveyard for burned-out stars

I remember my grandmother's talismans
15 the gourds she carved and painted
with symbols of rain   thunderheads
bowls of special stones   an owl feather
her prayers to those who came before
her silent offerings of corn

20 On the edge of First Mesa
heat lightning arcs

bridging earth and sky
In volcanic craters   miles away
there is a stirring in ancient shrines

25 Constellations shift
petrified colors spin out across desert sand
Kachinas filter through boundaries of time
dance in fields of blue corn.

                                                              1990

Ceremonials

We beseech the earth mother
she has been in mourning
We call upon the goddess
she has been in exile
5 We call out to one another
we have been confused

In circles we gather
redwood groves
        sea caves
10   meadow tipis

In moonlight
fires are kindled
    hands are joined
        legends honored

15 Our voices rise
chanting spells
    invoking grandmothers
        reclaiming ancient visions

We are sisters
20 We are witches
We are healers
    standing together
        weathering change
            forests of deep rooted trees

                                                              1990

Infinity

The idea of infinity makes me crazy
I tell my grandmother

after Uncle Eugene dies,
his soul spirited away
5 like smoke on the Santa Ana winds.
She leads me to her bedroom
sits me at her dressing table:
a shrine of crystal candleholders,
silver urns, and music boxes.
10 She lights candles
arranges the half-circle of mirrors,
tells me to look into the glass.

In the shimmer of shadow and light
I gaze at reflection after reflection,
15 watch myself shrink
until I nearly vanish.
Time shifts like a dream
rolling slowly out of control.

1990

Yusef Komunyakaa

(1947–   )

More Girl Than Boy

You'll always be my friend.
Is that clear, Robert Lee?
We go beyond the weighing
of each other's words,
5 hand on a shoulder,
go beyond the color of hair.
Playing Down the Man on the Field
we embraced each other before
I discovered girls.
10 You taught me a heavy love
for jazz, how words can hurt
more than a quick jab.
Something there's no word for
saved us from the streets.

15 Night's pale horse
rode you past common sense,

but you made it home from Chicago.
So many dreams dead.
All the man-sweet gigs
20 meant absolutely nothing.
Welcome back to earth, Robert.
You always could make that piano
talk like somebody's mama.

1993

Facing It

My black face fades,
hiding inside the black granite.
I said I wouldn't,
dammit: No tears.
5 I'm stone. I'm flesh.
My clouded reflection eyes me
like a bird of prey, the profile of night
slanted against morning. I turn
this way—the stone lets me go.
10 I turn that way—I'm inside
the Vietnam Veterans Memorial
again, depending on the light
to make a difference.
I go down the 58,022 names,
15 half-expecting to find
my own in letters like smoke.
I touch the name Andrew Johnson;
I see the booby trap's white flash.
Names shimmer on a woman's blouse
20 but when she walks away
the names stay on the wall.
Brushstrokes flash, a red bird's
wings cutting across my stare.
The sky. A plane in the sky.
25 A white vet's image floats
closer to me, then his pale eyes
look through mine. I'm a window.
He's lost his right arm
inside the stone. In the black mirror
30 a woman's trying to erase names:
No, she's brushing a boy's hair.

1993

Kenneth Sherman

(1950–   )

My Father Kept His Cats Well Fed

My father kept his cats well fed.
In back of the tailor shop
far from consumer eye
they'd stretch
5   on thick rolls of mohair,
on new blue synthetics from Japan.

And somehow he bought time
to keep fresh milk in the saucepan,
providing leftovers
10   from a hurried lunch.

Between the measurements and complaints,
between the clean sound of closing shears
they were his own animal symphony
purring at a conducted stroke
15   under the chin,
behind the ear.

The cats,
they sang my father's praise
in the fishbone throat of the coldest nights
20   where their lives, once lean,
curled fat and secure

and dreamt their gifted names:
No-Neck, Schvartz, Kaatz, Rabinovitz . . .
a regular *minyan*[1]
25   to greet his early mornings
when snow outside
dropped soft as padded paws
and the shop was a museum hush.

There they reclined,
30   impenetrable as sphinx,
the curious engines of their soft throats
running, their great eyes smouldering
in the precious twilight of my father's day

---

[1] the quorum needed in order to conduct a Jewish public worship service

before the startling ring
35 and the long unwinding of curses
and cloth.

Rita Dove

(1952–   )

Geometry

I prove a theorem and the house expands:
the windows jerk free to hover near the ceiling,
the ceiling floats away with a sigh.

As the walls clear themselves of everything
5 but transparency, the scent of carnations
leaves with them. I am out in the open

and above the windows have hinged into butterflies,
sunlight glinting where they've intersected.
They are going to some point true and unproven.

1986

Dusting

Every day a wilderness—no
shade in sight. Beulah
as her gray cloth brings
dark wood to life.

5 Under her hand scrolls
and crests gleam
darker still. What
was his name, that
silly boy at the fair with
10 the rifle booth? And his kiss and
the clear bowl with one bright
fish, rippling
wound!

Not Michael—
15 something finer. Each dust
stroke a deep breath and
the canary in bloom.
Wavery memory: home
from a dance, the front door

20 blown open and the parlor
   in snow, she rushed
   the bowl to the stove, watched
   as the locket of ice
   dissolved and he
25 swam free.

That was years before
Father gave her up
with her name, years before
her name grew to mean
30 Promise, then
Desert-in-Peace.
Long before the shadow and
sun's accomplice, the tree.

Maurice.

1986

Carl Phillips

(1959–   )

Still Life: Treadmill with Mirror

Oh, he was beautiful (even
a man, even here, can say it),

racing toward his own good idea
of what beauty must be when it goes
5 all steamy and determined
in place.

This is the last long afternoon of Kid Narcissus,
I was thinking,

any moment something different will happen.

10 Much later, I thought of that poem about the urn—

you know, where everyone's barefoot and pastoral
robes loose and slightly
raised, like there's really wind
or some kind of headway being made:

15 beauty, chasing tail forever.

1992

Goods

Bed-wetter, probably: solver of problems
in parts, only.

                Dreamer of trees always falling,
and the hard rains after,

5   I'm sure.

. . .

"Let's just say," he says, picking up speed,

the sun, from behind, doing a Hollywood thing
with his hair,

               "I am mostly not a bad man."

10 Still,

. . .

I can picture him
getting rough with the good china,

how I'll feel about that.

                                      1992

INDEX OF TERMS

INDEX OF AUTHORS AND TITLES

INDEX OF FIRST LINES